The Making of Miracles in Indian States

STUDIES IN INDIAN ECONOMIC POLICIES

India's Reforms: How They Produced Inclusive Growth

Reforms and Economic Transformation in India

State Level Reforms, Growth, and Development in Indian States

The Making of Miracles in Indian States: Andhra Pradesh, Bihar, and Gujarat

The Making of Miracles in Indian States
Andhra Pradesh, Bihar, and Gujarat

Edited by
Arvind Panagariya
and
M. Govinda Rao

OXFORD
UNIVERSITY PRESS

Oxford University Press is a department of the University of
Oxford. It furthers the University's objective of excellence in research,
scholarship, and education by publishing worldwide.

Oxford   New York
Auckland   Cape Town   Dar es Salaam   Hong Kong   Karachi
Kuala Lumpur   Madrid   Melbourne   Mexico City   Nairobi
New Delhi   Shanghai   Taipei   Toronto

With offices in
Argentina   Austria   Brazil   Chile   Czech Republic   France   Greece
Guatemala   Hungary   Italy   Japan   Poland   Portugal   Singapore
South Korea   Switzerland   Thailand   Turkey   Ukraine   Vietnam

Oxford is a registered trademark of Oxford University Press
in the UK and certain other countries.

Published in the United States of America by
Oxford University Press
198 Madison Avenue, New York, NY 10016

© Oxford University Press 2015

All rights reserved. No part of this publication may be reproduced, stored in
a retrieval system, or transmitted, in any form or by any means, without the prior
permission in writing of Oxford University Press, or as expressly permitted by law,
by license, or under terms agreed with the appropriate reproduction rights organization.
Inquiries concerning reproduction outside the scope of the above should be sent to the
Rights Department, Oxford University Press, at the address above.

You must not circulate this work in any other form
and you must impose this same condition on any acquirer.

Library of Congress Cataloging-in-Publication Data
The Making of Miracles in Indian States : Andhra Pradesh, Bihar, and Gujarat / edited by
Arvind Panagariya.
    pages cm. — (Studies in Indian economic policies)
Summary: "Examines India's economic growth at the state level"— Provided by publisher.
Includes bibliographical references and index.
ISBN 978-0-19-023662-5 (hardback)
1. Rural development—India.   2. Local government—India.
3. Economic development—India.   I. Govinda Rao, M., editor.
II. Panagariya, Arvind, editor.
HN49.C6S7698 2015
307.1'4120959—dc23
2014046315

1 3 5 7 9 8 6 4 2
Printed in the United States of America
on acid-free paper

To

Prime Minister Nerendra Modi
Chief Minister Chandrababu Naidu
Chief Minister Nitish Kumar

Leaders who brought relief and prosperity to millions of citizens in their respective states.

CONTENTS

Series Editors' Note   ix
Preface   xi
Contributors   xiii

1. Introduction: Understanding the Growth Miracles of Andhra Pradesh, Bihar, and Gujarat   1
   Arvind Panagariya and M. Govinda Rao
Chapter 1 References   17

PART I: Andhra Pradesh
   Mudit Kapoor and Rahul Ahluwalia
2. Andhra Pradesh: Setting the Stage   21
3. Growth and Economic Transformation   29
4. Poverty and Employment   59
5. Microfinance and Employment Guarantee Program in Rural Areas   77
6. Health and Education   88
7. Conclusions   102
Appendix 1: Implications of Bifurcation and Region-Wise Analysis of Andhra Pradesh   109
Part I References   117

PART II: Bihar
   Arnab Mukherji and Anjan Mukherji
8. Bihar's Economy in Historical Perspective   123
9. What Went Wrong?   152
10. What Changed?   167
11. Governance and Reforms Matter   199
12. Conclusions   212
Part II References   217

PART III: Gujarat
    Archana Dholakia and Ravindra Dholakia
13. Growth and Development in Gujarat: An Overview   227
14. Policy Reform in Economic Sectors   246
15. Urban Development   265
16. Fiscal Reforms and Performance   275
17. Elementary and Higher Education   285
18. Primary Healthcare and Medical Education   295
19. Governance, Efficiency, and Effectiveness   311
20. Lessons from the Gujarat Experience   320
Appendix 2: Sardar Sarovar Project (SSP) on the River Narmada   323
Appendix 3: The Earthquake and Its Impact on the Kutchh District   325
Part III References   327

21. Lessons from the States and Looking Ahead   333
    Arvind Panagariya and M. Govinda Rao

Index   341

SERIES EDITORS' NOTE

The Making of Miracles in Indian States: Andhra Pradesh, Bihar, and Gujarat, edited by Arvind Panagariya and M. Govinda Rao, is the fourth volume in the series Studies in Indian Economic Policies. This volume follows up on the third volume, which offered an overview of the 18 largest states of India and state-level reform priorities. It analyzes three highly successful states, Andhra Pradesh, Bihar, and Gujarat, in-depth with the view to understanding the link between state-level policies and economic outcomes. By implication, it also seeks to glean lessons for state-level policies that can be emulated elsewhere in India and, indeed, other countries with a federal structure of government.

Our purpose in launching the series Studies in Indian Economic Policies has been to bring out scholarly studies of the past and future economic policies and their impact on India. We are open to including volumes authored by single or paired authors as well as collections of essays by different authors devoted to closely related themes in the series. We are not wedded to any specific method of analysis or viewpoint but do seek a policy focus and high standards of economic and political analysis.

The series has originated in the Columbia Program on Indian Economic Policies, generously funded by the John Templeton Foundation. Beginning on October 1, 2009, the program has undertaken a number of research projects with the participation of leading economists. The first four volumes have come out of these projects.

We thank the John Templeton Foundation for supporting the Columbia Program and the Oxford University Press for bringing out the series. Terry Vaughn and Catherine Rae initially helped launched the series, and it is now in the able hands of Scott Parris and Cathryn Vaulman. We are grateful to them all.

Jagdish Bhagwati
and
Arvind Panagariya
October 2014

PREFACE

This volume, the fourth in the series Studies in Indian Economic Policies, is the product of a two-part study that we together initiated in January 2011. The first part was devoted to the study of overall economic development of the 18 largest states and state-level policy reforms in areas such as agriculture, industry, urbanization, infrastructure, education, and health that could help states transform and modernize faster. This part of the study has now appeared as the third volume of the series under the title *State Level Reforms, Growth, and Development in Indian States*. We are now pleased to offer the readers the second part of the study.

A key issue, which the first part of the study had eschewed, was the connection between the state-level policies and economic outcomes. This is a complex subject requiring in-depth analysis of policies in individual states and therefore could not be taken up in an overview volume that spanned over 18 states. The present volume fills the gap by looking at three very different states in terms of their per capita income levels, poverty, rural–urban split, and infrastructure. Yet, a common feature to them is that they have all registered 8% to 10% growth and massive reduction in poverty in recent years. As such, they make excellent candidates for case studies.

While gleaning the lessons for other states for state-level reforms is the key aim of this volume, we also see it as the first serious scholarly effort to analyze states in-depth, especially during the post-reform period. While the Indian press routinely carries contentious pieces on the relative performance of Gujarat versus Bihar or Gujarat versus Maharashtra versus Tamil Nadu, a deeper systematic analysis of various aspects of economic development in the states has been lacking.

We provide the summary of the volume in our introduction. Rather than repeat it, we note here that the work on the project leading to this volume is the result of a collaborative effort between Columbia University in the City of New York, where Panagariya is a professor and the National Institute of Public Finance and Policy (NIPFP) in New Delhi, which Rao directed until recently. Key to the success of the project were two workshops at the NIPFP on January 11, 2011, and October 1, 2011, and a two-day public conference at the India International Center in New Delhi on August 7–8, 2012. The Columbia Program on Indian Economic Policies and NIPFP jointly organized these events.

In bringing together this volume, we have greatly benefited from comments by many from different walks of the policy and scholarly worlds. Our thinking was naturally informed and refined by those commenting on the overview volume, *State Level Reforms, Growth, and Development in Indian States*. In addition, the comments on Bihar at an early stage at the first of our two workshops by N. K. Singh, who served as a member of Rajya Sabha until recently, were extremely helpful. Subsequently, at the conference in August 2012, we were fortunate to have the benefit of the comments by Satya Das, Professor, Indian Statistical Institute; Bibek Debroy, Professor, Center for Policy Research; Arunish Chawla, Ministry of Finance, Government of India; Rana Hasan, Principal Economist, Asian Development Bank; Manoj Panda, Director, Institute of Economic Growth; and Ajit Ranade, Chief Economist, Aditya Birla group. We are deeply indebted to these commentators.

We were also beneficiaries of three excellent anonymous reviews as a part of the OUP review process. These reviews led to several improvements in all studies at the final stage. All authors of the three studies have expressed their appreciation of the comments in these reviews.

We also wish to thank Michael Falco, Assistant Director, Columbia Program on Indian Economic Policies, whose flawless management helped the work progress smoothly at all stages. The financial support from the Templeton Foundation through the Columbia Program is gratefully acknowledged. The views expressed in the volume are entirely those of the authors and may not be attributed to the foundation.

Our final thanks go to the OUP editorial team, especially Scott Parris and Cathryn Vaulman, who have assisted us at various points in the preparation of the volume.

Arvind Panagariya
M. Govinda Rao
October 2014

CONTRIBUTORS

Rahul Ahluwalia, University of British Columbia, Vancouver

Archana Dholakia, Entrepreneurship Development Institute of India, Ahmedabad, Gujarat

Ravindra Dholakia, Indian Institute of Management, Ahmedabad, Gujarat

Mudit Kapoor, Indian School of Business, Hyderabad, Andhra Pradesh

Anjan Mukherji, National Institute of Public Finance and Policy, New Delhi

Arnab Mukherji, Indian Institute of Management, Bangalore, Karnataka

Arvind Panagariya, Columbia University, New York, New York

M. Govinda Rao, Member, Fourteenth Finance Commission, New Delhi

CHAPTER 1

Introduction

Understanding the Growth Miracles of Andhra Pradesh, Bihar, and Gujarat

ARVIND PANAGARIYA AND M. GOVINDA RAO

After independence in 1947, India adopted a federal rather than unitary structure of government. This structure has at least two important advantages over the alternative. First, as Alexis de Tocqueville stated as early as 1835 in his celebrated book *Democracy in America*, "The federal system was created with the intention of combining the different advantages which result from the magnitude and littleness of nations." A federal system makes it possible to reap economies of scale and scope while catering to the diversified characteristics of the regions and preferences of the people in different jurisdictions. For example, while defense for all component units is best provided at the federal level, law and order is best left to the individual units that can take into account the local customs and traditions. A multilevel fiscal system ensures more efficient resource allocation, promotes greater intergovernmental competition and innovation, enables better political participation, and has better reach in protecting basic liberties and freedoms.

Second, federalism also provides fertile ground for what economist Wallace Oates (1999) has called "laboratory federalism." Intergovernmental competition among different states and accompanying experimentation leads to innovations that can then result in the identification and eventual adoption of the best policies and practices by many or all states. Following the important work of Salmon (1987), the phenomenon is sometimes called "Salmon" mechanism in competitive federalism literature. In exercising their vote, people in a given jurisdiction benchmark themselves against the good policies and performances in other jurisdictions. This leads to pressure on the government to deliver similarly good policies and performance.[1]

The Constitution characterizes India as a "Union of States." In spite of significant centripetal bias in the assignment of powers and centralization in the working of the economy within its planning framework, states play a significant role not only in ensuring law and order but also the creation and maintenance of social and physical infrastructure. Within the federal structure, states have powers to legislate in areas such as education, health, land, labor, and agriculture. They also administer the myriad central government sponsored development schemes and projects. Therefore, state governments have an essential role in influencing the economic outcomes within their jurisdictions.

Interestingly, the new Prime Minister of India, Narendra Modi, who assumed office on May 26, 2014, had served as the Chief Minister of the state of Gujarat during the preceding 12 plus years. Having found the fiscal and legislative boundaries drawn by the central government excessively constraining, he has expressed much sympathy for granting greater flexibility to the states along both dimensions. This has raised expectations that in the forthcoming years, the spirit of federalism will revive and the states will see their domain expand. On the fiscal front, this would mean proportionately reduced expenditures on the centrally sponsored schemes or greater flexibility in shifting these expenditures across different schemes or both. On the legislative front, states will acquire greater freedom of legislation on subjects covered by the Concurrent List in the Constitution. This list contains important subject areas such as labor, land, education, and health in which both the center and states can legislate. But, in case of a conflict, central legislation takes precedence over the state legislation so that the center can effectively define boundaries of what the states can or cannot do. The Constitution empowers the center, however, to allow state legislation to prevail even when it is in violation of the central legislation through presidential assent. Therefore, the Modi government can impart greater legislative power to the states through such assents on specific legislative amendments by the states.

ON THE NEED FOR STATE-LEVEL ANALYSIS

Much of the scholarly work on India has been undertaken at the national level. At the beginning, this was natural since the economic reforms, initiated in 1991, were entirely national in nature and the immediate question was whether the reforms had served India as a whole well. But with the passage of more than two decades since the reforms and a wealth of state-specific

---

1. Also see Breton (1996) in this context.

information becoming available, it is important to ask how the post-reform experience has varied across states and what lessons can be derived from it. We might also ask how the policies and reforms undertaken by the states themselves may have impacted their performance. Additionally, there is the issue regarding what reforms the states themselves can undertake to accelerate growth, combat poverty, and promote social objectives such as education and health within the Indian federation.

In a recent book, the authors, with Pinaki Chakraborty (Panagariya, Chakraborty, and Rao 2014), have made a modest attempt to fill this important gap in the literature on reforms and economic development in India. We provide a comparative analysis of outcomes with respect to growth, industrialization, urbanization, poverty, household amenities, education, and health in the 18 largest states in the post-reform era. We demonstrate that every one of these states has improved the outcomes with respect to growth, poverty alleviation, and other social indicators following the economic reforms. We also discuss in detail the reforms the states can undertake on their own within the Indian federal structure in areas of agriculture, industry, urban development, education, and health.

An early influential assessment of the growth experience at the level of the states, Ahluwalia (2000), had reached the conclusion that reforms had benefited disproportionately the states that were already more prosperous relative to the lagging states. With their superior infrastructure and links to the world markets, these states were better able to take advantage of liberalizing reforms than the lagging states. Consequently, regional disparities rose sharply. The analysis in Panagariya, Chakraborty, and Rao (2014) shows, however, that while regional disparities have continued to rise on average during the last decade, the growth performance in some of the lagging states has defied this trend. While all the states had a significant acceleration in the growth rates in the 2000s, some of the low per capita income states took off in a major way matching or even beating some of the best performing richer states in terms of growth and poverty alleviation. This was particularly true of Bihar and Orissa.

A key question that our previous work had sidestepped is the link between state-level policy reforms and the economic and social outcomes. With the same set of national policies in place, why has the performance of different states been different? To some degree, the variation may be explained in terms of initial conditions relating to infrastructure, availability of a coastline that provides a direct link to the world markets, and the level of human and physical capital. But the response may also differ due to differences in governance, qualities of states' leadership, and policy initiatives taken by the states themselves.

In view of the absence of reliably quantifiable measures of governance and policy changes and the possibility of two-way causation, a quantitative assessment of the link between state-level policies and outcomes is fraught with difficulties. But some insight into such a link can be obtained through in-depth studies of individual states. Such in-depth study of the states was not possible in our previous volume in view of the large number of states we covered. Instead, that study was limited to a broad-brush comparative assessment of the experience of all major states prior to and following the national-level reforms.

This then provides the rationale for the present follow-up volume, which undertakes in-depth studies of three large states of India: Andhra Pradesh, Bihar, and Gujarat.[2] Each of the studies attempts to document the evolution of the major economic indicators, policies pursued at different points in time, and the link between the two. It is hoped that the narratives we have produced will offer helpful insights not only for the future development of the states studied but also for the other states. Here then is the possibility of stimulating "Salmon" competition among state.

WHY WE CHOOSE ANDHRA PRADESH, BIHAR, AND GUJARAT

An important question we must address at the outset concerns the choice of the states: why Andhra Pradesh, Gujarat, and Bihar? Several considerations have gone into the choice. First and foremost, given the scarce resources and the objective of in-depth investigation, we decided to limit ourselves to three states. Next, we opted in favor of confining ourselves to relatively large states. While there is much to be learned from small states as well, in our experience, any conclusions derived from the study of smaller states risk being dismissed as irrelevant to the bulk of India. For decades, Indian policymakers would dismiss the lessons of countries such as Singapore, Taiwan, and South Korea as being inapplicable to India because they were very small. This criterion then narrowed down the possible set to 10 states with populations of 60 million or more as per the 2011 census. In order of declining population, these are: Uttar Pradesh, Maharashtra, Bihar, West Bengal, Andhra Pradesh, Madhya Pradesh, Tamil Nadu, Rajasthan, Karnataka, and Gujarat.

---

2. Just as this volume went into the final stage of preparation, the central government had decided to split Andhra Pradesh into two separate states naming them Telangana and Andhra Pradesh. The latter includes two regions, Coastal Andhra and Rayalaseema so that they are jointly called Seemandhra in popular parlance. Telangana consists of the rest of the regions of the original Andhra Pradesh state with the qualification that Hyderabad is to serve as the capital of both new states for the next ten years. A separatist movement for the split had existed in the state for many decades.

Our next two criteria were that three states must have different levels of development and must have exhibited sustained high growth in recent years. These criteria identified Bihar as clearly the candidate from among the states with a low level of development that additionally include Uttar Pradesh, Madhya Pradesh, and Rajasthan. Going by per capita income, the choice of a rich state narrowed down to Gujarat and Maharashtra and that for a middle-income state among Tamil Nadu, Karnataka, Andhra Pradesh, and West Bengal.

Two factors guided our decision in favor of Gujarat to represent the richer states. First, it was a state much in the news on account of its flamboyant Chief Minister Narendra Modi, who had been articulating the successes of his state in various public forums. Simultaneously, his critics had been claiming that Gujarat suffered rather poor social indicators. Controversies surrounding the state made it an interesting case study in its own right. In retrospect, the force of this argument has magnified by the fact that the Gujarat Chief Minister ended up making a bid for the top national office, building his case on the progress achieved by his state, and is now the Prime Minister of the country. Second and perhaps more substantively, Mumbai, Thane, and Pune together accounted for as much as 46.8% of the Gross State Domestic Product of Maharashtra in 2012/13.[3] What happens in the state is heavily influenced by these three entities that represent only a tiny part of the geographical region and population of the state.

The choice among Tamil Nadu, Karnataka, Andhra Pradesh, and West Bengal turned more arbitrary. West Bengal could be eliminated because it has not performed very well. But the remaining three were all good candidates, and we chose Andhra Pradesh mainly because the state has a large agricultural sector, growing manufacturing base, and fast-growing modern services sector. The reform orientation of the state too has been much stronger than the other comparable states during the last decade. In addition, we were able to get an energetic young scholar to lead the study, so it seemed the best from among this group of states. In retrospect, the decision turned out right, since Andhra Pradesh had not only seen the information technology industry flourish just like Karnataka, it also did extremely well in agriculture. The former factor contributed to the decline in urban poverty and the latter in rural poverty.

To summarize then, all three states we have chosen are large with the smallest of them, Gujarat, having a population of 60.4 million as per the 2011 census. All three have also performed very well during the 2000s and beyond. But beyond these similarities, they are very diverse. They are located in three different parts of the country: Gujarat in western India, Bihar in eastern India, and Andhra Pradesh in southern India. While Gujarat and

3. See Government of Maharashtra (2014: 27, paragraph 3.18).

Andhra Pradesh have long coastlines, Bihar is landlocked. According to per capita income, Bihar is the poorest while Gujarat ranks third among the 15 largest states. Andhra Pradesh ranks in the middle group of states among these states.

SOME SALIENT FEATURES OF THE THREE STATES

All three states we have chosen to study have introduced state-level reforms in recent years and sustained them. Each has also achieved a very high rate of growth and, consequently, has been successful in cutting poverty significantly. Gujarat started out at a relatively high per capita income and grew particularly rapidly during the 1990s and 2000s and beyond. Bihar, on the other hand, started extremely poor and has had a long history of poor performance. While it remains the poorest in all-India and still has much catching up to do even with the other low-income states within India, it too has shown ultra-rapid growth since 2005. Andhra Pradesh began in the middle but has sustained a very high growth since the late 1990s and is a shining example of modernization and rapid reduction in poverty.

Among the three states, Gujarat is the most industrialized and urbanized, followed by Andhra Pradesh and Bihar in that order. Differences among the three states along these dimensions are vast. Despite rapid growth in recent years, the share of industry in the Gross State Domestic Product (GSDP) remains well below 10% in Bihar. According to the 2011 census, the proportion of population in urban areas in the state is a paltry 11.3%, the level prevailing in India as a whole in 1901. At the other extreme, industry accounts for more than 30% of the GSDP in Gujarat and census 2011 places urbanization in the state at 42.6%.

History played an important role in determining the economic outcomes in all three states. At the most basic level, consistent with Banerjee and Iyer (2005), the land tenure system under the British turned out to be a good predictor of subsequent performance in not just agriculture but also investment in education and health. To quote them (p. 1190), "Areas in which proprietary rights in land were historically given to landlords have significantly lower agricultural investments and productivity in the post-independence period than areas in which these rights were given to the cultivators. These areas also have significantly lower investments in health and education." Within the group of states analyzed in this volume, proprietary rights to land under the British were vested in the landlords in Bihar and with farmers in Gujarat. In Andhra Pradesh, the rights rested with farmers in 8 of the 10 districts in the Banerjee-Iyer sample. In the post-independence era, Gujarat and Andhra Pradesh have performed significantly better than Bihar in agriculture as well as education and health.

This is, of course, a highly stylized historical sketch. The studies in the volume offer much deeper and richer sketches of the role of history. The outcomes depend on not just what was inherited but also how political leadership in the states reacted to those legacies. In this respect, the studies also show that the leadership at the center as well in the states played a crucial role in determining the outcomes, given the initial conditions. At the center, the reforms that freed the states from the stranglehold of investment and import licensing owed much to the leadership of Prime Ministers Narasimha Rao and Atal Bihar Vajpayee. At the same time, the emergence of decisive and visionary leaders such as Chandrababu Naidu in Andhra Pradesh, Nitish Kumar in Bihar, and Narendra Modi in Gujarat at the helm was crucial to the turnaround or sustaining of growth in the states.

Before we proceed to offer a summary of the three state case studies, we note two points relating to the time period of the studies and the treatment of the data. First, consistent data series on the GSDP in Indian states begin in 1980/81. Therefore, setting aside the historical data and background, which each study provides, the formal beginning year of each study is 1980/81. Moreover, since the studies were launched in 2011, as editors, we made a conscious decision to make 2010/11 the terminal year of the studies. Therefore, much of the quantitative information provided in the studies spans 1980/81 to 2010/11. Where essential, occasional updating has been done, but this is in the nature of exception rather than the rule. One specific set of estimates that each study has updated relates to poverty. The estimates for 2011/12 turned out to be dramatically different from those available for the previous year, 2009/10, and were incorporated in the final drafts of the studies. Additionally, in the concluding chapter, we provide an update relating to the dramatic political developments in all three states during 2013 and, especially, 2014, and speculate on their implications for the future of the states.

The second point concerns the treatment of the data series. Here we have not tried to coordinate across the three studies. Therefore, depending on the decision each author made, the studies may use the GSDP or Net State Domestic product (NSDP). More importantly, the GSDP and NSDP data come in four different series: from 1980/81 to 1996/97 at 1980/81 prices, from 1993/94 to 2004/05 at 1993/94 prices, from 1999/2000 to 2009/10 at 1999/2000 prices, and from 2004/05 to 2010/11 at 2004/05 prices. In Panagariya, Chakraborty, and Rao (2014), we had converted these series to 2004/05 prices. In the present volume, we have not followed this approach, leaving the authors of each study free to present the data as they saw fit. Therefore, specific numbers on the GSDP and NSDP or per capita GSDP and NSDP in the studies in this volume will generally not match those in Panagariya, Chakraborty, and Rao (2014).

We are now in a position to present the highlights of the three studies.

ANDHRA PRADESH

The state was formed in 1956 by combining Telugu-speaking regions of the erstwhile Madras presidency and state of Hyderabad, which was also inhabited by Telugu-speaking population.[4] The state, which is analyzed in this volume in its pre-bifurcation form, is the fourth largest by area and fifth largest by population in India. It is also the largest of the four states in south India.

Mudit Kapoor and Rahul Ahluwalia, the authors of the study on Andhra Pradesh, highlight the success of the state by comparing it to the state of Uttar Pradesh. In 1993/94, Andhra Pradesh had a modest lead over Uttar Pradesh with its per capita income being 1.47 times that of the latter. This gap changed very little until 1997/98 but rose sharply thereafter. By 2004/05, the ratio of per capita income in Andhra Pradesh to that in Uttar Pradesh had climbed up to 1.93. This trend continued subsequently with the ratio reaching 2.27 by 2011/12.

Alongside, poverty also came crashing down. Based on the Tendulkar poverty line, the poverty ratio in Andhra Pradesh was just 3.7 percentage points below that in Uttar Pradesh. But the difference rose to 11 percentage points in 2004/05 and 20.2 percentage points in 2011/12. By 2011/12, the poverty ratio in Andhra Pradesh had dropped below 10% to 9.2%. The decline in rural poverty was even sharper.

How did this dramatic turnaround take place? Kapoor and Ahluwalia give much of the credit to the visionary leadership of Chief Minister Chandrababu Naidu of the Telugu Desam Party (TDP), who served as the Chief Minister of Andhra Pradesh from 1995 to 2004. Soon after taking office, he shifted away from exclusive focus on welfare schemes to economic growth and prosperity.[5] He recognized the potential of Information Technology (IT), biotechnology, healthcare, and the outsourcing services for Andhra Pradesh and the need for the development of major urban centers to attract investment into these industries.

---

4. The recent split of the state into two has taken place precisely along the lines of these two parts: the original state of Hyderabad has been named Telangana and the Telugu-speaking part of the old Madras presidency has inherited the name Andhra Pradesh.

5. A vision document adopted in 1999 articulated the importance of growth in promoting social objectives such as eradication of poverty and expansion of employment opportunities, education, and health in these lucid terms, "Economic growth will stimulate development in two ways. First, it will increase incomes for the people by creating employment opportunities. Second, it will generate additional resources for the Government. The Government will invest these resources mainly in social development, that is, eradicating poverty, improving education and health, promoting rural and urban development, and providing services such as housing, water, power, transportation, and so on."

Naidu invested in urban infrastructure, improved business environment through speedy clearances and sought out investors within and outside India. Hyderabad quickly found a place on the global map as an investment destination. Such IT majors as Microsoft, IBM, Dell, Computer Associates, and Oracle opened their offices in Hyderabad.

While his visionary leadership won him the 1999 election, Naidu unexpectedly lost the 2004 election. Y. S. Rajasekhara Reddy, popularly known as YSR, who belonged to the Congress, succeeded him. Although YSR had fought the election on the plank that the Naidu government had neglected agriculture, rural areas, and the rural poor, he did not reverse any of the policies of Naidu relating to industry and the services sectors. On the contrary, he significantly improved the pace of execution of the projects. Simultaneously, he took advantage of enhanced revenues due to high growth, the introduction of value added tax, higher tax devolution from the center, and lower interest payments on debt and debt write off by the center to increase spending on rural development and social programs. Among other things, Andhra Pradesh saw a rapid expansion of irrigation infrastructure, spread of microfinance, and the introduction of a major health insurance program called Aarogyasri in 2007. The focus on IT-based governance helped the state to implement the central programs much more efficiently and utilize the central grants much more effectively than most other states.

In summary, the analysis by Kapoor and Ahluwalia brings out the importance of three factors in accelerating growth and successfully combating poverty. First, state-level actions and governance are critical for catalyzing and sustaining rapid growth. Right from the time Naidu became the Chief Minister in 1995, the focus was on creating a market-friendly environment for entrepreneurs and modernizing administration to impart efficiency to governance and public service delivery. Although the leadership changed in 2004, policies to attract investments were continued and modified to ensure more balanced spread of investments to rural areas and social sectors.

Second, the focus on growth was important to reduce poverty in Andhra Pradesh. Acceleration in growth not only helped to reduce poverty directly but also created additional fiscal space to make investments in irrigation and expand health coverage. In turn, both these policies had the impact of reducing poverty, particularly of the disadvantaged groups at a faster rate than in most other states.

Finally, Andhra Pradesh's growth experience shows that leadership matters. While their appetites for populism differed, both Naidu and YSR worked hard toward creating an investor-friendly environment and actively courted entrepreneurs. Naidu, in particular, had a clear vision to build Hyderabad into a major urban agglomeration that would be a magnet for investors from within India as well as abroad. He fiercely competed against other states to bring investors to Hyderabad. His successor YSR continued his policies toward accelerating growth while using the additional fiscal space created by growth to spend more on agriculture and human development.

BIHAR

Throughout the post-independence era, Bihar has been the poorest among the 15 largest states in India. It has also grown well below the national average until recently. The ratio of per capita income in Bihar to that of the average of the country declined from 68% in 1980/81 to about a third in 1997/98 before recovering marginally to 38% by 2011/12. Low investment levels, large governance deficit, poor quality of human capital and frequent natural disasters had turned the state into a "basket case." The state has had the lowest per capita GSDP and one of the largest concentrations of poverty.

Arnab Mukherji and Anjan Mukherji analyze the trends in the growth performance of the state over the period 1980/81 to 2010/11 by dividing the time period into three phases. The first phase spanning 1980/81 to 1999/2000 is marked by stagnation and decline in the relative share of the state in per capita income. The second phase begins with the bifurcation of the state to carve out Jharkhand in 2000 with severe adverse impact on the economy of the state. The third phase coincides with the change in the government headed by Nitish Kumar in 2005 after 14 years of rule by the government headed by Lalu Prasad Yadav. This period is marked by rejuvenation of the economy through improved governance and economic management and consequent large acceleration in the growth of per capita GSDP and reduction in poverty.

Mukherji and Mukherji begin by recounting the rich heritage of Bihar, which had seen the rise and fall of many a flourishing kingdom during the past three millennia. Beginning as early as 600 B.C., the state has seen the succession of several kingdoms with the governance systems varying from the good, the bad, and the indifferent. It produced leaders some of whom were benevolent, some others exploitative, and still others ineffective. Two of the four religions originating in India—Buddhism and Jainism—originated in Bihar. And the first ruler to unify almost all of India under a single banner in the third century B.C., Chandragupta Maurya, came from Bihar. His advisor, Chanakya, produced the first treatise in statecraft that largely anticipated Machiavelli's *Prince*. Through the millennia, Bihar was the epicenter of the regimes that unified India, created and disseminated knowledge, and established institutions of learning.

In sharp contrast, modern Bihar has been steeped in low incomes, a vicious cycle of poverty, and poor human development. Mukherji and Mukherji summarize the matter thus, "Bihar's rich history . . . offers itself as an example of a society that underwent multiple expansions and contractions within different and evolving social structures and governance systems." Their analysis of history brings out the role that initial conditions and leadership play in development. History shapes the nature and quality of institutions that determine the structure of incentives that make or mar the growth process.

The history of Bihar during and following the colonial era offers important insights into the subsequent economic performance of Bihar. First, the permanent settlement system of revenue collection that the British instituted created a feudal system that was reinforced by the prevailing caste-based hierarchy. The constraints and rigidities implicit in the system impacted adversely on incentives and accountability besides causing inefficiency in resource use. The revenue collection system, which vested the land rights in the revenue collector called the zamindar eliminated the incentive to the tiller to make any improvements in land.

Second, the central government policies in the post-independence era also proved harmful to the development of a resource-rich state like Bihar. The policy of freight equalization, which fixed uniform prices of resources throughout the country by adjusting the net price received by the seller depending on the transport cost, not only rendered the resource-rich states poor by placing the entire burden of transport cost on them but also worked against industrialization in the states where the resources were located. Freight equalization eliminated any advantage the states with resources would have enjoyed in the manufacturing activity related to those resources.

Finally, it is possible to overcome the constraints posed by history with enlightened leadership and effective governance to protect life and property of the people and deliver public services efficiency as has been shown since 2004/05. When the state is a mute spectator and "roving bandits" are on the loose, there cannot be any incentive to save and invest and growth is simply not possible, a point the history of Bihar illustrates well.[6] The most important component of governance even in a minimalist state is to ensure law and order and protect life and property of the people, which provides basic incentives to save, invest, and grow.

As just noted, Bihar's per capita GSDP was just 68% of the national average in 1980/81. However, from the late 1980s and especially early 1990s, Bihar's relative position worsened steadily, and it was just about a third of the national average by the end of the millennium. During the period 1980/1998,

---

6. Mancur Olson (1993) distinguishes among economic effects of anarchy, dictatorship, and democracy. He argues that a roving bandit (anarchist) only has an incentive to steal and destroy and therefore is harmful to growth and development. A stationary bandit (dictator) has an interest in promoting saving and investment though the nature of the investment is designed to serve the interests of the bandit. It is only under participatory democracy that "encompassing" growth that serves the interests of the people at large is possible.

while the per capita income in India registered an average annual growth of 3.2%, the growth in Bihar was just about 1.1%. The corresponding decline in poverty in Bihar was also slower. The trend broadly continued after bifurcation of Bihar until 2004/05 when the National Democratic Alliance government led by an effective Chief Minister Nitish Kumar assumed the office. The subsequent period (2005–10) witnessed a significant improvement with Bihar's per capita GSDP increasing at 8.5% as compared to 7% in the country despite the devastating floods in 2007. In fact, the growth rate during 2010/12 in Bihar was over 14% as compared to about 6.8% in the country.

In addition to the permanent settlement and freight equalization policy, Mukherji and Mukherji point to three additional sources of the poor performance of Bihar. First, the failure to construct a dam across the Kosi River at the base in Nepal and the erection of a temporary barrage instead became a major source of devastation. This failure has meant that the river has been a continuous source of misery rather than livelihood.

Second, the authors highlight the poor governance and non-performing leadership as a factor in the poor performance of the economy until 2004/05. During the period 1990–2005, the state faced a serious law and order problem. The state effectively came to be infested with roving bandits, eliminating the incentives to save and invest. The leadership did not implement many of the anti-poverty programs on the premise that the upper castes too will gain from them. The vacant posts of teachers and health workers were not filled to ostensibly deny the benefit of employment to the upper castes and this severely constrained the delivery of public services.

Finally, inability of the fiscal transfer mechanism to offset the fiscal disabilities in Bihar arising from low revenue-raising capacity proved another important handicap. Because of this factor, the spending on social and physical infrastructure fell substantially below the national average. Indeed, lack of protection against natural disasters like floods has been one of the outcomes. In addition, unfavorable terms of bifurcation that left the state with three-fourths of the liabilities and but significantly smaller share of the assets left it yet poorer.

But the 2005 state election brought about a dramatic change in the circumstances. Bihar quickly became one of the fastest growing states in India. The acceleration was not accidental; instead, it resulted from the change of leadership. One of the first actions of the Nitish Kumar government was to ban the public display of arms and focus on law and order, which worked toward ending the regime of roving banditry. The attempt to augment social services by filling in the vacant positions of teachers and health workers helped to improve the social indicators. The attempt to improve the road infrastructure to enable people from every part of the state to reach Patna within six hours helped improve mobility, market access, and economic activity.

GUJARAT

In their comprehensive study, Archana Dholakia and Ravindra Dholakia discuss the development of Gujarat state in terms of agricultural growth, industrialization, urbanization, education, and health. While their emphasis is on the years following 1980/81, they offer important details of the evolution of the economy beginning with the formation of the state in May 1960. They show that during the first three decades the economic performance of the state was at best moderate relative to the average of the country but has been significantly better since the 1990s. The structural transformation in the economy is seen in terms of a significantly higher share of industry in GSDP as compared to the average of the country. The state has also achieved a much greater degree of urbanization than India as a whole. The only shortcoming seen in the state is the slow pace of movement of labor from agriculture into industry and services. Almost half of the workforce continues to rely on agriculture, as is the case in the country as a whole.

In terms of per capita GSDP, Gujarat performed moderately during the first three decades, but during the 1990s and 2000s the performance was significantly better than the national average. The state's rank among the largest 15 states moved from fifth in 1993/94 to third at the present, despite the devastating earthquake in 2001. In fact, the growth performance of the state since 2000/01 has been significantly higher than the average of the country in the primary, secondary, as well as tertiary sectors of the economy. The state has a much higher share of the industry sector in GSDP than the all-state average, and during the last decade and a half manufacturing employment has also shown a rapid increase. Commensurate with acceleration in growth, there has been a steady decline in poverty throughout the past two decades in both rural and urban areas and within all social groups including the Scheduled Castes and Scheduled Tribes. Rapid growth in the state has been achieved without increase in inequality and with the level of inequality continuing to be well below the country's average.

Over the years, there have been improvements in social indicators in Gujarat, more than the national average. The literacy rate in Gujarat, which was higher than the national average by 3 percentage points in 1961, improved to a lead of about 5 percentage points in 2011, and particularly large gains in this indicator have been made during the 2000s. In health indicators such as infant mortality, maternal mortality, and life expectancy too the performance of Gujarat has been better than the national average. The institutional deliveries in the state are much higher than the average for the country. Even in the much-debated indicator of malnourishment of children, the recent report of the Comptroller and Auditor General of India (CAG 2013) shows that Gujarat made the greatest progress in bringing down child malnutrition between 2007 and 2011. Thus, in terms of both economic and social indicators, there have been significant improvements.

As mentioned above, the growth performance of agriculture in the state since 2000/01 at over 6.4% has not only been much higher than that of the average of the country but also the volatility has been much lower. The reason for this has to be found in several policy initiatives taken by the state government, such as expansion in irrigation, thanks to the progress made in Sardar Sarovar project, water conservation, and water management; assured electricity supply to agriculture; emphasis on wheat, sesame and several non-food crops like BT Cotton, horticulture, castor beans, and sesame; marketing and information networking to help farmers; support to the livestock sector; and promotion of agricultural exports by creating a reliable infrastructure.

The policies to promote industrial development have been enunciated virtually every five years (1990, 1995, 2000, 2003, and 2009). While the first three policies had the emphasis on various incentives and subsidies for capital investment, sales tax, and geographical coverage of units, the last two policies were aimed at making Gujarat industries globally competitive, creating a global brand image of the state, and attracting mega investment projects into it. Not surprisingly, the annual industrial growth since 2000/01 has been 11.8% as compared to 8.8% nationally. This could be achieved due to a series of policy initiatives, particularly in co-opting the private sector to ensure competitive standards of physical infrastructure such as ports and roads, water, power, storage, and marketing. Interestingly, unlike in most other states, the industry sector in Gujarat is as important as services and a part of this is attributable to more lax application of labor laws within the overall constraint posed by the central labor legislation. Reduced inspector visits to industrial units, self-assessment coupled with heavy penalties for cheating, allowance of contract labor, speedy disposal of labor disputes, and the non-intervention policy of the state government have helped to improve the climate of industrial relations.

The government in the last two decades has focused on a variety of other policies to create an enabling environment for the growth of industry and services. These include facilitating the growth of urban areas, which are centers of production and distribution. The government repealed the Urban Land Ceiling Act early on, increased the land coverage in urban areas to reduce density of urban population, improved the provision of basic urban services including water supply, sanitation, and solid waste disposal, facilitated migration to urban areas to relieve pressure on land, improved urban road density and the quality of urban roads, and introduced mass rapid transportation system in Ahmedabad. Although the unprecedented earthquake in 2001 derailed the rigorous fiscal reforms program put in place in the late 1990s to achieve fiscal consolidation, the effort was renewed after the reconstruction phase. The rationalization and simplification of the tax system and later introduction of value added tax in 2005, the passage of fiscal responsibility legislation in 2005, adherence to the targets set in the medium-term fiscal plan, and, more important, effective power sector reforms helped to create significant fiscal space for spending on physical and social infrastructure and surplus power to industry and agriculture.

Higher public spending on social sectors has led to significant improvements in input-based measures of educational performance. However, much remains to be done in the areas of both elementary and higher education. Although there have also been significant improvements in most of the health outcome indicators in Gujarat, these were not commensurate with the economic growth in the state mainly because of the slow expansion of public health infrastructure during 1992–97 and its virtual stagnation during 2002–09. Since 2007/08, however, the government has made substantially increased public expenditure allocation to the health sector.

A major focus area of the state government has been effective governance. We have already mentioned expeditious decision-making and the provision of single-window clearance for industrial projects as some of the measures in this direction. Application of modern technology to deliver public services efficiently, judicial reforms to reduce pendency in courts, measures to improve transparency, accountability, and interdepartmental coordination have helped the state attract significant additional investments.

As Dholakia and Dholakia explicitly discuss, leadership has played a crucial role in the impressive performance of Gujarat. Narendra Modi, who became the Chief Minister of the state in 2001, has been behind the effective and largely corruption-free political leadership. A hands-on Chief Minister, he has personally led many of the initiatives taken during his rule. He participates in the agricultural fairs the state organizes every year to directly reach out to farmers and provide extension services. He also takes direct interest in the major industrial and infrastructure projects to ensure that clearances proceed expeditiously and without corruption. According to a famous story, when the Tata project of the Nano car ran into problems in West Bengal, Modi directly sent a text message to Ratan Tata, the head of the Tata Group, inviting the project to Gujarat. The car is now being manufactured in Gujarat. Modi also played active role in the organization and execution of the Vibrant Gujarat Summit, organized every other year, to bring investors from around the world to Gujarat. Under him, the state acquired the image of an investor-friendly destination around the world.

CONCLUDING REMARKS

The purpose of this volume is to study how and why different states evolve differently in a democratic country with a federal structure. The three states chosen for detailed case studies have had different histories and institutions.

In the initial year of study, 1980/81, they were at different stages of market development. They also followed different sets of policies and naturally the experience in regard to growth and development differed markedly. They exhibit different levels of per capita incomes, shares of industry in output, rate of urbanization, and education and health outcomes. Yet, recently, they have all managed to grow rapidly. This last fact points to some common factors across the three states. We shall return to identifying these common factors in the final, concluding chapter in this volume.

Presently, we note that even between the terminal year of the studies and the year of completion of the volume, important changes with serious implications for future developments have taken place in each of the three states. Andhra Pradesh, the largest southern state, has been divided into its two original component parts: Telangana which comprises of predominantly the original State of Hyderabad (Medak and Warrangal divisions) originally ruled by the Nizams, which has been named Telangana, and the Telugu-speaking part of the old Madras presidency consisting of coastal Andhra Pradesh and Rayalaseema, which has inherited the name Andhra Pradesh. Interestingly, Chandrababu Naidu has returned as the first Chief Minister of the new Andhra Pradesh.

In sharp contrast, Chief Minister Nitish Kumar has experienced a serious political setback. He broke the alliance with the Bharatiya Janata Party (BJP) in reaction to the latter's choice of the Gujarat Chief Minister Narendra Modi as its prime ministerial candidate in the May 2014 national parliamentary elections. The break-up proved devastating for his party and him personally. BJP, in alliance with a regional party (Lok Janashakti Party), won the vast majority of parliamentary seats, dramatically weakening the position of Nitish Kumar and his party. Feeling morally responsible for the defeat, Nitish Kumar resigned as Chief Minister with another member of his party replacing him. Even more surprisingly, the old friends turned foes, Nitish Kumar and Lalu Prasad Yadav, are now talking reconciliation.

In Gujarat, the change has been triggered by its Chief Minister Narendra Modi seizing control of the BJP national leadership. Recognizing his rising stature nationally, the party elevated him to the position of its prime ministerial candidate in the May 2014 parliamentary elections. He ran the most effective election campaign in the Indian history and went on to score a decisive victory. He is now the Prime Minister of India and has been succeeded in Gujarat by his protégé Anandiben Patel. This means that of the three states, Gujarat has the highest prospects of continuity in the economic policies. We will return to this and related issues in the concluding chapter.

CHAPTER 1 REFERENCES

Ahluwalia, M. (2000). "Economic Performance of the States in Post Reform Period." *Economic and Political Weekly*, May 6, 1637–1648.

Banerjee, Abhijit, and Lakshmi Iyer (2005). "History, Institutions, and Economic Performance: The Legacy of Colonial Land Tenure Systems in India." *American Economic Review* 95(4): 1190–1213.

Breton, Albert (1996). *Competitive Governments*. New York: Cambridge University Press.

CAG (Comptroller and Auditor General of India) (2013). "Report No. 4 of 2013: Government of Gujarat – Report of the Comptroller and Auditor General of India on General and Social Sectors." Government of India. http://www.saiindia.gov.in/english/home/Our_Products/Audit_Report/Government_Wise/state_audit/recent_reports/Gujarat/2013/Report_4/Report_4.html

Government of Maharashtra (2014). *Economic Survey of Maharashtra 2013–14*. Mumbai: Directorate of Economics and Statistics, Planning Department. http://www.indiaenvironmentportal.org.in/files/file/esm_2013-14_eng.pdf

Oates, Wallace (1999). "An Essay on Fiscal Federalism." *Journal of Economic Literature* 37(3): 1120–1149.

Olson, Mancur (1993). "Dictatorship, Democracy and Development." *American Journal of Political Science* 87(3): 567–576.

Panagariya, Arvind, Pinaki Chakraborty, and M. Govinda Rao (2014), *State Level Reforms, Growth and Development of Indian States*, New York: Oxford University Press.

Salmon, Pierre (1987). "Decentralization as an Incentive Scheme." *Oxford Review of Economic Policy* 3(2): 32–43.

PART I
Andhra Pradesh
MUDIT KAPOOR AND RAHUL AHLUWALIA

CHAPTER 2

Andhra Pradesh: Setting the Stage

In 1999, Andhra Pradesh's government took, what was for an Indian state government, the novel step of releasing a vision document for the state.[1] This document committed the state government to achieving a high quality of life for all its citizens by the year 2020. Its specific goals included the eradication of poverty, the empowerment of women and vulnerable groups, stabilization of its population, and the enablement of this population, through improved health and education, to participate in and fulfill the opportunities presented to it. While ambitious and unusual in their timeline and articulation at the state level, these goals are what any otherwise responsible government would aspire to. The vision document however, went on to clearly identify its engine of choice for achieving these goals—economic growth—and to envision a new paradigm for government, from being merely a controller of the economy, to an enabler of its growth.

> Economic growth will stimulate development in two ways. First, it will increase incomes for the people by creating employment opportunities. Second, it will generate additional resources for the Government. The Government will invest these resources mainly in social development, that is, eradicating poverty, improving education and health, promoting rural and urban development, and providing services such as housing, water, power, transportation, and so on.
>
> . . .

---

1. We would like to thank Arvind Panagariya for his extensive comments on multiple earlier drafts and JA Chowdary, BVR Mohan Reddy, Pramath Raj Sinha, Shamika Ravi, Sudip Gupta, Reuben Abraham, Rana Hasan, Srini Raju and participants of the National Institute of Public Finance and Policy-Columbia University Conference on August 7–8, 2012, and the Indian School of Business Seminar for extremely helpful comments.

> Finally, to promote rapid development, the State Government will need to transform itself and quickly adopt a new role: from being primarily a controller of the economy, it must become a facilitator and catalyst of its growth.

The political drive behind this reimagining of government's role came from Chandrababu Naidu, who became chief minister of Andhra Pradesh in 1994. The vision document was meant to demonstrate the targets that Andhra Pradesh had taken on for itself, to inspire the bureaucracy, and, at the same time, put in place metrics against which the achievements of the government could be measured.

Much water has passed under the Godavari bridge since 1999. Political administrations have come and gone, and on June 2, 2014, Telangana, the twenty-ninth state of India was created by splitting up Andhra Pradesh. Given the generally laudable nature of the goals laid out in the vision document however, we examine what the data says about the progress of Andhra Pradesh toward these ends. We also explore the means adopted to achieve them, with a view toward commenting on their effectiveness and identifying takeaways that can support policymakers in Andhra Pradesh, the new state of Telangana, and elsewhere.

Before its bifurcation, Andhra Pradesh was India's fourth largest state by area and fifth largest by population. With a population of 84.7 million in 2011, it was also the largest of the four states in south India. Tamil Nadu, Karnataka, and Kerala in that order followed it in population size. Unless otherwise specified, we will use "Andhra Pradesh" to refer to the state as it existed before it was split up in 2014. We address some of the implications of the split and provide a detailed breakdown of the economic performance of the different regional units of erstwhile Andhra Pradesh, including the region that is now the state of Telangana, in the appendix.

Andhra Pradesh was formed in 1956 by combining the Telugu-speaking regions of the erstwhile Madras presidency and the state of Hyderabad. Tamil-speaking regions of the south came to form Tamil Nadu, Malayalam-speaking regions formed Kerala, and Kannada-speaking regions became Karnataka. India-wide, Andhra Pradesh is the fifth largest state, preceded by Uttar Pradesh, Maharashtra, Bihar, and West Bengal in the northern half of the country. It accounts for 7% of the country's total population.

Ironically, the movement for the separate state of Telangana sought to split the state precisely along the lines of its original formation. Telangana state was formed from the regions that were a part of the original Hyderabad state, leaving Rayalseema and Coastal Andhra Pradesh, which were a part of Madras presidency, as a separate state.

Andhra Pradesh has been among the more rapidly transforming states of India since the launch of the economic reforms. This is perhaps best illustrated by a comparison between the evolution of growth and poverty in

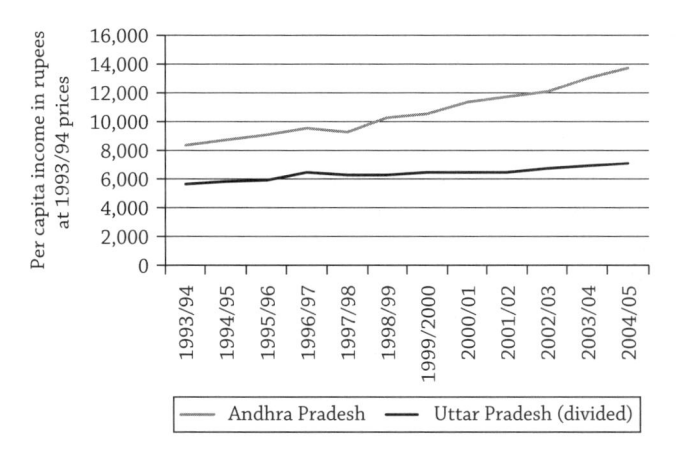

Figure 2.1: Per Capita GSDP in Andhra Pradesh and Uttar Pradesh, 1993/94 to 2004/05
Source: The author's construction based on calculations using the CSO data on the GSDP and census data on population.

Andhra Pradesh and Uttar Pradesh. In the early 1990s, the two states had comparable per capita incomes and poverty levels. But by the early 2000s, they looked dramatically different.

Before presenting the comparison, we may note that the Central Statistical Office (CSO) provides comparable Gross State Domestic Product (GSDP) data for years 1980/81 to 2011/12. Unfortunately, however, these data come in four series covering four partially overlapping sub-periods within these years. Each of these series measures the GSDP at prices relating to a different base year. In particular, we have GSDP estimates for years from 1980/81 to 1997/98 at 1980/81 prices; for those from 1993/94 to 2004/05 at 1993/94 prices; for 1999/2000 to 2006/07 at 1999/2000 prices and for 2004/05 to 2011/12 at 2004/05 prices. In principle, we can convert the four series into a single one at prices in any one of the four years at which these series are computed. But since the choice of the year and the precise overlapping years used for the conversion would impact the construction of the series, there is some arbitrariness involved in the conversion. Therefore, we choose to work with the series in the original form.

Accordingly, combining the GSDP estimates from the second of the above four series with corresponding population estimates, we depict per capita GSDP in Andhra Pradesh and Uttar Pradesh from 1993/94 to 2004/05 at 1993/94 prices in figure 2.1.[2] In 1993/94, per capita income in Andhra Pradesh was 1.47 times that in Uttar Pradesh. This proportionate gap remained approximately unchanged until 1997/98. But beginning in 1998/99, the gap widened rapidly

---

2. We calculate the population in any given year using the census populations just preceding and following that year and assuming a constant compound growth rate between the two censuses.

and the ratio of per capita income in Andhra Pradesh to that in Uttar Pradesh climbed up to 1.93 in 2004/05.

The process of widening of the gap continued in subsequent years. This is shown in figure 2.2, which depicts per capita incomes in the two states between 2004/05 and 2011/12 at 2004/05 prices. By 2011/12, per capita income in Andhra Pradesh as a proportion of that in Uttar Pradesh had climbed up to 2.27.

The differences in the performance of per capita GSDP between the two states also translated into differences in combating poverty. This is shown in figure 2.3, which exhibits the proportion of population below

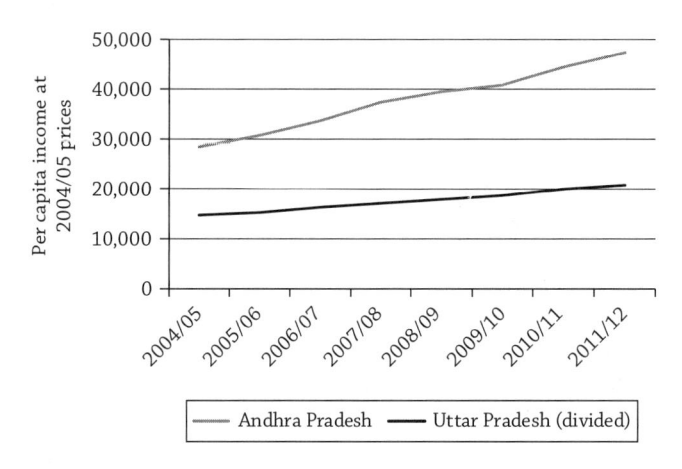

Figure 2.2: Per Capita GSDP in Andhra Pradesh and Uttar Pradesh, 2004/05 to 2011/12
Source: The author's construction based on calculations using the CSO data on the GSDP and census data on population.

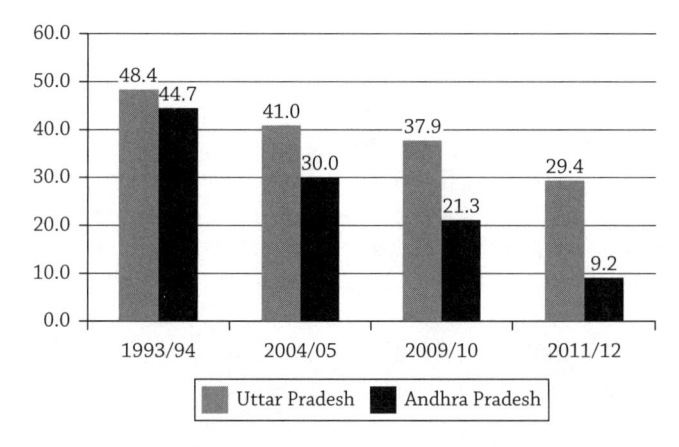

Figure 2.3: Poverty Ratios in Andhra Pradesh and Uttar Pradesh, 1993/94, 2004/05, 2009/10, and 2011/12
Source: Author's construction using poverty estimates from different NSSO surveys.

the poverty line in years 1993/94, 2004/05, 2009/10, and 2011/12 at the Tendulkar poverty line. The two states began with relatively small differences in poverty rates in 1993/94: just 3.7 percentage points. This difference rose to 11 percentage points in 2004/05, 16.6 percentage points in 2009/10, and 20.2 percentage points in 2011/12. The gap has become progressively larger.

Admittedly, some of the differences in the response to the central reforms that began in earnest in 1991 but continued until at least 2003/04 can be attributed to the differences in the initial conditions pertaining to such variables as population size, caste composition, initial income level, income distribution, geography, natural resources, and the composition of GSDP across sectors. But prima facie these factors seem insufficient to explain the sustained rise in the gap for nearly two decades. Therefore, it is a reasonable hypothesis that Andhra Pradesh government also took policy measures that allowed it to better exploit the opportunities opened up by the liberalization by the central government.

Deep down, the superior performance of Andhra Pradesh is to be traced to its superior leadership. The state has been lucky to have at least two excellent successive chief ministers. The beginnings of the divergent fortunes of Andhra Pradesh and Uttar Pradesh are to be traced to the mid-1990s when the state saw a change in the leadership, which also brought a dramatic change in the approach to development policy.

In 1995, Chandrababu Naidu, leader of the Telugu Desam Party (TDP), became the chief minister of the state. N. T. Rama Rao, a film actor who was popularly known as NTR, had founded the TDP in 1982. At the time, 32-year-old Naidu, who also happened to be NTR's son-in-law, was a member of the cabinet in the Congress government that ruled from 1978 to 1983 in the state. Although NTR asked Naidu to join the TDP, the latter chose to contest the 1983 election on the Congress ticket and lost his seat. NTR formed the first ever non-Congress government in Andhra Pradesh.

Soon after losing the election, Naidu joined the TDP. He became NTR's trusted lieutenant and quickly rose in stature. After a party crisis in 1984, NTR sought a new mandate and won a landslide victory. In the 1989 election, though Naidu won his seat on the TDP ticket, the party lost the election to the Congress. In the following election in 1994, the TDP captured power yet again, however. As the right-hand man of NTR, Naidu became the finance and revenue minister. On August 23, 1995, Naidu engineered an internal party coup against NTR and became the state's chief minister on September 1, 1995. He also became the president of the TDP.

Under Naidu, the political climate shifted away from near exclusive focus on welfare schemes to the promotion of economic growth and prosperity. Early in the game, he recognized the potential that information technology (IT), biotechnology, healthcare, and the outsourcing services held for

Andhra Pradesh. Simultaneously, he understood the need for the development of major urban centers to attract investment into these industries.

Naidu himself succinctly described his philosophy of the intimate link between these industries and major urban centers in a 2004 interview.[3] Responding to a question on his development philosophy, he stated, "I am very clear about my perception of development. If you want to develop a state, you have to make its main cities a showpiece. Hyderabad is the capital of Andhra Pradesh. Naturally, when a foreign investor is coming, if I ask them to go to Warangal, Tirupati or Vijayawada, they may not go. So for the key sectors like information technology, biotechnology, healthcare and various outsourcing services, we had to develop Hyderabad. Then from Hyderabad, we were taking and spreading development to other areas of Andhra Pradesh."

Consistent with this philosophy, Naidu gave the slogan "Bye-Bye Bangalore, Hello Hyderabad" and took his vision to the global and local business community. He invested in building infrastructure, especially in the cities, improved business environment in the state through faster government clearances and proactively pursued potential investors within and outside India. In a relatively short period, he placed Hyderabad on the global map as an important investment destination. Virtually all IT majors including Microsoft, IBM, Dell, Computer Associates and Oracle setup their shops in Hyderabad. So visible was the impact of his mission to turn Hyderabad into a hub of the IT industry that it came to be called Cyberabad.

Naidu's visionary leadership brought a new era of prosperity into the state. Incomes rose and poverty fell, as shown in figures 2.1 to 2.3. He was rewarded with victory in the 1999 election, which gave him another five years to implement his vision. Unfortunately, however, he unexpectedly lost the 2004 election. His own explanation of the defeat was a severe drought preceding the election. But perhaps superior campaign strategy of the Congress Party, which traditionally had an extensive and well-functioning campaign machinery, also played an important role. Some have suggested that Naidu's singular focus on urban development was the central cause of his defeat but this explanation runs into the difficulty that in the 2004 election the TDP lost in not just rural areas but major cities, including Hyderabad as well.

Y. S. Rajasekhara Reddy, popularly known as YSR and head of the Congress in Andhra Pradesh, had fought the election on a populist platform. The election outcome had also been widely described in the press as reflecting public disenchantment with Naidu's focus on the development of urban areas and the IT industry. Therefore, soon after his election, the business community was apprehensive that YSR would undo the economic reforms undertaken by his predecessor and focus exclusively on welfare schemes. But he proved

3. See http://www.rediff.com/news/2004/nov/11inter.htm.

himself to be an astute politician. He surprised the business community by not only leaving all of Naidu's economic reforms intact but also significantly improving the pace of execution of the projects. At the same time, he placed added emphasis on rural development programs and social spending. The financial discipline and accelerated growth under Naidu had helped generate significantly larger revenues, which made rural development programs and social spending on larger scale feasible. By staying the course on reforms, YSR was able to sustain and accelerate growth, which in turn allowed him to finance more anti-poverty programs and speed up poverty reduction.

We shall see in this study that accelerated growth under YSR was accompanied by accelerated decline in poverty all around: rural and urban Andhra Pradesh, among the disadvantaged groups known as the Scheduled Castes and Scheduled Tribes and different religious groups. Poverty reduction among the socially disadvantaged groups under the YSR regime turned out to be three to four times larger than that under Naidu. This is perhaps the single biggest achievement of the YSR regime.

In a nutshell, YSR efficiently continued the pro-growth economic agenda, whose foundation was laid by his predecessor Chandrababu Naidu, but at the same time he took the benefits of growth proactively to socially and economically backward sections of the society. It was no surprise therefore that in 2009 he was re-elected as the chief minister of the state and created history by being the only full-term chief minister of Andhra Pradesh to be re-elected.

Unfortunately, however, YSR met untimely death in a helicopter crash in 2009 resulting in political turmoil that has the potential to derail the process of economic growth and widespread prosperity. The demand of a separate state for Telangana re-emerged as a major political issue in the aftermath of his death. One of the key reasons put forward for this demand was the neglect of the economic development of Telangana under unified Andhra Pradesh. Ironically, our regional social and economic analysis shows that Telangana has been one of the biggest beneficiaries both in terms of economic growth and poverty reduction.

Although much has been achieved in terms of economic growth and poverty reduction since the early 1990s, there are certain areas of concern, particularly in terms of employment opportunities. In terms of overall output a large share comes from the services sector. But insofar as workers are concerned, agriculture with its lower growth and higher volatility remains their largest employer. Limited or no education on the part of the workers in agriculture and the concentration of nonagricultural growth in capital- and skilled-labor-intensive sectors have combined to discourage migration of workers out of the former into industry and services. The performance of the state in terms of education when compared to India as a whole is not exemplary and leaves a lot of room for improvement. The data on employment and unemployment also suggests an increased reliance on casual rather than regular employment in the recent years.

So far this has not become an issue because the growth of real wages of casual workers in rural and urban Andhra Pradesh is among the highest in India, but it does pose a question of sustainability. For example, in urban areas, a large percentage of the casual workers were in the construction sector, which experienced a massive boom from 2004 to 2009. But as growth in the construction sector slows down it would result in a slowdown in the growth in real wages thus adversely affecting the pace of poverty reduction.

We deal with these and other issues in greater detail in the remainder of this study. In chapter 3, we discuss the economic growth between 1981/82 and 2011/12, the associated transformation of the economy and the policies that can potentially explain them. In chapter 4 we examine how the situation of poverty and employment in the state has changed since 1993/94 and the factors that contributed to the changes. In chapter 5 we look at two areas where Andhra Pradesh has been a leader of sorts—Microfinance and the National Rural Employment Guarantee Act. In chapter 6 we look at two very important components of development—health and education. Chapter 7 summarizes and concludes while the appendix provides an analysis of the implications of the split and a region-wise economic analysis of Andhra Pradesh.

CHAPTER 3

Growth and Economic Transformation

In this chapter, we consider the economic growth and transformation of Andhra Pradesh during the three decades spanning 1981/82 to 2011/12. We divide this period into three distinct phases: Phase I from 1982/83 to 1993/94; Phase II consisting of 1994/95 to 2003/04, and Phase III beginning in 2004/05 and continuing. The latest year in Phase III for which we have data is 2011/12, which will also serve as the terminal year of Phase III for the purpose of this study.[1] For completeness, we should note that at the beginning of the period that we focus on, Andhra Pradesh was regarded as one of the less developed Indian states, and its per capita growth rate of 0.31 percentage points in the 20 years prior to our period of focus were a matter of some concern to economists (Rao 1988; Mukund 1989).

Although piecemeal reforms at the center had been undertaken throughout the 1980s with some acceleration in them during the second half of the decade, they became systematic and systemic only in 1991. Since 1991 was also a year of crisis, the impact of reforms in the early 1990s was minimal, thus justifying the inclusion of the years 1991–94 into the first phase.[2] Moreover, the choice of 1993/94 as the last year of Phase I also gives a close correspondence of Phase II with the Naidu era.

Prime Minister Atal Bihari Vajpayee, who served from 1998 to 2004, carried the reforms initiated by Prime Minister Narasimha Rao during the first half of the 1990s much further. Therefore, the last of the three phases was characterized by the most liberal policy regime at the national level. The same was equally true at the level of the state. While Naidu had laid down the

---

1. With the year 1981/82 chosen as the beginning year of the analysis, 1982/83 is the first year for which we can calculate the growth rate.
2. Throughout the study, a period such as 1991–94 refers to years from 1991/92 to 1993/94. Therefore, Phase I refers to years 1982–94, Phase II to 1994–2004, and Phase III to 2005–12.

foundation of the reforms in Andhra Pradesh, Y. S. Rajasekhara Reddy (YSR) strengthened them and gave the policy environment greater certainty.

The remainder of this chapter is divided into seven sections. In the next section, we discuss the pattern of overall growth in the economy over time. In the second section, we turn to the transformation in terms of shifts of output and workforce out of agriculture and into industry and services resulting in increased urbanization. In the third section, we turn to the policies in agriculture with a view to explaining the pattern of growth in this sector. In the fourth section, we discuss the policies in industry and in the fifth section the reforms in the power sector to explain why industrial growth during the 1990s was lackluster while turning significantly more robust in the 2000s. In the sixth section, we turn to an explanation of the success of the information technology (IT) sector. In the seventh section, we provide concluding remarks.

GROWTH IN PER CAPITA GSDP

Unless otherwise specified, growth rates in this study are based on the GSDP data at 1980/81 prices for years from 1982/83 to 1993/94, at 1993/94 prices for years from 1993/94 to 2004/05, and at 2004/05 prices for years from 2004/05 to 2011/12. The output shares for years 1981/82 to 1993/94 are derived from the first series, those for 1994/95 to 2004/05 from the second series, and those from 2005/06 to 2011/12 from the last one.

Figure 3.1 provides the summary of per capita GSDP growth during the three phases. The first set of bars shows the average growth rates in per capita GSDP and the second set the coefficient of variation of the growth rates. The figure shows that growth not only accelerated over successive phases, year-to-year fluctuations in it dramatically declined. The figure is

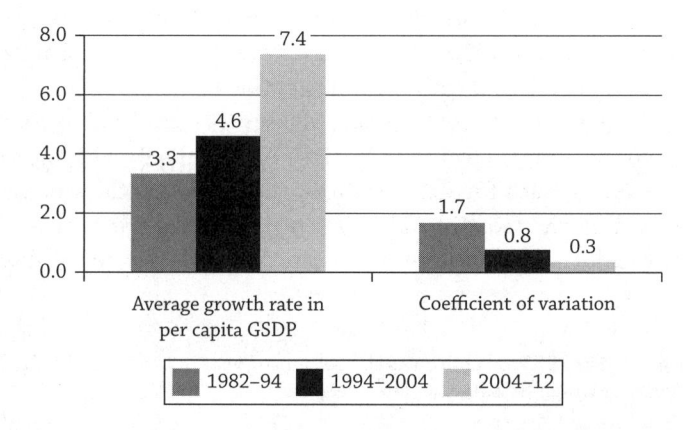

Figure 3.1: Average Growth Rate and Volatility of Growth of Andhra Pradesh GSDP
Source: Author's construction using the CSO data.

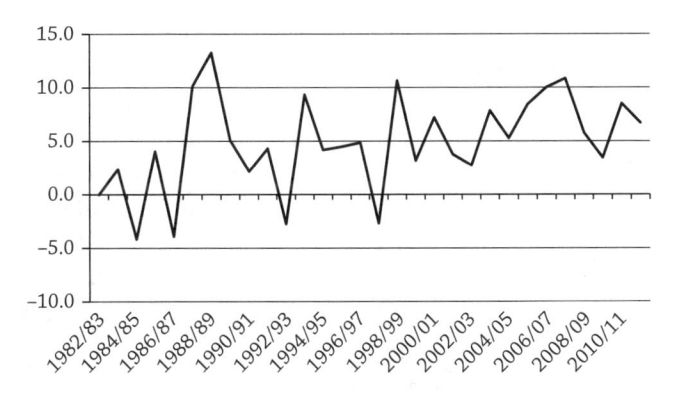

Figure 3.2: Per Capita GSDP Growth in Andhra Pradesh
Source: Author's construction using the CSO data.

also consistent with the view taken in the first chapter that the Naidu era laid down the foundation of the significantly higher growth that Andhra Pradesh was to experience in the third phase under YSR. Growth acceleration during the Naidu era itself was smaller principally because the effect of the reforms by him at the level of the state and those by Prime Minister Vajpayee were fully realized only beginning in 2003/04. What is significant about the Naidu era is that it laid down the foundation of a much more stable and higher growth rate in the YSR era.

Figure 3.2, which plots the annual growth rates in per capita GSDP, provides a graphic depiction of the steady decline in the volatility in the growth rate. During the first phase, growth rate turned negative on three separate occasions, 1984/85, 1986/87, and 1992/93. It also jumped above 10% during two years, 1987/88 and 1988/89, in this phase. In contrast, growth rate dropped below zero only once during Phase II in 1997/98 and not at all during Phase III. At the other extreme, the growth rate crossed the 10% mark only once during each of the last two phases. This declining volatility is neatly captured by the coefficient of variation, which dropped from 1.7 in Phase I to just 0.3 in Phase III.

THE ECONOMIC TRANSFORMATION

There are three key elements of economic transformation: a declining share of agriculture in the GSDP, movement of workers out of agriculture into industry and services, and increasing urbanization. It is generally the case that the movement of the workforce out of agriculture into industry and services often results in enhanced urbanization. The Pearl River Delta in China best illustrates this phenomenon. This region was almost entirely rural until the early 1980s. Once China opened it to foreign investment and private economic activity, however, it rapidly industrialized and is now among the most urbanized regions of China. But urbanization can also lead rather than follow the movement of workforce out of agriculture. The availability of cheap rental housing and good transportation within cities and rural–urban connectivity can facilitate migration of workers from rural to urban areas.

To study the transformation in terms of output composition, we divide the GSDP into three conventional sectors, Agriculture and allied activities, industry, and services. Agriculture and allied activities include agriculture, forestry, logging, and fishing. Industry includes mining and quarrying, manufacturing and electricity, and gas and water supply. All else, including construction, is counted among services.

In table 3.1, we report the average growth rate of each of these sectors during the three phases for Andhra Pradesh, Uttar Pradesh, and India as a whole. Alongside, we also show the coefficient of variation, which measures the fluctuations in the annual growth rate. Because manufacturing has a special role in transforming an economy from a traditional to a modern one, we show it separately in each case.

As expected, agricultural growth was slower and fluctuations in it larger than in industry and services during all phases in all three entities shown. But unlike Uttar Pradesh and India as a whole, the sector has seen a steady acceleration in growth in Andhra Pradesh. Not only did the average growth rate accelerate in the successive phases in the state, it also experienced considerably reduced fluctuations. In the third phase, agricultural growth in Andhra Pradesh is comparable to that in Gujarat, another state that has made impressive gains in this sector during the 2000s. During this phase, growth in agriculture did not become negative in a single year compared with four times during each of the first two phases.

Taking all three decades together, industry has grown faster in Andhra Pradesh than in Uttar Pradesh or India as a whole. But except during the first phase when it grew faster than the GSDP in Andhra Pradesh, it has barely kept pace with the latter. Fluctuation in industrial growth fell in Phase II but returned to its Phase I level in Phase III. Manufacturing growth shows a similar pattern though it exhibits a slightly steadier declining trend in the fluctuations. Broadly, industry shares the tepid performance relative to services with virtually all states in India.

A common feature across Indian states (Panagariya, Chakraborty, and Rao 2014) has been faster growth of services than industry and manufacturing. This is unlike the growth patterns observed in countries such as South Korea and Taiwan during the 1960s and 1970s and China more recently. In Andhra Pradesh, the emphasis by Naidu on the IT industry in the early stages of reforms and subsequent validation of that policy by YSR have meant that services have seen progressively higher growth in Phases II and III. During Phase III, they grew 10.1% on average, a hair's breadth faster than in India

Table 3.1. GROWTH RATES OF AGRICULTURE, INDUSTRY AND SERVICES, 1982–94 TO 2004–12

Sector	Growth Rate			Coefficient of Variation		
	1982–94	1994–2004	2004–12	1982–94	1994–2004	2004–12
Andhra Pradesh						
Agriculture and allied	2.4	3.5	4.7	3.6	3.5	1.2
Industry	8.7	6.2	8.3	0.7	0.5	0.7
Services	6.7	7.6	10.1	0.7	0.2	0.2
Manufacturing	8.8	5.8	8.3	0.8	0.7	0.6
GDP at factor cost	5.4	6.0	8.5	1.1	0.6	0.3
Uttar Pradesh						
Agriculture and allied	2.7	2.8	2.7	1.2	1.5	0.6
Industry	8.3	4.7	6.8	0.9	1.5	1.0
Services	5.1	5.4	9.0	0.6	0.4	0.2
Manufacturing	8.1	5.1	7.3	1.0	1.8	1.1
GDP at factor cost	4.4	4.3	6.9	0.7	0.7	0.1
India						
Agriculture and allied	3.2	2.9	3.3	1.6	1.8	0.8
Industry	5.7	6.3	7.6	0.5	0.5	0.5
Services	6.2	7.8	9.7	0.2	0.2	0.1
Manufacturing	5.3	6.7	8.3	0.7	0.6	0.5
GDP at factor cost	5.1	6.2	8.2	0.4	0.3	0.2

Source: Author's calculations using the CSO data.

as a whole. Fluctuations in services growth have declined steadily over the three phases.

Table 3.2 carries forward this analysis by considering the evolution of output shares of different sectors during the three phases in Andhra Pradesh, Uttar Pradesh, and India as a whole. Here we select the beginning year, 1981/82 of Phase I and the terminal years of the three phases. The shares for the first two years are calculated using the series at 1980/81 prices, those for 2003/04 using the series at 1993/94 and those for 2011/12 using the series at 2004/05 prices. This is important to remember because the change in the base year itself can alter the shares.

Table 3.2. EVOLUTION OF OUTPUT SHARES, 1981/82 TO 2011/12

Sector	1981/82	1993/94	2003/04	2011/12
Andhra Pradesh				
Agriculture and allied	44.7	31.2	24.9	19.3
Industry	15.0	21.7	19.8	17.2
Services	40.3	47.1	55.3	63.5
Manufacturing	12.2	17.8	14.3	12.0
GDP at factor cost	100	100	100	100
Uttar Pradesh				
Agriculture and allied	50.0	40.9	33.6	22.5
Industry	12.3	18.6	18.5	15.5
Services	37.7	40.5	47.9	62.0
Manufacturing	10.2	15.1	14.4	13.5
GDP at factor cost	100	100	100	100
India				
Agriculture and allied	35.7	28.3	20.3	14.0
Industry	18.8	20.1	20.1	19.2
Services	45.5	51.5	59.6	66.8
Manufacturing	14.4	14.6	15.2	15.3
GDP at factor cost	100	100	100	100

Source: Author's calculations using the CSO data.

Although the share of agriculture has steadily declined in all three entities shown, both Andhra Pradesh and Uttar Pradesh continue to exhibit significantly higher output share of agriculture than India as a whole. In both states, this partially reflects the much larger share in the initial year, 1981/82. Half of the output in Uttar Pradesh and 45% in Andhra Pradesh that year originated in agriculture compared with only 36% in India as a whole. In the case of Andhra Pradesh, the share of agriculture has declined slowly as well because of the superior performance of this sector.

The share of industry grew sharply in Andhra Pradesh during the first phase, rising from 15% to almost 22%, but it fell subsequently dropping to approximately 17% by 2011/12. The share of manufacturing showed a nearly identical pattern with its level being slightly lower. The share of services in Andhra Pradesh has grown during the last two phases at the expense of both agriculture and industry. This share has steadily gained 7 to 8 percentage points during each of the three phases. Overall, the main difference between Andhra Pradesh and India as a whole is in the approximately 5 percentage points' larger share of agriculture in the former. This translates into a 2 percentage points smaller share in industry and 3 percentage points smaller share in services.

Given the superior performance of services and the policy emphasis in Andhra Pradesh on the IT sector, it is useful to consider in greater detail the growth experience of the broad service sectors. To this end, table 3.3 provides the average growth rates of these service sectors and table 3.4 their shares. Two sectors that exhibit unusually high growth are communications, and banking and insurance. Communications grew at annual rates of 22.1 and 26.9% during the second and third phases, respectively. This is in keeping with the Naidu focus on the IT industry. Although the spread of cell phones, which also contributed to the growth in communications, is an India-wide phenomenon, this growth took off in a major way only after 2002. In terms of the share in the total services output, communications rose from a mere 1.5% in 1981/82 to 8.7% in 2011/12.

Banking and insurance grew at double-digit rates during each of the three phases in Andhra Pradesh. In the third phase, it reached an impressive 16.3%. The share of this sector in the total services output rose from 5.1% in 1981/82 to 12.1% in 2011/12. A third sector that has seen a large expansion in the share is real estate, ownership of dwellings and business services. It rose from just 8.8% in 1993/94 to 17.5% in 2011/12. Given that business services are a part of the software services that Andhra Pradesh greatly emphasized, this is not surprising. Nevertheless, it is important to note that the growth rates in this sector, shown in table 3.3, are not exceptionally high. It turns out that a significant part of the increase in the share in this case has resulted from the change of the base year from 1993/94 to 2011/12. This fact is graphically illustrated by the observation that the share of real estate, ownership of dwellings and business services in 2004/05 is 7.4% at 1993/94 prices but jumps to 19.5% when the base is shifted to 2004/05.

Table 3.3. GROWTH IN SERVICES SECTORS, 1982–94 TO 2004–12

Service Sector	1982–94	1994–2004	2004–12
Construction	3.9	8.3	10.1
Railways	3.3	5.7	6.0
Transport by other means and storage	5.6	6.6	10.8
Communication	7.4	22.1	26.9
Trade, hotels, and restaurants	7.7	6.0	8.0
Banking and insurance	12.6	11.4	16.3
Real estate, ownership of dwellings, and business services	4.3	6.2	8.5
Public administration	5.9	6.1	6.3
Other services	7.8	6.9	7.3
Services	6.7	7.6	10.1

Source: Author's calculations using the CSO data.

Table 3.4. SHARES OF DIFFERENT SERVICE SECTORS IN THE SERVICES OUTPUT

Service Sector	1981/82	1993/94	2003/04	2011/12
Construction	11.9	8.5	11.2	11.8
Railways	3.0	2.0	2.8	1.5
Transport by other means and storage	9.3	8.4	7.4	8.8
Communication	1.5	1.6	7.9	8.7
Trade, hotels, and restaurants	34.5	37.2	23.6	20.7
Banking and insurance	5.1	9.3	10.5	12.1
Real estate, ownership of dwellings, and business services	11.5	8.8	12.3	17.5
Public administration	8.9	8.1	7.9	5.7
Other services	14.3	16.1	16.4	13.2
Services	100	100	100	100

Source: Author's calculations using the CSO data.

Table 3.5. EMPLOYMENT SHARES OF USUALLY WORKING PERSONS IN THE PRINCIPAL STATUS AND SECONDARY STATUS IN AGRICULTURE IN RURAL REGIONS

State	1993/94	1990/2000	2004/05	2009/10
Andhra Pradesh	79.3	78.8	71.8	68.7
Uttar Pradesh[a]	80.0	76.2	72.8	66.9
India	78.4	76.3	72.7	68.0

[a] Data in 1993/94 and 1999/2000 relate to the undivided Uttar Pradesh and those in the remaining years exclude what is now the state of Uttarakhand.
Source: NSSO Employment-Unemployment Survey reports for the years shown.

As in much of India, the transition of workforce out of agriculture in Andhra Pradesh has been significantly slower than the shift in the output share. Table 3.5 provides the comparative data for Andhra Pradesh, Uttar Pradesh, and India on the proportion of the workforce in agriculture in rural areas at four different points in time. The transition is remarkably similar in the three entities. During the 16-year period, approximately 10 to 13 percentage points of rural workforce has shifted out of agriculture into industry or services in each case. The proportion of the rural workforce in agriculture in 2009/10 stood at a remarkably similar level in the two states and India as a whole. The same is also true of the proportion of the labor force in agriculture in rural and urban areas combined, which stood at 54.8% in Andhra Pradesh, 56.1% in Uttar Pradesh, and 53.2% in India as a whole in 2009/10.

Despite what appears to be a painfully slow transition, the data in table 3.5 are not without a silver lining. In each of the three entities shown, the bulk

Table 3.6. PROGRESS IN URBANIZATION, 1991 TO 2011

State	Total Population (million) 1991	2001	2011	Percentage Urban 1991	2001	2011
Andhra Pradesh	66.5	75.7	84.7	26.9	27.1	33.5
Uttar Pradesh	139.1	166.1	199.6	19.8	20.8	22.3
India	846.3	1,027.0	1,210.2	25.7	27.8	31.2

Source: Census of India, 1991, 2001, and 2011.

of the shift has taken place in the 2000s, the period of the fastest growth and higher per capita incomes. With higher and rising per capita incomes, prospects are perhaps bright for the workforce to move progressively out of agriculture into industry and services.

Finally, it is useful to consider briefly the progress in urbanization. This is done in table 3.6. Here Andhra Pradesh has done better than both Uttar Pradesh and India as a whole and significantly so relative to the former. By 2011, it was 33.5% urban exhibiting a relatively large jump by 6.4 percentage points in the preceding 10 years. India-wide average rate of urbanization stood at 31.2% and that in Uttar Pradesh at just 22.3% in 2011. The gap in urbanization between Uttar Pradesh and Andhra Pradesh considerably widened between 1991 and 2011. In view of the acceleration in urbanization in the latest decade, it is likely that we will see the transition out of agriculture speed up even more in the forthcoming years in Andhra Pradesh.

ACCOUNTING FOR THE PERFORMANCE OF AGRICULTURE

Agriculture has seen acceleration in the growth rate as well as reduced fluctuations in recent years. As figure 3.3 shows graphically, this has been particularly true during what we have called the third phase. There are three identifiable factors contributing to this change with the first being perhaps by far the most important.

Shift Toward High-Value Commodities

First and almost surely the most important, the acceleration and stabilization of growth in agricultural and allied output has been due to the steady shift in the production basket away from food grain and traditional commercial crops to high-value commodities including horticulture (fruits,

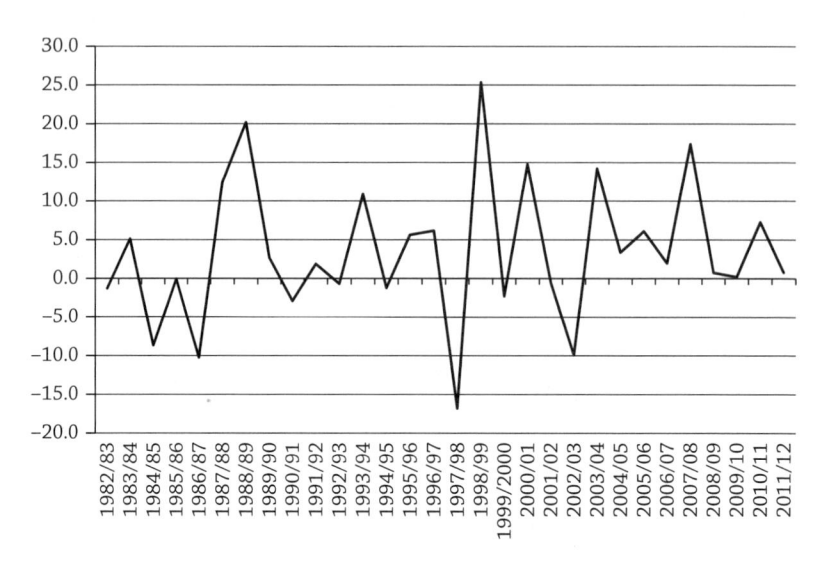

Figure 3.3: Annual Growth Rates of Agriculture and Allied Activities, 1982/83 to 2011/12
Source: Author's construction using the CSO data.

vegetables, and flowers); animal products including milk, eggs, and meat; and fish and prawns. According to the data assembled by Parthasarthy Rao et al. (2008), the share of the high-value commodities in the total value of agriculture and allied output rose from the average of 29.1% during 1980–83 to a modest 33.1% during 1990–93 and then to the significantly higher level of 50.3% during 2000–2003.

The 2011/12 Andhra Pradesh Socio-Economic Survey, published by the Government of Andhra Pradesh, reinforces this picture. The area under food grains has declined from a high of approximately 9 million hectares in the late 1970s and early 1980s to an average of 7 million hectares during 2009–11.[3] In contrast, the area under horticulture has expanded from just 370,000 hectares in 1982 to 2.5 million hectares in 2010/11. The area and production of horticulture grew at annual rates of 6.4 and 11.3%, respectively, between 2001/02 and 2010/11. Andhra Pradesh ranks first in the country in the production of fruits and spices and third in flowers. Figure 3.4 graphically depicts the progress in areas and output during the 2000s.

Progress in production of milk, meat, and eggs, shown in figure 3.5, has been similarly rapid. Between 2000/01 and 2010/11, the average growth was 7.4% in milk, 9.9% in meat, and 5.6% in eggs. These growth rates are significantly higher than those normally observed in crop production. According to the 2011/12

---

3. There has been a shift in favor of rice in recent years, however, with the area rising from an average of 2.9 million hectares during 2002–05 to 4 million hectares during 2009–12.

GROWTH AND ECONOMIC TRANSFORMATION (*39*)

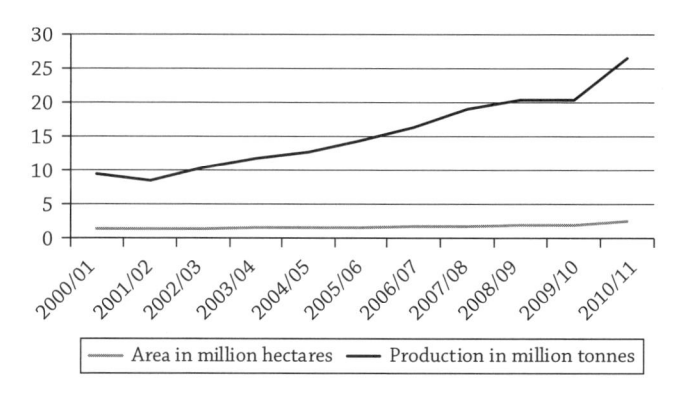

Figure 3.4: Area and Production in Horticulture, 2000/01 to 2010/11
Source: Author's construction using data in the Andhra Pradesh Social and Economic Survey, 2011/12, chart on p. 43.

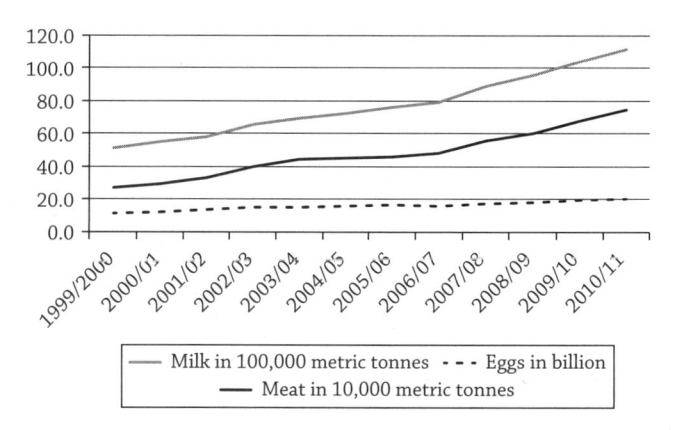

Figure 3.5: Production of Milk, Meat, and Eggs, 1999/2000 to 2010/11
Source: Author's construction using data in the Andhra Pradesh Social and Economic Survey, 2011/12, Annexure 5.19.

Andhra Pradesh Socio-Economic Survey (p. 46), livestock activity alone contributed 5.6% of the GSDP and 26% of agricultural output in 2010/11.

Andhra Pradesh also leads India in fish production. Once again, the 2011/12 Andhra Pradesh Socio-Economic Survey (p. 58) notes that the state ranks first in the country in brackish water shrimp and fresh water prawn. In the total value of fish and prawn production, it ranks second. Between 2000/01 and 2010/11, inland and marine fish production have grown at average rates of 12% and 4%, respectively. Inland and marine fish and prawn production during this period are shown in figure 3.6. Once again, these growth rates exceed the growth in crop production, the lead being especially large in the case of inland fish production. Fishing as a proportion of agriculture and allied output has risen from 9.5% in 2000/01 to 17.7% in 2011/12.

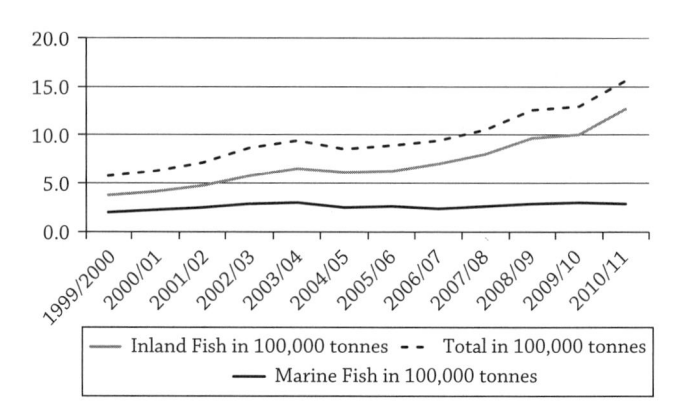

Figure 3.6: Production of Inland and Marine Fish and Prawn, 1999/2000 to 2010/11
Source: Author's construction using data in the Andhra Pradesh Social and Economic Survey, 2011/12, Annexure 5.22.

Both demand and supply side factors have played an important role in bringing about these developments. These are discussed in great detail in Parthasarthy Rao et al. (2008), and we briefly summarize them here. On the demand side, urbanization and rising incomes have been the key. Rising incomes have made the high-value commodities affordable to a rising proportion of the population and led to a shift toward these products. Going by the consumption patterns observed over time in India, rising incomes have led to declining absolute per capita consumption of cereals and rising consumption of fruits and vegetables, dairy products, fish, and meat. This shift is even more pronounced among urban consumers so that rising urbanization has led to yet further shift away from cereals and toward the high-value commodities.

It is useful to recognize that this demand-side effect has been a byproduct of the economic reforms. The impetus for rising incomes as well as acceleration in urbanization, which are the key demand-side factors, has originated in the liberalizing reforms. Seen this way, even though reforms have not made significant direct inroads in the area of agriculture, they have indirectly helped accelerate as well as stabilize its growth.

On the supply side, the government policies have reinforced the process unleashed by the shift in demand. Andhra Pradesh was among the early states to initiate the reform of agricultural marketing. As early as 1999, Andhra Pradesh had introduced the Rythu Bazars or farmer markets where farmers could sell their produce directly to consumers without the involvement of the middlemen. The main objective of these markets was to allow farmers to earn remunerative prices and consumers to have access to fresh fruits and vegetables. According to the 2012 Andhra Pradesh Socio-Economic Survey, 106 such markets currently exist where 45,000 farmers sell an average of 175,000 quintals of vegetables every week directly to customers. There also exist now mobile Rythu Bazars in Hyderabad and Vijaywada cities for selling graded vegetables.

Andhra Pradesh was also one of the early states to abolish the state monopoly on marketing agricultural produce through the adoption of the State Agricultural Produce and Marketing (Development and Regulation) Act, 2003. The act gave private companies the rights to procure produce directly from the farmers and farmers the rights for direct sales to the companies or consumers. Parthasarthy Rao et al. (2008) report the existence of a dozen retail players such as Reliance Fresh and Subhiksha in fresh fruits, vegetables, dairy, poultry, frozen foods, and other processed staples as of March 2007.

We may also briefly mention a series of additional measures the state has taken in areas of horticulture, dairy products, animal husbandry, and fisheries. There is no easy way to connect these measures to outcomes, but it is likely that they have played some role in promoting agriculture in general and easing up the shift into high-value commodities in particular.

With respect to horticulture, the government has undertaken activities focused on the adoption of modern technologies such as drip and sprinkler irrigation, post-harvest infrastructure facilities, and quality plant material. During 2010/11, 130,000 hectares were brought under drip or sprinkler irrigation. The same year, the government provided assistance for 13 cold storage units, 25 ripening chambers, and 560 turmeric-drying platforms. To promote quality plant material, the government has established 30 horticulture farms and 144 nurseries producing more than 1.5 million quality plants. The government has also identified floriculture as one of the focus segments of horticulture.

Andhra Pradesh government has extensive provision of veterinary and animal husbandry services. To protect animal health, the state has an extensive network of veterinary medical institutions including polyclinics, super specialty hospitals, regular hospitals, dispensaries, mobile clinics, and rural livestock units. During 2011/12 alone, these institutions treated 27 million cases and undertook 47.9 million vaccinations. Andhra Pradesh Livestock Development Agency runs a variety of programs from artificial insemination to distribution of frozen semen to organization of fertility clinics to improve the productivity of the livestock. In 2010/11, the state conducted 5.2 million inseminations with 1.9 million improved progeny born. The state also runs a livestock insurance scheme with 50% subsidy and another similar scheme specifically for sheep.

Finally, the state also runs a number of programs supporting fisheries. These include subsidized housing for fishermen, construction of fish landing centers, 100% subsidized insurance schemes, and a fish seed program with 50% subsidy. The rationale behind some of these schemes can be questioned on efficiency grounds, but they certainly work toward promotion of fishing industry.

Irrigation

Agriculture in general has also benefited from increased irrigation leading to a decline in the dependence on rain-fed cultivation in the third phase. The average net area irrigated for the five-year period 1990–95 was 4.12 million hectares. This increased marginally to 4.27 million hectares in 1995–2000 but fell down to 4 million hectares in 2000–05. During the years 2005–10, the average net area under irrigation rose to 4.51 million hectares, however. The net irrigated area in 2010/11 stood at 5.34 million hectares.

Table 3.7, which shows the annual gross area irrigated by sources of irrigation from 1997/98 to 2010/11, shows a similar trend. A sharp decline in the area irrigated by canals led to a significant overall decline in the gross area irrigated during 2002–05. In the subsequent years, not only did canal irrigation recover except for a brief blip in 2009/10, well irrigation steadily expanded rising to 3.67 million hectares in 2010/11 from 2.56 hectares in 2004/05.

Improved irrigation performance itself is to be explained in terms of better availability of credit and increased access to electricity. The former allowed farmers to rapidly expand the installation of tube wells while the latter allowed them to operate them to draw out ground water. Of course, this has led to declining water tables and contributed to a brewing crisis in the future availability of water that most Indian states need to urgently

Table 3.7. SOURCE-WISE GROSS AREA IRRIGATED, 1996/97 TO 2010/11 (IN MILLION HECTARES)

Year	Canals	Tanks	Wells	Others	Total
1996/97	2.20	0.97	2.39	0.22	5.78
1997/98	2.05	0.61	2.31	0.19	5.16
1998/99	2.29	0.93	2.64	0.23	6.09
1999/2000	2.21	0.72	2.60	0.22	5.75
2000/01	2.20	0.80	2.69	0.22	5.92
2001/02	2.09	0.63	2.62	0.21	5.55
2002/03	1.45	0.45	2.48	0.15	4.54
2003/04	1.51	0.54	2.57	0.16	4.78
2004/05	1.73	0.52	2.56	0.18	4.99
2005/06	2.23	0.76	2.80	0.21	6.00
2006/07	2.30	0.70	2.89	0.18	6.07
2007/08	2.25	0.67	3.17	0.19	6.29
2008/09	2.38	0.73	3.42	0.22	6.74
2009/10	1.87	0.37	3.34	0.19	5.77
2010/11	2.50	0.76	3.67	0.22	7.15

Source: Andhra Pradesh Socio-Economic Survey 2011/12, Annexure 5.8.

address. As we will cover in our later section on power, and as other commentators (Dev and Rao 2003) have noted, the subsidy given to the agriculture sector in the form of negligible power tariffs is exacerbating this issue, besides causing several others. Correcting these distortions in some manner, perhaps by tiered pricing—charging heavy users a higher price—is critical. Over the longer term, suggested strategies for adapting to water shortages include encouraging the shift of the economy away from a dependence on agriculture, shifting the pattern of cropping to less water-intensive crops, and creating supporting institutional frameworks for the most vulnerable (World Bank 2006).

Other Initiatives

The government has also been deeply involved in supporting food grain and other conventional crops through a number of initiatives though it remains difficult to assess their impact. A detailed discussion of these measures can be found in the Andhra Pradesh Socio-Economic Survey 2011/12. Here we briefly touch upon some of the more important ones.

The government has tried to reinvent its approach to extension services, introducing many new initiatives. The government annually organizes an event called Rythu Chaitanya Yatra or Farmer Empowerment Program in which the officials from various line departments in the Ministry of Agriculture reach out to farmers to educate them at grass-roots level. The focus of the education is on technology transfer, timely delivery of credit, effective input planning for the fall crop, agricultural mechanization, crop diversification, and water management. In 2011, the program reached out to 3.7 million farmers spread over 37,250 habitations.

The state has a systematic program of soil testing and recommendations for action that help enhance productivity including the mix of fertilizer use and soil treatment for any problems. Each of the 22 districts in the state has a soil-testing lab of its own. Additionally, the state has 2 regional labs, 2 national labs, 5 mobile labs, and 58 mini labs with the latter located at the agricultural market committees. These labs convey the results of the analysis to farmers through soil health cards, which contain the information on the nutrients present in the soil. Based on these nutrients, the card gives recommendations for the crop to be grown by the farmer. In 2010/11, more than half million such cards were issued.

The state also has had a crop insurance program. The first such program was introduced under the National Agricultural Insurance Scheme since the fall-season crop in 2000. But in 2008, Andhra Pradesh became the first and so far the only state to provide insurance treating the village as the unit in all districts of the state. According to the Andhra Pradesh Socio-Economic

Survey of 2011/12 (p. 32), the total claims paid to farmers under the two crop insurance schemes from the fall season crop of 2000 to fall season crop of 2010 was 41 billion rupees benefiting some six million farmers.

Finally, the state also has an extensive agricultural credit program. As recently as the early 2000s, this was a small program. For instance, the total credit disbursed in 2000/01 was only 48.7 billion rupees. In the year 2010/11, the amount had reached almost 10 times that figure at 479 billion rupees. Even accounting for inflation, this represents a very large expansion of the program.

POLICIES TOWARD INDUSTRY

Industrial policy at the state level was first implemented in 1989. The state government introduced the "Liberalized State Incentive Scheme" (LSIS) for a period of three years from 1989/90 to 1991/92. The scheme announced a set of incentives like sales tax deferrals aimed at achieving all round industrial development. It also included special incentives for new SSI units set up by entrepreneurs belonging to Scheduled Castes and Scheduled Tribes. A 25% rebate in power charges for the first three years of production was provided for certain new industries.

In the Industrial Policy announced in May 1992, the Government of Andhra Pradesh extended the LSIS incentives till 1997 by modifying the LSIS Scheme and calling it the "New Comprehensive Scheme of State Incentives" (NCSSI). This scheme was in force up to March 1997, and it extended many of the incentives given by LSIS and also introduced new ones. It provided incentives of sales tax deferral for 10 years for expansion and modernization projects. The scheme also provided an investment subsidy of 15% to 20% of fixed capital investment up to maximum of 150,000 to 200,000 rupees worth of investment. An interest subsidy that provided a reimbursement at 6% both on term loans and working capital loans was also given. The earlier LSIS scheme's power rebate of 25% up to a period of three years was also extended in this new scheme, and the special provisions for the Scheduled Caste and Scheduled Tribe entrepreneurs were maintained.

While specific entrepreneurs must have profited from these schemes, it is highly unlikely that they could have had noticeable impact on industrial growth in the state. It is more likely that the policy itself was responding to the gigantic 15.3% average annual growth of industry during the last three years of the 1980s spanning 1988/89 to 1990/91. Indeed, the growth rate of industry during 1991/92 to 1996/97 at 7.5% was much lower.

After 1997, a new policy was introduced to replace NCSSI after "partial modification" and it was called "Target 2000." In substance, it did not deviate significantly from the NCSSI, but it was applicable to a broader set of industries. The Scheme continued to offer an investment subsidy of 20% of the fixed capital investment as long as it did not exceed 2 million rupees. Target 2000 also provided for a deferment/tax holiday on sales tax limited to 135% of fixed capital investment for a period of 14 years. The rebate in electricity charges was continued, as were the special incentives for Scheduled Caste and Scheduled Tribe entrepreneurs. Sales tax deferral and exemption were also granted for expansion projects, diversification, forward integration projects, and backward integration projects. Interestingly, perhaps as proxy recognition of poor infrastructure provision by the state, investments in captive power plants, including cogeneration units, became eligible for capital investment subsidy at 20% on fixed capital investment and subject to the 2 million rupees ceiling. This policy applied to all new units, expansions, and diversifications (large, medium, or small) going into production after November 15, 1995, other than those located in Hyderabad, Vijayawada, and Visakhapatnam. The impact of these policies is difficult to trace, as the evidence is mixed. While industrial growth was ultra-high in the late 1980s as just mentioned, it decelerated in the 1990s. Indeed, during 1997/98 and 1999/2000, industrial growth was actually negative.

In 2001, the state government announced a new industrial policy. A key component of this policy was the provision for a law mandating a single-window registration and clearance for projects. The provision became reality in 2002 with the passage of the "Andhra Pradesh Industrial Single Window Clearance Act." This watershed legislation provided for speedy processing and issue of various approvals, clearances, and permissions for setting up of an industrial undertaking. It prescribed statutory time limits on various departments and introduced the concept of deemed approvals. The law mandated the setting up of a district level authority for clearing cases up to 10 million rupees worth of investment in plant and machinery, a state investment promotion committee to clear cases up to 250 million rupees, and a state investment promotion board to clear cases beyond 250 million rupees of investment. The law also stipulated that all procedures for inspection, maintenance of registers, and pollution control procedures be simplified. In sum, the Single-Window Act went a long way toward introducing an investor-friendly environment in the state

The 2001 industrial policy also mentions infrastructure provision in industrial areas, as had all prior industrial policies. It was also proposed to set up an Industrial Infrastructure Development Fund (IIDF) of 1 billion rupees to share costs of infrastructure development in non-industrial areas. Captive power generation was to be allowed for all industrial units, and up to 10% of water from existing and new projects was to be reserved for industrial purposes including existing industrial units. As an additional incentive, a 50% exemption was provided on Stamp Duty, Registration Fee, and Transfer Duty of lands meant for industrial use. The incentive of a 20% investment subsidy on capital investment in land, buildings, and plant and machinery up to a maximum of 2 million rupees to eligible SSI and Tiny units was also maintained.

This policy gave particular impetus to organized sector manufacturing or what is called registered manufacturing. For four consecutive years ending with 2000/01, registered manufacturing in Andhra Pradesh had experienced negative growth rate. But the situation turned around beginning in 2001/02. Not only has growth in registered manufacturing been strictly positive every single year beginning from 2001/02, the average growth between that year and 2011/12 has also been a respectable 9.5%. The number of registered units in Andhra Pradesh too has shown a sharp increase in the period post-2002 when the single-window facility was introduced.

The Andhra Pradesh Socio-Economic Survey 2011/12 (p. 74) reports that under the provisions of the Single-Window Act, the state had issued clearances to 55,983 units with proposed investment summing to 4.2 trillion rupees and employment potential of 1.3 million persons as of July 31, 2011. This is in contrast to the inconsistent response of industry to the industrial policies introduced in the 1990s. Prima facie, this would imply that reduction of administrative overhead and red tape has greater impact than "sops" for industry.

For completeness, we may mention that District Industries Centers are now empowered to clear proposals up to 50 million rupees investment in plant and machinery. In 2010, the government announced its new Industrial Investment Promotion Policy 2010–15, which has expanded many of the financial incentives to the industry while also adding new ones. These relate to investment subsidy on fixed capital, stamp duty on the purchase of land, rebate on land use in industrial estates and industrial parks and rebate land conversion charges.

THE KEY ROLE OF THE POWER SECTOR IN EXPLAINING THE PATTERN OF INDUSTRIAL GROWTH

In this section, we discuss the role of infrastructure in economic development. From our sectoral analysis, we see that the share of the service sector in the GSDP increased very significantly, but there was only a modest increase in the share of the manufacturing sector. Why has the manufacturing sector failed to take off significantly in Andhra Pradesh even after major reforms? Why did the service sector take off with modest reforms?

Recently Gupta, Hasan, and Kumar (2008) addressed this question in the paper "What Constrains Indian Manufacturing?" Using the Annual Survey of Industries data, they show that post-reforms the experience of the manufacturing sector has been very heterogeneous. Industries that depend on the infrastructure and external finance and those characterized by high labor intensity did not benefit much from the reforms. There have been other studies, notable among them being papers by Besley and Burgess (2004) and Aghion et al. (2005) that have looked at the performance of Indian manufacturing post-"license raj" era. They argue that the major impediment to the growth in the manufacturing sector is the labor laws.

Since both the state and the center are allowed to legislate in the area of labor under the Indian constitution, we find some variation in the stringency of labor laws across states. Some states have gone farther than the center in tilting the labor laws in favor of the workers while the others have leaned the other way. Exploiting this variation, the studies show that the states with pro-labor laws were associated with lower levels of growth in output and employment in the registered manufacturing sector. These studies rank Andhra Pradesh as one of the most pro-employer states. According to them the registered manufacturing sector in Andhra Pradesh should have been poised to take off post-reforms. However, the reality has been very different. Immediately following the 1991 reforms, growth in the registered manufacturing was lackluster and subject to wild fluctuations. It changed significantly only in the 2000s with average growth in registered manufacturing reaching 9.3% between 2001/02 and 2011/12 with minimal fluctuations.

How do we explain this pattern? Our hypothesis is that the answer is to be found in the poor infrastructure, in particular, in the unavailability of electricity at a reasonable price, in the state. For power is the key input the state provides to the industry though roads and connectivity to ports also play an important role.

In the 1980s, the Andhra Pradesh State Electricity Board (APSEB) increased its generation capacity from 1,890 megawatt to 4,500 megawatt. Sound commercial management accompanied this increase of over 140% in generation capacity, with the board breaking even or generating a surplus for most of these years. In 1982, the APSEB adopted a change in its policy for serving agricultural customers. It decoupled pricing from usage by charging a flat, low amount per irrigation pump rather than per kilowatt hour used. Predictably, this led to a sharp rise in agricultural consumption of electricity. The share of industrial customers, who in 1980 consumed 67% of the APSEB's power supply, dropped to 44%, while agricultural customers came to consume 39% against their earlier share of 17% (Shankar 2003). The increased share of agriculture was cross-subsidized by charging higher tariffs to industrial customers. From 1975 to 1990, the average industrial tariff increased by more than seven times, going from 0.22 rupees per kilowatt hour to 1.39 rupees per kilowatt hour. Average agricultural tariff over the same period decreased, going from 0.28 rupees per kilowatt hour 0.03 rupees per kilowatt hour.

In effect, a diminishing industrial customer base was paying for an expanding agricultural user base. In the early 1990s, this situation was further exacerbated for the APSEB by a gap in the revision of tariff from 1992 to 1995. This period was also characterized by lower capacity addition, with generation capacity increasing only 5%. During this time, the APSEB also went from a small surplus of 270 million rupees in 1991/92 to a deficit of 11 billion rupees in 1995/96. The APSEB was now, like most other state boards throughout the country, facing large losses. This deficit was met by the government of Andhra Pradesh through a subsidy instead of a revision of tariff. At least part of the reason for this could be that the tariff for industrial customers was already at levels that were unsustainable. For the "High Tension" industrial customers, electricity tariffs had doubled from 1990 to 1995. What is interesting is that in 1995/96, industrial customers were not only consuming a smaller share of the total power generated than they had in 1993/94, they were also consuming less power in absolute terms.

In the period that industrial growth was supposed to take off because of delicensing, industrial consumers actually *reduced* the amount of power they consumed from the APSEB. This is also reflected in the decline in the growth rate of the registered manufacturing sector. From 1986 to 1991, the average growth rate in the manufacturing sector was 12.7%, and it declined to 10% post-reforms from 1991 to 1996, the growth rate further declined to 3% from 1996 to 2001. In summary, the power sector was creaking under the weight of an increased agricultural subsidy, the slow addition of generating capacity, and most of all the unsustainable financial situation of the APSEB. All these factors necessitated reform, a subject we next examine.

Prior to 1990, electricity generation, like much else, was entirely in the hands of the government—both central and state. The total installed power-generation capacity of Andhra Pradesh in 1990 was approximately 4,900 megawatts. Of this, approximately 4,100 megawatts were being generated by APSEB and 760 megawatts by central government undertakings like the National Thermal Power Corporation (NTPC). In 1991, the central government, to encourage the participation of the private sector in power generation, introduced the "Policy on Private Participation in Power" and followed it up with the Electricity Laws (Amendment) Act. This was followed by a steady increase in the generation capacity of the state. By 2000, the total installed capacity available to the state had gone up by 53% to 7,500 megawatt, of which 466 megawatt was private capacity. This rate of growth, however, was not sufficient to meet demand, leaving an estimated peak energy deficit of 14.6% in Andhra Pradesh in 2000. Another significant legislation that attempted to rationalize the electricity tariffs, bring in transparent policies regarding subsidies, was the Electricity Regulatory Commission Act, which was enacted in 1998. The act called for the setting up of regulatory commissions at the central and state levels to take on the function of deciding the tariff.

As outlined earlier, the APSEB by 1995 was faced with its own set of issues, and the Andhra Pradesh government, in consultation with the World

Bank, passed the Andhra Pradesh Electricity Reforms Act in 1998. As with the central initiatives, this act too was an attempt to restructure the power sector and increase private sector participation in the state. Following the passing of this act, the Andhra Pradesh Electricity Regulatory Commission (APERC) was set up as an independent body to decide the power tariff. The APSEB was also restructured and split up into two independent entities: the Transmission Corporation of Andhra Pradesh Limited (APTransco) and Andhra Pradesh Power Generation Corporation Limited (APGENCO). The distribution function was later further separated from APTransco and divested with four distribution companies as subsidiaries to APTransco.

In 2003, the central government also introduced the Electricity Act of 2003, which did away with a requirement of licenses for setting up of power generation as long as generating stations met technical standards. Distribution and transmission of electricity, particularly in urban areas, would still require licenses. In addition to this, the central government released the National Tariff Policy in 2006, which suggested limiting cross subsidization of different categories of customers and recommended direct subsidies instead. The set of reforms undertaken by the Andhra Pradesh government in some sense also foreshadowed some of the requirements of the act, which made it mandatory for states to unbundle and restructure the state electricity boards. The power generation capacity of Andhra Pradesh almost doubled in the period from 2000 to 2010, with total installed capacity in March 2010 being 14,600 megawatt. The installed capacity of the private sector had also gone up to 3,223 megawatt, which was 22% of the total installed capacity. This is in contrast to the first decade of reforms (1990–2000), when the private sector capacity only came to 6% of the total installed capacity.

The independence of the regulatory commission is questionable, in the sense that the cross-subsidization of agricultural customers continues, even when a national tariff policy of 2006 had recommended limiting the cross-subsidization to within plus or minus 20% of the average cost of supply. For the financial years 2004/05 to 2007/08, tariff for domestic and agriculture category has remained at approximately 80% and 4–10% of the average cost of supply, respectively, and the non-domestic and industrial categories continue to pay much more than 120% of the cost of supply. What has changed, however, is that the industrial tariff has not increased as sharply as previously. The industrial tariff increased to 4.1 rupees per kilowatt hour in 2004/05 from 2.4 rupees in 1995, an increase of only 70% over 10 years. In 2006–08, the industrial tariff was reduced to 3.74 rupee per kilowatt-hour. The non-domestic or commercial sector, on the other hand, has continued to face higher tariffs, with tariff increasing from 2.3 rupees per kilowatt-hour in 1994/95 to 5.7 rupees per kilowatt-hour in 2004/05 (CRISIL 2010).

To try to trace how these changes translated to provision of power to the registered manufacturing sector, we look at data from the Annual Survey of Industries (ASI). The ASI collects a number of details regarding inputs, outputs, and costs incurred by factories. One of the data points that it collects is the electrical power that a unit generates on its own and also the electrical power that it purchases and consumes. Shukla et al. (2004) show that captive plants in India can be broadly attributed to the need for backup power arrangement, requirement for a better quality supply, and the need to generate electricity at costs lower than the high industrial tariffs set to cross-subsidize other categories of consumers. In effect, a unit would need to generate power on its own if the public provision of power is not good enough, or is priced too highly, both of which would indicate an environment that is not industry friendly. This enables us to use the ratio of power that units generate on their own to the total power they consume as an instrument that sheds light on the public provision of infrastructure. We make use of data collected by the ASI from the period 1996/97 to 2007/08. Figure 3.7 shows the ratio of own-generated electricity to the total electricity consumed during these years. In the figure, we indicate the year 1996/97 by 1997 and similarly for the other years.

In 1996/97 (indicated as year 1997 in the figure), factories in Andhra Pradesh were generating as much as 22.7% of the total power that they consumed. This number climbed to 24.6% in 1999/2000. Since that time however, we find that the ratio has declined to reach 15.7% in 2003/04, and then declined further to 13.1% in 2005/06, before increasing marginally to 13.3% in 2007/08. We also find that among the other pro-employer states that are noted by Aghion et al. (Andhra Pradesh, Karnataka, Kerala, Rajasthan, and Tamil Nadu), Andhra Pradesh was better than only Karnataka in 1998/99,

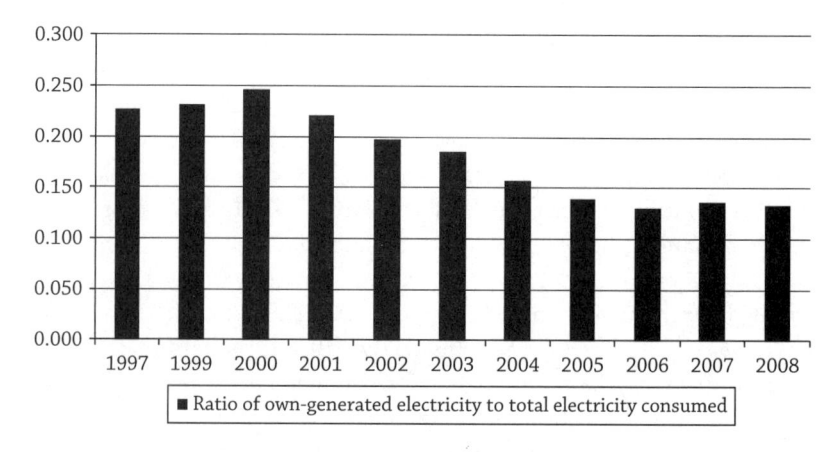

Figure 3.7: Ratio of Own-Generated Electricity to Total Electricity Consumed
Source: Author's construction using the Annual Survey of Industries data.

and worse than 10 other large states. By 2007/08, Andhra Pradesh was worse than only three other large states overall. This would point to power sector reforms in Andhra Pradesh having been a partial success, particularly from the point of view of infrastructure provision for industry. The increased growth of registered manufacturing during this period of improved infrastructure provision also indicates that the power sector reforms undertaken at the central level and in Andhra Pradesh have had a positive impact.

EXPLAINING THE SUCCESS OF THE IT SECTOR

The rise of the Information Technology Enabled Services (ITES) sector in the state has been one of the success stories of the state and makes a good case study of how a government that chooses to facilitate economic activity while letting private players manage it can create economic miracles. To some extent, the growth in IT is a reflection of broader trends that have been visible in the country as a whole. What is special about their occurrence in Andhra Pradesh is the active role played by the state government in creating an enabling economic environment that has allowed individuals to take advantage of growth opportunities and boosted Andhra Pradesh ahead of other states that began in similar or better positions.

In the mid-1980s, Texas Instruments (TI), a US-based company, pioneered the outsourcing model. Bangalore, recently renamed Bengaluru, became TI's preferred choice of destination over Chennai and Hyderabad for a number of factors. Bangalore already had a significant electronic industry (primarily public sector undertakings), which was an important advantage for two reasons—it provided potential clients for TI and, more importantly, it provided a pool of skilled manpower, which was critical to TI's operations. The presence of premium research and management institutes like the Indian Institute of Science and the Indian Institute of Management, Bangalore further improved the availability of human capital in Bangalore. Even its cool, temperate climate was to the advantage of the city.

Hyderabad did not have any of the same historical, manpower-related, or even climate-related advantages that Bangalore enjoyed and yet the ITES sector in Andhra Pradesh took off and as of today the state is one of the leading players in the sector in the country. The natural questions that come to mind are why and how did the ITES sector take off in Andhra Pradesh despite its initial disadvantages?

In 1992, Andhra Pradesh was substantially an agrarian economy—agriculture contributed 37% to the gross state domestic product and employed more than 70% of the usually working persons. In terms of per capita consumption, poverty rates, literacy rates and even in the distribution of workforce among broad industries Andhra Pradesh and Uttar Pradesh were quite similar. To the extent that any differences existed from the viewpoint of an IT investor, they favored Uttar Pradesh as the host. Uttar Pradesh is large in absolute terms and had the presence of institutes like the Indian Institute of Technology (IIT) in Kanpur, IT Banaras Hindu University, Motilal Nehru Regional Engineering College in Allahabad, and IIT Roorkee. Yet, it was Andhra Pradesh that emerged as a leader in the IT industry and came to enjoy the fourth position in terms of total software exports by 2009. In contrast, Uttar Pradesh could attract no IT industry whatsoever.

The year 1992 was a turning point in the Indian economy in terms of the large-scale liberalization program—the "license raj" was dismantled. For potential IT entrepreneurs in Hyderabad, this was a major step forward, since it meant spending less time dealing with the bureaucracy in Delhi to import essential items like computers and more time to expand business. However, this in itself was not sufficient to generate growth in the sector. The government was the only provider of communications services and it cost 4.5 million rupees to get a 64-kilobyte per second connection, which was prohibitive for most potential entrants.

Luckily, in 1992, the then Chief Minister of Andhra Pradesh N. Janardhan Reddy sanctioned an interest free loan of 10 million rupees and a plot of land for the development of a communication link. This significantly reduced the cost of doing business and perhaps was the turning point for the industry. Interviews with the IT industry leaders suggest that this policy initiative was the primary reason that the software technological park (STP) in Hyderabad took off while similar initiatives in other places such as Gandhinagar, Pune, Bhubaneshwar, and Trivandrum remained dormant.

Andhra Pradesh entered the second phase of the IT sector development under the visionary leadership of Chandrababu Naidu, the state's Chief Minister from 1994 to 2004. When Naidu came to power, the IT sector was in its very early stages with its contribution to the state gross domestic product being negligible. Rather than wait for industrialization to take its own course, Naidu assumed a proactive role to turn Hyderabad into a major investment destination. As mentioned earlier, he engaged a McKinsey team to aid the process of creating a Vision 2020 document for Andhra Pradesh. One of the assets McKinsey brought to the table was global experience. They had just finished a project for the Malaysian government focusing on the slowdown in growth that had been fueled by manufacturing. By a happy coincidence, McKinsey had also just identified the large potential of the IT and Business Process Outsourcing (BPO) sector in India in a joint report with India's National Association of Software and Services Companies (NASSCOM). When they presented some of their findings to Naidu and the Andhra Pradesh government, the latter concluded that business process outsourcing (BPO) would play to Andhra Pradesh's strengths and could help kick start investment in the state. The first companies to invest in Andhra

Pradesh were Genpact, Deloitte, and HSBC, all of which set up back office operations in Hyderabad, and were later followed by General Electric.

Naidu followed up this initial push with other initiatives to sustain and accelerate IT investments. One of the early initiatives that he undertook was related to the development of skilled manpower, a key ingredient for the growth and development of the IT sector. The idea of International Institute of Information Technology (formerly known as Indian Institute of Information Technology (IIIT)) was conceptualized in 1997 and within a year it was implemented. In 1998, IIIT was started as an autonomous, self-supporting institution with seed money from the government. The key objective was to impart broad-based high-quality interdisciplinary IT education. The government also encouraged the participation of the private sector in higher education, in particular, engineering colleges. The impact of these policies and initiatives is reflected in the fact that in 1995/96 there were 32 engineering colleges, which produced 8,000 engineers per year, but by 2009/10 there were 639 engineering colleges, which produced 218,915 engineers per year.

Another policy initiative was the promotion of telecommunication infrastructure, in particular, the laying down of optical fiber along state properties. The government believed that this would lead to promotion of the IT sector and more importantly it would enhance the quality of life of the citizens. The government was cognizant of the fact that creating broad networks required laying down of the optical fiber network along the national highways, state highways, and other road networks that belonged to the Road & Building, Panchayat Raj, Municipal Administration & Urban Development and Forest Departments. Any agency that intended to lay the optical fiber had to take permission from these departments. Given the fact that there were no general guidelines for the concerned departments on this issue, the matters were typically sent to higher authorities for approval and this led to major delays in the execution of the project. In light of this the government decided to "issue guidelines for issuing permissions to agencies, especially telecom operators, desirous of implementing optical fiber projects in the State."[4]

In 2000, the government took another major step by coming out with a first comprehensive Information Technology policy. The clear emphasis of this policy was placed on using IT as vehicle for economic growth and as a tool for improving both governance and human capital. The policy focused on creation of an enabling environment through clear demarcation of policymaking structure and responsibilities at different levels. The aim was to enable quick decision-making and prevent the government-related delays for which governments in India were so famous. To ensure swift decisions, the

---

4. Government Order M S 5, dated February 11, 2000. http://apit.ap.gov.in/pages/gort5.pdf.

chief minister came to head the apex IT policy body. Additionally, the policy committed the Andhra Pradesh government to minimizing the compliance burden faced by industry. Infrastructure availability to the IT sector was prioritized in the form of land allotment and Special Economic Zones (SEZs), increased ease of setting up communication infrastructure like the aforementioned optical fiber policy and in promotion of an international airport.

Interestingly, generation of social awareness regarding IT and its benefits was viewed as an instrument to spread IT across different government departments. E-governance was given great importance with computerization of government departments and IT enabled governance improvement schemes such as citizen services to be implemented. Human resource development was also made a priority. IIIT had already been established with the help of the Andhra Pradesh government, and other initiatives like networking different universities within the state were also suggested. Apart from this, there were also incentives introduced in 1999 for the IT industry. Under this incentive scheme, the IT Software industry was exempted from the purview of the Andhra Pradesh Pollution Control Act. Industrial power tariff and other admissible incentives and concessions applicable to industries in respect of power were also made applicable to the IT Industry, and it was exempted from statutory power cuts. To further reduce the impact of power on IT firms operating costs, a 25% concessional power tariff was also allowed to new IT Industrial units for a period of three years. Computer software was totally exempted from the payment of sales tax. IT Software Industry was exempted from zoning regulations for purposes of location. The government also agreed in principle to exemption to the IT Software Industry from the provisions of various Acts and Regulations such as Employment Exchange (Notification of Vacancies Act); Payment of Wages Act; Minimum Wages Act; Contract Labour (Regulation and Abolition) Act, Workmen Compensation Act; Andhra Pradesh Shops and Establishments Act and Employees State Insurance Act. General permission was accorded to run a three-shift operation to the IT Software industry.

Financial incentives were also provided in the form of a rebate in the cost of land allotted to an IT industry at 20,000 rupees per job created, and an investment subsidy for new IT (hardware and software) industries. An investment subsidy was provided up to 20% of the fixed capital investment or 2 million rupees. This was expanded for entrepreneurs belonging to Scheduled Castes and Scheduled Tribes to 25% of fixed capital or 5 million rupees. For mega projects, with investment exceeding 1 billion rupees, the government agreed to consider a special package of incentives on a case-by-case basis.

The government created a regulatory regime that was minimal in nature. This can be gleaned from the following statement in the policy, "Efforts shall be made to ensure that starting and running of businesses in the State in general and IT industries in particular, is fast and smooth and to see that the interface with Government is required to be minimal and positive. Efforts shall be made to put in place a regulatory regime that regulates the least!"

The government was also keen to use international consulting firms to build an "overall architecture" for IT to assess global trends and the competitive advantages of the state. This shows the positive, entrepreneurial, and reform-minded approach of the government in promoting the sector.

In 2002, the government issued another IT policy, which was in essence the continuation of the policy in 2000, with a few additional incentives and benefits.

The policy expressed an intention to introduce a "single-window system" to reduce the regulatory burden and smooth the interface between industry, business, and the regulatory agencies. In order to encourage IT businesses to participate in international events, the government would provide 30% subsidy on rent payable for these events to Small and Medium Enterprises (firms whose turnover in the preceding year did not exceed 100 million rupees). This was an attempt to help small firms to overcome the fixed cost of exploring international market opportunities. Preference for state e-government projects was given to firms that were headquartered in Andhra Pradesh.

Did the policy initiatives have any impact? The following observations suggest that they did.

- Total IT exports from Andhra Pradesh increased from a meager 2 million rupees in 1992 to 82,700 million rupees in 2004/05 (a cumulative annual growth rate of 130%).
- Microsoft set up an overseas software development center in Hyderabad, which was the first such center outside the US and the second largest anywhere in the world outside Seattle (headquarters of Microsoft).
- Some of the other big companies that invested in the state were General Electric, Oracle, Metamor, HSBC, Motorola, Infosys, Wipro, Tata Teleservices, Toshiba, TCS, and Ericsson, etc.
- In e-governance some of the key achievements were that state budgets were online, there was simple online file tracking system, eCops—online first information report (FIR) management.
- Establishment of e-Procurement for online tender processes—by 2004/05, 32 government departments participated in the process, total volume of transaction was 359 million and the cost of the tenders was 2,43,380 million rupees.

Central to these successes was the visionary political leadership of Naidu. His vision laid down the foundation of economic growth by introducing policies that were growth-oriented and also creating a business-friendly environment. However, on the eve of the general assembly elections in 2004, there was a general feeling that growth in Andhra Pradesh was taking place at the expense of rural development, which is where the majority of population resides. YSR promised to bring growth and prosperity to rural areas. For his promise, he was elected as the chief minister.

The common perception around this time was that the era of growth-oriented policies was at an end and once again welfare schemes would dominate the political agenda. But YSR proved his skeptics wrong—his political formula was not to disrupt the growth process; on the contrary, he gave another impetus to the growth process by expediting the projects that could enhance the growth process. However, the new twist he introduced was to use the growth process to increase the revenues of the state and then use the increased resources of the state for development projects. Even though YSR championed welfare schemes, he recognized the importance of growth to pursue this cause. Therefore, the growth process in the state continued uninterrupted during his tenure. The support provided by YSR and his ability to efficiently facilitate industry is reflected in the fact that from 2004 to 2009:

- The export turnover of the state increased from 82,700 million to 325,090 million rupees.
- The number of people directly employed in IT/ITES increased from 85,945 to 251,786.
- The total number of IT/ITES companies increased from 883 to 1,206.
- Andhra Pradesh's share of IT/ITES export turnover in the country went up from 8.64% to 15%.
- By 2009, there were 30 government services that were offered by e-governance.
- By 2009, 205 government departments participated in e-Procurement as against 32 departments in 2004. Total volume of transaction increased from 359 million in 2004 to 3,557 million in 2009. Total cost of tenders went up from 243.38 billion to 1,054.47 billion rupees.

CONCLUDING REMARKS

In looking at the economy of Andhra Pradesh over the period 1982–2012, we find that it was characterized by increasingly fast and stable growth as it progressed through the pre- and post-liberalization phases of 1981–94, 1994–2004, and 2004–12. Post-2004, on the foundation of reforms introduced by Chief Minister Naidu and later sustained by YSR, growth in Andhra Pradesh accelerated past what had been a comparable state in the 1980s— Uttar Pradesh—and also moved ahead of the all-India growth rate. The reduced volatility of economic growth in the later periods is also notable. The increased growth and reduced volatility were accompanied by an economic transition that simultaneously followed a pattern previously exhibited by other developing economies and possessed attributes specific to Andhra Pradesh. As with other developing economies (and India as a whole), Andhra Pradesh's economic growth came with increased urbanization (at a rate slightly faster than all-India and significantly more so than Uttar Pradesh) and the movement of workers from agriculture into manufacturing and services. India's experience in this matter has diverged from those of other countries however, in that this latter shift of employment out of agriculture has been slower and has depended more on services than on manufacturing. In 2009/10, 68% of India's rural workforce was still employed in agriculture; whereas, 78.4% had been employed in 1993/94. Of those that moved out, a greater share went to services than manufacturing. Here Andhra Pradesh's experience has been consistent with that of India, and in line also with Naidu's focus on IT and IT-enabled services.

When we take a deeper look at the individual sectors, we note the superior performance of agriculture in Andhra Pradesh which, unlike the performance of agriculture in India as a whole, saw accelerating growth and much improved stability over the post-liberalization period. Much of this performance can be traced to the shift toward high-value commodities (fruits, vegetables, fisheries, and animal products), the share of which grew quite slowly from 29.1% during 1980–83 to 33.1% during 1990–93 and then increased sharply post-liberalization to 50.3% during 2000–03. This growth can in turn be attributed to both the economic growth that preceded it, thereby increasing demand, and to supply-side reforms carried out by the government that increased farmers' access to markets and removed the state's monopoly in procurement. Further measures to support agriculture included increased irrigation, knowledge extension, crop insurance, and farm credit.

When examining the industrial sector, we find that industrial growth in Andhra Pradesh, though extant, has not been exactly stellar, and has responded only fitfully to financial incentives announced over the years. Interestingly, industry seems to have responded best after the single-window clearance act—a move to reduce bureaucratic red tape—was passed. As it costs nothing in foregone revenue, and can have a considerable upside, any such reform that reduces the delays and complexities involved in dealing with government would be generally advisable.

Another factor that constrained the industrial sector in Andhra Pradesh is infrastructure, in particular, power. Partial power sector reforms in Andhra Pradesh and at the national level have helped improve generation capacity in Andhra Pradesh and also the provision of power to industries, alleviating what was, and still remains, a bottleneck for industrial growth.

The services sector saw growth throughout India, and in Andhra Pradesh too the sector grew faster than agriculture and industry. The IT sector's growth in Andhra Pradesh, however, is particularly noteworthy. Total IT exports grew from 2 million in 1992 to 82,700 million rupees in 2004/05, a cumulative annual growth rate of 130%! This somewhat unlikely success story in Andhra Pradesh is widely credited to visionary political leadership and provides a striking example of what is possible with the right mix of dedicated entrepreneurs, relatively few infrastructure bottlenecks, and responsive national and state policies.

CHAPTER 4

Poverty and Employment

In this chapter, we consider in greater detail the impact that economic growth and social programs have had on poverty and employment in Andhra Pradesh. With respect to poverty, we ask: (1) What is the overall trend in poverty in rural and urban areas; and (2) What is the trend in poverty among the different social groups, most notably the Scheduled Castes and the Scheduled Tribes, in relation to the trend in poverty in the overall population? In Appendix 1, we consider the trend in poverty across different regions—Rayalseema, Telangana, and Coastal Andhra Pradesh. With respect to employment, we consider the participation rates, distribution of workforce across sectors in rural and urban areas and across male and female workers, employment in the organized sector and underemployment of workers.

POVERTY

We limit our analysis of poverty to the period from 1993/94 to 2011/12. The choice of the period is largely dictated by the fact that the Tendulkar poverty line, currently in use, is available from the official Planning Commission sources beginning in 1993/94 only. The reader interested in the evolution of poverty in earlier years using the Lakdawala line can consult Reddy, Galab, and Rao (2003) and Panagariya and Mukim (2013).

Overall Poverty Trends

Rapid decline in rural and urban poverty from 1993/94 to 2011/12 was one of the major achievements of Andhra Pradesh. The overall poverty declined by a massive 36 percentage points. This was the largest decline in poverty across all the states in India during this time period as shown in figure 4.1. Rural poverty

(59)

declined by a gigantic 37 percentage points during this period. Once again this was the largest decline among all the states in India as shown in figure 4.2. It fell from 48% in 1993/94 to 11% in 2011/12. This was significantly larger than both Uttar Pradesh, which was comparable to Andhra Pradesh in terms of per capita income and poverty levels in the early 1990s, and the India-wide average, as shown in figure 4.3. Andhra Pradesh is now within striking distance of entirely eliminating abject poverty from rural areas.

The trend in urban poverty is nearly identical. It fell by 29 percentage points from 35.1% in 1993/94 to 5.8% in 2011/12—the largest across all the states in India, as shown in figure 4.4. Once again, its performance has been an order of magnitude superior to both Uttar Pradesh and India as a whole.

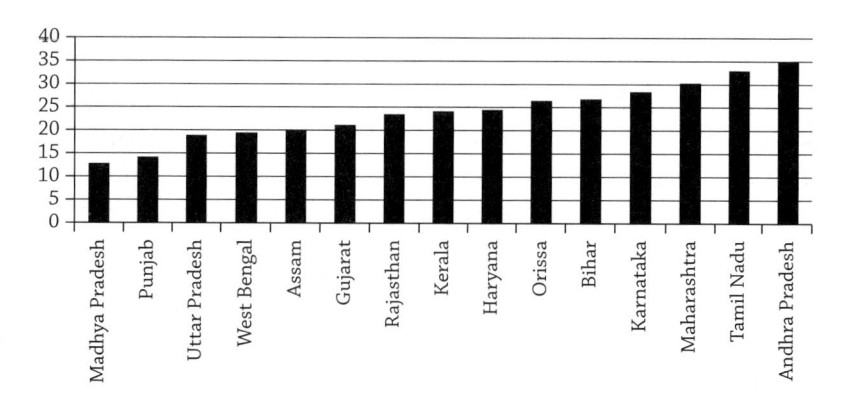

Figure 4.1: Percentage Point Decline in Overall Poverty for the Large States in India from 1993/94 to 2011/12 Based on the Tendulkar Poverty Line
Source: Planning Commission, Government of India.

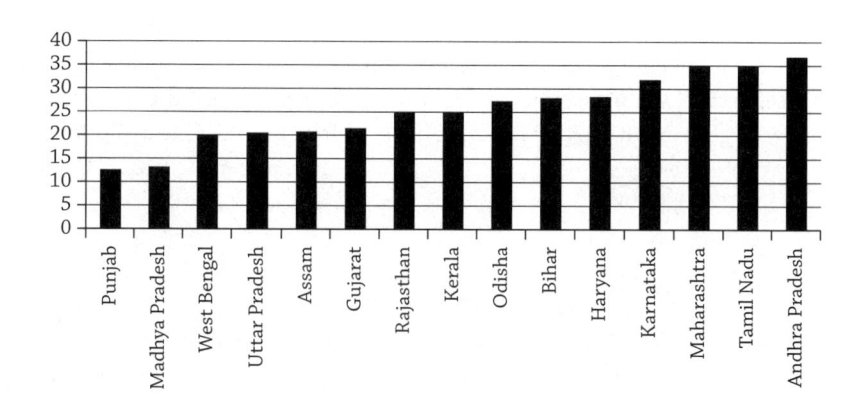

Figure 4.2: Percentage Point Decline in Rural Poverty for the Large States in India from 1993/94 to 2011/12 Based on the Tendulkar Poverty Line
Source: Planning Commission, Government of India.

POVERTY AND EMPLOYMENT (61)

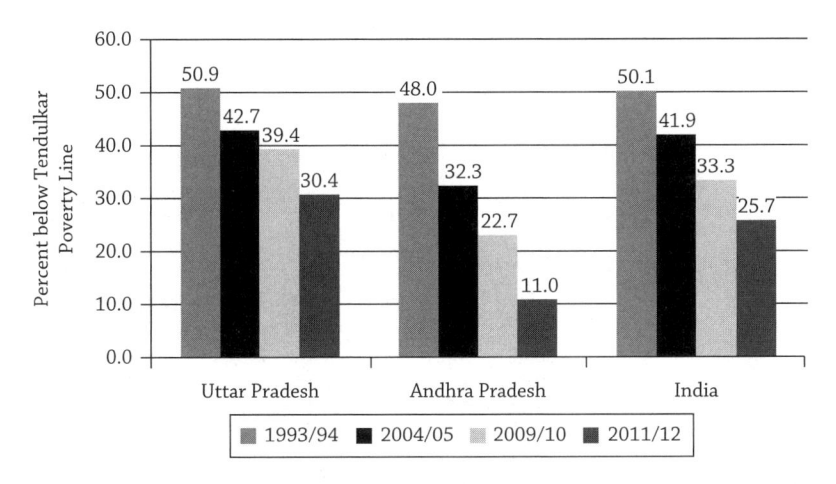

Figure 4.3: Poverty Ratio in Rural Uttar Pradesh, Andhra Pradesh, and India from 1993/94 to 2011/12 Based on the Tendulkar Poverty Line
Source: Authors' construction using estimates from the NSSO surveys.

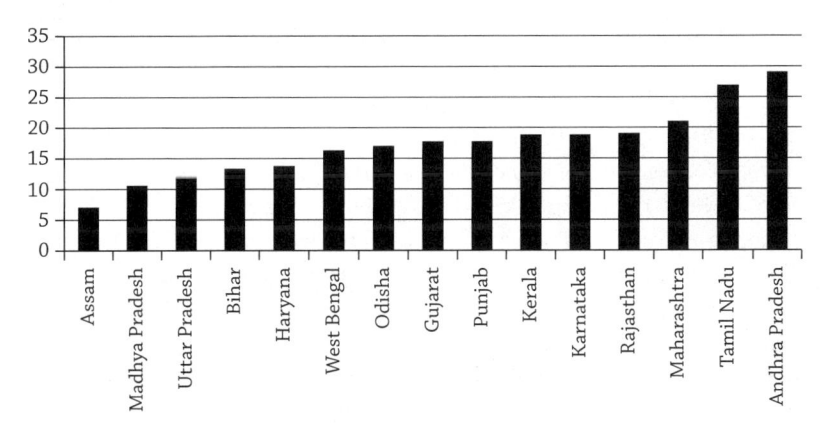

Figure 4.4: Percentage Point Decline in Urban Poverty for the Large States in India from 1993/94 to 2011/12 Based on Tendulkar Poverty Line
Source: Planning Commission, Government of India.

Uttar Pradesh began with urban poverty of 38.2% in 1993/94 and still suffered from 26.1% poverty ratio in 2011/12 as shown in figure 4.5.

The decline in poverty has been particularly sharp between 2004/05 and 2011/12. During these seven years, the total (rural plus urban) poverty fell by 21 percentage points in Andhra Pradesh, 16 percentage points in India as a whole, and 11 percentage points in Uttar Pradesh. The average growth rate in India during the relevant period spanning 2005/06 to 2010/11 was 8.6%. This is powerful evidence that growth has amply fulfilled its promise. Some may wish to argue that a significant part of the decline is due to increased social spending on public distribution system and the National

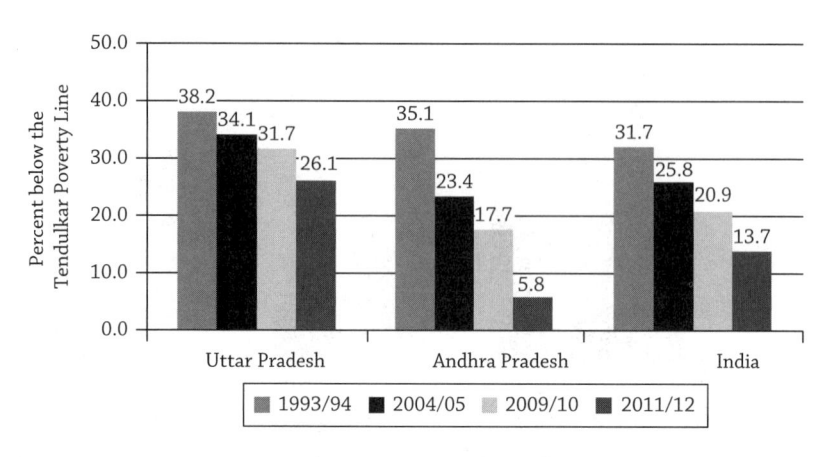

Figure 4.5: Poverty Ratio in Urban Uttar Pradesh, Andhra Pradesh, and India from 1993/94 to 2011/12 Based on the Tendulkar Poverty Line
Source: Authors' construction using estimates from the NSSO surveys.

Rural Employment Guarantee Scheme (NREGS), but it remains true that the rise in social spending itself was not possible without the massive growth.

A distinguishing feature of Andhra Pradesh has been a significantly larger reduction in poverty per percentage point growth. The rural economy is predominantly driven by the agricultural sector, therefore, per capita growth in agriculture is perhaps one of the important factors that could potentially lead to poverty reduction. We do find evidence that the agricultural growth in Andhra Pradesh was much higher as compared to the all-India level. In particular, from 1993/94 to 2004/05 the agricultural output per capita in Andhra Pradesh grew at compound annual growth rate (CAGR) of 1.9%, as compared to the CAGR of 0.6% for India as a whole. Our hypothesis, which remains to be rigorously examined, is that in rural Andhra Pradesh, this has been substantially due to the shift toward high-value commodities such as horticulture, animal husbandry, and fishing. This shift has plausibly led to increased productivity and higher real wages.

Datt and Ravallion (1999), in their study on why some Indian states have performed better than others in reducing rural poverty, identify growth rate of agricultural output as one of the significant explanatory variables. In addition, they note that initial conditions of the state in terms of infrastructure, female literacy rates, and infant mortality rates also play an important role in the relationship between poverty reduction and agricultural growth rate. We do not observe significantly better initial conditions in Andhra Pradesh compared to India as a whole. For example, the female literacy rate in 1991 in Andhra Pradesh was 33%, which was lower compared to the all India level of 39%. In terms of infant mortality rates in 1994, Andhra Pradesh was somewhat better at 65 per 1,000 live births compared to 74 for all-India. In terms of irrigation density in 1995/96, 38.8% of the agricultural land was irrigated while the corresponding number for the all-India level is 37.6%. This would suggest that difference in the performance of Andhra Pradesh compared to all-India is primarily driven by differences in agricultural growth.

Additionally, Andhra Pradesh is also said to have achieved a good track record in implementing the NREGS, which we study in a subsequent chapter. As for urban poverty, urban growth—for example, in the construction sector, which experienced a massive boom from 2004 to 2009—has done its job by pulling up urban wages.

Poverty Reduction among Social Groups

The all-around reduction in poverty in Andhra Pradesh is also seen in the decline in poverty across social and religious groups. Tables 4.1 and 4.2 report these estimates for years 1993/94, 2004/05, 2009/10, and 2011/12 for rural and urban areas in Andhra Pradesh and India as a whole.

According to table 4.1, rural poverty has declined in Andhra Pradesh between each pair of successive surveys for each social grouping. The same is also true in urban areas with one exception: Scheduled Tribes between 1993/94 and 2004/05. But even this exception may be simply due to the fact that with the Scheduled Tribes largely concentrated in rural areas, random sampling of households ends up picking too small a number of Scheduled Tribe households in urban areas to allow the estimation with a great deal of precision. Poverty rates in Andhra Pradesh also turn out to be consistently lower than the national average with the exception of Scheduled Tribes in urban areas in 2004/05 and Scheduled Castes in rural areas in 1993/94.

Importantly, reduction in poverty for each social group over the entire period from 1993/94 to 2011/12 has been much sharper in Andhra Pradesh than India as a whole. By 2011/12, the gap in the poverty rates between Scheduled Castes and all groups taken together in both rural and urban areas had been significantly reduced. Only the gap between Scheduled Tribes and others in rural areas remained substantial.

It is also interesting to note that among the states with a significant presence of Scheduled Tribe population in rural areas, Andhra Pradesh was among the top three states which experienced the highest decline in rural poverty as shown in figure 4.6.

When we compare the decline in rural poverty among the Scheduled Castes across the large states in India, we find that Andhra Pradesh experienced the most significant decline by 51 percentage points as shown in figure 4.7. It is also interesting to note that in 2011/12 the rural poverty rate among the Scheduled Castes in Andhra Pradesh was the lowest at 13.1% when compared with other large states including Kerala and Punjab.

Table 4.1. POVERTY RATIO BY SOCIAL GROUPS IN ANDHRA PRADESH AND INDIA

Rural Poverty among Social Groups	1993/94	2004/05	2009/10	2011/12
Scheduled Tribes				
Andhra Pradesh	58.1	60.3	40.2	24.1
India	65.7	64.5	47.4	45.3
Scheduled Castes				
Andhra Pradesh	64.2	41.8	25.7	13.1
India	62.1	53.6	42.3	31.5
All Groups				
Andhra Pradesh	48.0	32.3	22.7	11.0
India	50.1	41.9	33.3	25.7

Urban Poverty among Social Groups	1993/94	2004/05	2009/10	2011/12
Scheduled Tribes				
Andhra Pradesh	43.9	50.1	21.2	12.1
India	40.9	38.7	30.4	24.1
Scheduled Castes				
Andhra Pradesh	45.6	35.0	19.8	10.9
India	51.4	40.6	34.1	21.7
All Groups				
Andhra Pradesh	35.1	23.4	17.7	5.8
India	31.7	25.8	20.9	13.7

Source: Panagariya and More (2013); Panagariya and Mukim (2013).

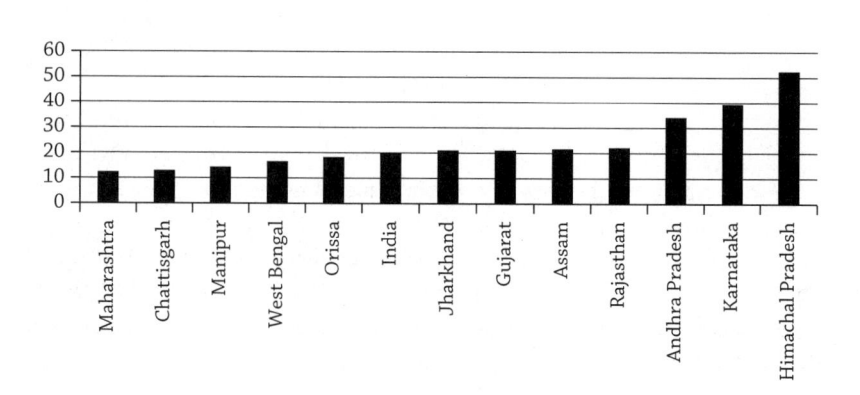

Figure 4.6: Percentage Point Decline in Rural Poverty: Scheduled Tribes from 1993/94 to 2011/12 in the States with Significant Scheduled Tribe Presence
Source: Panagariya and More (2013).

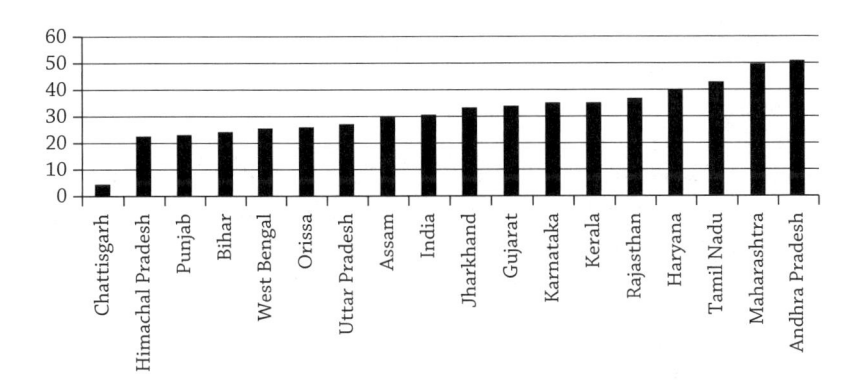

Figure 4.7: Percentage Point Decline in Rural Poverty among the Scheduled Castes from 1993/94 to 2011/12 in the Large States
Source: Panagariya and More (2013).

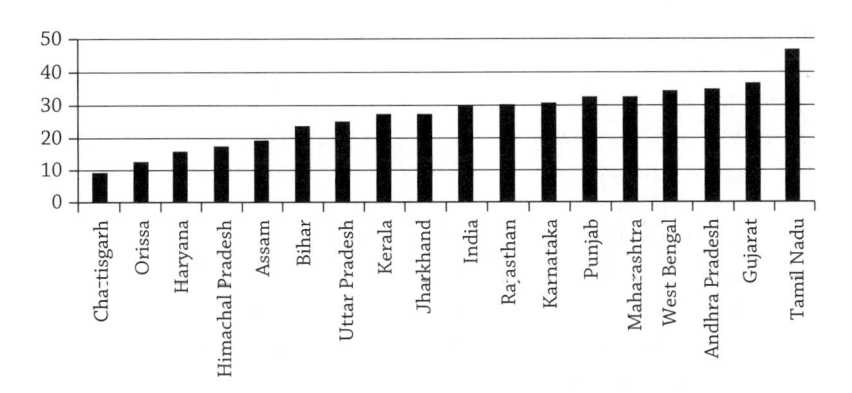

Figure 4.8: Percentage Point Decline in Urban Poverty among the Scheduled Castes from 1993/94 to 2011/12 in the Large States
Source: Panagariya and More (2013).

Furthermore, when we compare the decline in urban poverty among the Scheduled Castes across the large states in India, we find that Andhra Pradesh was among the top three states with the sharpest decline as shown in figure 4.8.

In order to understand this better, we look at the industries and the category in which the Scheduled Caste and the Scheduled Tribe workforce are employed. In 2009/10 73.6% of the rural men and 82.1% of the rural women were employed in the agricultural sector. Given the high employment in the agricultural sector and the fact that per capita growth in the agricultural sector was higher in Andhra Pradesh compared to India as a whole, it is clear from the previous discussion that poverty reduction in Andhra Pradesh among the Scheduled Castes and the Scheduled Tribes would be higher. It is also important to note that from 2004/05 to 2009/10 there was a movement of labor away from the agricultural sector to the construction sector. This phenomenon was also observed in urban areas. The construction sector grew faster than the agricultural sector; this may also have contributed to the rapid decline in the poverty among the Scheduled Castes and the Scheduled Tribes in rural and urban areas.

As we will later see, there has been a dramatic shift among the Scheduled Castes and the Scheduled Tribes from self-employment to casual employment between 2004/05 and 2009/10 relative to India as a whole. In particular, in rural Andhra Pradesh, in 2004/05, 40.8% of the Scheduled Caste and the Scheduled Tribe rural workers were casual while the corresponding number for all-India was 46.3%. By 2009/10, for Andhra Pradesh 60.9% of the rural Scheduled Caste and the Scheduled Tribe workers had turned casual, while for all-India it was 55.8%. Similarly in urban areas, in Andhra Pradesh there was an increase in casual workforce from 58.7% to 88.6% while for all-India there was an increase from 63.2% to 69.6%. We will later see that the real wages of casual workers in both rural and urban areas have risen sharply during this period, which possibly explains the sharp decline in poverty among the Scheduled Castes and Scheduled Tribes.

According to table 4.2, poverty rates have steadily declined across the major religious groups in rural and urban areas as well. Poverty rates among Muslims in rural areas in Andhra Pradesh are lower than the corresponding rates for Hindus during all four years shown. In the urban areas, the reverse is true. But the most remarkable development is that in each case, the gap between poverty rates for Hindus and Muslims has been dramatically reduced. In each region, the group with the higher initial rate of poverty has seen sharper reduction in it.

When we compare the performance of different religious groups in terms of poverty reduction across the large states in India, we find that Andhra Pradesh is a top performer. Andhra Pradesh experienced the sharpest decline in rural poverty among the Hindus from 1993/94 to 2011/12 as shown in figure 4.9. As a matter of fact among the large states the rural poverty rate among the Hindus was the lowest at 10.8% in Andhra Pradesh. Interestingly this was marginally lower than Kerala at 10.9%.

We repeat our analysis for the Muslims and find that Andhra Pradesh was among the top three states that experienced the sharpest decline in rural poverty among the Muslims as shown in figure 4.10. Furthermore, among the large states, Andhra Pradesh has one of the lowest poverty rates among the Muslims as of 2011/12.

Next we look at the decline in urban poverty from 1993/94 to 2011/12 for the religious groups and compare the performance of Andhra Pradesh vis-à-vis other large states in India. We find that Andhra Pradesh experienced the sharpest decline in urban poverty among the Hindus during this period as shown in figure 4.11. Moreover, as of 2011/12, Andhra Pradesh has the lowest urban poverty rates for the Hindus among large states including Kerala.

Table 4.2. POVERTY RATIO BY RELIGIOUS GROUPS IN ANDHRA PRADESH AND INDIA

Rural Poverty among the Religious Groups				
	1993/94	2004/05	2009/10	2011/12
Hindus				
Andhra Pradesh	48.0	32.4	22.9	10.8
India	50.3	42.1	33.5	25.6
Muslims				
Andhra Pradesh	44.2	28.4	20.3	10.6
India	53.4	44.6	36.1	26.9
Others				
Andhra Pradesh	65.2	63.4	22.7	
India	37.8	30.7	21.4	

Urban Poverty among the Religious Groups				
	1993/94	2004/05	2009/10	2011/12
Hindus				
Andhra Pradesh	33.8	22.1	16.0	5.6
India	29.5	23.1	18.7	12.1
Muslims				
Andhra Pradesh	44.5	32.7	24.7	7.2
India	46.4	41.9	33.9	22.7
Others				
Andhra Pradesh	19.4	11.6	3.2	
India	22.8	13.5	12.9	

Source: Panagariya and More (2013); Panagariya and Mukim (2013).

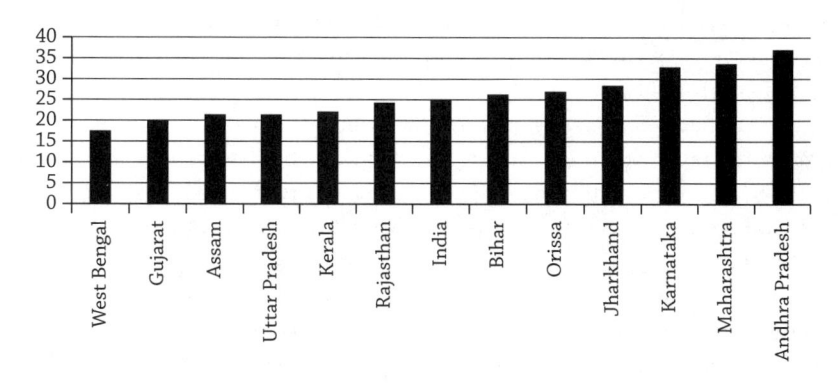

Figure 4.9: Percentage Point Decline in Rural Poverty among the Hindus from 1993/94 to 2011/12 in the Large States
Source: Panagariya and More (2013).

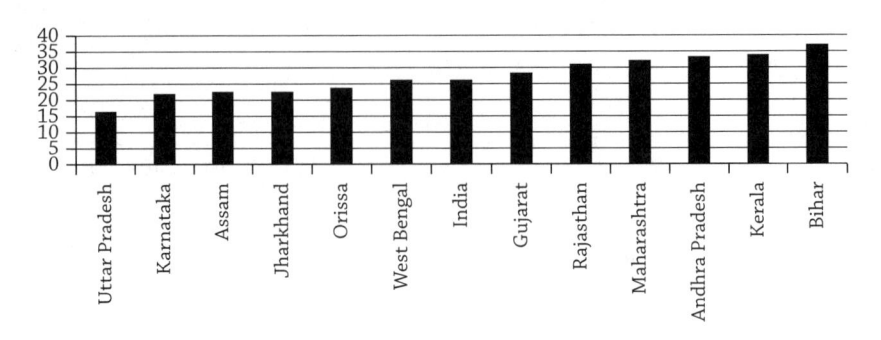

Figure 4.10: Percentage Point Decline in Rural Poverty among the Muslims from 1993/94 to 2011/12 in the Large States
Source: Panagariya and More (2013).

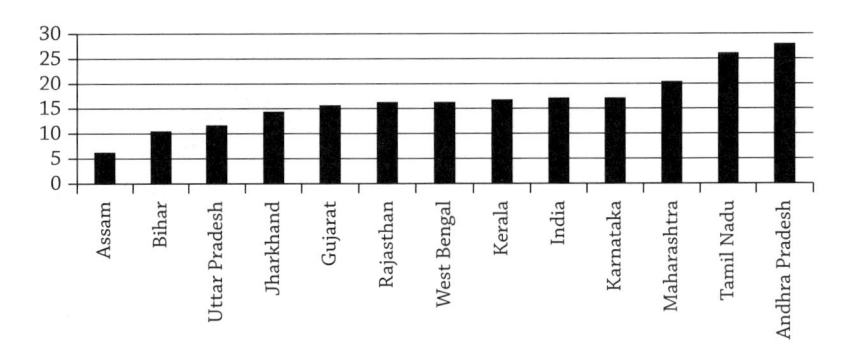

Figure 4.11: Percentage Point Decline in Urban Poverty among the Hindus from 1993/94 to 2011/12 in the Large States
Source: Panagariya and More (2013).

For the Muslims, we observe that Andhra Pradesh was in the top two states that experienced the sharpest decline in urban poverty as shown in figure 4.12. Moreover, as of 2011/12, Andhra Pradesh has one of the lowest poverty rates among the Muslims in urban areas, the other states being Kerala and Tamil Nadu.

In summary, the trends in poverty among the socially disadvantaged groups and religious minorities suggest that there has been a very significant decline in their poverty rates in both rural and urban areas. This decline is very impressive when we compare it to the all-India level. Furthermore, we find that during the period from 2004/05 to 2009/10, when growth was substantially higher, the decline in both rural and urban poverty was significantly higher than the previous period. Also the decline in the poverty rates of groups that had higher initial levels of poverty has been sharper than the average across all groups. At least in terms of poverty, there seems to be a narrowing of the gap between the socially disadvantaged and religious minority groups on the one hand, and the general population on the other.

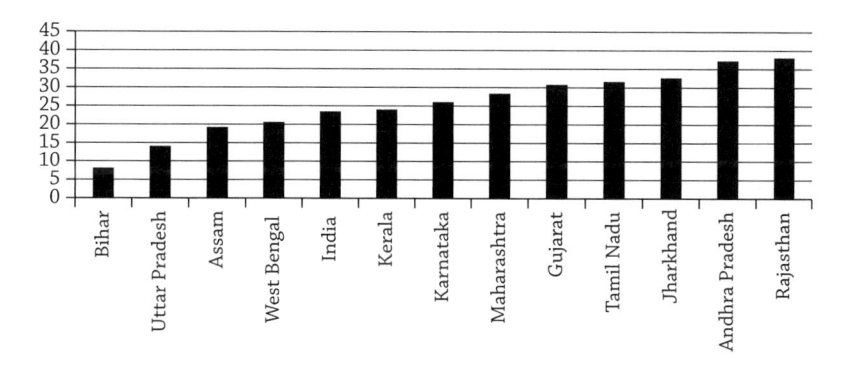

Figure 4.12: Percentage Point Decline in Urban Poverty among the Muslims from 1993/94 to 2011/12 in the Large States
Source: Panagariya and More (2013).

EMPLOYMENT

In this section, we analyze the employment situation in Andhra Pradesh. First, we analyze the workforce participation rate in rural and urban areas. Second, for rural and urban persons we look at the distribution of employment by sectors. Third, we look at overall employment by broad industry division, and then do a similar analysis for rural males and females and urban males and females. Next we look at the category of employment for rural males and females and urban males and females. We also extend our analysis to a consideration of employment in the organized sector, and that in the public and private sector. Lastly, we look at the unemployment and underemployment situation in the state. The data for this part of the analysis is largely from the National Sample Survey (NSS) for the years 1983 (NSS 38th round), 1987/88 (NSS 43rd round), 1993/94 (NSS 50th round), 1999/2000 (NSS 55th round), 2004/05 (NSS 61st round), and 2009/10 (NSS 66th round). Our study extends the analysis by Dev and Mahajan (2003).

Workforce Participation Rate and the Total Workforce

The workforce participation rate (WPR), which measures the number of workers as a percentage of population, has been significantly higher in rural Andhra Pradesh than rural India as a whole. In urban areas, the rate has closely tracked that in India. Table 4.3 shows the participation rates in Andhra Pradesh and India as a whole during various years from 1983 to 2009/10. It shows that the rural participation rate in Andhra Pradesh has consistently exceeded that in India by approximately 10 percentage points or more.

The total workforce was 35.7 million in 1993/94 and rose by 1.2 million people by 1999/2000 despite a small decline in the WPR due to rising population. The rise between 1999/2000 and 2004/05 was slightly larger at

Table 4.3. WORKFORCE PARTICIPATION RATES

Year	Andhra Pradesh Rural	Andhra Pradesh Urban	India Rural	India Urban
1983	53.5	34.8	44.5	34
1987/88	53.3	35.8	43.4	33.7
1993/94	57.7	37.6	44.4	34.7
1999/2000	54.2	34.8	41.7	33.7
2004/05	54.4	39.2	43.9	36.5
2009/10	52.1	36.4	40.8	35.0

Source: NSSO tables.

2.7 million. This trend was reversed between 2004/05 and 2009/10 with the workforce declining 0.4 million. This decline was primarily driven by the drop in the WPR of women both in rural and urban areas.

Distribution of Employment by Sectors

We have previously reported the evolution of the share of workforce in agriculture in rural areas. We now consider this compositional change in greater detail, reporting it in both rural and urban areas. Recall that the output share of agriculture has been declining rather sharply. The same is not true, however, of the employment share. This can be gleaned from tables 4.4 and 4.5.

In terms of employment, Andhra Pradesh still remains a heavily agrarian economy, where approximately 53% of the total workforce engaged in agricultural activities till as late as 2009/10. More specifically, we look at the trend in employment in the sectors of the economy in the rural and urban areas. In 1983, 79.7% of the rural workforce was engaged in agricultural activities and by 1999/2000 the share had declined only marginally to 78.5%. But in the 2000s the decline was more pronounced, it fell to 69% by 2009/10. In industry, the share of employment in the rural areas increased from 9.8% in 1983 to 16% in 2009/10; it is interesting to note that this increase has primarily happened from 1999/2000 to 2009/10. In the services sector, the share of employment in rural areas has increased from 11.9% in 1983 to 15% in 2009/10, with this increase once again taking place between 1999/2000 and 2009/10. It is clear, that in terms of employment composition in the rural areas, the economy has begun to move out of its agrarian structure only after 1999/2000.

In urban areas, across all time periods, the service sector is the largest employer followed by industry and agricultural in that order. From 1983 to 2009/10 the share of the service sector has increased only marginally

Table 4.4. EMPLOYMENT IN ANDHRA PRADESH BY BROAD INDUSTRY DIVISION (MILLIONS)

Industry	NSS round	Rural Male	Rural Female	Urban Male	Urban Female
Agriculture	2009/10	10.62	9.49	0.29	0.25
	2004/05	11.27	10.51	0.46	0.46
	1999/2000	12.56	11.04	0.37	0.30
	1993/94	12.03	10.76	0.58	0.55
Industry	2009/10	2.97	1.83	2.63	0.98
	2004/05	2.48	1.56	2.09	0.71
	1999/2000	1.64	0.99	1.67	0.59
	1993/94	1.60	1.09	1.54	0.54
Services	2009/10	3.27	1.12	4.60	1.17
	2004/05	3.26	1.34	4.15	1.43
	1999/2000	2.69	1.07	3.21	0.88
	1993/94	2.29	0.99	3.00	0.71

Source: Authors' calculations based on NSSO tables and census data.

Table 4.5. DISTRIBUTION OF EMPLOYMENT IN ANDHRA PRADESH BY SECTORS ACCORDING TO USUAL STATUS

Year	Rural Persons Agriculture	Industry	Services	Urban Persons Agriculture	Industry	Services
1983	79.7	9.8	11.9	14.3	29.6	56.1
1993/94	79.3	9.3	11.3	16.4	30.0	53.7
1999/2000	78.5	8.9	12.6	9.5	32.2	58.2
2004/05	71.7	13.1	15.2	9.6	30.0	60.5
2009/10	69.0	16.0	15.0	5.2	36.2	58.6

Source: NSSO tables.

from 56.1% to 58.6%. The share of the industry during the same period has increased from 29.6% to 36.2% and the share of agriculture has declined from 14.3% to 5.2%.

Employment in the Organized Sector

Employment in the organized sector has marginally increased from 1.9 million people (5.4% of the total workforce) in 1995/96 to 2.1 million (5.4% of the total work force) in 2009/10. This clearly suggests that a very significant proportion of the workforce (approximately 94%) is in the unorganized sector. It is important to keep in mind here that when it comes to labor, most social security laws are applicable only in the organized sector.

Furthermore we look at the employment in the public and the private sector. In 1995/96 the share of employment of the private sector in the total employment in the organized sector was approximately 25%. By 2009/10 this share had risen to approximately 36%. It has also been observed that the growth of employment in the private sector is much higher than that of the public sector. Indeed, growth rate of employment in the public sector has been negative from 1999/2000 to 2009/10.

Category of Employment

In this section, we look at employment in three categories: (1) self-employed, (2) regular wage and salary, and (3) casual workers. Table 4.6 reports the relevant data.

During 1993/94 to 2004/05, self-employed workers increased from 16.4 million to 18.7 million. In contrast, from 2004/05 to 2009/10, there was a sharp decline in this number from 18.7 million to 15.6 million (a reduction of self-employed workers by 3.1 million). The numbers of workers with a regular wage or salary has steadily increased from 3.9 million in 1993/94 to 6.5 million in 2009/10. From 1993/94 to 2004/05, the number of casual workers remained more or less the same at 15.4 million. In contrast, from

Table 4.6. EMPLOYMENT IN ANDHRA PRADESH BY CATEGORY OF EMPLOYMENT (MILLIONS)

	NSS round	Rural Male	Rural Female	Urban Male	Urban Female
Self-Employed (ps + ss)[a] Workforce	2009/10	7.06	4.90	2.63	1.01
	2004/05	8.21	6.32	2.86	1.27
	1999/2000	8.17	5.58	1.88	0.69
	1993/94	7.82	5.82	1.95	0.83
Regular Wage/Salaried Employees	2009/10	1.57	0.46	3.61	0.83
	2004/05	1.65	0.54	2.58	0.78
	1999/2000	1.28	0.47	2.21	0.50
	1993/94	1.29	0.24	2.05	0.31
Casual Labor	2009/10	8.23	7.07	1.28	0.56
	2004/05	7.11	6.52	1.24	0.55
	1999/2000	7.43	7.05	1.17	0.57
	1993/94	6.81	6.79	1.11	0.66

[a] "ps" stands for principal status and "ss" for secondary status.
Source: Authors' calculations from NSSO and census data.

2004/05 to 2009/10 the number of casual workers increased from 15.4 million to 17.1 million (an increase of 1.7 million). This suggests that in the more recent years, in particular from 2004/05 to 2009/10, there has been increased casualization of the workforce. It is also interesting to note that this increased casualization of the work force from 2004/05 to 2009/10 is primarily a rural phenomenon. In particular, there was an increase in the number of rural male casual workers by 1.1 million, while there was a decline in the number of the self-employed by approximately the same magnitude. Similarly for the rural females, there was a decline in the self-employed by approximately 1.4 million, though the number of female casual workers increased by 0.6 million. Similar trends can be observed when we look at the ratios of the workforce in the category of employment. A primary force that could be driving this casualization of the workforce from 2004/05 to 2009/10 is the introduction of the National Rural Employment Guarantee Scheme beginning in 2006, which guaranteed 100 days of wage-employment in a financial year to an adult member of each rural household.

In rural and urban areas of Andhra Pradesh, from 2004/05 to 2009/10, there has been a very dramatic increase in real wages for casual labor as shown in table 4.7. For example, the real wages of casual labor in rural areas has increased at the CAGR of 8.3% during this period and this is significantly higher than the CAGR of 3.8% for India as a whole. Furthermore, a similar phenomenon has been observed in the urban areas during this period—the real wages of casual labor in urban areas has increased at the CAGR of 8.6% while the corresponding number for all-India is 1.9%. This clearly suggests in terms of the growth of real wages for casual labor, the Scheduled Castes and the Scheduled Tribes in Andhra Pradesh have done much better than the rest of India.

It is also interesting to note that in Andhra Pradesh the real wages of the casual workers grew much faster than the real wages of the workers with a regular wage and salary. One explanation for this phenomenon could be that

Table 4.7. DAILY WAGES IN RUPEES IN ANDHRA PRADESH (2004/05 PRICES)

	Rural 2004/05	Rural 2009/10	Urban 2004/05	Urban 2009/10
Regular Wage/Salaried				
Scheduled Castes and Scheduled Tribes	74.8	100.9	141.3	177.4
All	90.5	114.5	167.0	216.1
Casual Labor				
Scheduled Castes and Scheduled Tribes	40.8	60.9	58.7	88.6
All	41.6	65.0	55.9	91.0

Source: Calculated from NSS unit level data. 2009/10 prices deflated using CPI-AL for Andhra Pradesh.

a large portion of the urban casual workforce was engaged in the construction sector, which grew extremely rapidly. This suggests that integration of the socially disadvantaged group into rapidly growing sectors can have a very important impact on poverty reduction. Secondly, for rural areas, this could also reflect the impact of National Rural Employment Guarantee Scheme (NREGS). Rural households may register themselves and receive a job card, subsequent to which they can ask for and receive work. In Andhra Pradesh, 43.4% of all rural households had job cards. The proportion of the Scheduled Caste and the Scheduled Tribe households that had job cards, on the other hand, was significantly higher at 56.7%. At the all-India level, the percentage of the Scheduled Caste and the Scheduled Tribe households with job cards was much less at 47.9%. The NREGS program in Andhra Pradesh was also able to provide employment to a higher proportion of the Scheduled Caste and the Scheduled Tribe households when compared to the all-India level, 46.3% against 35.2%, respectively. The Scheduled Caste and the Scheduled Tribe households in Andhra Pradesh were on average provided work for 46.5 days. The Scheduled Caste and the Scheduled Tribe households all over India could only find employment for 37.2 days under NREGS on average. These numbers suggest that the Scheduled Castes and the Scheduled Tribes in rural Andhra Pradesh have benefited much more from NREGS than the Scheduled Caste and the Scheduled Tribe households in the rest of India. The data also suggests that within Andhra Pradesh, the Scheduled Castes and the Scheduled Tribes were the biggest beneficiaries of the program.

Unemployment and Underemployment

The potential impact of NREGS also shows up in the unemployment and underemployment rates. Unemployment rate is defined as the proportion of the labor force that is unemployed, and this is a proportion that has not changed significantly in rural Andhra Pradesh over the past two of decades. The number of people who are usually unemployed in rural Andhra Pradesh has typically remained in the neighborhood of 1% to 1.5% of the number of people who are seeking employment. As table 4.8 shows, the unemployment rate in rural Andhra Pradesh has remained largely constant, but what is interesting is that underemployment has come down.

Underemployment can be thought of as being incomplete utilization of the time that a person is available for work. For instance, if a person is seeking work 300 days of the year, but finds employment only for 250, they are said to be underemployed. Underemployment can be measured by the proportion of time that a person classified as usually employed is looking for work without success. According to the NSSO data, a usually employed man in rural Andhra Pradesh would still be unemployed and seeking work 5%

Table 4.8. UNDEREMPLOYMENT: PER 1,000 DISTRIBUTION OF PERSON-DAYS OF USUALLY EMPLOYED (PRINCIPAL + SUBSIDIARY) BY CURRENT DAILY STATUS IN RURAL ANDHRA PRADESH

Year	Rural Males				Rural Females			
	1993/94	1999/2000	2004/05	2009/10	1993/94	1999/2000	2004/05	2009/10
Employed	898	881	870	894	722	739	723	781
Unemployed	50	67	86	55	53	59	97	54
Not in labor force	53	51	44	51	226	202	180	165

Note: Unemployed here refer to person-days out of 1,000 that usually employed people cannot find employment.
Source: NSSO reports.

of his time in 1993/94. This proportion increased to 6.7% and then to 8.6% in 1999/2000 and 2004/05, respectively. However, this rising trend was arrested in 2009/10 with the proportion coming down to 5.5%. A similar trend was also observed among rural females. This result is consistent with the fact that the aim of NREGS was to provide additional employment to agricultural labor principally during off-season.

Unemployment rates in Andhra Pradesh tend to be lower than those in India as a whole if one considers the usual status of those surveyed. The unemployment rate for men in urban Andhra Pradesh has also seen a reduction to 2.6% in 2009/10 from 4.3% in 1999/2000. However, this same trend has been reversed for urban women, who faced an unemployment rate of 5.8% in 2009/10, as opposed to 4.4% in 1999/2000.

CONCLUDING REMARKS

Poverty reduction has been one of the signal achievements of the state of Andhra Pradesh between 1993/94 and 2011/12. The rural poverty rate has fallen from 48% to 11%, and the urban rate from 35% to 6%. It is also pertinent to note that this reduction has been across the board—poverty in Andhra Pradesh has fallen for socially disadvantaged classes (Scheduled Castes and Scheduled Tribes) as well as for religious groups. Groups with larger proportions of poor at the beginning of the period have seen sharper declines, so there is also greater parity among various social groups, at least in terms of poverty.

Our hypothesis is that the shift to high-value agricultural commodities, and the subsequent high growth of Andhra Pradesh's agricultural output, has driven the drop in rural poverty in Andhra Pradesh. While this is yet to be rigorously studied, it is given weight by past empirical findings that growth rate of agricultural output is one of the significant explanatory variables in determining which Indian states have performed better at reducing rural poverty. At the same time, it is important to keep in mind that this shift is inextricably linked with the broader economic growth in the state and country that led to increased demand for such high value commodities in the first place. Besides driving this demand, economic growth has also enabled higher urban wages and led to a reduction in urban poverty.

Another potential factor in the dramatic reduction in rural and urban poverty is the increase in per capita development expenditure of the state. Datt and Ravallion (2002) provide empirical evidence that high growth rate and high development expenditure of the state reduce the incidence of poverty. In 1994, per capita development expenditure in Andhra Pradesh was 1,237 rupees—lower than the all-India average of 1,560 rupees. By 2008, per capita state development expenditure in Andhra Pradesh had risen to 3,123 rupees, which was higher than the all-India average of 2,901 rupees.

It is important to mention that the increase in per capita development expenditure in Andhra Pradesh has not happened at the expense of revenue or the fiscal deficit of the state. As a matter of fact, since 2001 revenue and fiscal deficit of the state have been declining as a percentage of the GSDP. This suggests that high GSDP growth rates in the 2000s and the taxation reforms such as the introduction of the value added tax (VAT) have played an important role in expanding the states revenues, which could then be used for development.

This highlights the value of growth as a strategy to promote socioeconomic development. Policies pursuing higher growth can simultaneously enable the government to pursue its social and development agenda, while the reverse might not be true. That the period of high growth between 2004/05 and 2011/12 coincided with the sharpest declines in poverty is powerful evidence that economic growth is important for helping the poor.

In terms of employment, Andhra Pradesh still remains a heavily agrarian economy, with just over half of the total workforce of approximately 39 million people engaged in agricultural activities in 2009/10. The movement of people from agriculture into industry and services has been slow, but most of it has taken place in the past decade, and it has been accelerating. In urban areas, 59% of the workforce is engaged in services and 35% in industry. In rural areas, 69% of the workforce is still employed in agriculture, and the remaining 31% are nearly evenly split between agriculture and industry. The bulk of the workforce however, in both rural and urban areas, was still engaged in the unorganized sector, where they fall entirely outside the protections that India's harsh labor regulations aim to provide. Reform of labor regulations is thus a pressing need.

CHAPTER 5
Microfinance and Employment Guarantee Program in Rural Areas

The microfinance industry in Andhra Pradesh is the largest among all Indian states in terms of client outreach and loan portfolio. At the same time, it has come under attack recently from the state government for lack of delivery of financial services at an affordable cost to the economically weaker sections of the society. These facts make Andhra Pradesh's experience in microfinance an interesting case study. In a similar vein, Andhra Pradesh has been one of the most successful states in providing employment in rural areas under the central scheme known as Mahatma Gandhi National Rural Employment Guarantee Act (MNREGA). Given the perceived potential importance of these instruments in combating poverty, we discuss them in some detail in this chapter.

MICROFINANCE

It is commonly believed that financial inclusion can play a vital role in poverty reduction.[1] One of the key players in the spread of microfinance is the group of organizations known as Microfinance Institutions (MFIs). In recent years MFIs have partnered with different financial providers to take formal financial services like remittances, savings, credit, and insurance services at an affordable cost to the unbanked, under-banked, and

---

1. In its report of January 8, 2008, the Rangarajan Committee on Financial Inclusion, appointed by the Government of India, defines financial inclusion as "delivery of financial services at an affordable cost to the vast sections of the disadvantaged and low-income groups." Full report of the committee can be found at http://sksindia.com/downloads/Report_Committee_Financial_Inclusion.pdf (accessed on January 21, 2014).

vulnerable populations. In this section, we explore in greater detail the overall status of the microfinance industry and the role played by the MFIs in Andhra Pradesh.

Size of the Industry in Andhra Pradesh Relative to India

Microfinance started out as a relatively modest attempt to provide credit in the form of small loans to poor families and businesses that were outside the reach of the formal banking system. Over time, it has grown into a multi-billion-dollar industry that operates at a scale beyond what was possible for charity-led NGOs or regional governments. The microfinance industry in India too has grown very dramatically from 2001 onward. In 2001, the loans made available through MFI totaled 645 million rupees. By 2011, this figure had grown more than 300 times to 207.56 billion rupees. In terms of client outreach, in 2001, merely 300,000 clients were served by MFIs but by 2011, the number of clients served by the MFIs increased by more than 100 times to 31.8 million.

A large part of this growth has come from Andhra Pradesh, which is the largest among all states in India in microfinance, both in terms of loan disbursement and client outreach. In Andhra Pradesh, the total loan portfolio outstanding as of March 2011 was 52.05 billion rupees, representing one-quarter of the total loans outstanding for India as a whole. In terms of client outreach, 5.75 million clients were served by the MFIs in 2011 in Andhra Pradesh and represented approximately 19% of the total clients served by the MFIs across the country. Of the top nine of a total of 172 MFIs, which accounted for 80% of the loan portfolio, five—Spandana, SKS, Share, Asmitha, and BASIX—are headquartered in Andhra Pradesh. These shares highlight the importance of Andhra Pradesh in the microfinance industry. As home to such a large part of the microfinance sector, it is perhaps not surprising that the controversy surrounding the sector in 2010 also had its roots in Andhra Pradesh.

Evolution of Microfinance in Andhra Pradesh

Examples of NGOs extending credit to Self-Help Groups (SHGs) in India had existed since at least the Self-Employed Women's Association (SEWA) started providing loans to women in the 1970s. Over the years, the SHGs evolved to incorporate features that are now well known in microfinance literature—socialization of risk through joint liability, regular repayments, and lending to women. Institutional support from the Reserve Bank of India (RBI) came in the form of a rural pilot in 1992, which linked SHGs (under the tutelage of NGOs) to banks that could provide them credit with this system formalized in the later part of the 1990s. SHGs with bank finance subsequently surged from 10,000 in 1996/97 to 1 million in 2004.

Andhra Pradesh, in particular, had a very large number of SHGs—by 2002, over 50% of those in India as a whole. One of the primary reasons for this was that the Telugu Desam Party (TDP) of Chandrababu Naidu, which was in power in the late 1990s and early 2000s, was pursuing reforms with the support of the World Bank. The reforms involved both a reduction in subsidies and bank credit in rural areas (Rao 2008). This drawdown in state largesse was offset by a promotion of SHGs as a means of access to credit and a link to the ruling party at the state level. SHGs were encouraged with logistical and financial backing under a new program called *Velugu*. The state government also saw SHGs as one of the methods that could be used to dispense patronage and circumvent local power structures such as the Panchayati Raj system (Johnson et al. 2005). The state government thus helped form a large base of SHGs. But only about 25% of them ended up receiving microloans and they tended to be the more affluent groups (Mooij 2002).

This set up a situation in which a large number of SHGs were present on the ground but only a small proportion of them was taking loans. The imbalance presented an opportunity for NGOs which began transforming into for-profit MFIs and acting as financial intermediaries—raising funds from banks and private investors and lending them to SHGs at lucrative rates of interest. The potential of a large unmet demand for credit and the apparent scalability of the for-profit model led to a rapid expansion of MFIs. This growth came to a head with the highly publicized IPO of SKS microfinance, one of the largest MFIs in the industry. The IPO was hugely successful, oversubscribed by 14 times of what was on offer.

SKS was not alone in seeking external funds. MFIs systematically sought external investors as shareholders (Sriram 2010) and as a result, where they had previously been concerned primarily with SHGs and their clients, they had now gained a significant new stakeholder and a new mission—profit. For profit provisioning of microcredit in turn reportedly led to a new, more aggressive paradigm of microfinance in Andhra Pradesh. Loan officers were incentivized for expanding the number of loans made and for ensuring high repayment rates. SHGs were preferred candidates for lending because they were ideal for socializing risk. Loan officers would either lend to already existing SHGs from the government's Velugu program, or lend again to people who had already taken financing from other MFIs. This state of affairs is highlighted by the fact that while the total number of households in Andhra Pradesh was only 16 million, MFIs and SHGs counted 23.55 million people among their clients and credit members (Srinivasan

2010). It has been pointed out that the problem that this could give rise to lay not so much in multiple borrowing per se but in the over-indebtedness caused by a lack of proper credit infrastructure and the resulting inability of MFIs to judge the suitability and creditworthiness of the borrowers (Chakrabarti and Ravi 2011).

Indeed, not long after the SKS IPO, Andhra Pradesh experienced around 30 suicides that were allegedly linked to indebtedness and the collection practices of MFIs. The political backlash from this series of suicides saw a precipitous decline for the entire microfinance industry in Andhra Pradesh, a fall from grace made worse by the state having been its biggest success story thus far. The MFIs faced local political persecution followed by the Andhra Pradesh Microfinance Institutions (Regulation of Money Lending) Ordinance, 2010, later ratified by the state assembly. The new law threw the entire MFI operating model into jeopardy. It mandated that MFIs limit collections to monthly schedules as opposed to the weekly norm and that collection meetings be held in public panchayat offices.

Prior to the ordinance, MFIs had used various methods to ensure repayment. Most of these methods, however, depended on social sanctions. Borrowers continued to repay loans because most of their peers thought it necessary to do so and did so themselves (Bannerjee and Duflo 2011). In the period following the suicides, however, there was a widespread political campaign maligning the MFIs as loan sharks. This had the predictable effect of delegitimizing the MFIs and causing repayments to drop. Combined with the restrictions placed on their activities by the ordinance, MFIs in Andhra Pradesh saw their repayment rates fall to below 30 percent from more than 90 percent before the ordinance (Chakrabarti and Ravi 2011).

As a result of the crisis, 20 small MFIs in Andhra Pradesh closed down operations. Even large operators like SKS microfinance laid off 1,200 of their 3,400 employees in Andhra Pradesh and closed 78 of their 180 branches. Total client outreach in Andhra Pradesh and its neighboring states in South India saw declines instead of the large increases to which the industry had hitherto been accustomed. Bank lending to MFIs after the Andhra Pradesh crisis slowed down or stopped entirely.

The crisis compelled the RBI to set up the Malegam committee to look into establishing policy that would aid in regulating the microfinance sector. The Malegam committee's recommendations stipulate that MFIs be classified under a separate category of non-banking financial corporations and steps be taken to prevent over-borrowing and borrowing from multiple sources. It remains to be seen how the final law for regulation of the microfinance sector, currently under consideration by the central government, will impact the industry.

Impact

Given the rapid spread of the MFI in Andhra Pradesh, there is still an intense debate on the impact of MFI on poverty reduction. In spite of the importance of this issue, there have been very few rigorous research analyses to test the impact. In a seminal contribution, using data from the Grameen Bank in Bangladesh, Pitt and Khandker (1998) (hereinafter PK) show that microcredit does reduce poverty. This finding has, however, been challenged by Roodman and Morduch (2009) (hereinafter RM). Their main criticism is that using the same data, they were unable to replicate the important PK results, and this is primarily because the identification issue was not addressed adequately by the latter. The main conclusion of the RM study was that "30 years into the microfinance movement we have little solid evidence that it improves the lives of clients in measurable ways."

More recently, Banerjee, Duflo, Glennerster, and Kinnan (2010) have attempted to address this question using randomized control trials. Their study was based in Hyderabad, which is the capital of Andhra Pradesh. They find heterogeneous impact of microcredit—existing businessmen increase their expenditure on durable goods and microcredit clients who have a higher propensity to become new business owners increase their expenditure on durable goods. Households with lower propensity to become new business owners increase their non-durable expenditure. Last but not least, they find no impact of microcredit on health, education, or women's decision-making.

MAHATMA GANDHI NATIONAL RURAL EMPLOYMENT GUARANTEE ACT (MNREGA)

In 2005, the government of India launched a very ambitious development initiative called the National Rural Employment Guarantee Act (NREGA), renamed as Mahatma Gandhi National Rural Employment Guarantee Act (MNREGA) in 2009. The fundamental objective of this act was the "enhancement of livelihood security" to rural households by guaranteeing up to 100 days of wage employment (minimum wage, fixed by the state government) in a financial year to rural households which have adult members willing to do unskilled manual work.

EVALUATION

As Dutta et al. (2012) point out, there are many distinct ways in which this scheme attempts to alleviate poverty: (1) It provides employment and extra income to the poorest rural households. (2) The scheme is "self-targeting"—non-poor might not want to do manual work for a minimum wage and also if better opportunities emerge then poor people can turn away from the scheme. (3) The scheme enforces a minimum wage for all casual work by enhancing the bargaining power of the poor in the labor market and benefits even those who might not be participating in the program. (4) The scheme could also potentially provide insurance against the many risks faced by rural poor households.

Nevertheless, for this grand scheme to fulfill its objectives effectively and efficiently the key challenge was of implementation and monitoring at the ground level, and this was primarily the job of the state government. Andhra Pradesh has gained a reputation for being one of the states where the scheme was successfully implemented (Kannan and Breman 2013). Indeed, we do observe that some states, in particular Andhra Pradesh, have done much better than others in taking the benefits of this central scheme to the poor. The data points below are based on the National Sample Survey of 2009/10.

1. The participation rate (defined as the share of rural households working in the MNREGA) in Andhra Pradesh is 35.4%, which is significantly higher than the corresponding national average of 24.9% for all-India (figure 5.1). Andhra Pradesh is in the top 5 states among the 20 large states. It is also important to mention that the participation rate for the poor in Andhra Pradesh is 51.3%, while the corresponding number at the all-India level is 32.5%. Among the top 20 states, there are only 3 other states that have done better than Andhra Pradesh. This clearly suggests that poor people are

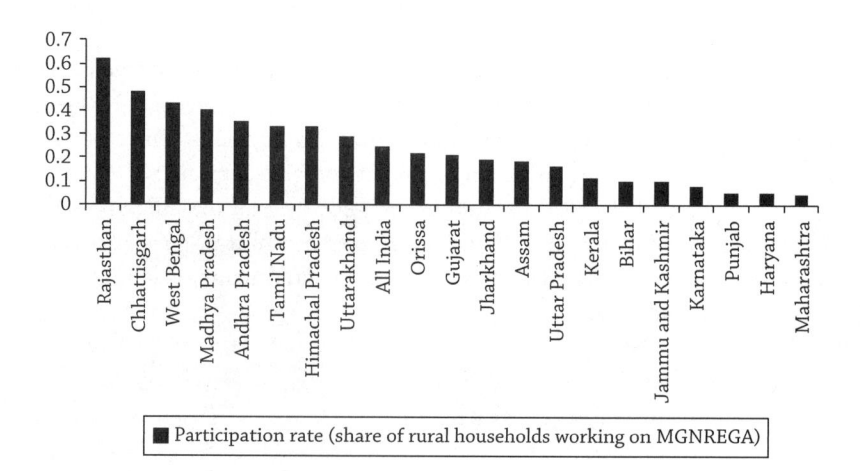

Figure 5.1: Participation Rate in MGNREGA across Different States in India
Source: Based on data from Dutta et al. (2012).

significant beneficiaries of the scheme. Furthermore, in Andhra Pradesh, participation rates among the Scheduled Castes, Scheduled Tribes, and the Other Backward Castes (OBCs) are 56.7%, 43.4%, and 38.2%, respectively. Once again, Andhra Pradesh is among the top 4 states when compared to the 20 large states.

2. "Targeting differential" (TD) has been suggested as a measure to predict the impact of the program on poverty. In the context of MNREGA, Dutta et al. (2012) define TD as the difference between the participation rate among the poor and the non-poor. They show that TD for Andhra Pradesh was much higher at 19.1% when compared to the all-India rate of 11.5% (figure 5.2). Among the large 20 states only 2 other states did marginally better than Andhra Pradesh. This suggests that relative to other states Andhra Pradesh has been much better at taking the scheme to poor households.

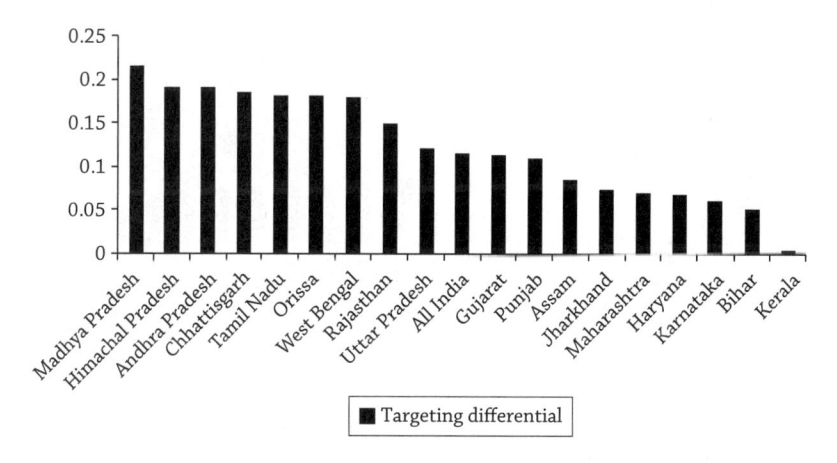

Figure 5.2: Targeting Differential in Different States
Source: Based on data from Dutta et al. (2012).

3. If we look at the rationing rate, defined as the share of the rural households who wanted work but could not get it, Andhra Pradesh does much better at 24.9% compared with the all-India average of 44.4% (figure 5.3). When compared to the other large 20 states, Andhra Pradesh is among the lowest in terms of rationing rate. Among the poor, the rationing rate in Andhra Pradesh is 21.5%, which is much lower when compared to the all-India average of 42.8%. There are only 2 other states that have a lower rate when compared to Andhra Pradesh.

4. In Andhra Pradesh, the female share of employment as a percentage of total person days is 58.1%, which is significantly higher than the all-India average of 48.1% (figure 5.4). Moreover, Andhra Pradesh is among the top 3 states in term of female participation in the program.

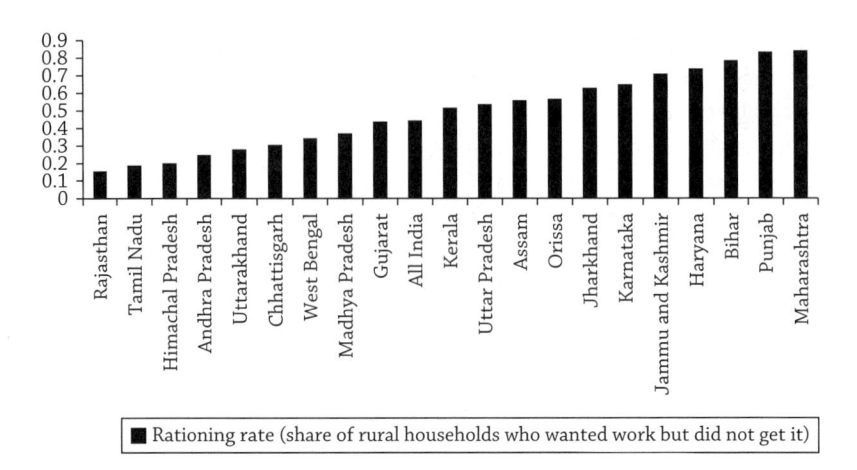

Figure 5.3: Rationing Rate in Different States
Source: Based on data from Dutta et al. (2012).

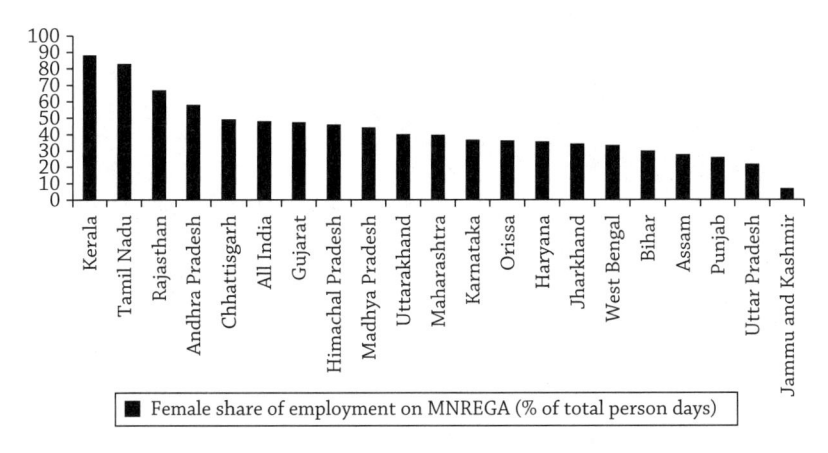

Figure 5.4: Female Share of Employment on MNREGA in Different States
Source: Based on data from Dutta et al. (2012).

Lessons from Andhra Pradesh

These numbers clearly suggest that in terms of various indicators Andhra Pradesh has outperformed other states, and it becomes imperative to understand why. Some of the key lessons following from the Andhra Pradesh experience are: the use of information technology for process flow, monitoring, and the role of NGOs.

Use of Information Technology (IT) for Process Flow

In order to efficiently implement the scheme, Andhra Pradesh has used a very comprehensive IT infrastructure that provides an end-to-end solution.[2] Some of the key features of the program, like issue of job cards, generation of work and cost estimates, issuing the work commencement letters, creation and update of muster rolls, and the measurement and generation of pay orders and slips, have been fully computerized. At the mandal (block) level, there is a computer center, which is manned by two operators and this information is updated on a daily basis. This allows efficient centralized implementation and monitoring of the program by the Program Officer (PO) and District Program Coordinator (DPC). This has also led to a fixed payment cycle where it takes approximately 13 days from the opening of the muster roll to the disbursement of the wages. Andhra Pradesh has also pioneered software that can be used for the preparation of technical estimates and the generation of the work estimates. This, in turn, has reduced the dependency on engineers at the panchayat level, a human resource that is not easily available at the village level. Computerization has also facilitated the grouping of similar works, which in turn leads to more efficient implementation and better supervision.

Andhra Pradesh has also pioneered the creation of a system called electronic Muster and Measurement System (eMMS). This allows for the use of the mobile phones to obtain live data from the worksite and to update it to the mandal computer on a day-to-day basis. This to a certain extent addresses the issues related to the fudging of muster rolls and distortions in measurement and reduces delays in wage payments.

The state also uses an electronic Fund Management System (eFMS) for online money transfers. All the mandal computer centers are networked to a central server and therefore have online access to central funds. Once a pay order is generated, all the payments are transferred to the accounts online, which allows efficient utilization of funds. First, this system avoids deficient or excess funds at the mandal level; second, the mandal staff reliance on paperwork (maintenance of checkbook and accounts) is reduced significantly; and lastly, this prevents fraud.

Even before the universal identification card was issued, Andhra Pradesh had pioneered the issue of smart cards relying on biometric identification. Each worker is issued a smart card where his fingerprint is stored for identification. With the help of this card, wage payments are credited automatically to the accounts of the beneficiaries and the bank arranges the cash payment using a business correspondent.

For efficient implementation of the MNREGA, the computerization has also been used to help tie up with other relevant departments - like the tribal welfare department, forest department, and horticulture department - to use their expertise in implementation of the projects without incurring any other additional expense.

---

2. Tata Consultancy Service (TCS) was hired to provide an end-to-end IT solution and to automate the implementation in Andhra Pradesh.

In summary, IT has played a very instrumental role in the monitoring and the implementation of the scheme on a continuous daily basis. This has introduced transparency, minimized frauds, and improved the efficiency in the processes, thereby reducing the total cost of implementation.

Monitoring

In order to monitor the program, social audits have been set at the village community level. Furthermore, an external Society for Social Audit, Accountability and Transparency (SSAAT) with eminent people as board members has been formed. Some of the key steps that have been taken at the ground level are:

1. Social audit of every village is carried out once in six months.
2. The social auditors inspect all the muster rolls and the projects.
3. All persons who have been paid wages are contacted at their residence and the amount of money that is deposited in their accounts is validated.
4. Program Officers provide the social auditors with all the relevant documents.

Another interesting feature of the social audits is that these reports are read out in a public meeting held at the village level. All the local government officials are required to attend these public hearings. In case of any misappropriation of funds, decisions like filing the First Information Report (FIR) and collection of the amount from the erring officers are made on the spot by the presiding officers.

Every month, information regarding the work and payment are written on the walls in the villages and a gram sabha is conducted to take feedback.

Role of NGOs

Last but not least, Andhra Pradesh NGO Alliance (APNA) has been formed with 483 civil bodies. The NGOs are appointed to find facts in those areas where there are complaints. The debriefing session happens at least once a month at the village, block, and the district level.

This suggests that there is a genuine effort to ensure that the program is reaching out to the true intended beneficiaries and any issue related to implementation and misappropriation is dealt with quickly and efficiently.

CONCLUDING REMARKS

The implication of our discussion on microfinance is that so far there is no academic evidence to suggest that microfinance has any impact on poverty.

Even though the microfinance industry in Andhra Pradesh has exploded in the 2000s and this is also the time period when the state experienced a dramatic decline in poverty, there is no reason to believe that there was any causality. The impact of microfinance on poverty still remains an open-ended question. The political backlash against MFIs in the aftermath of a spate of suicides allegedly linked to microfinance related indebtedness provides a compelling case study of the risks inherent in microfinance, and careful study is warranted before aggressively pushing microfinance.

In the case of MNREGA, which was launched in 2007/08, available data only tells us that Andhra Pradesh has been one of the best implementers of the scheme. It has remained in the top five states in terms of maximum participation, minimum rationing, female participation, and targeting of poorer households. Its experience in implementation, including the use of IT and monitoring through local bodies, offers us a useful example to emulate for successful targeting of welfare programs.

CHAPTER 6
Health and Education

In this chapter, we turn to the key social sectors: health and education. Our main finding is that though Andhra Pradesh has done spectacularly well in combating poverty, its progress in health and education has been less than satisfactory. In part, the explanation lies in its late start: Andhra Pradesh was behind the average of India right from the time comparable data on health and education are available. But the progress during the recent decades also raises concerns and calls for more concerted effort in both sectors.

HEALTH OUTCOMES

Health outcomes in Andhra Pradesh have been consistently superior to those in India as a whole, but progress has been uneven. This is best illustrated by the evolution of the infant mortality rate (IMR), which measures deaths of children before reaching 1 year of age per 1,000 births. The IMR in Andhra Pradesh in 1971 was 106 deaths per 1,000 live births (see figure 6.1). The corresponding IMR for all-India was 129. By 1981, Andhra Pradesh had brought down the IMR to 86 representing a reduction of nearly 25%, while the all-India IMR had come down by a similar absolute margin to 110, which represented a reduction of 18%.

After these early gains, however, the improvement in Andhra Pradesh's IMR has slowed down in comparison with the all-India figures. In 1991, all-India estimates of IMR had come down nearly 40% to 80 deaths per 1,000 live births, while Andhra Pradesh had made only a 17% reduction to move to 73. This trend continued for the next two decades as well, and in 2009, the IMR in Andhra Pradesh was 49, while the all-India IMR was 50.

These trends may suggest that initial gains in bringing the IMR down are merely low-hanging fruit and that once the easy steps have been taken, the subsequent reductions are harder to achieve. But the case of Tamil

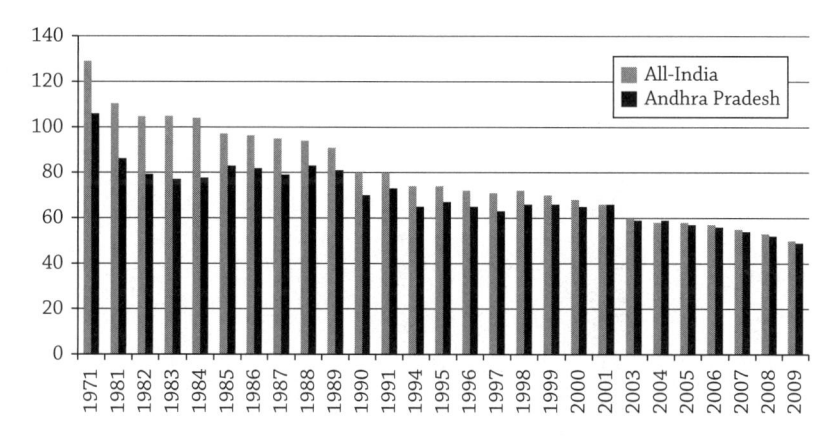

Figure 6.1: IMR Trends in Andhra Pradesh and All-India, 1971–2009
Source: Authors' construction using data from Sample Registration System Bulletins.

Nadu brings this hypothesis into question. Tamil Nadu started off in 1971 with an IMR of 113, which was higher than the corresponding figure of 106 for Andhra Pradesh. Until 1981, the reduction in IMR in Tamil Nadu was fairly similar to that in Andhra Pradesh, but from the 1980s onward, Tamil Nadu has consistently made bigger percentage reductions in IMR than Andhra Pradesh. This has resulted in the IMR in Tamil Nadu in 2009 being 31, which is significantly lower than the corresponding estimate for Andhra Pradesh.

Kerala offers another example of the possibility of achieving high percentage reductions in IMR, even when starting with a low initial IMR. The IMR for Kerala fell from 58 in 1971 to 12 in 2009. It is thus clear that Andhra Pradesh cannot wish away its average performance in reducing the infant mortality rate.

Estimates of life expectancy at birth tell a similar tale. This is shown in figure 6.2, which shows the evolution of life expectancy in Andhra Pradesh, India as a whole, and Tamil Nadu. Andhra Pradesh, Tamil Nadu, and India had virtually identical life expectancy at birth during 1970–75, the earliest period for which we have comparable data. But by 2005–10, Tamil Nadu had pulled well ahead of Andhra Pradesh and India as a whole while Andhra Pradesh had fallen a tad behind the average of India. In view of the trends in the IMR, this should not be surprising. Life expectancy at birth is highly correlated to the IMR, since the differences in survival rates across populations are far less at 1 year of age or later than in the first year of life.

The reasons for uneven progress in Andhra Pradesh are not altogether clear. As far as the slow progress since 1981 is concerned, one possible explanation is the relative stagnation of the public health infrastructure in Andhra Pradesh. The availability of government doctors has increased from 8 per 100,000

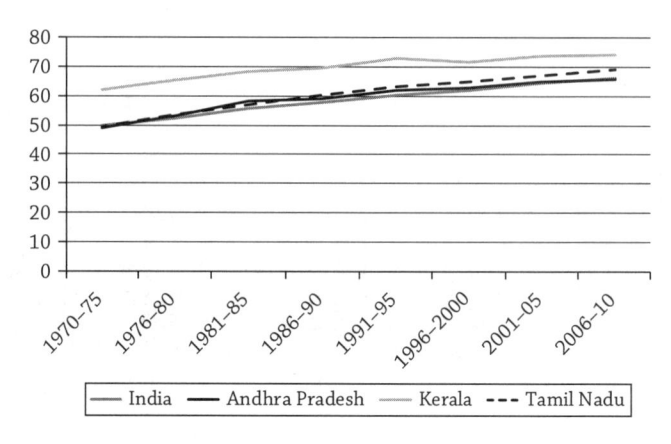

Figure 6.2: Life Expectancy at Birth, 1970–75 to 2006–10
Source: Authors' construction based on data from the SRS Bulletins
Health Care: Public versus Private.

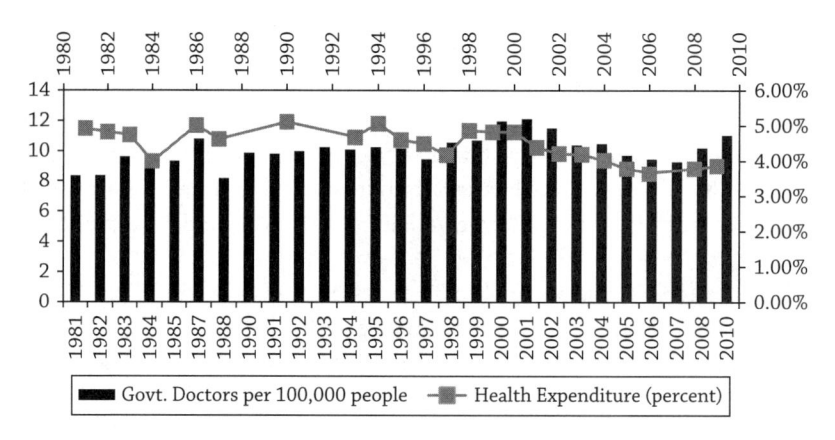

Figure 6.3: Healthcare Inputs in Terms of Government Doctors and Expenditure, 1981–2010
Source: Various Andhra Pradesh statistical abstracts.

people in 1981 to 11.7 doctors in 2010 (figure 6.3). The number of hospital beds available in the public sector has also remained practically constant at approximately 47 beds per 100,000 people over this period. Overall (public plus private) health expenditure as a percentage of the GSDP has declined over the period from 1981 to 2010 from almost 5% in 1981 to just below 4% in 2010.

National Sample Survey data show that as in much of the rest of India, the slack in public provision of health services as reflected in the shortage of government doctors has been taken up in Andhra Pradesh by private providers. Andhra Pradesh's private sector share in hospitalization was the highest in India at 70% in rural and 62% in urban areas in the 1986/87 survey. In outpatient services as well the share of private providers was quite high at approximately 80% for both rural and urban areas. This was again higher than the national average, which was around 74% in 1986/87. In 2004, the picture in Andhra Pradesh was little changed, with the share of private sector in hospitalization showing small increases (of the order of 3 percentage points), and the share of private sector in outpatient care remaining practically unchanged at 80%. In terms of expenditure, per capita public expenditure on medical care at current prices went from 75 rupees in 1993/94 to 188 rupees in 2004. The NSS surveys for the same periods reveal that per capita household expenditure increased from 244 rupees in 1993/94 to 518 rupees in 2004. This shows that on average, roughly 75% of health expenditure in the state was out of pocket expenditure by households. This is consistent with the all-India levels of public and private expenditures. Interestingly, the more developed states tend to have a higher proportion of private spending in healthcare, indicating that those who can afford it prefer private care.

The National Family Health Surveys (NFHS) paint a similar picture on the type of medical attendance at the time of delivery. The three NFHS surveys were held in 1992/93, 1998/99, and 2005/06. The percentage of deliveries in Andhra Pradesh taking place in institutions (public or private) during these three periods was 34%, 54%, and 68.6%, respectively. In 1992/93, the private sector accounted for 58% of these institutional deliveries, and by 1998/99, this proportion had increased to three-quarters of all institutional deliveries. The corresponding share for India as a whole in 1998/99 was only 52%.

The data from both NSS and NFHS thus show that the majority of the population in Andhra Pradesh seeks treatment in private facilities rather than public ones, even though treatment in public facilities is highly subsidized. The high proportion of care seekers that utilize private healthcare providers points to the likelihood that the only people who seek care at public health facilities are those who cannot afford the private option and this in turn provides an insight into the quality of service provided at the government facilities. It has also been argued that the poor quality of service delivery in the public health sector and the consequent preference of care-seekers for private medical services suggest that attempts to strengthen the public system may not be the most cost-effective way to improve healthcare in India.

IN-PATIENT CARE AND HEALTH INSURANCE—RAJIV AAROGYASRI

Perhaps in recognition of the delivery limitations of public health services, Andhra Pradesh shifted to the innovative approach of introducing a health insurance scheme in 2007. Known as Rajiv Aarogyasri, henceforth referred to as Aarogyasri, it is the flagship healthcare scheme of the Andhra Pradesh state government. The scheme's stated mission is to improve access of Below

Poverty Line (BPL) families to quality medical care for treatment of diseases involving hospitalization. Under Aarogyasri, the state government pays a premium of 210 rupees for those households that hold ration cards. This enables cashless hospitalization of people included on those ration cards in health facilities (public or private) that have been empanelled by the government insurance scheme. Aarogyasri is also one of the few publicly funded insurance schemes in India to focus on tertiary care.

Aarogyasri Implementation System

The innovative scheme makes effective use of information technology. The ration cards provided to those who qualify for them are biometric, using fingerprints and ID scans to minimize abuse of the system through issuance of multiple ration cards. To enable utilization of services by those sections of people who may find the procedural aspects of availing the insurance a barrier, assistants called "Aarogyashris" are present at empanelled hospitals to facilitate the treatments.

The e-governance solution used to administer the system includes a standardized empanelment process, an accounting module to keep track of funds spent by the Aarogyasri trust, audit trail based workflows to make stakeholders more accountable, exception based management system for workflow approvers to detect possible misuse, and ability to capture and view evidence at every stage of process flows thereby ensuring better monitoring. Medical and public audit mechanisms are in place, although their effectiveness is unclear at this stage. The program website is a repository of shared information that includes statistics of treatments provided under the insurance scheme which are posted online on a daily and cumulative basis with workflow diagrams and feedback systems. These statistics also reinforce the view that private healthcare facilities are the preferred options for care seekers, with 90% of outpatients and 75% of inpatients who availed the scheme being treated at private facilities.

Benefit to the Poor versus Non-Poor

In spite of the extensive use of IT to attempt and reduce abuse, Aarogyasri provides insurance coverage to approximately 85% of the population of Andhra Pradesh or roughly 71 million people (Planning Commission 2011). When we consider that the proportion of poor people in Andhra Pradesh in 2010 was only around 20%, or approximately 17 million people, it is clear that the scheme has expanded well beyond its stated objective to serve those below the poverty line.

We look at the district wise distribution of claims by ranking the 23 districts of Andhra Pradesh by the proportion of Andhra Pradesh poor that they contain. Warangal was the district with the smallest proportion of poor in Andhra Pradesh (2.1%) and Kurnool was the one with the highest proportion (8.8%). If the poor were benefiting the most from the scheme, one would expect that the amount claimed per poor person under Aarogyasri would remain the same as we go from districts that have a smaller proportion of Andhra's poor to districts where the proportion is higher. However, we find that the poorest districts are not those that are benefiting the most. In fact, exactly the opposite phenomenon is seen, with the amount claimed per poor person in districts that have a higher proportion of poor typically being much lower than in districts with a smaller proportion of Andhra's poor (see figure 6.4).

In terms of treatment, 3.7 million people had received outpatient treatment, and 1.6 million had received treatment that required hospitalization. Of these, 1.4 million were surgeries. The total amounts preauthorized for procedures over the five years the scheme has been in operation (April 2007–April 2012) came to 38 billion rupees. The lion's share of this amount, 30 billion rupees, was pre-authorized for private hospitals, and 8 billion for public hospitals.

Impact

Early studies point toward Aarogyasri having made some difference to the out-of-pocket health expenditure incurred by people in Andhra Pradesh. Aarogyasri has resulted in a significant reduction in the inpatient expenditure incurred and has also increased the likelihood that fewer people incur outpatient expenditures. However, the impact of Aarogyasri on impoverishment and

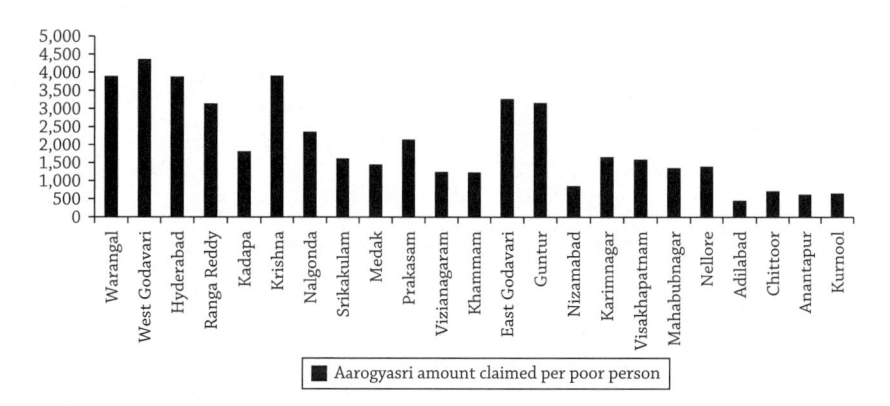

Figure 6.4: Amount Claimed under Aarogyasri per Poor Person in District. Districts arranged in order of the proportion of Andhra Pradesh's poor that they contain. Lowest proportion is Warangal on the left.
Source: Author's construction using data from Aarogyasri website.

catastrophic health expenditure is not clear (Fan et al. 2012). One possibility is that the Aarogyasri scheme may not be reducing the regular financial burden on families who benefit from it because the scheme is designed to insure the poor against disruptive medical emergencies. It has also been suggested that better referral mechanisms and strengthening the primary level health care system would still be required to improve the overall healthcare provision in the state (Mitchell, Mahal, and Bossert 2011). The efficacy of public health insurance schemes in India in general is also contested, with schemes in India having been found to actually increase catastrophic headcount and out-of-pocket expenditure on health and hospitalization (Selvaraj and Karan 2012).

EDUCATION

We next turn to education in Andhra Pradesh, beginning with the literacy rate and moving on to a discussion of school, student and teacher statistics, the rise of private schools, a possible way to improve learning outcomes, and the potential impact of India's recently passed Right to Education (RTE) Act, 2009 on Andhra Pradesh's education sector.

Literacy

The literacy rate in Andhra Pradesh has shown great improvement over the past 4 decades, but it has consistently stayed below the all-India average. As shown in table 6.1, the overall literacy rate has increased from 21% in 1961 to 68% according to the latest numbers released in the 2011 census, but this is still behind the all-India average of 74%. In fact, the literacy rate

Table 6.1. LITERACY RATES(PERCENTAGE OF POPULATION THAT WAS LITERATE) IN ANDHRA PRADESH AND INDIA, 1961–2011,

Year	Andhra Pradesh			India		
	Person	Male	Female	Person	Male	Female
1961	21	30	12	28	40	15
1971	25	33	16	34	46	22
1981	30	39	20	44	56	30
1991	44	55	33	52	64	39
2001	61	71	51	65	76	54
2011	68	76	60	74	82	65

Source: Census data.

in Andhra Pradesh is among the bottom five states in the country. This, however, is a slight improvement from the bottom three position it occupied in the 2001 census. A positive aspect of literacy trends in the state is that there has been a sharper increase in the female literacy rate, which has reduced the gender gap. Interestingly, literacy levels are generally uniform across different regions of Telangana, Rayalseema, and Coastal Andhra Pradesh.

Access and Enrollment

In order to meaningfully implement the RTE and achieve universal access in school education, the state government has aimed to provide elementary school facilities within 1 kilometer of all habitations and to provide secondary education within 5 kilometers of all habitations. By 2010/11, the state had achieved 99% access at the elementary education level and 91.25% at the secondary level. Table 6.2 provides the total number of primary schools, upper primary schools, high schools, and higher secondary schools. From the table we can see that private unaided schools play a very significant role in Andhra Pradesh.

According to the Andhra Pradesh Socio-Economic Survey 2011/12, approximately 13.3 million children were enrolled in schools in 2010/11. Of these students, 53% were enrolled in primary schools, 19% in upper primary, 25% in secondary, and the balance 3% in pre-primary and higher secondary.

Total enrollment in primary schools has been falling (see figure 6.5), but this is consistent with a decline in population in the relevant age group and hence not a cause for concern. The gender gap also seems to be narrowing in Andhra Pradesh. The number of girls enrolled is nearly 50%

Table 6.2. NUMBER OF SCHOOLS IN ANDHRA PRADESH BY MANAGEMENT TYPE AND LEVEL OF EDUCATION, 2010/11

Management Type	Primary	Upper Primary	High Schools	Secondary Schools	Total
Central Government	21	2	41	49	113
State Government	5,043	383	1,814	93	733
Mandal/Zila Parishad	50,487	8,374	8,348	—	67,209
Municipal	1,637	158	312	—	2,107
Private Aided	2,110	420	830	—	3,360
Private Unaided	7,536	6,084	7,431	33	21,082
Total	66,834	15,421	18,776	173	101,204

Source: Socio-Economic Survey of Andhra Pradesh 2011/12.

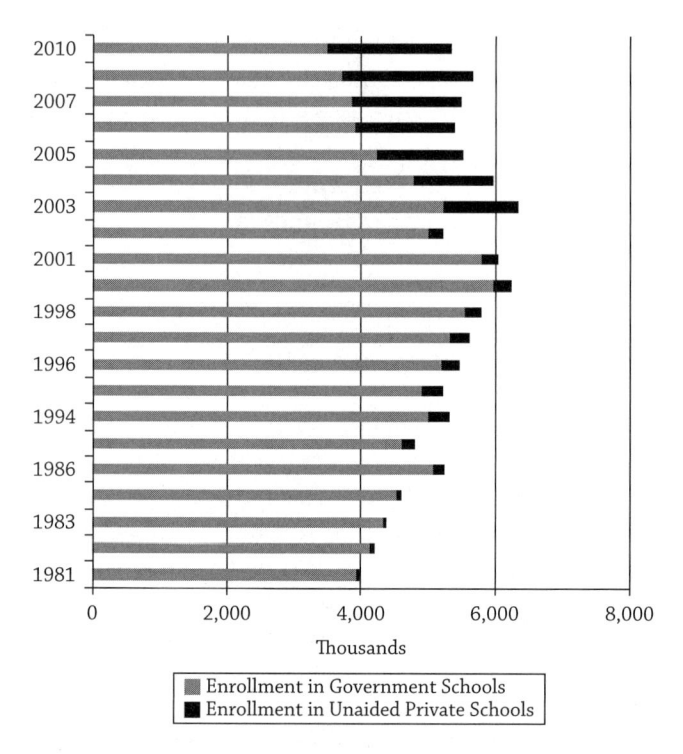

Figure 6.5: Enrollment in Primary Schools in Andhra Pradesh, 1981–2010
Source: Various Statistical Abstracts of Andhra Pradesh.

of total enrollments at all levels of schooling in 2008. This is an improvement from approximately 40% in 1981. The ratio of girls to boys in primary school has improved from 42% in 1981 to approximately 50% in 2010. The Gross Enrollment Ratio (GER) for primary schools reported by the Directorate of Education has been above 100% since 2001. However, using the enrollment data from the directorate and using population data for the appropriate age group from the 2001 census, the GER came out to be approximately 70%. This discrepancy repeats in the case of upper primary schools as well, where the reported enrollment ratio was 81%, yet calculations using census data indicate that the enrollment ratio is closer to 50%.

The ratio of girls to boys enrolled in upper primary school has improved from 37% in 1981 to approximately 48% in 2008 but is still lower than the ratio for primary education, suggesting that more girls drop out of school after primary education. Reported enrollment ratio in secondary school was 81% in 2008, up from a reported 48% in the year 2000. Enrollment ratio calculated for 2001 from the census data is approximately 49%.

Public versus Private Schooling

From the enrollment data on schools available with the Directorate of Economics and Statistics, we observe an interesting phenomenon—the share of private unaided schools in the total enrollment of primary school children has been rising sharply post-liberalization in 1991 with children enrolled in private unaided primary schools reaching 34% of all school-going children in 2010. The share of private unaided schools in the total enrollment of upper primary schoolchildren has also risen over time, increasing faster after liberalization in the 1990s with the proportion reaching 37% in 2008. This pattern is seen again at the high school level, with the share of private unaided schools in the total enrollment of high school students at 33% in 2008.

These figures are consistent with the documentation of an increase in private school enrollment by researchers such as Kingdon (2007) and independent assessments such as PROBE. However, while Kingdon has noted that official sources tend to underestimate the enrollment in private institutions, National Sample Survey data on education for Andhra Pradesh from 2007/08 report a similar proportion of students in private unaided schools as the official data.

The rise in private education in India and in Andhra Pradesh can be explained by a number of different factors, but primary among them is the higher effectiveness of private schools. Numerous studies across India have found that private schools outperform government schools even after controlling for student intake (Bashir 1994; Govinda and Varghese 1993; Kingdon 1994, 1996; Tooley and Dixon 2003). While these studies cannot control for all the unobservable student and family characteristics that lead to selection of private schools, they do establish that learning outcomes at private schools are better than those in public schools. This is not all that surprising a finding for those who are familiar with the government education system in India. Poor infrastructure, insufficient teachers and high teacher absenteeism are endemic. Accountability and incentives for teachers are also completely absent or minimal, due to increasing unionization and involvement of teachers in the political process. All these factors have led to a very low quality, both actual and perceived, of education in the public sector (Dreze and Sen 2002; Kingdon and Muzammil 2001). Not only do government schools and teachers perform poorly, they do so for much higher salaries and with much greater job security than the teachers in private sector (Kingdon 2007). Andhra Pradesh fits this pattern well. The structure of the education sector thus suggests high returns to exploring a school choice program that can work in a way and through a platform similar to the Aarogyasri health insurance scheme.

A key human capital requirement for educational system is the availability of the teachers. In 2010/11 altogether there were 476,555 teachers

Table 6.3. NUMBER OF TEACHERS IN ANDHRA PRADESH BY MANAGEMENT TYPE AND LEVEL OF EDUCATION, 2010/11

Management Type	Primary	Upper Primary	High Schools	Higher Secondary Schools
Central Government	164	17	898	1,670
State Government	9,006	1,552	19,310	1,192
Mandal/Zila Parishad	96,977	37,632	99,231	—
Municipal	3,680	600	4,122	—
Private Aided	6,834	2,532	7,809	—
Private Unaided	57,408	50,670	73,809	1,442
Total	174,069	93,003	205,179	4,304

Source: School Education Department.

in Andhra Pradesh. In table 6.3, we provide the breakup of the number of teachers across management type and by the level of education of schools.

It is interesting to note that after the mandal/zila parishad schools the highest number of teachers are employed by the private unaided schools. Once again this highlights the fundamental role of the private sector in the educational sector.

A Novel Experiment: Teacher Performance Pay in Andhra Pradesh

A key issue in the educational policy is the relative effectiveness of input-based or incentive-based policies for improving the quality of education. Muralidharan and Sundararaman (2011) examine this question rigorously using randomized control in government schools in Andhra Pradesh. They study four interventions: two interventions were based on providing school with additional inputs (extra contract teachers and a cash block grant) and the other two were based on providing incentives to teachers for better performance (group and individual bonus programs for teachers based on student performance). The authors find evidence that performance-based bonuses to teachers led to significant improvements in students' test scores with no evidence of any adverse impacts of the program. Second, the additional input provision also had a positive impact on the students' test scores, but the teacher incentive program was three times more effective. In a nutshell, if the teachers are even modestly incentivized, it can have very large impacts on the students' learning outcomes. Even though this experiment was in the context of government-run rural primary schools, it is important to mention that it basically shows that incentives matter. This finding also supports the idea of privatization or introduction of a school choice program. Based on these results it is easier to understand why private schools, which are better placed to incentivize teachers, promise superior educational outcomes than public schools. We believe that private schools, as the most cost effective and yet high performing intervention, need to be encouraged. This could be done perhaps, as mentioned earlier, through a voucher-based school choice program that allows the poorer sections to access private education. However, this does not imply that government has no role to play in the supply of education. As a matter of fact, the government should focus its energy in those areas where the private sector is unlikely to enter.

Right to Education Act

The Indian parliament passed the Right of Children to Free and Compulsory Education Act, 2009. Notwithstanding the inherent contradictions in "Right" and "Compulsory" being used in the same sentence, there is no doubt that this act has noble intentions. Education plays a very important role in expanding individual capabilities and therefore affects individual freedom. In the case of children, it can be argued that the government needs to adopt a paternalistic attitude to ensure that their individual freedom is expanded. This is particularly true for children who unfortunately, due to no fault of theirs, are born in socially and economically backward families. These children deserve an equal opportunity for education, which enables them to participate productively in society and take advantage of the opportunities, and the act aims to provide this compensatory justice.

However, it is not the intention of the act that we question here but the manner in which it is implemented. It places the bulk of the responsibility on the state government to expand access to schools. As we have noted earlier, governments in India and Andhra Pradesh have proven themselves to be poor providers of education, and those parents that can afford it prefer private education. In the face of such a track record, an alternative system of scholarships and/or cash transfers to those who cannot afford private schools would have been a better option. To compound this misstep, the RTE, in general and also as implemented by the Andhra Pradesh government, lays particular emphasis on inputs like the teacher–student ratio. As we saw earlier, such interventions have been definitively shown to provide, at best, a modest benefit. The act also places no emphasis at all on student outcomes like learning. In fact, students explicitly cannot be held back to repeat a class and cannot face a state-level examination until they reach secondary school. In effect, the government system is accountable only for building schools and paying teachers, not actually teaching students—exactly the issues that have led government schools to perform so abysmally in the past.

The act also requires private unaided schools to admit at least 25% of the students in class 1 from weaker and disadvantaged groups in the neighborhood and provide free and compulsory education till completion. In the context of Andhra Pradesh, private unaided schools are very important and substantial players in the provision of education. These schools are not beneficiaries of any kind of aid or grants from the government to meet their expenses. In light of this we strongly believe that such a provision in the act in principle violates the freedom of such schools in terms of whom they admit.

It might seem perfectly fine for the government to sacrifice individuals or individual organizations for the larger interest of the society. However, the state doing so to deflect its own responsibilities onto, and at the cost of, these individual organizations is in sharp contradiction to the fundamental role of the government in a representative democracy. Our belief is that the role of the government in a representative democracy is to protect individual freedom and if this freedom has to be limited then it must be for the sake of more freedom—"freedom can only be sacrificed for the sake of more freedom."

Thus, from a philosophical point of view too, it becomes important that the alternative government policy could have been to incentivize the private unaided schools to admit children from weaker and the disadvantaged group of the society rather than forcefully impose a quota on them. Such a provision in the law would not only have enhanced the opportunity for the children from the weaker and the disadvantaged section, but at the same time it would have preserved the freedom of the private unaided schools.

CONCLUDING REMARKS

Andhra Pradesh's performance in the spheres of both health and education has been, at best, average especially when we consider it alongside the poverty reduction that has taken place in the state. Infant mortality rates have fallen, life expectancy, literacy rates and enrollment rates have risen, but only at about average or below average India-wide rates of progress. In both healthcare and education, studies have shown that government delivery of services has been consistently substandard and people are turning *en masse* to the private sector to provide these services by paying from their own pocket.

Studies have also shown, in education especially, that the private sector performs better, is more responsive to the needs of the users of the service, and is more cost-effective. Unfortunately, the private sector is not affordable for everybody, although we believe that the government should look to provide school vouchers or conditional cash transfers to the poor and enable them to switch to private schools if they prefer.

Turning to health, in the case of in-patient healthcare, the Andhra Pradesh government decided to tackle this program through the innovative step of paying for health insurance for those who cannot afford to take the private option. While early studies indicate some impact on out-of-pocket expenditure, the results are still ambiguous on measures such as catastrophic spending for in-patient care. Targeting of the scheme to the poor is also proving to be a chimera. However, the scheme at least reflects a willingness to think outside the box for providing healthcare solutions to those who cannot pay out of their own pocket for more advanced care.

On the other hand, experience in the areas of primary healthcare and education does not demonstrate any evidence of such willingness to innovate. On the contrary, in its implementation of the RTE Act, the state government, for all its good intentions, has placed an extra burden on private schools, boosted input costs for government schools, and relaxed accountability for learning outcomes. Such steps will only make it more difficult for the people of Andhra Pradesh to receive the social services that they need.

CHAPTER 7
Conclusions

The central lesson from the recent experience of Andhra Pradesh is that political leadership is of fundamental importance in bringing about change in a representative democracy. In the early 1990s, Uttar Pradesh and Andhra Pradesh had very similar economic backgrounds. Both these states were suffering from low per capita income and a high incidence of poverty. But their paths diverged subsequently. By 2011, Andhra Pradesh had surged ahead of Uttar Pradesh in terms of economic growth and a dramatic decline in poverty.

We argue in this study that the success of Andhra Pradesh is to be traced to a vision and its effective execution by the state's two key political leaders: Chief Ministers Chandrababu Naidu and his successor Y. S. Rajshekhar Reddy popularly known as YSR. In 1995 Naidu engineered an internal party coup against the then Chief Minister N. T. Rama Rao and became the Chief Minister of the state. He brought with him a paradigm shift in the approach to economic development in the state. He believed that the government should facilitate rather than undertake all aspects of development. He promoted an environment in which private enterprise could flourish. His approach was continued by YSR with the twist of greater attention paid to agriculture.

It is important to remember that when Naidu came to power, Andhra Pradesh was largely an agrarian economy. By that time, promises of subsidies and doles of various kinds as means to gaining and maintaining power had been tried and tested. He was quick to realize that these short-term populist measures that relied on state subsidies such as rice sold at 2 rupees per kg would not deliver economic and social development. Instead, his vision was to promote investment and economic growth in the state that would lead to long-term socioeconomic development.

To experiment with a new vision for the government was a very courageous and bold step. After all, there was no guarantee that it would succeed or its benefits would reach the larger population. Nevertheless, he was willing to take the chance. Perhaps an important implication is that transformation of a state requires experimentation and learning through trial and error.

In the early 1990s, even though Andhra Pradesh was an agrarian economy, the government was creative and entrepreneurial enough to encourage investment in new sectors such as Information Technology (IT), biotechnology, healthcare, and the outsourcing services. This was nothing short of a bold "experiment." And a clear impact of this was a phenomenal increase in IT exports of the state from 2 million rupees in 1992 to 325 billion rupees in 2009. The rise of the IT sector also led to further experimentation—the conceptualization and implementation of "smart governance," which introduced transparency and in turn played an important role in the efficient implementation of a national scheme like Mahatma Gandhi National Rural Employment Guarantee Scheme (MNREGS).

In addition, the government initiated reforms. For example, in the agricultural sector we witness a steady shift in the production basket away from food grain and traditional commercial crops to high-value commodities including horticulture (fruits, vegetables, and flowers); animal products including milk, eggs, and meat; and fish and prawns. There were demand factors like rising income and urbanization that played a role in this shift but equally important were reforms that influenced the supply. Andhra Pradesh was among the early states to initiate the reform of agricultural marketing. As early as 1999, Andhra Pradesh had introduced the Rythu Bazars, or farmer markets, where farmers could sell their produce directly to consumers without the involvement of the middlemen. The main objective of these markets was to allow farmers to earn remunerative prices and consumers to have access to fresh fruits and vegetables. Andhra Pradesh was also one of the early states to abolish the state monopoly on marketing agricultural produce through the adoption of the State Agricultural Produce and Marketing (Development and Regulation) Act, 2003. This shift in the production basket resulted in a significant increase in the growth rate of the agricultural and the allied activities. Moreover, the growth rates were far more stable, which is indicated by the dramatic decline in the coefficient of variation.

In addition to the agricultural sector, the government also initiated reforms in the industrial sector. For example, in 2001, the state government announced a new industrial policy. A key component of this policy was the "Andhra Pradesh Industrial Single Window Clearance Act" mandating a single window registration and clearance for projects. This watershed legislation provided for speedy processing and issue of various approvals, clearances, and permissions for setting up of an industrial undertaking. It prescribed statutory time limits on various departments and introduced the concept of deemed approvals. As a result, the number of registered manufacturing units in Andhra Pradesh has shown a sharp increase in the period post-2002 when the single-window facility was introduced. Overall industrial sector growth has been over 10%. Even in terms of employment, as we have seen earlier, most of the change in the workforce composition toward a higher share of the industrial sector has taken place in the period between 1999/2000 and 2009/10. This is in contrast to the inconsistent response of industry to the industrial policies introduced in the 1990s suggesting that reduction of administrative overhead and red tape has greater impact than "sops" for industry.

Overall, the "experimentation" and the "reform" process of the government had a significant impact on the growth rate and the stability of the economy. The average growth rate more than doubled from 3.3% between 1984 and 1994 to 7.7% between 2004 and 2012. What was also impressive was the dramatic decline in the coefficient of variation of the growth rate, indicating greater stability.

It is also important to recognize the role of the common people in the representative democracy. Without their broad approval, the "experimentation" and the "reform" process of the government would not have been possible. In 1999, the common people of the state did relate to Chandrababu Naidu's vision for the state and he was once again elected as the Chief Minister.

With prosperity came higher expectations. Even though the state had started to perform much better, there was a growing perception, particularly in the rural areas, that much of the development and growth had happened only in urban areas. On the eve of the election in 2004, this was the perception not only at the state level but also the national level. Furthermore, for two years prior to the election, there was a decline in the agricultural sector due to drought, which further aggravated the adverse perception that the focus of growth and development had only been restricted to the urban areas. Overwhelmingly the mood in the state and also the rest of the country was that growth had been "exclusive." YSR, the leader of the opposition Congress Party, exploited this sentiment and promised to bring prosperity to the rural areas and also to those people who had not benefited from the growth process in the urban areas. He decisively defeated Naidu in the assembly election in 2004.

There were apprehensions in the business community that YSR would undo the growth-oriented policies of the past, which would be detrimental for the future investment in the state. But once in power, YSR did not undo any policies of the past; on the contrary, he was savvy enough to reinforce the growth momentum that the state had acquired, pushing the policy regime further in the growth-friendly direction. By using the enhanced revenues that growth was making possible to alleviate poverty and promote agricultural growth, he additionally secured political support for growth-friendly policies for industry and services.

One of the single biggest achievements of Andhra Pradesh has been the sharp reduction in both rural and urban poverty. Nor have benefits of overall growth in the economy been restricted to the exclusive few, as is often alleged. Poverty has sharply fallen among the socially disadvantaged groups — the Scheduled Castes and the Scheduled Tribes—and also among different religious groups. As compared to India as a whole, rural and urban poverty in Andhra Pradesh declined much more rapidly. Rural poverty declined by a gigantic 37 percentage points between 1993/94 and 2011/12. It fell from 48% in 1993/94 to 11% in 2011/12. Andhra Pradesh is now within striking distance of entirely eliminating abject poverty from rural areas, as it had set out to do in its vision document in 1999. The trend in urban poverty is nearly identical. It fell by 29 percentage points from 35.1% in 1993/94 to 5.8% in 2011/12. A distinguishing feature of Andhra Pradesh has been a significantly larger reduction in poverty per percentage point growth.

Furthermore, we find that during the period from 2004/05 to 2010/11, when growth was substantially higher, the decline in both rural and urban poverty was also significantly higher than the previous periods. Also the decline in the poverty rates of socially disadvantaged groups, the Scheduled Castes and Scheduled Tribes that had higher initial levels of poverty has been sharper than the average across all groups. At least in terms of poverty, there seems to be a narrowing of the gap between the socially disadvantaged and religious minority groups, on the one hand, and the general category, on the other. In our opinion this is powerful evidence that growth has amply fulfilled its promise. This result was not an accident, but a deliberate outcome of the growth-friendly "experimentation" and the "reform" process that were initiated by Naidu who was the Chief Minister of the state from 1995 to 2004 and continued by YSR, who was the Chief Minister of the state from 2004 to 2009.

Andhra Pradesh cannot claim such spectacular success in all areas, however. In terms of employment, Andhra Pradesh still remains a heavily agrarian economy, with just over half of its workforce still engaged in agricultural activities in 2009/10, although the pace with which people are moving out of agriculture has been increasing. The majority of Andhra Pradesh's workforce is still in the informal sector, and as such does not benefit from India's harsh labor laws. We believe it is worthwhile to try and reform these laws in an attempt to encourage formal sector enterprises. The attempt should be to at least provide a few important protections to many workers, instead of many protections to very few.

Health and education are two other areas in which Andhra Pradesh's performance has been average at best. Important indicators like infant mortality rate and life expectancy are close to the Indian averages, and literacy rates are actually below the all- India levels. Both areas have suffered on account of persistently sub-par service delivery from government hospitals and schools. In recognition of this lacuna, as incomes have risen, patients and parents have increasingly turned to the private sector for service delivery. For those who cannot afford the out-of-pocket expenditure that this entails, the in-patient segment for healthcare saw the introduction of an innovative healthcare insurance program called Aarogyasri, launched during YSR's period.

While the jury is still out on the effectiveness of the program, and its expansion to a very large proportion of the population instead of effectively targeting the poor is questionable, the attempt to experiment with a new form of service delivery to the poor is a highly positive development. A similarly innovative education voucher or conditional cash transfer system to enable the poor to provide private schooling for their children—an alternative that research has shown to be unambiguously better than the public system— would have been heartening. Unfortunately, in education the latest move by the government— the Right to Education Act, 2009—has no such positives. It places the onus for service delivery on government, focuses on inputs, dilutes accountability for outcomes, and places an additional burden on what is otherwise a burgeoning private sector. While the RTE is an act of the Government of India, the Andhra Pradesh government would have been well within its rights to modify it for implementation, and we believe that it should have done so.

In a nutshell, Andhra Pradesh was fortunate to have two Chief Ministers who saw that economic growth was the engine that could usher in greater prosperity for its citizens. Naidu set Andhra Pradesh on the path to greater economic activity, and YSR sustained, and, in some respects, even accelerated the pro-growth economic agenda. At the same time, he took the benefits of growth to socially and economically backward sections of the society, which Naidu had not been able to do as effectively. We believe that the political vision of "experimentation" and "reforms" and continuation of that vision across political platforms for a sustained period of time from 1994 to 2009 has resulted in widespread economic prosperity and reduction in poverty. To put this in perspective,

- In 1993/94, among the 15 large states in India, Andhra Pradesh was ranked seventh and eleventh in terms of average monthly per capita consumption expenditure in rural and urban areas, respectively. By 2009, Andhra Pradesh was ranked fourth in rural and urban areas.
- From 1993/94 to 2009/10: Andhra Pradesh was among the top four states that have achieved the highest decline in rural and urban poverty. Andhra Pradesh is among the top three states that have experienced the highest decline in poverty among the socially disadvantaged groups, the Scheduled Castes and the Scheduled Tribes.
- When one compares Andhra Pradesh to Uttar Pradesh in 1993 and 2009— as mentioned earlier the two states were very similar in various economic dimensions in 1993, but by 2009 Andhra Pradesh was well ahead in terms of per capita income, monthly per capita consumption, and also in its fight against poverty.

To summarize the important lessons we believe can be taken away from the experience of Andhra Pradesh:

(1) Policy "experimentation" and "reforms" matter. Development of the IT sector happened because the political leadership in the state was willing to take chances. More often than not, policymakers, just like entrepreneurs, have to make decisions in an uncertain environment where success is not guaranteed. However, this did not dissuade the political leadership under Naidu from experimenting and learning using the trial and error process. In the words of Alvin Toffler, "It is better to err on the side of daring than the side of caution."

(2) Creating an enabling regulatory environment is extremely important. There was a clear shift in the political mindset of the government toward the promotion of business. Accordingly, businessmen were given due respect as important economic agents that could bring a socioeconomic revolution in the state. In recognition of this, the state leadership took deliberate steps to create an enabling regulatory environment by cutting bureaucratic red tape and hence lowering entry barriers. The approach of the government is aptly summed up in Friedrich Hayek's words, "Government plays a very important role in creation of institutions such that unknown individuals who are most suited to that particular task are attracted to it. It is not important to 'find' the individual but rather the creation of institutional arrangements."

(3) Growth and socioeconomic developments are interrelated. The experience of Andhra Pradesh clearly indicates that growth and socioeconomic developments are interrelated. The government policy should not aim at any singular objective, that is, it should not focus exclusively on policies that promote growth or redistribution. Both these objectives have to be pursued simultaneously. Both Naidu and YSR recognized the virtues of growth and used it to great effect in their fight against poverty and for the socioeconomic development of the state in a relatively short period of time. They proactively pursued policies that promoted investment and growth but also paid attention to socioeconomic development. It can be argued that it is not growth per se that is "inclusive" or "exclusive" but instead the government policies that should be inclusive. Perhaps government policies in a representative democracy whether they aim at growth or poverty reduction or redistribution should be judged from the perspective of its impact on individual freedom. If a policy expands individual freedom, then it should be encouraged; but if a policy limits individual freedom, then it should happen only for the sake of more freedom—"freedom can only be sacrificed for the sake of more freedom."

Last but not least, now that the political uncertainty around the bifurcation of Andhra Pradesh has been resolved, it provides a golden political opportunity for the two new Chief Ministers to introduce bold, major reforms that are otherwise infeasible in a large state. One of these men—Chandrababu Naidu—features prominently in this volume. The other, Telangana state's first Chief Minister K. Chandrashekar Rao, has so far focused on achieving statehood for Telangana. However, it is interesting to note that the first major demand from both the Chief Ministers is a loan waiver for farmers. This might result in short-term political brownie points, but in the long run this could be a very slippery slope. This is also in sharp contrast to Naidu's former vision when he became the Chief Minister for the first time of erstwhile Andhra Pradesh. During that time, he emphasized the promotion of investment and growth as a long-term strategy for human development. Even though he did not reap the political benefits of the policies he initiated, there is no doubt that his vision and policy reforms created an enabling economic environment, which resulted in one of the most dramatic declines in poverty seen in the country, particularly among the socially disadvantaged groups and the minority. It took tremendous political courage for Naidu in the past to steer the state away from the culture of dependency to the culture of promoting individual enterprise. In our opinion the two Chief Ministers will have to exhibit that same courage to propel the two new states further along the path of development.

APPENDIX 1
Implications of Bifurcation and Region-Wise Analysis of Andhra Pradesh

While the movement asking for a separate state of Telangana is as old as Andhra Pradesh itself, in recent years there has been intense political activity around the issue and on June 2, 2014, Telangana, the twenty-ninth state of the Indian capital was created. The fundamental imperative for the demand of a separate state, as argued by C. H. Hanumantha Rao (*The Hindu*, January 8, 2007), was the perception among the people of Telangana that in an integrated state they did not have equal access to water, jobs, business, career opportunities, and, more important, political process. This sense of injustice was the key driving force for the demand for the separate state of Telangana. Now that the demand has been fulfilled, the key challenge for the new state is to create an enabling political, social, and economic environment, which promotes investment, growth, and human development. It is useful in this context to look at the experience of the new states that were formed in the year 2000. In each case the component parts have outperformed the original state's trend growth. From 2002 to 2010, grwoth rates of Chhattisgarh, Jharkhand and Uttarakhand higher than those of their mother states, Madhya Pradesh, Bihar and Uttar Pradesh respectively. Uttarakhand's performance is partly due to the industrial sector, which grew rapidly during the period. This can be attributed to the special category status (and consequent tax concessions) it enjoyed as a hilly state. In recent years however, post 2006, Jharkhand and Chhattisgarh have both seen slower growth than their respective mother states. Division of states is thus reason for cautious optimism but not a guarantee of higher economic growth and better human development. The outcome will depend on the initiatives the states undertake to create an enabling social and economic environment. In our opinion the bifurcation provides a golden political opportunity to introduce bold, major reforms that are otherwise politically infeasible in a large state. For example, Telangana could encourage labor reforms in the state, which in turn would promote labor-intensive manufacturing. This would provide an opportunity for the agricultural workers to migrate to semi-skilled manufacturing. Just as Chandrababu Naidu in his early years as Chief Minister in the 1990s had envisioned Andhra Pradesh as a major IT hub, we would need a similar vision for the state of Telangana and the new Andhra Pradesh with respect to labor-intensive manufacturing. We hope that the new Chief Ministers would lay the foundation for their states to become a major hub for labor-intensive manufacturing sector, which could then be a model for other states to follow.

Another important issue is the "special category status" for five years for the new Andhra Pradesh. The former Prime Minister Manmohan Singh made the commitment for this in February 2014. However, it is important to mention that this commitment was made with the objective of the political gains in the future elections, in particular, to make up for lost ground in the Coastal Andhra Pradesh and Rayalseema regions where people were opposed to the bifurcation of the state. Irrespective of the intention, the key advantage of the special category status to the new state would be that it would receive 90% of the central assistance in the form of grants and 10% in the form of loans, whereas, for other non-special category status states 30% of central assistance is in the form of grant and the rest 70% is the form loans. In addition the special category status states also receive a favorable treatment from the Finance Commission with respect to the devolution of the central tax revenues. If the special category status is granted to the new Andhra Pradesh, it will favorably help the financial position of the state. This will help the state to grant tax concessions to the industrial sector to promote investment and growth, which is akin to what Uttarakhand had done. But the key obstacle to this is that the new state does not meet the criteria set by the National Development Council,[1] such as low resource base, hilly and difficult terrain, low population density, sizeable share of tribal population, and strategic (hostile) location. In the event it happens, it will be a major boost to the financial position of the state and help it in developing the requisite infrastructure to promote investment, growth, and human development.

Another important issue to mention is the subtle hostility between the people of Telangana origin and the people of the Seemandhra region. Anecdotal evidence suggests that there is an attempt by the government of Telangana to promote the business interests of local Telangana people at the expense of the outsiders, in particular, people from the coastal Andhra region. In our opinion this could be detrimental for the state; on

---

1. The National Development Council is the country's key planning body headed by the Prime Minister and made up of Cabinet Ministers, the Chief Ministers, representatives of the Union Territories, and members of the commissions.

the contrary, the objective should be to promote investment, growth, and efficient utilization of resources, which lead to local job creation irrespective of the origin of the businessmen. If implicit subsidies are granted to local businessmen, then it might lead to inefficient allocation of resources and rent-seeking opportunities. Shortsightedness on the part of the new government might lead to long-term distortions, which are irreversible and very expensive.

To provide some data and analysis on the performance of Andhra Pradesh and the new state of Telangana, in this appendix we compare and contrast the economic performance of the different regions of erstwhile Andhra Pradesh: (1) Rayalseema, (2) Telangana, and (3) Coastal Andhra Pradesh. The new state of Telangana comprises the 10 districts of what was the Telangana region of Andhra Pradesh, and Coastal Andhra Pradesh with 9 districts, and Rayalseema with 4 districts comprise the new state of Andhra Pradesh.

REGION-WISE ANALYSIS OF ECONOMIC GROWTH

In this section, we examine the GDP of the three regions by looking at data taken from the "District Domestic Products" publication of the Department of Economics and Statistics of Andhra Pradesh. The data in this series is available only for the time period 1992/93 to 2007/08. We divide these years into two periods 1992/93 to 1999/2000 and 2000/01 to 2007/08.

1992/93 to 1999/2000

In this period, the average annual growth rate in Rayalseema was much lower compared to Telangana and Coastal Andhra Pradesh and the volatility of the growth rate was very high. Rayalseema grew at an average annual rate of 2.3% while Telangana and Coastal Andhra Pradesh grew much faster at 7.29% and 5.17%, respectively. The volatility of growth rate in Rayalseema was also much higher at 11.37 when compared with Telangana and Coastal Andhra Pradesh where it was 4.95 and 4.78, respectively. The sectorwise growth rate and volatility are provided in table A1.1 and discussed in detail later in this section.

From figure A1.1, it is obvious that in terms of economic growth and performance, Telangana was the fastest growing region during this period, while Rayalseema lagged behind. There were four years (1994, 1996, 1997, 1999) when the growth rate in Rayalseema was negative. In Telangana, while the growth rate did fluctuate from year to year, there was never an episode when it was negative. Similarly, in Coastal Andhra Pradesh, except for 1997, the growth rate in every year was positive.

Table A1.1. REGIONAL AVERAGE GROWTH RATES AND STANDARD DEVIATIONS OF DIFFERENT SECTORS, 1993–2000 AND 2000–2008

		Rayalseema		Telangana		Coastal	
		Average Growth	Volatility	Average Growth	Volatility	Average Growth	Volatility
Agriculture	1993–2000	0.2	29.2	7.2	23.0	2.8	7.0
	2000–2008	10.8	24.5	8.1	18.2	5.1	5.7
Industry	1993–2000	4.9	7.6	6.6	5.2	7.9	9.9
	2000–2008	13.3	18.0	8.1	5.3	10.1	5.6
Services	1993–2000	4.7	3.4	8.7	4.2	6.2	1.6
	2000–2008	8.8	4.0	9.1	3.6	7.8	2.2

Source: Calculated from Andhra Pradesh Department of Economics and Statistics data.

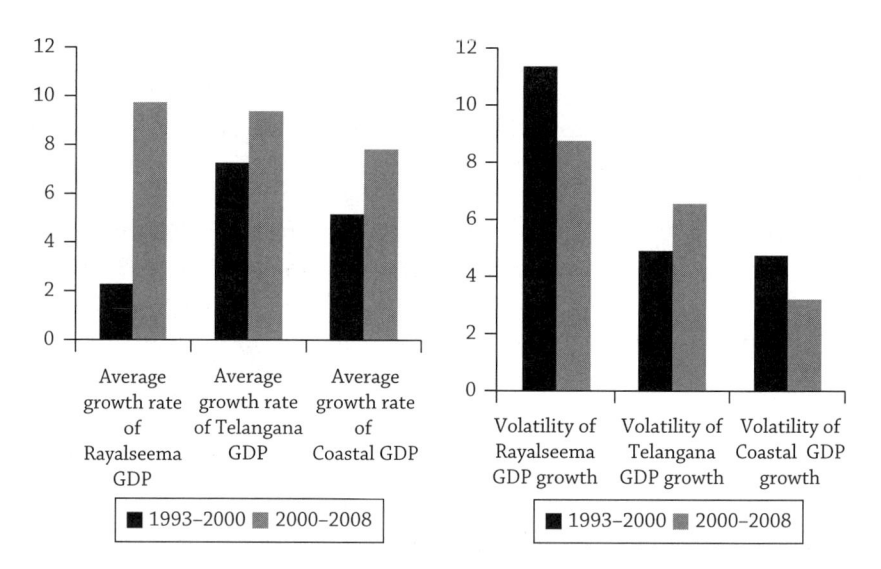

Figure A1.1: Growth Rate and Volatility of Growth of Different Regions in Andhra Pradesh, 1993–2000 and 2000–2008
Source: Authors' calculation based on data from Andhra Pradesh Department of Economics and Statistics.

In terms of the composition of the sectors we find that Rayalseema and Coastal Andhra Pradesh are very similar. For example, the average share of the agricultural sector in Rayalseema over this period is 35%, while it is 37% in Coastal Andhra Pradesh, and only 23% in Telangana. Similarly, the share of the industry sector in Rayalseema and Coastal Andhra Pradesh is 15% while it is 24% in Telangana and where the share of services sector in Rayalseema is 50%; it is 53% in Telangana. In contrast the share of agriculture sector in Coastal Andhra Pradesh is 49%, the share of the industry sector is 30%, and the share of the services sector is 47%.

During this period the average growth rate of agriculture in Rayalseema was merely 0.18% and the volatility was very high at 29.21. In contrast, Telangana's agriculture sector on average grew at 7.23% and the volatility was much lower at 22.98. In Coastal Andhra Pradesh, the average growth rate in agriculture sector was 2.84% but the volatility of the growth rate was much lower at 7.04 when compared to the other two regions. It is also important to mention that in three years (1994, 1997, 1999) there was a decline in the agriculture sector by more than 20% in Rayalseema while decline of such magnitude happened only once in Telangana (in 1997) and never in Coastal Andhra Pradesh.

In industry, the performance of Rayalseema is much better compared to that in agriculture; however, it still lags behind Telangana and Coastal Andhra Pradesh. More specifically, the average annual growth rate in Rayalseema was 4.88% while in Telangana it was 6.56% and in Coastal Andhra Pradesh it was 7.90%. When we look at volatility of the growth rate we find than Rayalseema and Telangana have lower volatility (7.61 and 5.15, respectively) compared to Coastal Andhra Pradesh (9.87).

In services, the scenario is very similar to that in industry. In Rayalseema the average annual growth rate was much lower at 4.74% when compared to Telangana and Coastal Andhra Pradesh where the growth rate was 8.74% and 6.16%, respectively. However, in terms of volatility of growth rate, it is much higher in Telangana (4.22) when compared to Rayalseema (3.44) and Coastal Andhra Pradesh (1.63).

Period from 2000 to 2008

In sharp contrast to the previous period, the economic performance of Rayalseema improved very dramatically across all sectors during this second period. As a matter of fact, Rayalseema grew much faster in all sectors when compared with Telangana and Coastal Andhra Pradesh.

In agriculture, the average annual growth rate in Rayalseema was 10.75% whereas in Telangana and Coastal Andhra Pradesh it was 6.56% and 5.13%, respectively. As compared to the previous period, volatility of growth rate came down in Rayalseema (24.50), though it remained much higher than those in Telangana (18.16) and Coastal Andhra Pradesh (5.72).

In the industry sector, the average annual growth rate in Rayalseema was 13.33%, while it was 8.11% in Telangana and 10.11% in Coastal Andhra Pradesh. However, in terms of volatility, Rayalseema was much higher at 17.95 relative to Telangana (5.30) and Coastal Andhra Pradesh (5.58). For two successive years, 2005 and 2006, industry in Rayalseema grew at a very impressive rate of 20.68% and 54.38%, respectively.

In the services sector, the economic performance of Rayalseema was comparable to Telangana and Coastal Andhra Pradesh. The average annual growth rate was 8.75% in Rayalseema, 9.05% in Telangana, and 7.80% in Coastal Andhra Pradesh. Even in terms of volatility, the performance is approximately comparable at 4.02 in Rayalseema, 3.60 in Telangana, and 2.23 in Coastal Andhra Pradesh.

In summary, we note that in the 2000s, in sharp contrast to the earlier period, the performance of Rayalseema improved very significantly relative to Telangana and the Coastal Andhra Pradesh. Moreover, across all regions and sectors, the economic performance in terms of average annual growth was much higher in the 2000s than during 1993 to 2000.

POVERTY TRENDS ACROSS REGIONS IN ANDHRA PRADESH

In this section, we look at the rural and urban poverty trends from 1993/94 to 2009/10 in the three regions: Rayalseema, Telangana, and Coastal Andhra Pradesh. In 1993/94, rural poverty across the three regions was very similar: 46.6% in Rayalseema, 45.8% in Telangana, and 49.2% in Coastal Andhra Pradesh (figure A1.2). In 2009/10, rural poverty in Rayalseema fell to 31.1%, in Telangana to 27%, and in Coastal Andhra Pradesh to 15.1%. These trends clearly suggest that even though the level of rural poverty was similar across regions in the beginning of 1993/94, the decline in rural poverty was very different. Coastal Andhra Pradesh seems to have done much better than the other regions.

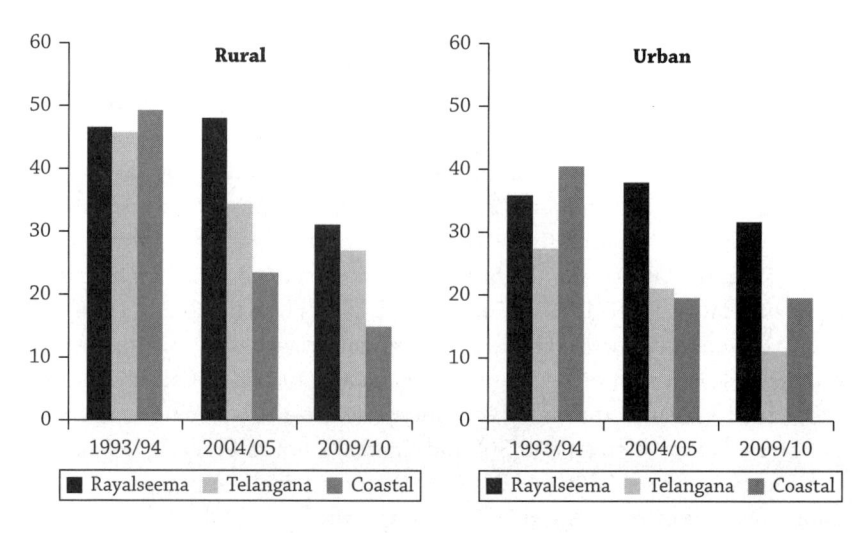

Figure A1.2: Rural and Urban Poverty in Various Regions of Andhra Pradesh, 1993/94 to 2009/10
Source: Calculated from NSSO unit level data using Tendulkar committee poverty lines.

In terms of urban poverty, in 1993/94, the data shows that it was the highest in Coastal Andhra Pradesh at 40.5%, followed by Rayalseema at 35.8%, and then Telangana at 27.5%. However, in 2009/10, urban poverty in Coastal Andhra Pradesh declined very sharply to 19.7%, whereas in Telangana it fell to 11.3% and in Rayalseema to 31.6%. Similar to rural poverty trends, the urban poverty trend showed a faster decline in the Telangana and the Coastal Andhra Pradesh regions when compared to Rayalseema.

PART I REFERENCES

Aghion, P., R. Burgess, S. J. Redding, and F. Zilibotti (2008). "The Unequal Effects of Liberalization: Evidence from Dismantling the License Raj in India." *American Economic Review* 98(4): 1397–1412.

Banerjee, A., and E. Duflo (2011). *Poor Economics: A Radical Rethinking of the Way to Fight Poverty*. New York: PublicAffairs.

Banerjee, A., E. Duflo, R. Glennerster, and C. Kinnan (2010). *The Miracle of Microfinance? Evidence from a Randomized Evaluation*. Cambridge, MA: J-PAL and MIT.

Besley, T., and R. Burgess (2004). "Can Regulation Hinder Economic Performance? Evidence from India." *Quarterly Journal of Economics* 119(1): 91–134.

Chakrabarti, R., and S. Ravi (2011). "At the Crossroads: Microfinance in India." *Money & Finance*, July 2011: 125–148.

CRISIL (2010). *Study on Analysis of Tariff Orders & Other Orders of State Electricity Regulatory Commissions*. http://www.forumofregulators.gov.in/Data/study/STUDY_ON_ANALYSIS_OF_TARIFF_ORDERS&OTHER_ORDERS_OF_STATE_ELECTRICITY_REGULATORY_COMMISSIONS.pdf.

Datt, G., and M. Ravallion (1999). "Why Have Some Indian States Performed Better than Others at Reducing Rural Poverty?" World Bank e-Library, http://elibrary.worldbank.org/doi/book/10.1596/1813-9450-1594.

———. (2002). "Is India's Economic Growth Leaving the Poor Behind?" *Journal of Economic Perspectives* 16(3): 89–108.

Deaton, A., and J. Dreze (2002). "Poverty and Inequality in India: A Re-Examination." *Economic & Political Weekly* 37(36): 3729–3748.

Deaton, A., and A. Tarozzi (2000). "Prices and Poverty in India." Princeton, NJ: Research Program in Development Studies. https://www.princeton.edu/rpds/papers/pdfs/deaton_tarozzi_prices_poverty.pdf.

Dev, M. S., and V. Mahajan (2003). "Employment and Unemployment." Hyderabad: Andhra Pradesh Development, Centre for Economic and Social Studies.

Dev, M. S., and C. H. Hanumantha Rao (2003). "Andhra Pradesh Development: Economic Reforms and Challenges Ahead." Hyderabad: Centre for Economic and Social Studies.

Drèze, J., and A. Sen (2002). *India: Development and Participation*. Oxford: Clarendon Press.

Dutta, P., R. Murgai, M. Ravallion, V. Walle, and P. Dominique (2012). "Does India's Employment Guarantee Scheme Guarantee Employment?" World Bank Policy Research Working Paper No. 6003. Washington, DC: World Bank.

Fan, V., A. Karan, and A. Mahal (2012). "State Health Insurance and Out-of-Pocket Health Expenditures in Andhra Pradesh, India." *International Journal of Health Care Finance and Economics* 12(3): 189–215.

Govinda, R., and N. V. Varghese (1993). *Quality of Primary Schooling in India: A Case Study of Madhya Pradesh, India*. Paris: UNESCO International Institute for Educational Planning.

Gupta, P., R. Hasan, and U. Kumar (2008). "What Constrains Indian Manufacturing?" Macroeconomics Working Papers 22162, East Asian Bureau of Economic Research.

Johnson, C., P. Deshingkar, and D. Start (2005). "Grounding the State: Devolution and Development in India's Panchayats." *Journal of Development Studies* 41(6): 937–970.

Kannan, K., and J. Breman (2013). *The Long Road to Social Security: Assessing the Implementation of National Social Security Initiatives for the Working Poor in India*. Delhi: Oxford University Press.

Kingdon, G. (2007). "The Progress of School Education in India." *Oxford Review of Economic Policy* 23(2): 168–195.

Kingdon, G., and M. Muzammil (2003). *The Political Economy of Education in India: Teacher Politics in Uttar Pradesh*. Delhi: Oxford University Press.

Kingdon, Geeta G. (1996). "Private Schooling in India: Size, Nature and Equity Effects." *Economic and Political Weekly* 31(51): 3306–3314.

Mitchell, A., A. Mahal, and T. Bossert (2011). "Healthcare Utilization in Rural Andhra Pradesh." *Economic and Political Weekly* 46(5): 15–19.

Mooij, J. (2002). "Welfare Policies and Politics: A Study of Three Government Interventions in Andhra Pradesh, India." Working Paper 181. London: Overseas Development Institutes.

Mukund, K. (ed.) (1989). *Andhra Pradesh Economy in Transition*. Hyderabad: Centre for Economic and Social Studies.

Panagariya, A., and V. More (2013). "Poverty by Social, Religious and Economic Groups in India and Its Largest States 1993–94 to 2011–12." Working Paper No. 2013-02, New York: School of International and Public Affairs, Columbia University.

Panagariya, A., and M. Mukim (2011). "Growth, Openness and the Socially Disadvantaged." Working Papers 1113. New York: School of International and Public Affairs, Columbia University.

Pitt, M., and S. Khandker (1998). "The Impact of Group-Based Credit on Poor Households in Bangladesh: Does the Gender of Participants Matter?" *Journal of Political Economy* 106(5): 958–996.

Planning Commission of India (2011). "A Critical Assessment of the Existing Health Insurance Models in India." Government of India. http://planningcommission.nic.in/reports/sereport/ser/ser_heal1305.pdf.

Rao, L. (1988). *Economic Growth of Andhra Pradesh*. Allahabad: Chugh Publications.

Rao, P., P. Joshi, S. Kumar, K. Ganguly (2008). "Agricultural Diversification in Andhra Pradesh, India: Patterns, Determinants and Implications." Published jointly with International Food Policy Research Institute, IFPRI, Report No. 2, Patancheru, Andhra Pradesh, India: International Crops Research Institute for the Semi_arid Crops (ICRISAT): 100.

Rao, S. (2008). "Reforms with a Female Face: Gender, Liberalization, and Economic Policy in Andhra Pradesh, India." *World Development* 36(7): 1213–1232.

Roodman, D., and J. Morduch (2009). "The Impact of Microcredit on the Poor in Bangladesh: Revisiting the Evidence." Working Papers 174. Washington, DC: Center for Global Development.

Shankar, T. (2003). "Power Sector: The Rise, Fall and Reform." *Economic and Political Weekly* 38(12–13): 1171–1178.

Shukla, P. R., D. Biswas, T. Nag, A. Yajnik, T. C. Heller, and D. G. Victor (2004). "Impact of Power Sector Reforms on Technology, Efficiency, and Emissions: Case Study of Andhra Pradesh, India." PESD Working Paper No. 20. Stanford, CA: Stanford University.

Srinivasan, N. (2010). *Microfinance India: The State of The Sector Report 2010*. New Delhi: SAGE Publications.

Sriram, M. S. (2010). "Commercialization of Microfinance in India: A Discussion of the Emperor's Apparel." *Economic & Political Weekly* 45(24): 65–74.

Reddy S., S. Galab, and P. Rao (2003). "Trends and Determinants of Poverty in Andhra Pradesh: 1957–58 to 1999–2000." *Economic and Political Weekly* 38(12–13): 1262–1273.

World Bank (2006). "Overcoming Drought: Adaptation Strategies for Andhra Pradesh, India." World Bank e-Library (e-ISBN: 978-0-8213-6665-3).

PART II

Bihar

ARNAB MUKHERJI AND ANJAN MUKHERJI

CHAPTER 8

Bihar's Economy in Historical Perspective

Bihar has existed either as a kingdom or a state within the Republic of India from the earliest time that written records on India can be found (Thapar 1966; Rangarajan 1992). Romila Thapar, a distinguished historian, begins an account of the history of ancient India by describing events in regions which largely make up Bihar. Achievements of ancient India in

---

An earlier version of this study, Mukherji and Mukherji (2012), was presented at the National Institute of Public Finance and Policy-Columbia University conference on "Growth, Poverty and Human Development in Indian States: Selected Issues" on August 7–8, 2012, at the India International Centre, New Delhi. We are indebted to our discussants Satya Das and Arunish Chawla for very helpful comments. We also benefited from comments received from Chetan Ghate, Arvind Panagariya, Sudipto Mundle, and M. Govinda Rao. We are particularly grateful to M. Govinda Rao for setting us straight on matters relating to state finances during the preliminary stages of preparing this paper. For very helpful suggestions on this and earlier versions, we are indebted to Pinaki Chakraborty, Sanchia de Souza, Sushant Joshi, Rajalaxmi Kamath, Mritiunjoy Mohanty, and Subhashish Ray. Discussions at various stages with Shaibal Gupta, Chirashree Das Gupta, Prabhat P. Ghosh, Chanchal Kumar, Chinmaya Kumar, Anup Mukerji, Arvind Panagariya, Amal Sanyal, and Ghanshyam Tiwary have been extremely educative and helpful. In particular Anup Mukerji and Arvind Panagariya provided detailed comments and insights from their respective areas of expertise. We gratefully acknowledge the help received from B. D. Pandit (DES, Government of Bihar), and Amit Bakshi (CEPPF, ADRI) in procuring data. We thank Shiladitya Chaudhuri and Nivedita Gupta for sharing their district-level poverty estimates for Bihar. We also thank Esha Chhabra and Amarjyoti Mahanta for assistance on many counts. The current version also reflects the very helpful comments from the set of three readers of the Oxford University Press and help from Manish Gupta is gratefully acknowledged. The views expressed here are the authors' own and should not be attributed to their employers, associates, or those acknowledged here. Finally, we are greatly indebted to Thapar (1966) and Sinha (2011): our dependence on these works will be clear.

education, governance, society, culture, and religion that are celebrated around the world today have had their roots in Bihar. Astonishingly, however, the mega achievements of Bihar in virtually all major spheres of life within the state and outside have left no living legacy in today's Bihar—a past so alien as to be either viewed as incredible or simply forgotten.[1]

A more recognizable, if rather dramatic picture of Bihar is the one seen in a 2010 article on the changes in the state:

> For decades the sprawling state of Bihar, flat and scorching as a griddle, was something between a punch line and a cautionary tale. . . . Criminals could count on the police for protection, not prosecution. Highwaymen ruled the shredded roads and kidnapping was one of the state's most profitable businesses. . . . Its government, led by politicians who used divisive identity politics to entrench their rule, was so corrupt that it required a newly coined phrase: the Jungle Raj. Polgreen (2010)

This is an idea of Bihar that the majority of contemporary readers have encountered over and over again, especially after the 1980s. In the article, Polgreen (2010) goes on to describe, however, not the decay of a once successful nation-state, but rather a more remarkable change—the veritable signs of development and growth in a state that had once been considered a basket case, or more delicately, a failed state (see figure 8.1).

The goal of this study is to understand how this reversal took place in the state of Bihar and to study the role of governance and public policy in making this change possible. There are many ways to describe this experience. For instance, we could profile individuals instrumental to the process of economic and organizational change in Bihar, or alternatively, focus on a range of statistics that capture the underlying structural change in the economy. A third possibility is to focus on political and social movements within which Bihar underwent many of these changes. While each of these approaches has its merits, we focus on using validated secondary data to quantitatively assess the pace of change and how robust this change has been and how likely it is to maintain the current trend. We believe that by focusing on changes in economic measures and their determinants, we are best able to discuss Bihar's experience as it relates to the complex process of governance. It is

---

1. An anecdote puts the matter in perspective. A few years ago at a Right to Food seminar in Delhi, a speaker asserted that the idea of this "right" could be traced to President Roosevelt and his New Deal. In a brief intervention, one of the authors reminded the audience that the idea went far back and read out several passages from *Arthashastra*, a text from 350 B.C. by a scholar-administrator of the Mauryan Empire based in Bihar, that laid down a basis for providing food for the needy as well as the definition of the needy—a definition startlingly close to the one proposed in the seminar!

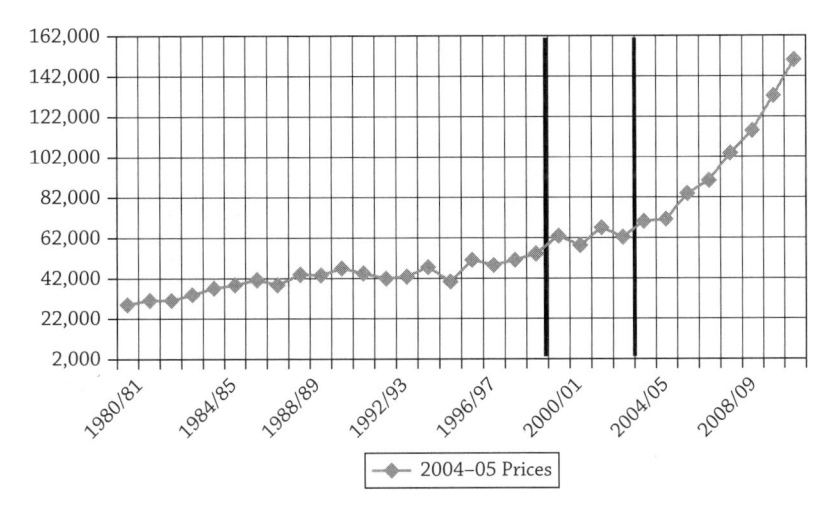

Figure 8.1: Evolution of Per Capita Income for Bihar, 1980/81 to 2011/12
Source: Authors' construction based on data from Central Statistical Organization, Government of India.

also a more fruitful approach from the viewpoint of replicating Bihar's experience in other regions in similar situations.

Our study is divided into five chapters. In the present chapter, we first provide a historical narrative of Bihar to set the context and then proceed to focus on its contemporary economy. This helps us to better understand the moribund state of its economy over much of the 1980–2005 period and its subsequent rejuvenation in a number of important dimensions. Chapter 9 documents different public policies that had significantly negative implications for Bihar's economy and continue to haunt it today. In chapter 10, we identify a number of important policy and institutional reform initiatives that were adopted in the post-2005 period in Bihar. In chapter 11, we discuss a range of issues that still need to be tackled to accelerate growth in agriculture, reduction in poverty, and absorption of labor outside the agricultural sector. Finally, in chapter 12, we conclude the study with some of the broad lessons that Bihar's experience offers.

A HISTORICAL SKETCH

In our short sketch of the history of Bihar, we limit ourselves to some key aspects necessary to convey the dramatic ups and downs in the economic fortunes that the state has seen.[2] As far back as 600 B.C., republics and kingdoms were being established and it is only then that the "details of Indian

2. Romila Thapar's (1966) *A History of India*, vol. 1, devotes significant coverage to the history of Bihar while initiating the discussion on Indian history.

history began to emerge with greater clarity" (Thapar 1996: 50). At this time, two forms of political organizations coexisted: republics and monarchies. The monarchies were based in the Indo-Gangetic plain while the republics skirted around the monarchies. Thapar (1996) documents that frequent skirmishes aimed at consolidation among the monarchies and republics culminated in the emergence of four rival states—the three kingdoms of Kashi, Kosala, Magadha (modern south Bihar), and the republic of Virjis (covering Janakpur in Nepal and the Muzaffarpur district of Bihar).

Over the next hundred years, Magadha emerged as the dominant state in the region. The first ruler of repute of Magadha was Bimbisara. He was not only a skillful and ambitious monarch but also an efficient administrator and was responsible for setting up a decentralized bureaucratic structure for governance rooted in the idea of autonomous village economies unified within a monarchy. Bimbisara was also responsible for expanding the dominion of the kingdom to control passage and commerce on the river Ganges. Through alliances created by marriages (for example, with the Kosala and Kashi), he was able to extend the reach of the Magadha kingdom to what today constitutes east Uttar Pradesh, Bihar, Jharkhand, and parts of Nepal. Many important changes began during his rule; towns and cities were built, international trade began, and commerce prospered. Over time, Magadha emerged as the main state among the earlier competing entities. While monarchy had won over the republic, its survival over the next few centuries was based as much on good leaders as on a well-oiled governance apparatus.

In 493 B.C., Ajatashatru, son of Bimbisara, ascended the throne and continued the expansionist initiatives of his father. It is believed that he imprisoned and starved Bimbisara to death. He continued the expansion of Magadha and built a fort near the river Ganges that grew into Pataliputra, which eventually became what is today known as Patna, the capital of Bihar. The importance of Magadha grew; it came to control the lower Ganges with trade and commerce providing revenue to the kingdom and a thriving business and trade community was established. The death of Ajatashatru in 461 B.C. was followed by a rapid succession of five weak kings. According to Thapar (1996: 57), each of these kings ascended the throne through patricide. In spite of such upheavals, the administrative set-up of the kingdom of Magadha proved robust and society and commerce continued to flourish. Domestic and foreign trade grew and led to rapid changes "in another sphere; that of religion and philosophical speculation. The conflict between established orthodoxy and the aspirations of newly rising groups ... resulted in a remarkable richness and vigour in thought rarely surpassed in centuries to come" (Thapar 1996: 63). Of the many sects that flourished, the Jains and the Buddhists matured into distinct religions and remain widely practiced world religions even today. Members of the Kshatriya (warrior) ruling class "who were opposed to brahminical orthodoxy" supported both of these religions

(Thapar 1996: 67). It should also be pointed out that the founders of both religions were approximate contemporaries of Bimbisara and Ajatashatru.

After the fifth patricide, the people of Magadha decided that they had enough; they revolted against the ruling dynasty and installed the royal viceroy as the king. This proved to be a temporary arrangement with a number of other rulers appearing one after another until the arrival of Mahapadma Nanda. Thapar (1996: 57) describes the Nanda dynasty as the "first empire builders of India" as under their rule the boundaries of the Magadha kingdom expanded to include parts of central India, modern Orissa (then called Kalinga), and further east toward present-day Bengal (Anga, approximately the eastern part of present-day Bihar).

At the same time, Alexander and his Greek army entered India from the northwest; they conquered much of northwest India but their progress eastwards stopped at Punjab from where they returned. The Greeks left written accounts of what they found and these documents greatly contributed to the myths and wonders of India. Although Alexander left the Indus Valley without challenging Nanda, the Greeks left detailed accounts of the fantastic army that the Nandas had built. This was also a period in which trade between various Greek colonies to the west of the Indian subcontinent was firmly established and this continued even as various dynasties waxed and waned in their rule of the Indian subcontinent.

The Nandas prospered with a complex and effective administrative machinery built on the structures they had inherited from Bimbisara and his successors. This was used to collect taxes that not only enriched the treasury but also allowed the Nandas to maintain large armies as well as build canals and institute complex irrigation projects. The Nanda dynasty held the throne of Magadha until 321 B.C. when Chandragupta Maurya overthrew it. Under the Mauryas, Magadha attained truly great heights. According to Thapar, "the imperial idea found expression" under the rule of Chandragupta Maurya and his heirs. He was able to rapidly extend the reach of Magadha in the west and in the northwest, due to the vacuum left behind by the departure of Alexander.

The success and rise of Chandragupta Maurya is attributed to the shrewd advice of the teacher-philosopher-administrator, Chanakya, also known as Kautilya. Historians credit Chanakya with being the key strategist in establishing the vast empire covering nearly all of the Indian subcontinent. He also authored the treatise *Arthashastra* that codified, for the first time in known history, norms associated with good governance. Waldauer et al. (1996) document how key ideas in the modern theory of international trade, taxation theory, and the labor theory of value have their origins in the *Arthashastra*. Written more than 2,000 years prior to Adam Smith and David Ricardo, the manuscript was never referred to by the latter authors; they were never aware that such a text existed. The role of "just" wages in society, crime and punishment, corruption within bureaucracy, right to food and a deep responsibility of the ruler to his people are all ideas that *Arthashastra* develops in a rich framework with the overall goal of expanding the wealth of the nation state and leading it to prosperity.

Chandragupta Maurya, with the counsel of Chanakya, soon controlled both the Indus and the Ganges valleys and much of the north of the Indian subcontinent. Chandragupta died around 297 B.C. and was followed by his son Bindusara who brought central India (the Deccan) under Maurya rule. By the time of his death, 272 B.C., extensive parts of the subcontinent were being ruled from Pataliputra. Ashoka, his able son, succeeded Bindusara. Ashoka expanded the empire to bring virtually the entire subcontinent of India under Maurya rule.

Under Ashoka, society, economy, foreign trade, diplomacy, religion, and administration reached their zenith. After initial years of war, the death of thousands in the battle of Kalinga led Ashoka to renounce violence and accept Buddhism. This proved instrumental in the spread of the religion outside India. However, by this time the expanse of the Magadha kingdom was already large—it was bounded by the Himalayas in the north, it covered areas well into Pakistan, Baluchistan, parts of eastern Iran and Afghanistan in the west, Assam, in the east, and most parts of the south of India. Small parts of the south that did not come directly under his empire paid tribute to him, as did Sri Lanka, and Myanmar. The extent of the kingdom is marked by inscriptions on rock pillars found in Peshawar (in Karoshthi script), Kandahar (in Greek and Aramaic), and, indeed, all over India in the Brahmi script. These inscriptions not only proclaim the reach of Ashoka's kingdom but also provide an understanding of public policy of the time in terms of the commitments of the king to his people.

Unfortunately, the Magadha Empire did not survive Ashoka long. Within 50 years of his death, in 232 B.C., the Maurya kingdom withered away. A second coming for an empire centered on Magadha was during the course of the Gupta dynasty that ruled over the period A.D. 320 to 550. Again, at its peak, the empire covered substantial portions of South Asia, although its reach into south India was more limited than during the time of Ashoka. Better documentation of the military strength and complexity of governance exists for the Gupta period than for the Maurya period (Mookerji 1959). At its peak, the empire was divided into 26 administrative units called Desas that were managed by governors. Each Desa was subdivided into districts that were administered by the district officer (Vishayapati). Mookerji (1959) notes that additional officers were assigned at the district level to help with different departments such as Saulkika (revenue officer), Gualkika (forest officer), and others. Apart from placing an administrative structure, a range of other initiatives, either through the state or through public philanthropy, such as rest houses, grants of land for educational institutions, hospitals, roads, temples of worship, and repairs of embankments provided a semblance of public service delivery.

In sharp contrast to the description of Bihar provided by Polgreen (2010), Fa-Hien, a Buddhist traveler from China during the Gupta age, notes how "the people were allowed by the government considerable individual freedom not subject to vexations from its Officers in the shape of registration, or other regulation; economic liberty with unfettered mobility of labour, so that agriculturalists were not tied to land like serfs; and humane criminal law" was practiced (Mookerji 1929: 59). During the Gupta dynasty, we also see the creation of an international university at Nalanda that flourished from the fifth to sixth century until the eleventh century and was a major contribution to academic life, society, and religion (Dutt 1962; Scharfe 2002). A range of other contributions in mathematics (most notably the work of Aryabhatta), large public works and engineering practices (irrigation and embankments), and art and theater are available from this period.

The decline of the Gupta dynasty set in during the late fifth century when a range of invaders including the Hepthalites and the Huns broke through its defenses, and other dynasties from within the subcontinent began to challenge it. The subsequent centuries did not see the emergence of any unifying empire till the rise and establishment of the Moghuls much later in the fifteenth century. A natural question that emerges is how do these periods of consolidation and growth emerge? These periods saw not just economic consolidation but also cultural and social consolidation as well. In a growing series of investigations that explore why civilizations, economies, and societies of the past have failed or succeeded, Bihar's case is undeniably important.

On a much smaller scale, consider the Chaco Phenomenon: a pre-Columbian society with thriving economic, political, and religious activity that spread out over more than 1,000 square miles in the Chaco Canyon over the A.D. 850–1150 period (Vivian 1990). The Chaco people built irrigation networks 150 times larger than any known before (Friedman et al. 2003). They constructed huge houses, with hundreds of rooms, and built more than 250 miles of roads. Over the three centuries of the civilization's existence, thousands of trees were transported great distances for building (Lekson 1986; Lewin 1993; Adovasio with Page 2002), and in the process the forests around the canyon were denuded. While no other pre-Columbian society reached this level of maturity, the Chaco Canyon civilization was unable to take the next step and become a nation-state. Attempts at state formation were unsuccessful. Today, what remains are the ruins and a mystery: Where did they go wrong? Was it the denuding of the forests around the canyon or something much more systematic?

Scholars from various disciplines, including physicists, historians, mathematicians, archaeologists, computer scientists, biologists, sociologists, and economists, explain the Chaco Phenomenon and its subsequent failure through the science of complexity. They explain it in terms of the evolution of an entity whose different parts interact and generate order and chaos and where nonlinearity in processes is the norm rather than the exception. State formation and governance are quite clearly such complex processes, wherein multiple agencies, institutions, and organizations interact as parts of a larger whole so that nonlinear evolution and unpredictable behavior are the norm. Bihar's rich history goes much further back in time compared to the Chaco civilization; it thus offers itself as an example of a society that underwent multiple expansions and contractions within different and evolving social structures and governance systems.

Our investigation attempts to realize only a part of this potential. We focus on contemporary Bihar; while the government of Bihar celebrated 2012 as the 100th year of the state's creation, the state of Bihar that was carved out of the Bengal Presidency in 1912 is not today's Bihar. Contemporary Bihar actually came into being within the federal republic of India through the Bihar Reorganization Act of 2000 that separated Jharkhand from the original entity carved out of the Bengal Presidency. It is mainly on this 12-year-old Bihar that much of our analysis focuses. However, to appreciate what exactly is happening today, we do need to go back to the earlier Bihar.

AN OVERVIEW OF THE ECONOMY: 1980–2010

By most measures, contemporary Bihar has been the poorest among the larger states of India. Not only in terms of per capita income and output but also in terms of almost each and every indicator of relevance such as the Human Development Index, access to infrastructure, healthcare, education, and law and order, the gap between Bihar and the average of India has been so large that from the mid-1980s, many have characterized Bihar as a "basket case."

Of course, poor achievements do not imply stagnation. Nor do they imply a lack of structural change. The economy of Bihar has surely been evolving with many of the changes resembling those in the larger Indian economy. The key difference relates to the extent of the change and the resulting levels of different indicators. In our overview, we partition the period 1980–2010 into three separate time periods: 1980–2000, 2000–2005, and post-2005. The basis of this classification is analytical rather than statistical. The data are comparable within each of these periods but not necessarily across them.

The first period represents the last 20 years prior to bifurcation of the state into Jharkhand and the current Bihar. It represents a period when the structure of the economy, its endowments, and its politics were markedly different from current Bihar. The districts that constitute Bihar and Jharkhand today have always been socially and economically different; thus, for example, while Jharkhand's population is largely tribal with limited caste identity, caste has historically been the basis for polarization and exclusion in Bihar (Sharma 1976).[3] In addition, with a substantial portion of its land on the Chota Nagpur Plateau, Jharkhand is rich in mineral deposits and has been the home to manufacturing activity. On the other hand, districts constituting the current Bihar have large swathes of alluvial soil, often replenished by floodwaters, which are particularly suitable for agriculture.

Years 2000–2005 represent the immediate post-bifurcation period that can be juxtaposed against the third phase beginning in 2006. Social dynamics, political demands for separation, and political expediency on the part of Rashtriya Janata Dal (RJD), which ruled in Bihar in 2000, and the National Democratic Alliance (NDA), which ruled at the national level, provided the movement for Jharkhand an opportunity in the 1990s that had not existed in the prior decades (Rorabacher 2008). While the economy of the bifurcated Bihar could no longer be compared with that of the 1980–2000 Bihar, RJD continued in power and this provides a period of political and policy continuity with the past that is important.

The third phase begins following the 2005 elections in Bihar in which the RJD was defeated and Nitish Kumar and his political party Janata Dal (United) (JD (U)) in a coalition with the Bharatiya Janata Party (BJP) came to power. This period saw major changes in policy, administration, and overall governance. The period marks a clear break from the past, in both a statistical and policy sense. While many of the structural changes seen in the past continued, and the relative position of Bihar among other states remained unchanged, there was a dramatic jump in economic growth and an associated decline in poverty.

PHASE I: 1980–2000

Like much of the rest of India, Bihar's economy was largely agricultural in terms of output as well as employment until the 1980s. After the mid-1980s, with Bihar's economy growing at a much lower rate than India's, we see a decline in the ratio of per capita output in Bihar to that of India (see figure 8.2). Lalu Prasad of the RJD came to power in 1990. The declining trend in per capita income in Bihar relative to India continued throughout the 1990s though less

---

3. Sharma (1976) provides an early account of how the Jharkhand movement took shape on the basis of administrative unity between the districts that form Jharkhand today, their exploitation by north Bihar, and the ethnic differences between the two. This distinct *Jharkhandi* identity had arguably been in place even in pre-independent India and is based on real and identifiable differences between the areas forming present-day Bihar and Jharkhand (Prakash 2001). The political angle leading to the bifurcation is discussed later.

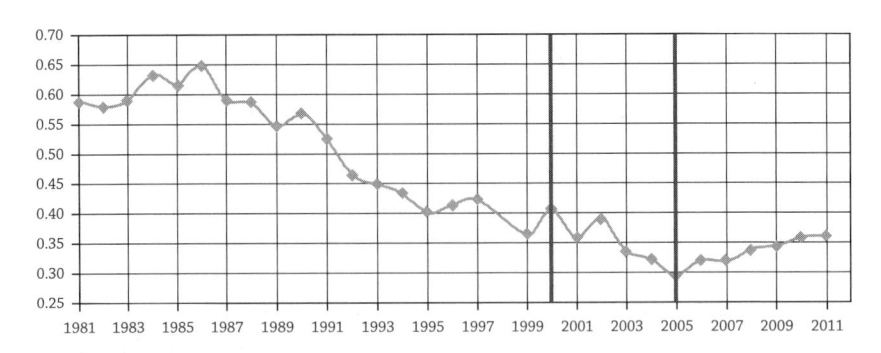

Figure 8.2: Ratio of Per Capita Incomes in Bihar to India (1981–2011)
Source: Authors' construction using the CSO data.

sharply than during the second half of the 1980s. This trend continued until 2005, the last year of the RJD rule. It was only after 2005 when Nitish Kumar took charge of the state that per capita income in Bihar relative to that in India returned to an upward trend again.

Growth: Absolute and Relative

In 1980/81, Bihar had a per capita income of 917 rupees, which was 60% of the national average. The CSO data on state-level per capita income show that Bihar was the poorest state in terms of per capita income that year and has remained so to date. In addition, the Planning Commission (2002) data shows that even in 1981, Bihar had the lowest Human Development Index (HDI) among all 15 major states of India. Bihar's poor performance was reasonably well recognized by 1980, and any explanation of such absolute backwardness must pre-date the 1980s. However, at this point in time, Bihar was far from being seen as an endemic failed state—its per capita income grew at the annual rate of 5.3% between 1980/81 and 1984/85 and was among the fastest across Indian states.

Figure 8.2 shows that the relative per capita income of Bihar exhibited an upward trend from 1980/81 to 1986/87 with the ratio reaching 0.65 by the latter year. Ghosh and Gupta (2010: 40–41) argue that Bihar failed to capitalize on the subsequent process of liberalization and opening of the Indian economy noting, "the growth rate of the Bihar economy during the post-reform era was the lowest among the states of India in any of the decades." Thus, while the average growth rate in India accelerated, it slowed down in Bihar, increasing the divergence in the per capita incomes between Bihar and the rest of the country. This, in fact, is the period when Bihar was transformed from being simply a poor performer to one for which recovery appeared to be increasingly out of the question.

The gap between India and Bihar, which started emerging in the latter half of the 1980s, expanded rapidly, so that by the end of the century per capita output in Bihar was as low as a third of the national average. Even more dramatically, the level of per capita income in Bihar actually fell from 1,197 rupees in 1990/91 to 1,073 rupees in 1997/98. For the period 1980–1998, the compound annual growth rate (CAGR) of per capita income in India was about 3.2% while it was a meagre 1.1% in Bihar. These rates of growth are significantly different when seen cumulatively over time. While in India, the average Indian could see her income double in 22 years (i.e., at least twice in her lifetime), for an average Bihari, it would take 63 years; with life expectancy well below 63 years over this period, citizens of Bihar were unlikely to ever see their incomes double.

Structure of the Economy

While the economy suffered from overall stagnation, there was nevertheless substantial change in the structure of the economy; from being largely an agricultural economy, it became one in which services and industry made significant contributions. Figure 8.3 plots the composition of national income for the years 1980/81, 1990/91, and 1997/98. Two observations follow from this figure: (1) even in 1980/81, the share of the services sector in Bihar's State Domestic Product (SDP) was larger than the share of the industrial sector, and the gap between the two increased over time; and (2) by 1997/98,

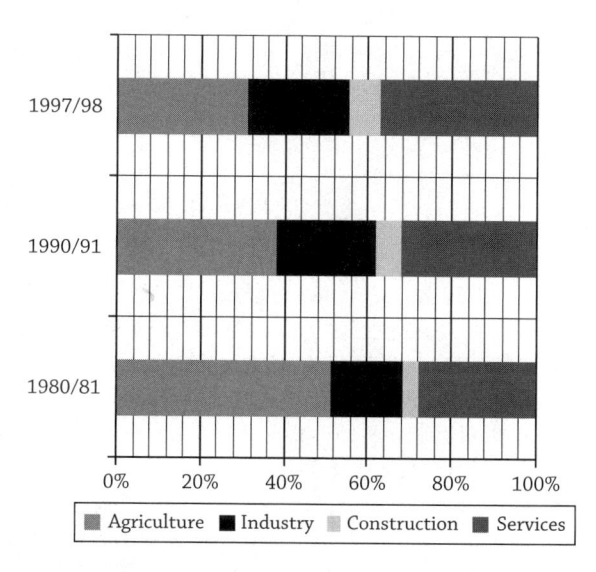

Figure 8.3: Composition of the GDP in Bihar, 1980/81, 1990/91, and 1997/98
Source: Authors' construction using the CSO data.

the share of services inclusive of construction had grown to just a little below twice that of industry. Qualitatively, these features of the Bihar economy were similar to those of the national economy. While Bihar remained more agrarian in output than India, its transformation into a services-led economy like that of the rest of India was clearly underway.

This large restructuring of the economy during the first phase is quite striking not only because of the very limited expansion of economic output accompanying it. But this change brought very limited change in employment structure with it. As we will discuss later, employment in Bihar remained overwhelmingly agrarian even in 1999/2000, with little qualitative change from its distribution in 1977/78. In 1999/2000, over 715 out of every 1,000 employed rural males and 845 out of every 1,000 employed rural women were engaged in agriculture. In comparison, the services sector for rural men employed a meagre 161 out of every 1,000 employed rural males, and the number was lower for women. Given the low level of urbanization in Bihar, these allocations of rural labor force serve as reasonable approximation of the overall allocation of the labor force in the state.

Ghosh and Gupta (2010) argue that the limited expansion in output in Bihar may be primarily attributable to the lack of expansion in the non-agricultural sector. Employment statistics clearly show that the non-agricultural sector was unable to draw people out of agriculture. Kishore (2004) documents that agriculture in Bihar performed better than the national average in the 1980s but had begun to stagnate in the mid- to late 1990s; this substantiates Ghosh and Gupta's (2010) and Sharma's (1995) arguments that the failure of growth in Bihar was largely a failure of the services and industrial sectors to expand. This in turn raises questions about the nature of the prevailing policy environment in Bihar during the 1990s, particularly because during the 1990s, Bihar's access to mineral resources was largely intact.

Poverty

Incidence of poverty in Bihar has always been significantly higher than the national average (see figure 8.4). The gap between poverty rates in Bihar and India rose during the decade from 1973/74 to 1983. The poverty ratio fell in India but remained stagnant in Bihar during this period. While the poverty ratio did fall between 1983 and 1987/88, it rose again in 1993/94 in Bihar. Therefore, the period from 1973/74 to 1993/94 exhibits a rising trend in the difference in poverty rates between Bihar and India. Unfortunately, due to a sample design change, we do not have comparable poverty estimates at the level of the state until 2004/05 again. Therefore, we cannot ascertain the evolution of poverty in Bihar till the end of the first phase.

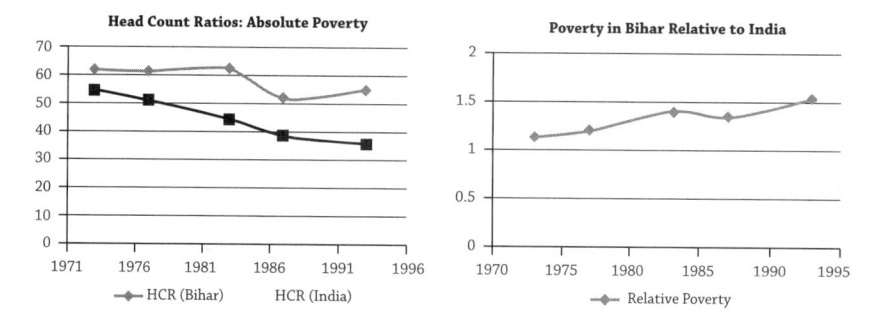

Figure 8.4: Poverty Trends in Pre-bifurcation Bihar, 1971–1996
Source: Authors' construction using the estimates by the Planning Commission.

Poverty in Bihar has been chronic and exists largely within the context of an agrarian economy. The literature on poverty for pre-bifurcation Bihar has centered on the performance of the agricultural sector and why its gains have been so limited. The lack of land reforms, poor agricultural productivity, fragmentation of land holdings, and caste rigidities are among the reasons frequently cited. An interesting hypothesis advanced by Kishore (2004), based on a careful study of six villages, is that more than the classic sources of agrarian failure, public investment in agriculture has been unstable and erratic. Sharma (1995: 2587), on the other hand, argues that "the state's backwardness is more related to the iniquitous and exploitative socioeconomic structure, lack of political leadership, and almost total collapse of administrative law and order machinery—to the point that it is said that in Bihar 'the state has withered away.'" While it is difficult to be definitive about the single most important reason for the minimal decline in poverty in the 1990s in Bihar, it is quite clear that with regard to many key aspects, incentives were often perverse and institutions of governance weak. It was also during this time that a sense of hopelessness about Bihar's economy started setting in and Bihar became increasingly identified as a failed state.

Social Indicators

Human development in Bihar followed national trends during this period. While there was modest improvement in all indicators, a large gap between national and Bihar-specific achievements has remained throughout the period. Table 8.1 reports literacy rates in Bihar and India according to each census beginning with the one in 1951 and ending with that in 2011. The gap between Bihar and India at 5 percentage points was small at independence but steadily rose during the following decades. It reached 11 percentage points in 1981 and 14.7 percentage points in 1991. Male literacy has always been higher than female literacy in most parts of India and this pattern is

Table 8.1. LITERACY RATES IN BIHAR AND INDIA, 1951–2011 (PERCENTAGES)

Year	Bihar Persons	Bihar Males	Bihar Females	India Persons	India Males	India Females
1951	13.5	22.7	4.2	18.3	27.2	8.9
1961	22.0	35.9	8.1	28.3	40.4	15.4
1971	23.2	35.9	9.9	34.5	46.0	22.0
1981	32.3	47.1	16.6	43.6	56.4	29.8
1991	37.5	51.4	22.0	52.2	64.1	32.2
2001	47.5	60.3	33.6	64.8	75.3	53.7
2011	63.8	73.4	53.3	74.0	82.1	65.5

Source: Census of India.

Table 8.2. LIFE EXPECTANCY AT BIRTH, 1981–85 TO 2011–16 (YEARS)

Period	Male Bihar	Male India	Female Bihar	Female India
1981–85	54.2	55.4	51.5	55.7
1992–95	60.2	60.1	58.2	61.4
1999–2003	61.6	61.8	59.7	63.8
2002–2006	62.2	62.6	60.4	64.2
2011–2016	69.9	70.0	69.1	71.1

Source: Sample Registration System Data. Estimates for 2011–16 are projections.

seen in Bihar as well. The gap in literacy rates between males and females in Bihar peaked in 1981 at 30.5 percentage points and has been declining since. The essential difference in gender-specific literacy rates between Bihar and India stems from the much lower rates of literacy for both sexes, rather than starkly larger gender gaps.

Two common indicators of health are life expectancy at birth and infant mortality rate (IMR). Because the probability of death is often the highest in infancy, these two indicators are closely related: a high IMR is associated with a low life expectancy. Interestingly, the gap between Bihar and the all-India average with respect to these indicators is smaller than in other indicators. Nevertheless, there is an anomaly with respect to gender-specific life expectancy: as shown by table 8.2, Bihar exhibits a significant gender bias. Nationally, women have a higher life expectancy than men; however, in Bihar it is the other way around. During 1981–84, the average man in

Bihar had a life expectancy at birth of 54.5 years, while the average man in India had a life expectancy of 55.2 years. Among women, however, life expectancy in Bihar was 51.5; whereas, in India it was 55.7 years. This gender gap against women in Bihar and in India narrowed in the 1990s, but persisted even during the 1999–2003 period when life expectancy for women in Bihar was 59.7 years, but for women in India it was 63.8 years.

In terms of infant mortality statistics, Bihar follows national trends very closely. In fact, as figure 8.5 shows, in much of the pre-bifurcation period, infant mortality in Bihar was slightly lower than the national average. It is only in the post-bifurcation period that we see infant mortality rates turning higher in Bihar than the national average levels.

These trends in poverty, education, and health translate into a relatively poor showing of Bihar in terms of the UN Human Development Index (HDI). As shown in table 8.3, HDI estimates reported by the Planning Commission

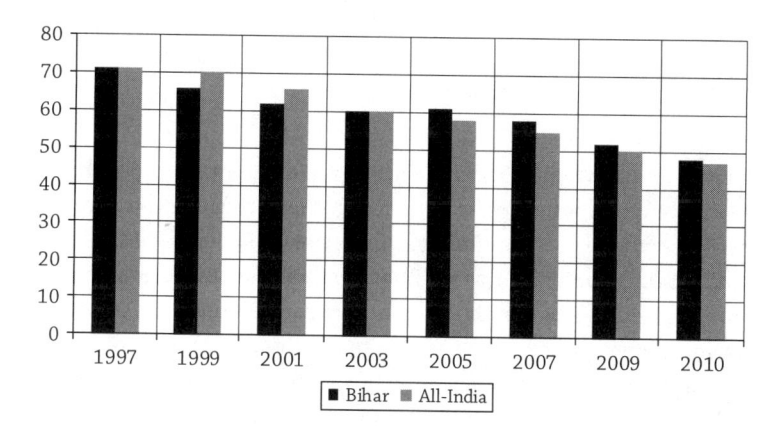

Figure 8.5: Infant Mortality Rate, 1997–2010 (per 1,000)
Source: SRS various issues.

Table 8.3. HUMAN DEVELOPMENT INDEX IN BIHAR ACROSS THE YEARS

Year	Bihar	India	Ratio
1981	0.237	0.302	0.784768
1991	0.308	0.381	0.808399
2001	0.367	0.472	0.777542
2005	0.449	0.575	0.78087

Source: National Human Development Report 2001 and Meghalaya 2008 Human Development Report.

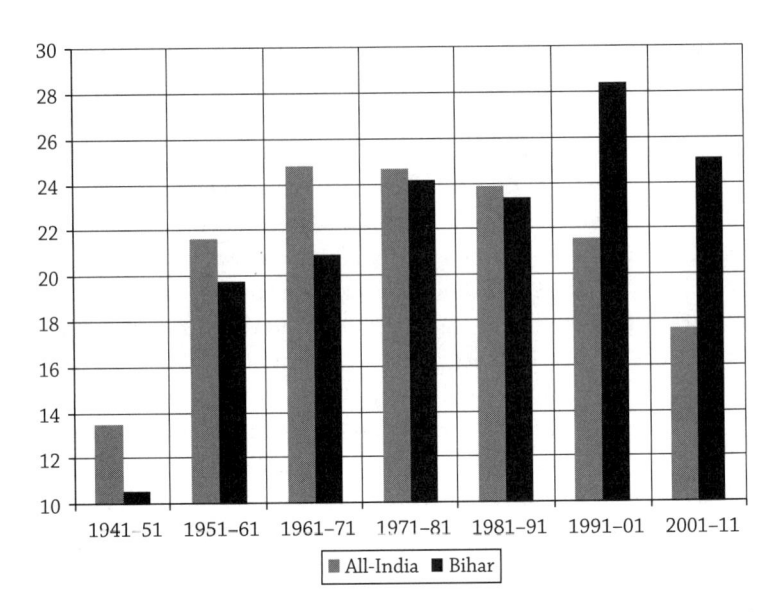

[Chart: Decadal Population Growth Rates comparing All-India and Bihar across 1941-51, 1951-61, 1961-71, 1971-81, 1981-91, 1991-01, 2001-11]

Figure 8.6: Decadal Population Growth Rates, 1941–1951 to 2001–2011
Source: Authors' construction using the census data.

systematically rank Bihar the lowest among the major states of India. HDI in Bihar has been improving over time indicating progress, but the improvement is not sufficiently large to close the gap with the national average.

Finally, demographic trends in Bihar have been a few decades behind the national trend as shown in figure 8.6. Since India's independence, India's population growth story is a good example of demographic transition in a country in the early stages of development—an initial decade of slow growth in the 1940s was followed by four decades of high growth during 1950–90. India's population growth then slowed down in the 1990s and decelerated significantly in the 2000s. The same transition began late in Bihar: its population grew at significantly lower rate than India's during the 1950s and 1960s and caught up with the national rates during the 1970s and 1980s. However, during the years 1991–2011, Bihar's population growth rate significantly exceeded that of India. This means that Bihar has a significantly younger population today than India as a whole, allowing for a range of opportunities including additional time to prepare for maximizing the benefits of transition to a large working-age population.

PHASE II: 2000–2005

The political bifurcation of erstwhile Bihar into today's Bihar and Jharkhand brought to the fore the need for norms on how financial and infrastructural resources would be shared. For practical reasons, and also to ease up the transition for the newly created state of Jharkhand, which consisted of a large proportion of tribal population, this process of bifurcation was very asymmetric. While all physical assets were distributed on an "as is, where is" basis, financial liabilities were distributed using population proportions (Bihar Economic Census, various rounds). This resulted in Jharkhand, which accounted for only one-fourth of the population of the erstwhile Bihar, inheriting three-fourths of its assets. The new Bihar grew absolutely and relatively poor overnight purely on account of this division. At the time of bifurcation, serious concerns were expressed about whether the "reduced" Bihar could even form a viable state on economic grounds (Bhattacharya 2000; Rorabacher 2008).

To give an idea of the magnitude of this loss in the size of the economy, it is useful to compare NSDP estimates before and after bifurcation in 2000. While in 1999/2000, CSO estimates that the cumulative NSDP for Bihar and Jharkhand was 763 billion rupees, this declined to 536 billion rupees in 2000/01 for divided Bihar (all in 1999/2000 prices); the economy shrank by 30% after the bifurcation.

Nevertheless, we can compare the structure of the economy for two consecutive years, one before and one after bifurcation, to get an idea of the structural differences between the economies of divided and undivided Bihar. According to table 8.4, bifurcation implied a huge setback to the industrial sector in Bihar—it had constituted 12% of NSDP for undivided Bihar but only 6% of NSDP for divided Bihar. Thus, bifurcation implied an accentuation of the role of the services and agriculture in national income. Thus, the economy of Bihar changed in a major way, losing virtually the entire industrial sector to Jharkhand in the bifurcation. Recognizing the critical role of the industrial sector in development, the prospects for growth turned significantly against Bihar in the post-bifurcation period. Of course, poverty

Table 8.4. STRUCTURAL CHANGE BETWEEN UNDIVIDED AND DIVIDED BIHAR

Sectors	Values (Rs. Million)		Composition (%)	
	Pre-bifurcation (1999/2000)	Post-bifurcation (2000/2001)	Pre-bifurcation (1999/2000)	Post-bifurcation (2000/2001)
Agriculture and Allied	136,550	214,960	32	41
Construction	19,170	18,720	4	4
Industry	52,570	33,560	12	6
Services	21,929	25,448	51	49
GSDP	427,580	52,173	100	

Source: CSO and authors' calculations; all rupee values are in 1999/2000 prices.

Ratio of Bihar PCY to All-India PCY

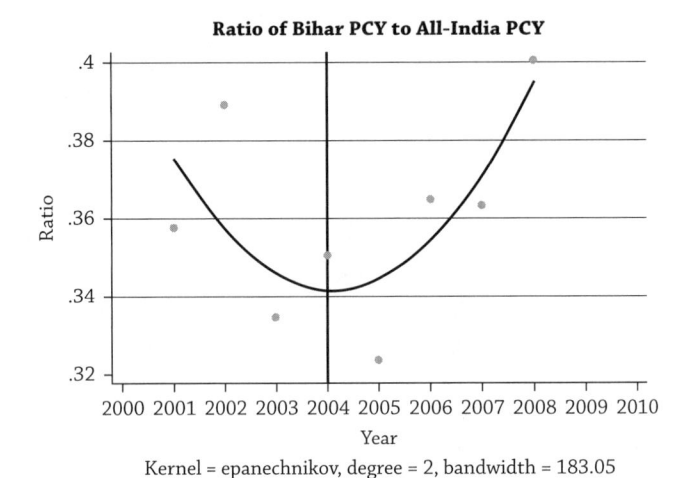

Figure 8.7: Bihar's GSDP Per Capita Relative to India Post-Bifurcation, 2000–2010
Figure 8.7 shows the ratio of per capita incomes of Bihar to all-India in the post-bifurcation period; over 2000–2005 this ratio continued to decline indicating slower growth than the Indian economy.
Source: Authors' construction using the CSO Data. We superimpose a quadratic fit to the time-series on per capita relative output. All data are at 1999/2000 prices.

ratios, per capita incomes, and HDI across these two time frames also show Bihar being in a disadvantageous position.

One of the immediate consequences of bifurcation for Bihar was that its economy became much more sensitive to shocks such as floods. While earlier about 55% of Bihar had been flood-prone, with the reduction in land area due to bifurcation, 73% of the area became flood-prone. What this meant was that the opportunities to tackle the shortfall due to floods declined and had to be forthcoming from a much smaller area. A raw indicator of this increased volatility is that the coefficient of variation of Net State Domestic Product (NSDP) increased from 6.2% in 1991–98 to 11.8% over the period 2000–2008. This is probably one of the key reasons that Bihar's economic growth shows more frequent peaks and troughs after bifurcation. In fact, some authors, such as Das Gupta (2010), worry about higher volatility of Bihar's economy post-bifurcation. The left panel of figure 8.8 captures the variation in annual growth rates of NSDP for Bihar and this concern is apparent. Two points can be made on this profile—one is of measurement and the other pertains to theory. The measurement issue relates to the appropriate time unit to look at growth; without disputing the high variation in annual growth if we look at compounded annual growth rates over longer periods of time, as in the right panel of figure 8.8, the trend of accelerating growth is very clear. On this basis alone, one can argue that while annual fluctuations may have increased, so has growth of domestic product in Bihar. The theoretical point stems from the fact that fluctuation in output alone is not the key concern, but rather

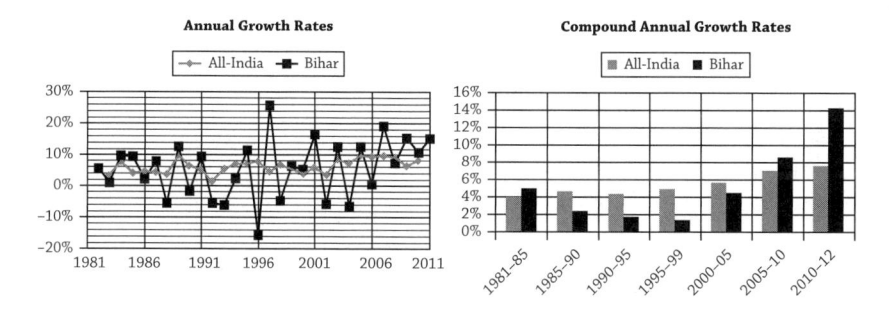

Figure 8.8: Per Capita NDP and NSDP Growth Rates for India and Bihar
Note: We use Net Domestic Product at factor cost (at 2004/05 prices) for Bihar and India.

the point of interest should be whether there has been sustained increase in economic activity.[4] The right panel of figure 8.8 shows that right after bifurcation, during the period 2000–2005, there is a sharp increase in the growth rate to 4.51% per annum in comparison to the 1.44% per annum seen over the period 1995–99. Benchmarking this growth against India's growth over the same period and the same time duration, we find that India grew faster than Bihar at 5.69% per annum even during this period and the gap between Bihar and India continued to increase. This was true in spite of the fact that in the first five years after bifurcation Bihar grew much faster than it had grown ever since the mid-1980s. It is only in the 2005–10 period and after that we find that Bihar bridging the gap between itself and India by growing faster.

As just discussed, Bihar's economy was substantially transformed when it was bifurcated into Bihar and Jharkhand under the Bihar Reorganization Act of 2000. Most of the manufacturing units and capacity to generate power were located in southern Bihar, and these went to Jharkhand. Thus, the share of industry (excluding construction) dropped from 22.5% to 4.6% of NSDP, and there was a parallel increase in the share of the services sector from 36% to 50% overnight. The share of the agricultural sector in the economy increased modestly from 36.5% to 40.4%. A natural consequence of the loss of the industrial sector was a substantial drop in the state's own share of non-tax revenue from this sector. During 1991–95, the industrial sector in Bihar had contributed 611.19 billion rupees to the state (i.e., about 10% of the total revenue); this declined marginally to 7% of the total revenue during 1995–2000. However, during 2000–2005, non-tax revenue from industry accounted for a mere

---

4. In an appendix in Mukherji and Mukherji (2012), an earlier version of this manuscript, we analyze growth patterns at the district level. There we establish that the growth profile for all districts in the 2005–08 period was better and more widespread than had been the case in the 2001–05 period. This suggests that Bihar's growth process was broader based than it would appear by looking at state-wide growth numbers alone.

123.44 billion rupees and was no more than 1% of the total revenue (Economic Survey, Government of Bihar, various issues). Thus, an additional consequence of bifurcation was a shrinking of the fiscal space within which the state could finance development, relief, and poverty alleviation activities.

The bifurcation artificially reinforced Bihar's transformation into a services driven economy that is also one of India's poorest economies. Simon Kuznets, in his 1971 Nobel Prize lecture, notes that one of the key features of modern economic growth seen in an economically dominant nation is the structural "shift away from agriculture to non-agricultural pursuits and, recently, away from industry to services; a change in the scale of productive units, and a related shift from personal enterprise to impersonal organization of economic firms, with a corresponding change in the occupational status of labour" (Kuznets 1971). Bihar's income now comes mostly from the services sector, but there was little movement of agricultural labor to opportunities outside of agriculture. Thus, while Bihar's NSDP is driven by the service sector, it remains overwhelmingly rural, with 64% of its workforce employed in agriculture (National Sample Survey Office, NSSO 2011). While this structural imbalance exists in the entire country, its extent is much greater in Bihar.

With no comparable estimates around the year 2000 available, we cannot judge progress in poverty reduction during 2000–2005. The best we can do is to compare poverty levels between 1993/94 and 2004/05. As table 8.5 shows, the proportion of the population below the poverty line shows a decline between these years in both Bihar and India as a whole. However, the extent of poverty in Bihar is significantly higher.

Careful work by Chaudhuri and Gupta (2009) enables us to look at district level poverty in 2004/05, and we use this information to plot the ranks of the districts in Bihar among the set of all districts in India in figure 8.9. It is immediately obvious that districts in Bihar tend have some of the highest headcount ratios in India and almost all of them have high head count ratios.

Table 8.5. POVERTY RATIOS AT OFFICIAL POVERTY LINES IN BIHAR AND INDIA

Year	Lakdawala Line Bihar	Lakdawala Line India	Tendulkar Line Bihar	Tendulkar Line India
1983	62.20	44.50		
1993/94	55.00	36.00	60.50	45.30
2004/05	41.40	27.50	54.40	37.20
2009/10			53.50	29.80
2011/12			33.74	21.92

Source: Planning Commission.

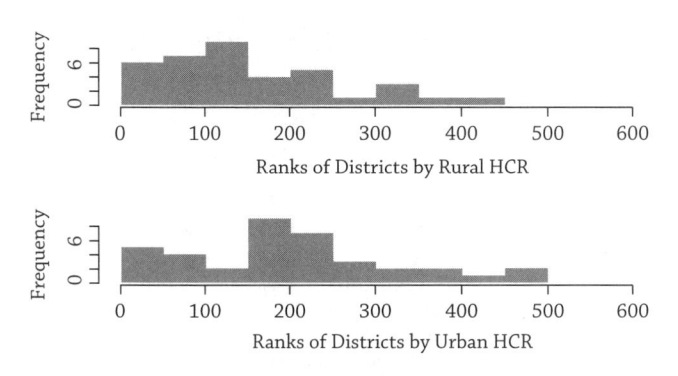

Figure 8.9: All-India Rankings of Bihar Districts by Poverty Ratios
Source: Author constructed figure from data reported in Chaudhuri and Gupta (2009).

Table 8.6 reports district level rural and urban monthly per capita expenditure (MPCE), poverty, and the Gini coefficient for all districts in Bihar in 2004/05. The Gini coefficient measures inequality with a higher value indicating greater inequality. A value of 0 for the coefficient represents entirely equal distribution and a value of 1 indicates the highest possible inequality such that all income is concentrated in one individual or household.

Rural inequality in Bihar ranges from 0.1139 (in Sheohar) to 0.2534 (in Saharsa) with a rural average of 0.2054 for Bihar; this is on the low side with 15 out of the 20 states showing higher average Gini coefficients than the highest in rural Bihar in Chaudhuri and Gupta (2009). Urban inequality ranges from 0.1144 (Banka) to 0.4231(Gaya) with an average of 0.3289 for all of urban Bihar. While the average urban inequality in Bihar is comparable to other states, within Bihar, urban areas of Saran, Patna, Aurgangabad, and particularly, Gaya, have very large levels of inequality. Thus, while rural Bihar tends to be quite egalitarian, urban Bihar is much less so, with some parts of urban Bihar having very high inequality.

In a similar fashion one can look at poverty (head count ratios at the Lakdawala line) estimates at the district level; rural poverty ranges between 7.68% (in Madhepura) to 76.9% (in West Champaran). These numbers make sense as the rural monthly per capita consumption expenditure in Madhepura is the second highest in Bihar and is the lowest for West Champaran. Urban poverty is even more widely dispersed although it is also the case that some of the more extreme values show low reliability due to low sample sizes; with a 10.8% urbanization rate and much of it centered on Patna, this is not surprising. It however does indicate that even Bihar needs serious effort at urban poverty alleviation with 25.7% of urban Patna being in poverty. While table 8.6 provides a snapshot of the distribution of poverty from 2005, this pattern remains of policy interest in view of the general pattern of persistence with poverty trends.

Table 8.6. DISTRICT LEVEL POVERTY AND INEQUALITY, 2004/05

District Name	MPCE (Rs.) Rural	MPCE (Rs.) Urban	Lorenz Ratio Rural	Lorenz Ratio Urban	Head Count Ratio Rural	Head Count Ratio Urban
West Champaran	319.57	449.90	0.1621	0.2758	76.90	71.70*
Muzaffarpur	382.75	545.90	0.2327	0.3346	65.25	56.30*
Kishanganj	362.97	768.90	0.1729	0.3042	62.32	30.60*
Banka	361.65	354.60	0.1650	0.1144	59.83	88.39
Madhubani	355.73	629.20	0.1632	0.3305	59.23	41.23
Begusarai	369.76	495.90	0.1488	0.2468	56.67	47.62
Saran	381.80	701.40	0.1990	0.3409	55.85	34.70
Aurangabad	371.84	647.80	0.2424	0.3744	55.41	53.60
Araria	362.32	649.40	0.1421	0.2510	54.60	35.58
Jehanabad	373.16	464.50	0.2048	0.2114	54.19	57.06
Buxar	354.34	552.10	0.1508	0.2365	54.18	33.31
Samastipur	388.00	480.00	0.2009	0.2397	52.28	62.08
Jamui	389.85	401.60	0.1638	0.1788	46.30	68.09
Bhagalpur	381.68	687.20	0.1731	0.1997	45.15	14.88
Nalanda	397.92	525.70	0.1673	0.2029	44.77	39.58
Patna	420.24	907.60	0.2364	0.3444	44.67	25.77
Darbhanga	427.71	627.80	0.2411	0.2922	42.16	40.74
Kaimur	387.51	662.40	0.1793	0.1849	41.99	21.74
Vaishali	411.27	525.90	0.2135	0.2865	41.64	54.34
Bhojpur	398.69	553.10	0.1877	0.2492	41.55	43.60
Nawada	431.29	563.20	0.1942	0.2319	38.83	48.66
Lakhisarai	457.25	591.10	0.1887	0.2621	38.59	41.72
Gaya	433.50	889.80	0.2236	0.4231	37.48	33.50*
Katihar	426.16	884.00	0.1940	0.3052	36.54	13.25
Munger	436.93	600.70	0.1574	0.2547	35.63	44.20
Rohtas	407.11	440.40	0.1679	0.2053	34.62	62.11
Siwan	455.36	634.20	0.1798	0.2615	30.18	41.41
Purnea	495.49	815.30	0.2167	0.2431	29.04	8.55
Sheikpura	433.06	506.20	0.1908	0.1599	28.64	39.27
Sitamari	450.56	586.60	0.1699	0.2377	28.08	39.27
Gopalganj	444.96	645.70	0.1962	0.2829	27.36	28.56
Saharsa	586.10	938.90	0.2534	0.2299	21.05	1.40*
East Champaran	473.61	592.10	0.1629	0.2128	20.05	35.18
Supaul	543.28	502.60	0.1933	0.2159	20.00	35.30
Khagaria	495.17	617.00	0.1568	0.1496	16.72	3.98
Sheohar	483.77	603.80	0.1139	0.2300	14.79	32.51
Madhepura	563.01	509.30	0.1582	0.2703	7.68	37.10*

* Indicates estimates reported by Chaudhuri and Gupta (2009) with low reliability due to high root mean square errors in these estimates.
Note: MPCE is the monthly per capita consumption expenditure. The Head Count Ratio is calculated using Planning Commission determined poverty lines. The Lorenz ratio is computed for each state or district using state-specific MPCE percentile classes and not for all-India MPCE classes.
Source: Chaudhuri and Gupta (2009).

BIHAR: POST-2005

Figure 8.1 captures, in a very raw sense, the rapid pace of growth in per capita income in Bihar in the post-2005 period. While there have been annual fluctuations in the rate of growth, the period 2005–10 saw a compounded annual growth of 8.6% for Bihar that was significantly higher than the growth seen for India (7.04%) over the same period. This growth further accelerated over the period 2010–12 when Bihar registered compound annual growth rates in per capita income of almost 14%.

For a state that has been systematically growing well below the national average, this has been a significant change in the level of economic activity since 2005. Thus, as figure 8.7 graphically captures, this is a period when Bihar has begun catching up with the rest of the economy. This being said, it remains true that Bihar has much catching up to do and this will require sustaining high growth rates over a considerable period into the future. A number of authors have expressed concern about how real this growth has been and how sustainable this process is.

We present evidence that leads us to believe that while the growth process has been robust, there still remain certain concerns. One such concern relates to uneven growth at the level of the district.[5] In figure 8.10, we plot district specific box plots of district domestic products (DDP) to capture the heterogeneity across districts. Districts such as East Champaran, Vaishali, Madhubani, Begusarai, or Saharsa experience years in which DDP grows rapidly or contracts rapidly. However, there are also districts where fluctuations in DDP have been small or have not been sharply contracting. Table 8.7 captures the changes in the ranks of districts according to per capita income between 2001 and 2007. Ranks of a range of large districts such as Patna, Begusarai, Nalanda, Jehanabad, and Sheohar have remained unchanged. A number of remoter districts such as Jamui, Khagaria, and Sheikhpura have made significant gain in relative terms over this period. Finally, districts such as Madhubani and West Champaran have significantly lost out. Many of these districts also saw significant contractions in their economies due to floods and droughts over this time span.

Thus, a significant amount of heterogeneity and volatility exists in the growth process at the district level. Policies aimed at diversification of economic activities could help stabilize these fluctuations. Even then a qualitative difference between the growth process between pre- and post-Nitish Kumar periods exists. Simple calculations show that prior to Nitish Kumar, the chances of a high-growth district in a given year staying in high-growth

---

5. This was done in the appendix to Mukherji and Mukherji (2012). This paper is available online as http://www.nipfp.org.in/media/medialibrary/2013/04/WP_2012_107.pdf.

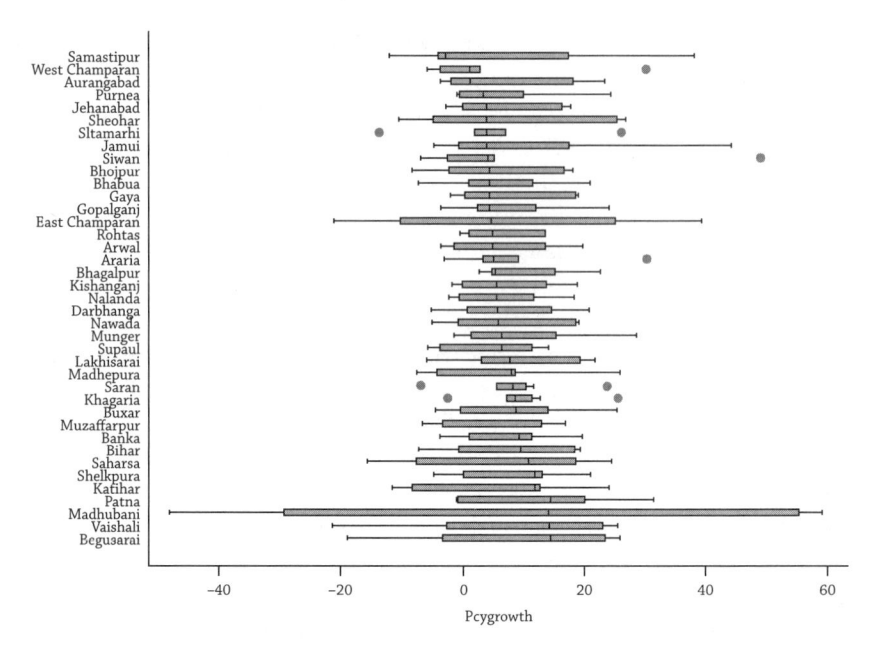

Figure 8.10: Box Plots for District Level Growth Rates, 2000/01 to 2007/08
Note: The box plots are sorted by median district growth rates.
Source: Department of Economics and Statistics, Government of Bihar.

regimes next year were almost nonexistent. In contrast, after Nitish Kumar became the Chief Minister, there were virtually no periods when growth was very low. Almost 77% of the districts with high growth in a given year continued in the high-growth zone the next year.

In terms of sectoral growth, it is also clear that the post-2005 period saw acceleration in each sector within India. While the construction sector maintained its high levels of growth in Bihar, agriculture, industry, and services, each grew faster in the post-2005 period. Thus, not only was the economy growing faster, but each of its key sectors was also growing faster in the post-2005 period. While construction as a sub-sector was clearly the fastest growing, the services sector, the largest contributor to income in Bihar, was also growing at a compound annual growth rate of 11.9%.

With almost 60% of NSDP coming from the services sector, we disaggregate this service sector into its various components in table 8.8 In sheer levels, the most important services sector for Bihar is Trade, Hotels, and Restaurants contributing about 27.3% of NSDP in 2010. Other Services, capturing professional incomes of lawyers, doctors, and income from teaching in nongovernmental educational establishments (including tuition centers) also remain important. The fastest growth within this sector has been in the Communications sub-sector establishing the importance of a nascent ITE&S sector in Bihar as well.

Table 8.7. CHANGES IN RELATIVE PERFORMANCE OF DISTRICTS IN POST-BIFURCATION BIHAR

District	PCY (2001)	PCY (2007)	2001 Ranks	2007 Ranks	Difference in Ranks
Jamui	4,600.000	7,975.000	35	17	18
Khagaria	5,226.563	9,013.423	23	9	14
Lakhisarai	5,587.500	9,108.696	16	8	8
Sheikpura	4,660.377	7,559.322	34	26	8
Buxar	5,442.857	8,696.202	19	12	7
Araria	4,310.185	6,778.656	38	32	6
Saran	4,824.615	7,575.342	28	23	5
Darbhanga	5,421.212	7,983.607	20	16	4
Banka	4,366.459	6,767.567	37	33	4
Bihar	6,680.000	10,435.420	7	5	2
Gopalganj	5,060.465	7,619.247	24	22	2
Vaishali	4,926.470	7,566.456	26	24	2
Siwan	4,752.768	7,330.065	31	29	2
Nawada	4,751.381	7,078.432	32	30	2
Gaya	5,858.790	8,854.637	12	11	1
Patna	24,919.490	49,831.140	1	1	0
Munger	9,263.158	15,543.310	2	2	0
Begusarai	8,102.127	12,974.070	3	3	0
Bhagalpur	7,260.331	12,252.710	4	4	0
Nalanda	5,641.350	8,052.631	15	15	0
Jehanabad	5,391.305	7,701.923	21	21	0
Sheohar	3,884.615	5,666.667	39	39	0
Rohtas	6,902.041	9,789.091	5	6	−1
Muzaffarpur	6,850.667	9,642.856	6	7	−1
Arwal	4,779.661	6,800.000	30	31	−1
East Champaran	4,500.000	6,089.324	36	37	−1
Bhojpur	6,629.464	8,869.047	8	10	−2
Aurangabad	5,542.289	7,843.478	17	19	−2
Purnea	5,468.504	7,722.973	18	20	−2
Kishanganj	5,030.769	7,414.474	25	27	−2
Saharsa	5,993.377	8,473.989	10	13	−3
Katihar	5,933.055	8,431.655	11	14	−3
Kaimur	5,736.434	7,885.135	13	18	−5
Madhepura	4,823.529	6,675.978	29	34	−5
Sitamarhi	4,723.881	6,077.419	33	38	−5
Supaul	4,919.075	6,417.91	27	35	−8
Samastipur	5,716.814	7,401.028	14	28	−14
Madhubani	5,321.229	6,132.029	22	36	−14
West Champaran	6,065.790	7,562.146	9	25	−16

Table 8.8. STRUCTURE OF THE SERVICES SECTOR
(AS A PERCENTAGE OF NSDP)

Services Sub-Sector	2000/01	2005/06	2009/10
Trade, Hotels, and Restaurants	14.94	20.18	27.30
Other Services	14.25	14.17	10.20
Public Administration	7.09	6.59	5.34
Real Estate, Ownership of Dwellings, and Business Services	3.80	4.14	3.19
Banking and Insurance	3.46	3.87	4.69
Communication	1.37	2.84	4.76
Railways	3.01	2.35	2.14

Table 8.9. SECTORAL DISTRIBUTION OF WORKFORCE
(PER 1,000 WORKERS)

Year	Agriculture	Manufacturing	Construction	Services
2007/08	637	105	53	203
2004/05	638	111	46	202
1999/2000	672	101	35	191
1993/04	692	101	28	178
1987/88	686	108	33	167
1983	718	102	20	156
1977/78	733	100	15	150

Note: The original data reports gender and rural–urban disaggregated numbers; we use gender and urbanization ratios to construct table 8.9 from NSSO (2011).
Source: Authors' calculations using data in NSSO (2011).

The key issue for the economy, of course, remains that in spite of this growth much of the employment profile within Bihar remains largely rural, in the agricultural sector, and dominated by male participation. Table 8.9 captures the changing employment structure in Bihar from 1983 onward, while figure 8.11 disaggregates these numbers by region (rural and urban) and gender. While there has been a move away from agriculture over this two and half decade time frame, the changes are modest given the vast changes in the share of agriculture in NSDP in Bihar. Contrasting the employment structure in table 8.9 with the output structure figure 8.3 and figure 8.12 gives a sense of the extent of the imbalance between worker and output shares in Bihar.

As previously noted, population growth in Bihar is expected to remain high in the next decade, as a key determinant of the population growth rate is the total fertility rate. In a healthy population, the total fertility rate consistent with stable population over time is 2.1 children per woman. Data from the National Family Health Surveys (NFHS) shows that while the total fertility rate for women in India went down from 2.68 children per woman in

BIHAR'S ECONOMY (149)

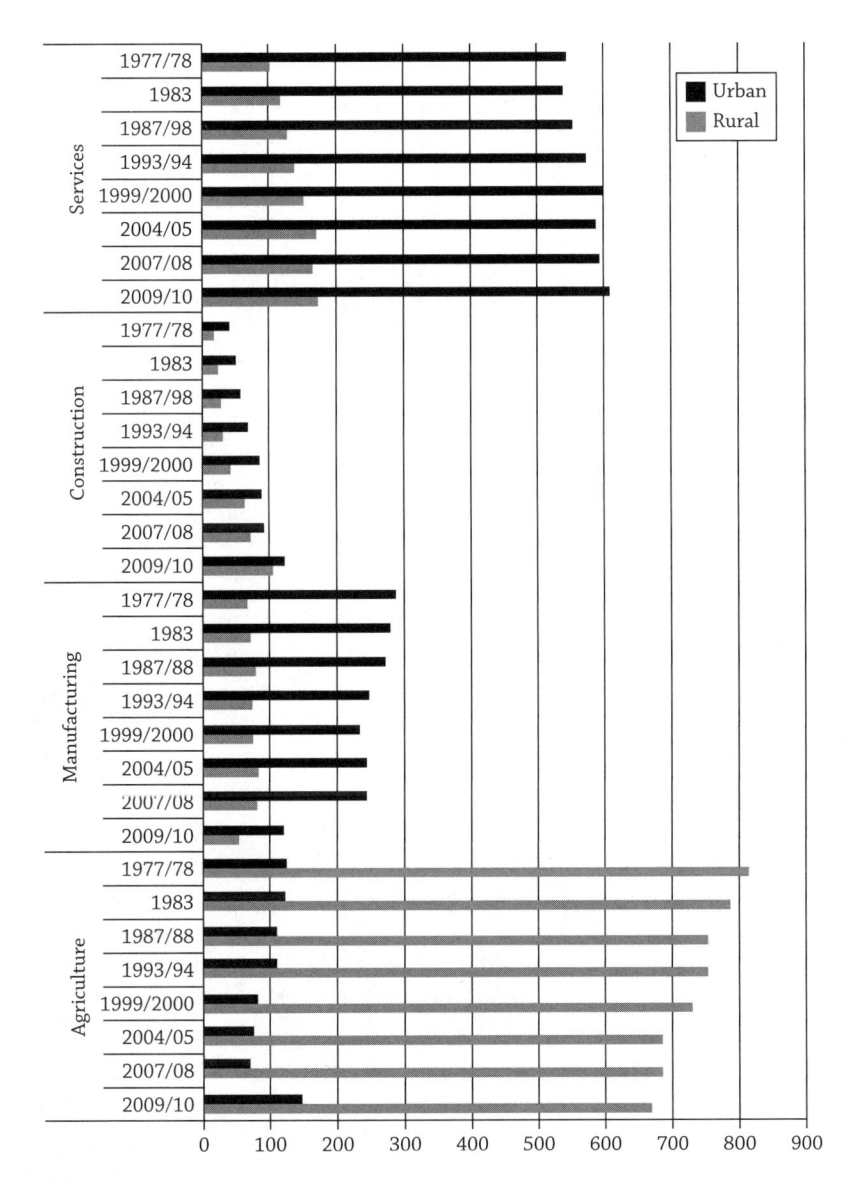

Figure 8.11: Labor Employment per 1,000 Workers in Bihar

1998/99 to 2.50 children per woman in 2005/06, in Bihar it went up from 3.7 to 4.0 children per woman over the same period. Among other states, Kerala and Tamil Nadu have a total fertility rate of 1.7 children per woman, Andhra Pradesh, Delhi, Himachal Pradesh, Maharashtra, Punjab, and West Bengal have 1.9 children per woman and Karnataka 2.0 children per woman. The fertility rate is still at 3.9 children per woman in Bihar and population projections suggest that Bihar will attain the replacement rate only by 2027—one of the slowest states to achieve it.

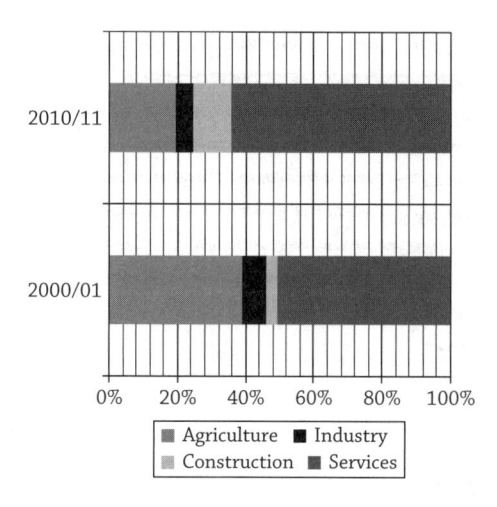

Figure 8.12: Composition of Output in Bihar, 2000/01 and 2010/11

There is a strong negative association between education and fertility rates. The NHFS-3 data shows that the fertility rate for women without education is about 4.6, while for those with 5–9 years of education, it is 3.2 children per woman; finally, for those with 10 or more years of education, it is 2.4 children per woman. Considerable evidence in favor of this inverse relationship is found in the demography literature from the late 1970s, and this only re-emphasizes the role of education in demographic transition. Thus, there are important complementarities between demographic structure and education.

One of the implications of Bihar's population growth rate and fertility rate is that Bihar's workforce is and will remain one of the younger workforces in the future. Projections of India's demographic dividend suggest that the working age ratio (i.e., the ratio of people working to those not working) began to increase in 2001 and will continue to do so until 2025–40 (Aiyar and Mody 2011). Bihar's working age ratio will continue to increase well past India's, as it will only hit the replacement rate in 2027. This gives Bihar a delayed demographic dividend and a window of opportunity to try to ensure that its workforce has the highest possible productivity when the demographic dividend unfolds. This has important implications for creating systems for savings, pensions, and planning for a future when a larger and larger proportion of the population is elderly and retired.

CONCLUDING REMARKS

In this chapter, we have performed two tasks: (1) we provided a brief sketch of the rich history of Bihar; and (2) we described in greater detail the evolution of the economy in its various aspects during the last 30 years spanning

1980/81 to 2009/10. In performing the first task, we have described rulers and empires that flourished and faded away with special emphasis on administration and governance. We saw that whenever governance was of a high order, the ruler prospered and the empire flourished; conversely, whenever governance weakened, the empire faltered and eventually disappeared.

In performing the second task, we have provided an overview of the Bihar's economy over the period 1980–2010, the period of main focus. We split this period into three distinct phases: the first 20 years is the first phase. The next 10 years are split into two phases of 5 years each. The first 20 years constitutes the pre-bifurcation Bihar. In 2000, the mineral-rich southern part of Bihar was carved out to create Jharkhand, while the remaining northern districts retained their identity as Bihar. We discussed how resource endowment and occupational and income structure altered due to this split. While there was a geographic bifurcation, the next five years (2000–2005) maintained continuity in political leadership, public policy, and in governance practices. In the last five years, on the contrary, while geographic continuity of the state was maintained with the previous five years, there were important political, governance, and policy changes, and these in turn were followed by a dramatic change in the indicators of the Bihar economy. It is this change that we study in chapter 10.

CHAPTER 9

What Went Wrong?

INTRODUCTION

Economic growth and development, like other dynamic processes, are intrinsically nonlinear in nature. Nonlinearity for any indicator implies that if we plot it over time, it need not necessarily exhibit a consistently rising or declining pattern; instead, it may rise during some periods and fall in others. Such processes often exhibit a "sensitive dependence to initial conditions" or hysteresis (Easterly et al. 1993; Quah 1993). Initial conditions frequently determine the course of the entire trajectory and slight deviations in the past can lead to great divergence later on. Bihar's progress or the lack of it, even relative to the rest of the country, may be traced not only to policies in place in the recent past but also to those from the distant past that led to unique "initial conditions" at the time of its formation and after independence.[1]

The intended and unintended consequences of several policies existing over decades, some over centuries, led to systemic disadvantages for Bihar for economic development and wealth accumulation. Such policies can be traced to a number of negative consequences for Bihar's economic potential. With many of these disadvantages persisting over long periods of time, we argue that they have collectively hampered progress in Bihar relative to the rest of the country, and more important, continue to do so even today. The policies that we worry about most are:

1. The *Zamindari* System and the Permanent Settlement of 1793.
2. The stepmotherly treatment meted out to Bihar by the Central Administration during the British Rule as well as during the Plan periods after independence.

---

1. Tripathy (2007) explains this as follows: "To those who grew up in Bihar in the 1960s and 1970s, it remains puzzling how things could have gotten *this* bad. Is it entirely because of neglect or is there an element of wilfulness to Bihar's decay?" This section argues that there was both ample neglect and willful omission in Bihar—not only in the recent past but also in colonial times.

3. The Freight Equalization Policy of 1948.
4. The unwritten policy of non-performance during the 1990–2005 period.

Apart from the disadvantages arising from the policies mentioned above, Bihar's economy has historically been faced with a number of challenges—the loss of resources from bifurcation, repeated flooding, and Naxal insurgency, to name a few. In fact, the state government has been attempting to negotiate a "special category" status with the central government to access central government and other funds on more favorable terms, citing challenges such as the Kosi floods. While there may remain ambiguities about whether Bihar merits support under the "special category" status, usually reserved for states with hilly and difficult terrain and low levels of infrastructure, there is little doubt that Bihar has faced significant barriers to growth. Two key factors that made these barriers insurmountable were the lack of support from the central government in both pre- and post-independence era and the lack of leadership in the state itself. The latter factor meant that the meagre resources available for relief and rehabilitation were often wasted and Bihar frequently performed not only far below its potential but also far below what was required for it to catch up.

PERMANENT SETTLEMENT

As the East India Company's, and later the British Raj's, trade and commerce expanded, it required a large amount of capital, of which there was a perennial dearth (Ghosh 2007). In due course, the Company came to realize that a possible source of financing for its administration in India as well as enhancing its trade was the agricultural revenues generated within India. In 1765, the East India Company's revenue inflow was made secure through access to land revenues from the Bengal Presidency.[2] This revenue was used to fund commercial activity and to support two other Presidencies within India (Madras and Bombay); it is said that this revenue was used even to buttress the Company's treasury in Canton! The larger the amount of land revenue collected, the greater would be the amount that was available to finance trade. Hence, there was always inherent pressure on the Company to increase

---

2. The Bengal Presidency is a reference to a colonial administrative unit that originally contained today's Bangladesh, Assam, Meghalaya, Tripura, Orissa, Bihar, and Jharkhand. In 1874, Assam was split from the Bengal Presidency, and later in 1912, Bihar and Orissa were separated too. Bihar further split into Bihar and Jharkhand in 2000. Thus, a discussion of long persistent challenges for Bihar requires a discussion of the Bengal Presidency, as it too suffered from a systematic policy of exploitation in comparison with other administrative units with better institutions for land revenue collection (Banerjee and Iyer 2005).

land revenues in India. In fact, from 1765 to 1793, the demand for revenue to finance the Company's various activities almost doubled (Kumar 1982).

A key challenge for the East India Company was that such revenue creation was vastly decentralized. There was an obvious need for a mechanism that would concentrate revenues and funnel them into administrative coffers through an easy-to-monitor institutional arrangement. The British East India Company eventually consolidated revenue collection by turning to the *zamindars* who were already collecting revenue from peasants for either the Mughal Empire or for independent kingdoms. By making the *zamindars* pay revenues for the right to collect revenues from their tracts of land, the British overcame the revenue aggregation problem. Thus, greater and greater amounts of land revenue were extracted from the Bengal Presidency. However, it soon became apparent that there was a declining trend in agricultural production in India and, therefore, a declining trend in revenue collection.

Lord Cornwallis saw the declining agricultural productivity as a serious threat to revenue collection and, in response, implemented the Permanent Settlement Act of 1793. Under this act, the tax revenues were fixed in perpetuity for each *zamindar* at 90% of his collections for 1793. Fixing the rent was meant as an incentive for *zamindars* to invest in land, as there would be no further increase in rent beyond the amount settled on in 1793 (Chaudhuri 1982). It would also stabilize the Company's revenue, which would no longer be subject to the vagaries of rainfall, flood, or drought—in short, the vagaries of agricultural conditions. If this fixing of the rent had worked, taxation would have been simpler and more transparent, requiring less overseeing and administration.

Unfortunately for Cornwallis, nothing of the sort actually happened; although the rent was to decline from the excruciating 90% of the 1793 level to about 28% by the end of the eighteenth century, few farmers were prompted to invest in land. Chaudhuri (1982) argues that, on the contrary, the very high rental rates made *zamindars* demand higher and higher rents from the tillers of the land; at times, the *zamindars* could not meet the requirements placed on them and even defaulted.[3] Thus, there were changes in the land ownership pattern, with some *zamindars* increasing their holdings; many of those with increased holdings were, in fact, not originally farmers but acquired large estates, as land became a more important asset under the Permanent Settlement. The Permanent Settlement, paradoxically, did not stop land taxes from increasing as the East India Company secured increases in it from time to time. The estates of defaulting *zamindars* were transferred to the government. An interesting point to note regarding incentives comes

---

3. See Ghosh (2007), for example, for a discussion of the consequences of the Permanent Settlement Act giving little incentive to the tiller to invest in agricultural land. In this connection see Banerjee and Iyer (2005) and earlier references to the same.

from huge wastelands in the transferred *zamindari* estates, which had not been included while considering the Permanent Settlement. These now became profitable with the spread of cultivation as they were rent-free, and soon there was a property market with escalating land prices. In principle, the income from the rent-free lands was to be spent on public account, to establish or support facilities such as temples, mosques, and educational institutes. In Patna district, between 1790 and 1870, the revenue from the rent-free lands increased by as much as 48% (Chaudhuri 1982). However, outside of these rent-free lands, the bulk of agricultural land continued to remain under Permanent Settlement.

Thus, delinking the amount of revenue from the actual output, which was one of the main features of the Permanent Settlement, was the undoing of Cornwallis's intentions; for years, the Permanent Settlement areas of the Bengal Presidency saw no investment by *zamindars* or farmers in improving the productivity of land. Agricultural output fell, and to meet rental obligations, the cultivation of cash crops such as indigo was encouraged. In Bihar, a single crop was generally produced; thus, any shock arising from either inclement weather or crop failure allowed a very limited chance of recovery. The impoverishment of farmers and tillers continued throughout; small landowners sold out, farm labor became indentured, and the dismal situation of the already poor was made worse. More important, since wages or rewards were unrelated to output, the work culture was destroyed in the Permanent Settlement areas: there was no incentive to work hard and even the spirit of entrepreneurship was dampened. As a result of the efforts of the Zamindars in extracting the maximum possible out of the farmer incentives for agriculture investment decayed; Banerjee and Iyer (2005) document lower agricultural investment and agricultural yields, and lower attainments in health and educational outcomes in areas under Permanent Settlement compared to other areas.

That the Permanent Settlement itself was detrimental was understood all around; one of the government's earliest post-independence acts, undertaken by state governments, was to abolish the *Zamindari* system. Bihar was among the first states to enact such legislation, abolishing the *Zamindari* system as early as 1947. The problem seems to have been in the implementation of the act, since the parties concerned with implementation were also those who would be adversely affected. Some argue that the *Zamindari* system was never really eliminated in Bihar, in the sense that large landowners continued to wield enormous power and influence till well after independence.[4]

---

4. See Sharma (2005) for a discussion of how the failure of land reforms continues to plague Bihar with agrarian relations rigidly locked within the ex-*zamindar* class; this continues to hamper agriculture and the economy in Bihar.

The problem that the *Zamindari* system created for the Eastern region can be best understood by looking at what transpired in other parts of the subcontinent, where this system was not in vogue.[5] In particular the differences across provinces in terms of tax burdens and the quality of public services were considerable. These differences never reduced since "precedent was followed rather than any principle" (Kumar 1982: 909). The main source of the differences in taxation and public services was the differences in the land revenue systems. While the *Zamindari* system prevailed in the Eastern region, the *Ryotwari* system was followed in the Madras Presidency and later in the Bombay Presidency. The *Ryotwari* system determined the revenue in relationship to agricultural output; this had to be carefully estimated, and the government had an incentive to ensure that agricultural productivity increased. Consequently, there was a greater concentration of administrative efforts in the *Ryotwari* areas, leading to an advantageous position for them vis-á-vis the Permanent Settlement areas. As a result, for example, the per capita expenditure of the government on items such as health, education, or infrastructure was much higher for the Bombay Presidency than for the others, and Bihar and Orissa, in contrast, spent much less.

It would, thus, appear that the tenure system chosen by the British continues to cast a long shadow on aspects of life in these regions even today. To some extent, the gap between former *Ryotwari* and former *Zamindari* areas has been narrowed in regions where land reforms have been effective, but wherever this is not the case,[6] the tiller is faced with perverse incentives, and differences in economic outcomes continue to persist.

STATE FINANCES

We know that public (or government) expenditure plays an important role in determining national income and therefore the size of the economy. Equally important, depending on the pattern of expenditure, it can also be used as a policy tool to stabilize and accelerate growth, encourage private economic activity, and enhance equity within the economy. Transfers made by the British government in India prior to independence and under various norms by the central government post-independence have largely defined the size

---

5. Banerjee and Iyer (2005) argue that the choice of tenurial system followed in particular regions was determined by the period in which they were conquered. They suggest that since in independent India, there is no agricultural income tax, the choice of tenurial system 150 years ago continues to affect the regions in question. The tenurial system also affected the social state at the time of independence, since areas with *zamindars* had an elite class that was absent in other areas and created inequalities of a type absent in other places.

6. And in Bihar land reforms were not undertaken in any meaningful way.

of Bihar's public expenditure. Rao (2009: 145) argues that in an economy with significant differences in institutions and resource endowments, the transfers are important for balanced and cohesive development; he goes on to add that the transfers may not be adequate for the purpose. We discuss the implications of these for Bihar's economy in this section.

Pre-Independence Concerns

Prior to independence, the British government in India set governance goals and the patterns of public expenditure were largely geared to support it. Kumar (1982) and Rao and Singh (2005) (see chapter 3) note that while the fiscal system was highly centralized till the 1870s, it evolved into a decentralized one following the Government of India Acts of 1919 and 1935. This change was possible due to (1) the emerging conflict among provincial governors over financial powers, much like the debates associated with the awards of each Finance Commission today; and (2) the political opposition to British rule, which implied increasing financial devolution to the provinces. Tax revenue allocation accruing to a province was not based on any uniform norms; thus, in 1887, we find that Bombay received 60% of all its land revenue, a key revenue source, while Bengal (including Bihar) and Madras received only 32% and 29%, respectively, and the relative poverty of Bihar and Orissa was apparent only after they were formed in 1912.

The Memorandum for the Indian Statutory Commission (1930) on the *Working of the Reforms in Bihar and Orissa* noted that the standard expenditure in Bihar and Orissa, worked out on the basis of actual expenditure prior to 1912, came to just 800,000 rupees per million of the population against 1.3 million rupees per million of the population in Bengal. It must be noted that the expenditure on administration in Bengal itself was the lowest in British India, in contrast to the Bombay or Madras Presidencies; and within this hierarchy of low expenditure, Bihar was accorded the lowest priority. Similarly, as Ghosh (2007) notes, citing the original 1930 report, while there was one police officer for every 776 individuals in the Bombay Presidency, in Bihar (and Orissa) there was one police officer for every 2,372 individuals.

This led to a relative deficit of institutional capacity for governance in Bihar, as compared to the other states of India, during the colonial period. Kumar (1982) argues that over time, these initial differences were reinforced and even magnified as precedent was followed in allocating revenue to states, leading to "rough inequality" that was far from any nominal notion of equality for states such as Bihar.

Table 9.1 succinctly presents the provincial distribution of public expenditure under key heads and shows the historic scarcity in public expenditures for Bihar in pre-independence India. In 1876/77, when Bihar and Orissa

Table 9.1. PER CAPITA EXPENDITURE ON KEY SERVICES IN PROVINCES OF BRITISH INDIA

Province	General Administration		Education		Health	
	1876/77	1927/28	1876/77	1927/28	1876/77	1927/28
Bombay	374	411	325	345	285	141
Central	185	169	197	131	142	53
Madras	159	193	112	166	139	98
Punjab	244	103	145	199	135	126
United	140	103	110	123	78	51
Bengal	100	100	100	100	100	100
Assam	159	136	117	120	82	121
Burma	470	292	295	276	260	201
Bihar and Orissa	—	75	—	83	—	51

Notes: (1) Expenditure on Bengal is taken as the base for all years (Bengal = 100 by construction); and (2) Bihar and Orissa were a part of the Bengal Presidency in 1876/77.
Source: Gyan Chand, *The Essentials of Federal Finance* (Madras, 1930), cited by Kumar (1982).

were a part of the Bengal Presidency, the lowest expenditure on General Administration and Education was in Bengal. Expenditures in the Health domain are distributed differently, with the United Provinces and Assam seeing lower expenditure than Bihar, but these three are together the lowest in the Health domain in 1876/77. By 1927/28, Bihar and Orissa had been separated from Bengal and clearly had access to the least financial support for developing public services in each domain. While this is unequivocal for both General Administration and Education, the pattern is different for Health, with a few other states' (United Provinces and Central Provinces) expenditures on Health almost as low as Bihar's.

Post-Independence Concerns: The Plan Period

Unfortunately for Bihar, even after independence, the pattern of poor allocation of public resources continued; this raises serious questions about political processes that were then in operation. After 1947, the union–state relationship in India was codified under the Constitution of India.[7] In contrast to the systematic allocation of responsibilities to the union and states, the financing and assistance given by the union central government

---

7. Details of this are available under the Central List, the State List, and the Concurrent List in the 7th Schedule of the Constitution.

over the first three plans were ad hoc and based on the needs of ongoing schemes, many of which were initiated by the union government (Planning Commission1997). In fact, much of the distribution of resources continued in line with the same sharing norms that existed before independence; the colonial past institutionalized inequality and uneven regional development, and the immediate post-independence period only accentuated it further, much to the detriment of Bihar (Kumar 1982; Ghosh 2007).

Three distinct channels of transfers exist in India: the Finance Commission, a constitutional body, recommends the sharing of central tax receipts between the center and states and among the states inter se, and grants for non-plan purposes; the Planning Commission directly gives funds to support developmental plans, all loans in this category having been discontinued since 2005/06 after the recommendations of the Twelfth Finance Commission, and finally, different central ministries give grants to their state counterparts to support various central sector and centrally sponsored schemes. Both the Finance Commission and the Planning Commission transfers are formula based and allow for little discretion, while the Ministry-specific transfers tend to be determined within the Ministry and thus, are more discretionary. Rao (2009: 152) documents that while transfers have been increasing over time, fraction of transfers through formula-based channels such as the Finance Commission and the Planning Commission have been declining while the discretionary transfers have been rising. More recent data from the Thirteenth Finance Commission suggests that these discretionary transfers may be declining, even though they still constitute above 30% of all transfers to the states (Thirteenth Finance Commission 2009: ch. 4, para. 4.54, p. 60). While this in itself is not problematic, the discretionary funding allows for the possibility of large disparities in inter-state transfers across states. Rao and Singh (2005) and Rao (2009) discuss the differential role that each of these channels of inter-state transfer plays in equalizing access to resources and in promoting development expenditures. They argue that while the Finance Commission transfers tend to have a strong equalizing effect, while the transfers from discretionary sources as well as for state plan schemes do not help balance fiscal abilities across states.

How do these discretionary transfers work? Discretion favors political alignment. Kletzer and Singh (1997) provide an analytical framework for fiscal federalism, within which they examine the opportunistic behavior of state governments that has led to discretionary transfers increasing as a proportion of total revenue. Assuming uniform lobbying abilities across states, such an increase in discretionary transfers is, in principle, fair. However, this assumption was far from accurate, particularly when parties in power at the center varied from those in the state, as was the case during and after the 1990s. Rao and Singh (2005: ch. 11) present a model of political influence of inter-state transfers, and they also summarize a set of papers, including their own work, that documents the negative effects of political influence on the balancing nature of inter-state transfers.

Guruswamy (2007) documents the nature of inequality in access to funds that such discretionary schemes have generated by comparing funds allocated under various Plans for Bihar with those for Punjab. Punjab's per capita income tends to be about five times greater than that of Bihar, and Guruswamy (2007) explains this in terms of differential public investment in these two states. Using data reproduced in table 9.2, he argues that Punjab systematically got more than the national average for public investment while Bihar received progressively less than the national average over various Plans. It is estimated that there is a total deficit of 771.61 billion rupees over time in what Bihar should have received. This does not even factor in the sort of benefits that the state of Punjab would have got through subsidies for its overwhelming use of fertilizer and electricity for agriculture and benefits from the Bhakra Nangal dam. These numbers are merely indicative and suggest that there has been gross oversight in providing resources to Bihar.[8] Arulampalam et al. (2009), using data for 1974/75 to 1996/97, estimate that a state that was politically aligned with the central government and also a swing state was likely to receive 16% greater inter-state transfers than states which are not aligned and are not swing states.

Finally, Biswas et al. (2010) also contribute to this debate by constructing some interesting measures of political lobbying in attempting to identify the causal effect of political lobbying on central government assistance. While they control for a number of observable and unobservable sources of bias in a panel regression context, one of their key innovations is the construction of measures for both lobbying and central government assistance (which we reproduce in table 9.3). It is interesting to note that while Bihar ranks sixth from the top in terms of engaging in lobbying activities, it ranks the lowest in terms of the central assistance index developed by these authors. In no other state is the disparity between effort and money disbursement so great, suggesting that there were rigidities in transfers that Bihar simply could not negotiate.

While this literature provides evidence to suggest that political lobbying plays an important role in determining inter-state finances, it is also the case that cumulatively, across the three channels, the volume of inter-state transfers for each poor state tends to be larger than richer states.[9] However, these

---

8. Particularly pertinent in this connection is the piece, "A Bend in the River," in N. K. Singh (2009: 58–60), which documents how the permanent solution to the flooding from Kosi was sought as early as 1956; experts had suggested building of a high dam in Nepal with a barrage downstream; the suggestion was shelved in favor of a temporary solution of building a barrage in Nepal; during the same time the Bhakra-Nangal project was taken up for implementation. Although during this period Bihar was politically aligned it was not a swing state and thus, taken for granted.

9. Rao and Mandal (2009) report that Bihar received 982 rupees per capita in central transfers in 2002/03. That year, the average per capita central transfers for richer states was 816 rupees. In their comprehensive study of the larger Indian states, Panagariya et al. (2014: ch. 4) provide a detailed up-to-date analysis of the role the inter-state transfers and own revenues play in determining the development expenditures of different states.

Table 9.2. CENTRALLY PLANNED INEQUALITY—PUNJAB AND BIHAR

Five Year Plan	I. Actual Plan Allocation Punjab	I. Actual Plan Allocation Bihar	II. Projected Plan Allocation Punjab	II. Projected Plan Allocation Bihar	Gap between I and II Punjab	Gap between I and II Bihar
First FYP 1951–56	124.00	104.00	52.71	423.22	71.29	(−)318.82
Second FYP 1956–61	1,263.00	194.20	110.37	465.40	1,152.63	(−)271.20
Third FYP 1961–66	231.40	337.04	189.53	793.08	41.86	(−)456.04
Fourth FYP 1969–74	293.60	531.28	371.60	1,703.61	(−)78.04	(−)1,172.33
Fifth FYP 1974–79	220.80	368.67	655.84	2,732.92	(−)434.97	(−)2,364.25
Sixth FYP 1980–85	1,957.00	3,225.00	2,492.91	10,374.40	(−)535.91	(−)7,149.40
Seventh FYP 1985–90	3,285.00	5,100.00	4,108.92	18,777.12	(−)823.92	(−)13,677.10
Eighth FYP 1992–97	6,570.00	13,000.00	4,373.63	18,609.38	2,196.37	(−)5,609.38
Ninth FYP 1997–2002	11,500.00	16,680.00	8,288.61	36,850.72	3,211.39	(−)20,170.70
Tenth FYP 2002–07	18,657.00	21,000.00	13,715.51	46,972.25	4,941.49	(−)25,972.30
TOTAL	44,101.80	60,540.59	34,359.63	137,702.10	9,742.19	(−)77,161.50

Source: Guruswamy (2007).

Table 9.3. MONEY DISBURSEMENT AND LOBBYING FOR CENTRAL ASSISTANCE

States	Money Disbursement Index	Average Lobbying Index
Punjab	1	3
Haryana	2	1
Orissa	3	7
Rajasthan	4	5
Gujarat	5	9
Kerala	6	12
Karnataka	7	2
Uttar Pradesh	8	4
Andhra Pradesh	9	8
Madhya Pradesh	10	11
Tamil Nadu	11	13
West Bengal	12	14
Maharashtra	13	10
Bihar	14	6

Note: Money Disbursement Index for state *j* in year *t* was calculated as $(mjt/\Sigma jmjt)/populationjt$, where *mjt* is the amount of money disbursed to a state under the discretionary head in state *s* and year *t*. The Political Lobbying Index is calculated as $(hjt/\Sigma jhjt)/populationjt$, where *hjt* is the total representation of the *jth* state in the council of ministers in time period *t*.
Source: Working paper version of Biswas et al. (2010), available online at http://www.csh-delhi.com/team/downloads/publiperso/state_lobbying_at_the_centre_and_discretionary_finance_in_india.pdf (accessed October 15, 2011).

transfers are too low to adjust for the differential ability of poorer states to raise revenues from their own sources.[10] With aggregate receipts being determined by both central transfers and revenues from each state's own sources, aggregate public expenditure under development heads and total expenditure in Bihar tends to be far lower than in the richer states. The magnitude of these differences is disturbingly large; per capita own revenues for Bihar

10. In an important contribution, Bagchi and Chakraborty (2004) consider among other things, Actual Statutory Transfers during the Tenth and Eleventh Finance Commission recommendations and report it as a percentage of the Normative Statutory Transfers (see their table 6); the figures for Bihar are 48.7% during the Tenth Finance Commission and 47.76% during the Eleventh. Normative Statutory transfers are defined to be central transfers "which would help bridge both horizontal and vertical imbalances in the system to a reasonable extent." Clearly for the case of Bihar, bridging the gap even to reasonable extent has not been possible.

tend to between one-seventh and one-tenth of the average for high-income states. This has led to large and systematic differences in per capita development expenditures that Bihar has been able to make; per capita total expenditures in Bihar are almost half the national average. Figure 10.1 presents a time series of the ratio of per capita development expenditure for Bihar and all-India. At less than 50% of the national per capita development expenditure, the average the standards of public service and the ability to encourage economic activity must necessarily be far poorer in Bihar. Economist Amaresh Bagchi submitted the following dissenting note to the report of the Eleventh Finance Commission:

> [I]n Bihar the per capita NPRE (excluding interests and pensions) for the year 2000–01 works out to be less than 60 per cent of the average for the general category States. Similar is the case with a few other low income States. Even with the State's share in Central taxes recommended by the Commission, the per capita revenue capacity of Bihar remains well below the group average for the year 2000–01. Paradoxically, Bihar does not get any non-Plan revenue deficit grant although its revenue capacity, even after it is augmented by statutory transfers, that is to say its revenue availability in the non-plan account falls significantly below the national average.[11]

Even more worryingly, Chakraborty (2011) shows that while the recommended targets for managing fiscal deficits and other targets for fiscal consolidation remain attainable for Bihar, they also imply a substantial contraction in developmental expenditure, as this remains one of the few places where cutbacks can be made. Such policy-induced cuts in development expenditure will restrict the growth potential for Bihar even further.

THE FREIGHT EQUALIZATION POLICY

The Freight Equalization Policy (FEP) was set in place in 1948 and was finally withdrawn in 1991. Under this policy, basic raw materials like steel and coal, abundantly available in Bihar prior to bifurcation, were made available at the same price across the entire country to encourage development countrywide (Rao 2009: 149). This meant that these raw materials in Bihar and Punjab or Maharashtra cost the same. The policy nullified the comparative advantage of mineral-rich poorer states in industrialization by implicitly subsidizing the cost of transporting raw materials to developed states at the expense of the mineral-rich but extremely poor states like Bihar. As the country itself

---

11. Quoted from a Ministry of Finance, Government of Bihar document that was the basis of a state presentation made to the Thirteenth Finance Commission.

followed inward-looking import-substituting industrialization policy, competitiveness was not a consideration in calibrating the policy.

The asymmetry was acute, since there were no reciprocal benefits in terms of either industrial or agricultural goods and services that Bihar might have needed but did not have. There was no parallel industrial incentive given for capital to enter Bihar either. In the process, for a period slightly longer than four decades, the policy environment directly hurt industrialization and growth possibilities in Bihar and other mineral-rich states and created the paradox of a mineral-rich state also being among the poorest in incomes. This policy continued till 1991 when it was repealed.[12]

Once one accounts for the gains reaped elsewhere through forward and backward linkages associated with industrialization and manufacturing, the cumulative losses that Bihar experienced appear dramatically large, even though there are no estimates of them available. Even after the withdrawal of the FEP, the industrial agglomeration bias continued; no significant policy was introduced at the national level to reverse decades of discrimination against Bihar that denied it the right to build up its "dynamic comparative advantage" during the era of licensing and controls. Thus, even in the post-liberalization era, the gap between Bihar's manufacturing capacity and that of other states continue to further widen, particularly, after the mineral-rich south of Bihar bifurcated to form Jharkhand. Apart from direct losses, this vicious cycle of "low investment, low growth" within which Bihar had to function also limited its internal resource-raising capacity. As we saw in the earlier section, this systematic inability to raise its own tax revenues has so severely affected Bihar that the current inter-state transfer system is unable to address this.

GOVERNANCE FAILURE BY DESIGN

Glaeser and Shleifer (2005) argue that James Michael Curly, four-time mayor of Boston, deliberately used public redistribution to favor his constituents and, at the same time, used incendiary rhetoric to encourage the rich to leave the city. This not only consolidated his support base but also led to significant economic stagnation in the city of Boston. Thus, deliberately failing economically may well be the strategy of a leader who seeks to consolidate his political position. Bihar's experience, Mathew and Moore (2011) argue, is a similar case of "state incapacity by design," where the ruling establishment under Lalu Prasad and his party the Rashtriya Janata Dal (RJD) deliberately limited government presence through reduced hiring and expenditures in an attempt to

---

12. The repeal of the law has created additional losses for industries that are now no longer cost-competitive in the absence of state-subsidized raw materials. For anecdotal evidence on losses in Batala, Punjab, see a report by Dhaliwal (2010).

ensure that upper castes did not benefit. Such a strategy also had value when looked at through the lens of electoral politics, as it enabled the crystallization of a number of poorer and historically oppressed groups into vote banks that would see Lalu Prasad as their champion. Mathew and Moore write,

> Such was the scale of poverty among this core electoral coalition that Yadav had limited prospects of maintaining its cohesion and allegiance through the normal processes of promising "development" and using networks of political patronage to distribute material resources to supporters. More important, that strategy would have involved a high level of dependence on the government apparatus, that was dominated by people from a number of historically-dominant upper castes.

Lalu Prasad apparently preferred to mobilize his supporters on the basis of continual confrontation with the historically oppressive elite. Thus, he kept public sector jobs vacant rather than appoint qualified people, who were often from the upper castes. Attempts to micro-manage the state apparatus from the Chief Minister's office were aimed at ensuring that state benefits did not accrue to the upper castes. He denuded the public service of staff and education and health sectors the much-needed teachers and health workers. Not surprisingly, the system did not deliver "development." It is reported that the Bihar government sacrificed large potential fiscal transfers from the government of India designed for anti-poverty programs because it was unable to complete the relevant bureaucratic procedures.[13] Thus, it would appear that Lalu Prasad knowingly undermined the capacity of the state apparatus. While the sheer size of the government and economy of Bihar dwarfs the city of Boston, the consequences of deliberately distorting government capacity had a not too dissimilar outcome in terms of political consolidation and economic degeneration.

CONCLUDING REMARKS

In this chapter, we asked the question where things went wrong for the state of Bihar. We proposed four distinct and complementary public policies that

---

13. See, for example, Mathew and More (2011: section 3). They write: "Bihar has the country's lowest utilisation rate for centrally funded programs, and it is estimated that the state forfeited one-fifth of central plan assistance during 1997–2000. . . . The state's Annual Plan expenditure was revised downwards in the course of every year between 1992/3 and 2004/5, sometimes radically. . . . Between 1997 and 2006, of the 96 billion rupees allocated to Bihar by the Central government in Delhi, over 22 billion rupees could not be drawn and, of the money received, only 64 percent could be spent."

had long-lasting negative impacts on Bihar's growth potential. First and foremost among them was the land revenue system known as the Permanent Settlement. This system of land revenue is what the British adopted during the colonial period for much of Eastern India including Bihar. It robbed the region of almost any incentives to make improvements to the land or otherwise increase agricultural productivity. The second factor was the systematic neglect of the Bihar region from colonial times to the present day in terms of provision of public goods. The third impediment was a set of policies adopted by the central government since independence that went against the interests of Bihar. And finally, the set of policies followed within Bihar and the nature of leadership in Bihar for a fairly long spell, until 2005, has been found to be significantly wanting; in some instances such failure even appears to have been a deliberately planned one.

CHAPTER 10

What Changed?

INTRODUCTION

The process of identifying determinants of growth has a rich history with successive authors offering a large number of competing variables as candidates. Hirschman, in his classic 1958 book, begins by noting that one discouraging result of economic development has been an ever-lengthening list of factors, conditions, obstacles, and prerequisites for growth, all broadly labeled determinants of growth. In Bihar's case these determinants can be broadly classified into those related to political changes and key changes in governance and public service delivery by the state government. As a result of these changes, a number of social and human indicators have changed in the period after 2005.

POLITICS: A TALE OF TWO LEADERS

A number of events in the late 1990s were responsible for not only ebbing political viability of the JD/RJD government in power but also for the creation of Jharkhand and the exit of the RJD from power in the 2005 elections.

After a humiliating defeat in 1977, the Congress Party returned to power in Bihar with a slim majority in one of the most violent elections in the history of the state. Toward the end of that year, B. P. Mandal, a Member of Parliament from Saharsa in North Bihar, who had chaired the Second Backward Classes Commission, submitted the commission's recommendations to Prime Minister Indira Gandhi recommending 27% reservation in all government jobs and educational institutions for the Other Backward Classes (OBCs). The Prime Minister decided not to act on these recommendations, as they went against the traditional voter base of the Congress: the upper castes, the Dalits (previously called the untouchables), and the Muslims. Bihar continued to be ruled by upper caste Chief Ministers hailing from Congress.

Throughout the 1980s, the Congress remained in power in Bihar. Although the office of the Chief Minister changed hands among nearly half a dozen Congress leaders in the state, they were all from the upper castes. In the 1990 election, Lalu Prasad, who had championed the cause of the OBC, unexpectedly won the election and became the Chief Minister.[1]

The subsequent story of Bihar is one of two friends, Lalu Prasad and Nitish Kumar, beginning their political careers together initially but parting ways eventually. Here we offer the broad contours of this fascinating story.[2] Lalu Prasad Yadav and Nitish Kumar were young leaders of the Lok Dal with Lalu Prasad having already won an election as a Member of Parliament in 1977. Nitish Kumar had less success winning elections in his early political career. His first victory came in 1985 when he won a seat in the Bihar Assembly. This was a bit unusual since a sympathy wave in favor of Congress, following the assassination of Prime Minister Indira Gandhi, had been sweeping the nation that year.

In the legislative assembly of 1985, the Lok Dal established itself as the largest party in the opposition with its leader Karpoori Thakur leading the opposition. Later, the Yadav community was to rise to a position of pre-eminence catapulting Lalu Prasad into the role of the leader of the opposition. At the Centre, V. P. Singh, a member of the Rajiv Gandhi cabinet, had been pursuing various corruption cases that allegedly involved many leaders and friends of the Congress including the Prime Minister himself. This fact led Rajiv Gandhi to push Singh out of his cabinet, which in turn led the latter to exit the Congress and mobilize various parties, including the Lok Dal, to form what came to be known as the Janata Dal. Singh was successful in winning enough seats in the 1989 parliamentary elections to form the government and become the Prime Minister. Nitish Kumar became a Member of Parliament that year and was appointed the Minister of State for Agriculture.

The differences between Nitish Kumar and Lalu Prasad, which had been brewing for some time, came out in the open when Singh decided to revive the Second Backward Classes Commission, popularly known as the Mandal Commission, and implement its recommendations. Nitish wanted the Bihar formula to be implemented whereby the EBC (Extremely Backward Classes) would be given a quota within the quota and the children of income-tax-paying other backward castes would be denied reservation.[3] Lalu Prasad wanted none of these restrictions favoring the recommendations of the Mandal Commission to be fully implemented without modification. Nitish Kumar first decided to go along despite his reservations, but some angry speeches from Lalu Prasad led to widening of the gulf between the two.

1. See Sinha (2011: 143) about the manner in which Nitish Kumar, as an observer appointed by the central government of the time, oversaw this process!
2. For a detailed account, see Sinha (2011: Part 1).
3. See Sinha (2011: 146) for details.

By January 1993, Nitish Kumar felt he was ready to make a move; in a meeting in the Gandhi Maidan in Patna, he publicly declared that if the Bihar formula proposed by Karpoori Thakur was not implemented, "we shall come out in the street and oppose it tooth and nail."[4] At this point, Lalu Prasad put aside his plans to bypass the Bihar formula. For the first time, it was felt that Lalu Prasad could be dislodged.

Nitish Kumar addressed a mammoth rally, once again in Gandhi Maidan in February 1994 and warned the powers in Delhi and Patna that neglect of the Kurmis would lead to disastrous consequences.[5] Himself a Kurmi, Nitish Kumar apparently did not wish to be seen as a mere leader of the Kurmis and had kept himself aloof from Kurmi causes but at this stage, he felt he had to take on the leadership of the Kurmis, since that gave him a handle against Lalu Prasad. But there were hardly any among the Janata Dal leadership who would support Nitish Kumar, and in April 1994 he left the party and together with George Fernandes and a few others formed Janata Dal (George). In October 1994, with the desertion of some more members of the Janata Dal, a new party called Samata Party came to replace the Janata Dal (George). The Assembly elections of 1995 were around the corner at the time and Samata Party wanted to make an impact. Nitish declared law and order as his topmost priority and resource mobilization as his second priority and presented a strong developmental platform in the campaign. Nitish Kumar and Lalu Prasad had distinct approaches. As Sinha (2011: 167) eloquently put it, "Nitish addressed the hungry stomach. Lalu conversed with the angry and fearful mind." Lalu Prasad won convincingly in this election and the Samata Party lost badly.

In 1996, the parliamentary elections were due. This election brought the Congress Party, which had led the outgoing government, in contention with two alliances: the National Democratic Alliance (NDA) made up of the BJP, the Samata Party, and some others led by Atal Bihari Vajpayee and the United Front made up of the Janata Dal and the Left parties. Lalu Prasad's dominance in the state of Bihar made him the automatic choice for the post of president of the Janata Dal. The NDA won the largest number of seats in the election with Nitish Kumar winning a seat in the Parliament as well. Although invited to form the government, the NDA failed to prove its majority on the floor of the parliament, paving the way for the emergence of a minority coalition government with Deve Gowda of Janata Dal as the Prime Minister and the Congress supporting the coalition from outside (i.e., without actually joining the government).

In the state of Bihar in the meantime, mismanagement became the daily headline news. Lalu Prasad's family members turned themselves into

4. See Sinha (2011: 162).
5. Sinha (2011: 164–65).

extra-constitutional centers of power with kidnapping for ransom becoming common. Then followed the so-called *fodder scam* in which millions of rupees were siphoned off from the state treasury as payment for fodder supplies to poor peasants—supplies that never arrived. Income tax officials found large stocks of cash in the homes of several officials and in offices. There was even a report of cash having been found in airline baggage.[6] Lalu Prasad was sent the files for necessary action, but he never acted upon them. The fodder scam, together with the general atmosphere of lawlessness that prevailed in Bihar worried the Janata Party leadership; it was clear that the investigation into the fodder scam would implicate the Chief Minister.

In 1997 the Governor of Bihar granted the Central Bureau of Investigation (CBI), the prime investigation agency pursuing the trail of the fodder scam, permission to file a charge sheet against Lalu Prasad. He refused to quit and contended that this was a conspiracy to get him because he was the champion of the backward classes. He organized a massive rally in front of the Patna high court. Nitish Kumar and other state leaders of the NDA took out processions against him. In June 1997, the Governor gave the CBI permission to prosecute Lalu Prasad. The then Prime Minister Inder Gujral, who had succeeded Gowda following the loss of support from the Congress, belonged to the alliance of which Lalu Prasad was an influential leader, but he did not come to the latter's rescue.

Lalu Prasad was thus forced to resign from the Chief Minister's post but insisted on retaining the party presidency of the party so that he could choose his own successor. Unable to seal this matter quickly, in July 1997 he organized a meeting of his supporters and announced the formation of a new party, the Rashtriya Janata Dal (RJD), and assumed its leadership. He formed an alliance with the Congress and was intent on continuing to rule Bihar. He did not resign and kept filing appeals, one after another; they were all rejected and soon it was clear that he would not be able to avoid being arrested. In July 1997, he nominated his wife, Rabri Devi, a housewife all her life and completely unprepared for the job, his successor. Lalu was sent to judicial custody but was released on bail in December. The mismanagement of Bihar continued unabated.

In the 1998 parliamentary elections, Samata and Janata Dal ended up eating into each other's voter base leading Nitish Kumar to forge unity between them. The result was the birth of the Janata Dal (United) or JD(U). Nitish Kumar himself had won his parliamentary seat in the 1998 election, however. Moreover, the NDA won enough seats to form the government bringing Atal Bihari Vajpayee to the helm as the Prime Minister. Nitish was rewarded with the prestigious Railway Ministry in this government. As for Bihar, it was

---

6. See Sinha (2011: 158).

withering fast under Rabri Devi leading Polgreen to make the observation quoted in chapter 8.

The grip of Lalu Prasad and the RJD government on Bihar was firm, but there was some evidence of weakening. Lalu Prasad continued to rule from the wings and his wife blamed the officers, who were mainly high caste, for all the shortcomings. Meanwhile, Nitish Kumar grew in stature and his decision to befriend BJP proved to be a masterstroke. The 1999 parliamentary elections saw the BJP-JD(U) alliance register a big victory in the Bihar parliamentary seats; Nitish Kumar, of course, won but what was unexpected, Lalu Prasad lost. It was clear that Nitish Kumar would become the Chief Ministerial candidate for the alliance in the state elections slated for 2000.

Meanwhile, at the center, the NDA began a clear stint of five years with Vajpayee at the helm. Nitish Kumar was first the cabinet minister in charge of surface transport and then later put in charge of agriculture. The gain in stature for Nitish Kumar was substantial. Almost simultaneously, Lalu Prasad had started losing. He first lost face and then apparently lost heavily but yet pulled off a master coup.

It all began with many leaving the RJD fold because the poor backward classes saw that while the people surrounding the RJD leader were people from their own community, they were not really interested in improving the lot of the common man. But mutual rivalries among his rivals strengthened Lalu Prasad, and he was successful in retaining power in the 2000 state assembly election and installed Rabri Devi as Chief Minister.[7] The surprising end was helped by Nitish Kumar pulling out Samata Party from the JD(U) while remaining within the NDA fold. The NDA emerged as the largest coalition in the election, but this was not enough for a majority. RJD supported by the Left parties was closer to a majority and the Congress decided to support them from outside. This Congress support cost the people of Bihar dearly, since the NDA government at the center passed the Bihar Reorganization Bill, which saw the bifurcation of Bihar and creation of Jharkhand in August 2000. We have already seen how costly the break up was to what is now known as Bihar.

The creation of Jharkhand reduced BJP membership in the Bihar assembly; in the NDA fold, the larger group was the Samata Party and JD(U) combination. Nitish Kumar saw the writing on the wall and to avoid the mistake of the 2000 election, set about transforming Samata Party into the JD(U) and by the end of 2000, the process was complete with some detractors having quit.[8] Meanwhile though Rabri Devi's government disintegrated, the RJD continued to hold on to power with Lalu Prasad making the major decisions.

In the 2004 parliamentary elections, the NDA, which had seemed invincible at the center, lost to the United Progressive Alliance that included the

7. For details of this maneuvering and resultant intrigue, see Sinha (2011: ch. 8).
8. Chiefly, Ram Vilas Paswan, who quit to form his own party.

Congress and RJD winning enough seats to form a government with the outside support from the Left parties. Although the Congress President Sonia Gandhi was to become the Prime Minister, she decided to bow out of it at the last minute paving the way for Manmohan Singh to take the office. Lalu Prasad managed to win sufficiently large number of seats in the Parliament to stake a claim to home ministry. While that claim did not translate into reality, he did land the important portfolio of Railways. Nitish Kumar had stood for election from two constituencies, Barh and Nalanda, and lost from the former but won from the latter. While Lalu Prasad seemed to have returned with a bang yet again, he did so at some cost; his ally Ram Vilas Paswan who was denied the chance to be the Railway Minister, parted ways with him.

The February 2005 Bihar Assembly elections brought a hung house with no party receiving a clear majority. This led the central government to temporarily impose the president's rule. In the ensuing months, the NDA gained ground.[9] Nitish Kumar went on a Nyaya Jatra, or March for Justice, publicly pleading throughout Bihar that he had enough support from smaller parties, which the governor had ignored when imposing the president's rule. It was during this march that Nitish Kumar began to plead to voters that they should rise above caste considerations, that a hung Assembly was good for no one and that they should vote for a strong government. These pleas seemed to have had an effect in the repeat Assembly election in November 2005 when the NDA won an absolute majority and Nitish Kumar became Chief Minister of Bihar. Lalu Prasad had been finally unseated: the unthinkable had happened. The NDA continued to go from strength to strength and won an even larger victory in 2010 and Nitish Kumar continued his rule defying the anti-incumbency nature of electoral politics that has been common over the past two decades.

PUBLIC SERVICE DELIVERY

A World Bank report dated 2005, presumably aimed at the winner of the 2005 election, identified three important challenges for Bihar (Sundberg et al. 2005). These were: catalyzing and sustaining rapid growth; strengthening social service delivery; and strengthening public administration and governance. Social service delivery and public administration and governance jointly reflect the ability of the state government to provide high-quality public services in the state. Not only was the ability to provide these services low due to understaffing in the preceding years, the state was also guilty of gross negligence of its duties all around (Mathew and Moore 2011;

---

9. See Sinha (2011: ch. 9) for details.

Mukherjee 2010). In addition, there was little expectation that the government machinery would provide services for the citizens. A result of this was that on many indicators public services were abysmally poor when the Nitish Kumar government took over in 2005.

When it took over, not only did the Nitish Kumar government have to contend with low levels of achievement but also, the public service delivery mechanism that was needed to create improvements was in disarray. In spite of limited existing capacity for delivery, the Nitish Kumar government made a number of important improvements. Below, we discuss the changes in managing public finances and reforms of government expenditures to enhance fiscal space while improving public service delivery, changes in law and order, and public investments in building infrastructure after 2005. All of these changes created an important enabling environment for economic activity.

FISCAL REFORM AND RESTRUCTURING OF PUBLIC EXPENDITURES

Creative use of the state's finances is critical to ensuring that the government works to promote social and developmental goals. This has long been understood as a part of the National Plan process, and in principle, each state has its own State Planning Board to ensure that the government spends and achieves its goals. One of the first things to note is that during the decade of the 2000s, India as a whole grew rapidly with the growth rate during the second half being even higher than in the first half. Rising national incomes have also meant larger tax revenues that can and have been redistributed in this time frame. The report of the Twelfth Finance Commission recommended significant write off of states' indebtedness to the central government in return for enacting and implementing Fiscal Responsibility and Budget Management (FRBM) Acts. This not only reduced the indebtedness but also the interest payments of the states including Bihar. Besides, strengthening the income-tax information system at the center and expansion in the base of service tax resulted in a significant improvement in tax revenue buoyancy, and the states' share in central taxes increased sharply during the period from 2004/05 to 2007/08. Furthermore, a number of other schemes were created to retire expensive debt of the states. All these factors contributed to improving the fiscal space of the states. While the potential was created by the central government, it was left to individual states to convert it into actual revenues.

Bihar seized on this opportunity and undertook many changes that have improved its fiscal space. It approved its own FRBM Act in 2006 in response to the national FRBM Act and committed to containing the fiscal deficit to 3% of GSDP by 2008/09, a target that it achieved. It also committed to a range of other goals, such as eliminating the revenue deficit altogether by raising

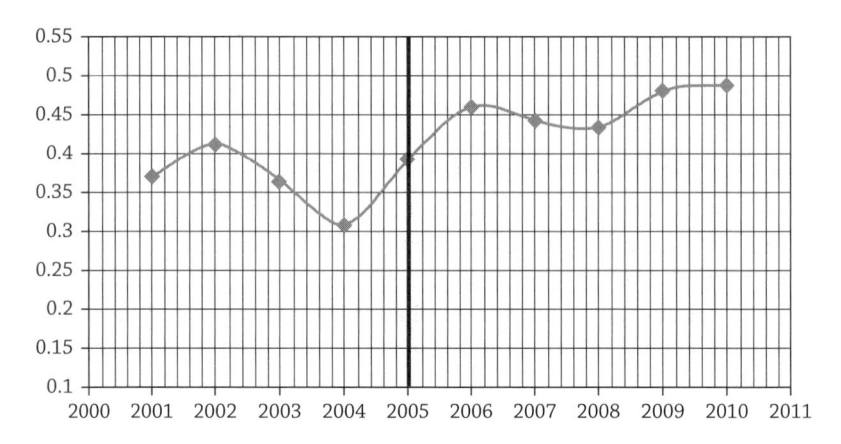

Figure 10.1: Ratio of Per Capita Development Expenditure in Bihar to that in India, 2000–2011

non-tax revenues while maintaining costs, retiring expensive debt, and increasing developmental expenditures to match the national average by 2015.

Between 2001 and 2004/05, Bihar's per capita public expenditure on developmental heads was between Rs. 943 and Rs. 1,138 in 1999/2000 prices. This amounted to between 30%–40% of the national average per capita public expenditure. Figure 10.1 plots the per capita development expenditures in Bihar as a proportion of that in India as a whole. As can be seen, the ratio rose from the 30%–40% range during 2001–2005 to the 40%–50% range during 2005–10. However, the fact of the matter remains that Bihar still has only half of what is being spent nationally on developmental heads. This not only leads to poor economic prospects today, it also has future effects in terms of lack of public infrastructure and investments in human capital. It is important to note, however, that whatever little gain Bihar was able to make in its per capita development expenditures relative to India, it met these goals within the ambit of its FRBM commitments so that it was able to convert its revenue deficit to a modest surplus and keep fiscal deficit well below the 3% of GSDP.

Apart from being able to expand fiscal expenditure due to increasing central government assistance, the government of Bihar has worked hard at reallocating expenditure away from non-developmental heads to developmental heads to further raise the amount of expenditure on development in the state.[10] Figure 10.2 shows that until about 2004/05, about half of all expenditure was on developmental activities and the other half was on non-developmental activities. From 2005 onward, there has been a concerted effort to redirect expenditure

---

10. However, it may be recalled in the light of our earlier discussion on state finances in chapter 9, these increases were never enough to make up for the state's fiscal disabilities.

```
0.7
0.6
0.5
0.4
0.3
     2001  2002  2003  2004  2005  2006  2007  2008  2009  2010
        ◆ Developmental Expenditures    □ Non-Developmental Expenditures
```

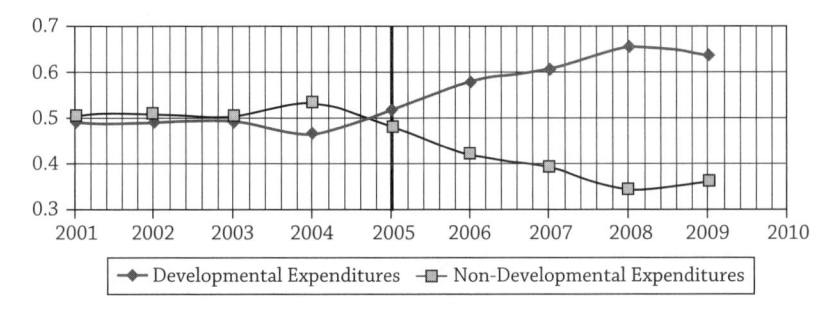

Figure 10.2: Expenditure on Developmental and Non-Developmental Heads, 2001–2010

toward developmental heads. Figure 10.2 shows that Bihar was able to ensure that development expenditure went up by cutting down non-development expenditures. One of the key challenges on this account will be how the fiscal space changes once there is shift from the current indirect tax system to the Goods and Services Tax (GST). Preliminary estimates by Chakraborty (2011) show that "higher than proposed" GST rates will have to be explored if Bihar is to maintain its revenue levels. A fall in revenue levels may lead to a decline in the development expenditures of the state government when it is already far below the national average. This is likely to significantly constrain growth.

LAW AND ORDER AND CRIME STATISTICS

Law and order, while easy enough to conceptualize, is also extremely difficult to measure, as the very extensive literature on this in political science, legal studies, economics, and public administration shows (see Nardulli, Peyton, and Bajjaleih 2011). Bihar had a particularly poor perceived record with respect to crime incidence throughout the 1990s and later. One unambiguous way to track law-and-order conditions in Bihar is to track crime statistics in Bihar. Crime incidence in Bihar was higher than for India in some key categories, such as murder, dacoity, and kidnapping.

Figure 10.3 plots this ratio of crime rates in Bihar to crime rates in India for a number of key categories of crime. Crimes such as burglary and theft are about half as frequent in Bihar as in the rest of the country; however, murders, kidnappings, dacoity, and robbery happen more frequently. Looking at this ratio for each crime type over time, we see that this rate increased till 2004/05 and has systematically declined since then for all categories except burglary and theft, which is unchanged throughout this time frame, and these crime types are less frequent in Bihar than nationally. Crimes that were more frequent in Bihar than in the rest of the country prior to 2004/05 now occur less often. However, absolute levels remained

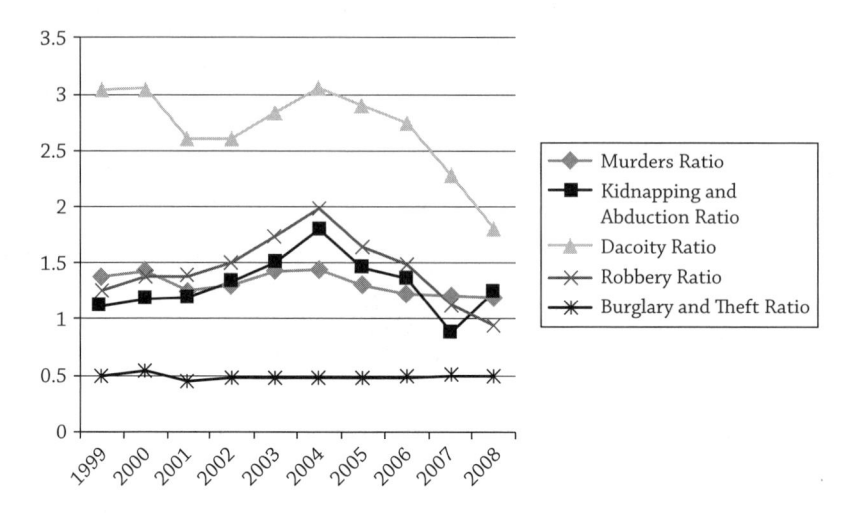

Figure 10.3: Ratio of Incidence of Key Crimes in Bihar to Those in India, 1999–2008
Note: For each crime category, we plot the ratio of crime rate in Bihar to crime rate in India; the crime rate is the ratio of the counts of a category of crime to the population. Data for 1999 and 2000 are for both Bihar and Jharkhand.
Source: http://ncrb.nic.in/ciiprevious/main.htm.

higher than the national rates; for example, even in 2008, dacoity in Bihar was twice as likely as in India, down from three times as likely in 2003.

Table 10.1 presents the changing crime rates within Bihar across a much wider range of crime categories over the period from 2001 to 2010. Thefts are the only category of crime for which crimes per 100,000 people have actually gone up systematically in this time period. From figure 10.3, we know that thefts and burglaries are well below the national average in Bihar, and this may indicate that with improving law and order within Bihar, crime may decline in categories such as kidnapping and dacoity and there may be a move toward more thefts and burglaries. For almost all other categories, there are very sharp declines over this time period. All high-profile crimes that were often reported in the media, such as kidnapping for ransom, dacoity (at home and on the road), bank robbery, and murder, have much lower incidence rates in 2006–2010 as compared to the 2001–05 period.

In parallel with diminishing crime rates, there have been major changes in prosecutions under the Indian Penal Code (IPC) as well as under the Arms Acts. Table 10.2 presents the number of cases registered, counts of convictions made, and the distribution of punishments given out for the 2006–09 period. Interestingly, over this time span, cases registered under the IPC have increased rapidly in number, as there has been a sharp decline in cases involving firearms and explosives that are typically covered under the Arms Act.

Much of this is attributed to changes made in managing law and order in Bihar after Nitish Kumar came to office (Mukherjee 2010). One important

Table 10.1. CHANGING CRIME RATES PER 100,000 PEOPLE BY DIFFERENT TYPES OF CRIME IN BIHAR, 2001–2010

							Kidnapping		Road		Bank	
Year	Murder	Dacoity	Robbery	Burglary	Theft	Riots	for Ransom	Rape	Dacoity	Robbery	Dacoity	Robbery
2001	4.37	1.56	2.62	3.66	11.45	10.28	0.46	0.90	0.31	1.56	0.03	0.02
2002	4.27	1.48	2.63	3.72	11.50	10.30	0.46	1.03	0.30	1.55	0.03	0.02
2003	4.21	1.39	2.79	3.37	11.88	9.44	0.39	0.93	0.28	1.65	0.02	0.02
2004	4.37	1.47	3.29	3.61	13.04	10.42	0.47	1.20	0.32	2.12	0.03	0.03
2005	3.81	1.33	2.65	3.52	13.15	8.58	0.28	1.08	0.25	1.46	0.03	0.01
2006	3.53	1.06	2.34	3.86	14.33	9.35	0.21	1.19	0.23	1.37	0.02	0.01
2007	3.19	0.70	1.86	3.51	13.26	8.61	0.10	1.21	0.16	1.19	0.02	0.01
2008	3.21	0.68	1.63	3.54	15.00	8.70	0.07	1.10	0.15	0.95	0.02	0.01
2009	3.28	0.68	1.69	3.71	15.84	8.90	0.08	0.97	0.21	1.00	0.01	0
2010	3.44	0.66	1.57	3.52	15.92	9.02	0.07	0.81	0.21	1.08	0.01	0

Source: http://biharpolice.bih.nic.in/asp/cr12.asp and NCRB for mid-year population estimates to calculate rates.

Table 10.2. CONVICTION OF CRIMINALS, 2006–2009

Year	Number of New Cases IPC	Number of New Cases Arms Act	Number Convicted IPC	Number Convicted Arms Act	Hanging	Life	≥ 10 Years	< 10 Years	Major Punishment	Total Convictions
2006	2,178	1,156	5,230	1,609	17	366	1,389	5,067	1,772	6,839
2007	3,695	800	8,774	1,154	39	680	2,168	6,966	2,887	9,853
2008	4,461	706	10,994	1,018	27	610	2,307	9,063	2,944	12,007
2009	5,556	391	12,406	535	12	375	1,824	5,831	2,211	13,163

Source: Economic Survey 2010/11 and http://biharpolice.bih.nic.in/recent/strial.pdf.

act of the government was the creation of the State Auxiliary Police (SAP) force, staffed entirely by ex-army personnel who were trained in conducting warfare and were better prepared than the State Police to stand up to criminals and armed radicals. Beginning with a few thousand personnel, this force played a major role in controlling not only criminals but also the Leftist extremists. Although the SAP carried much of the burden of enforcing law and order, the government did not neglect the police and allocated an increased amount of funds to them during the first term. Police administration and training were strengthened via measures such as the establishment of the Bihar Police Academy in 2007/08, increased intake into the police force, and deliberate monitoring from the Chief Minister's Office to ensure limited political interference in routine police activities.[11]

Further, Speedy Trial Courts have been set up to effectively expedite convictions of hardened criminals across a range of cases (PTI 2007 and Balachand 2008). Speedy trials of cases were finally passed into law under the Bihar Special Courts Act of 2008. This Act pertains to crimes in which there "is prima-facie evidence of the commission of an offence alleged to have been committed by a person, who has held or is holding public office and is or has been public servant within the meaning of section 2(c) of the Prevention of Corruption Act, 1988 in the State of Bihar."[12] A number of well-known criminals and criminals-turned-politicians have been successfully investigated and prosecuted under the Bihar Special Courts Act. While this act became law in 2009, much of the background for it was motivated by careful action from 2006 onward. Speedy trials and the SAP together helped restore to some extent the image of the government of Bihar. But, more important, in the aftermath of the installation of the new government, police and the criminals were made aware that it would not be business as usual. Mukherjee's (2009) interview with Mr. Abhayanand, the then Additional Director General of Police in Bihar, captures a number of ways in which the police service creatively responded to the poor law-and-order situation and prosecuted criminals across party lines. While there still remain significant challenges to gain control over the crime situation, there was a noteworthy qualitative change in reputational and operational aspects of maintaining law and order.

Progress has also been made in combating the less visible but equally potent problem of graft and corruption under Nitish Kumar. A large number of high-profile entrapment cases since 2006 have exposed scams in public offices and led to prosecution of the officials involved. In 2006, a total of 66 persons were arrested on the basis of 60 entrapment cases; in 2007, this rose to 126

---

11. See Mukherjee (2010) for more on this.
12. Quoted from the text of Bihar Special Courts Act of 2009; for further details, see the text of the Bill available online at http://vigilance.bih.nic.in/docs/Bihar-Special-Court-Bill-2009-EN.pdf.

arrests from 108 cases; and in 2008, there were another 99 cases. A steady increase in registration of anticorruption cases is reported in the Economic Survey of 2010/11. A number of innovations in dealing with vigilance concerns have been tried out in Bihar. These include setting up additional special courts for entrapment cases, empowering District Magistrates to apprehend government employees taking bribes, and rapid prosecutions under disproportionate assets cases. Public officers and elected and non-elected bureaucrats are currently expected to list all assets on government websites to encourage transparency (Singh 2011). Apart from focusing on better policing, the state government has also put in place measures for improved jail administration. The earlier laxity of having criminals operate with mobile phones while jailed has been replaced with active placement of phone jammers in jails and better monitoring, as a part of national (not state) judicial reforms originally initiated by the Supreme Court of India in 2005. Occupancy rates have ranged between 125% to 523% of total capacity across various district and central jails in the state. The state government has been working toward improved conditions and rehabilitation programs for the entire jail system in Bihar.

Another major problem that the government of Bihar had to tackle is the Maoist insurgency. In this particular case, the government of Bihar took steps that were at variance with those by the government of India. The speedy trials described above were used even in the case of Maoists insurgents. Beginning with two dozen Maoist cases in 2006 and 2007, as many as 109 were convicted in speedy trials between 2007 and 2009 (PTI 2010). As an example of even-handedness, members of various landlord militias (some of whom even enjoyed the protection of members of the alliance forming the government) were also put on speedy trials. In the latter cases, those proved to have engaged in massacres were given death sentences.

In the face of abductions and killing of policemen and villagers, the government of Bihar experimented with a strategy called *Apki Sarkar Apke Dwar*, which translates as "your government at your doorstep." This was introduced at a public meeting in Sikaria, in Jehanabad district in January 2006, within two months of the new government taking office. The basic premise was to maximize all possible developmental activities: build roads, irrigation canals, houses, schools, health clinics, in other words, social security, anything which provided benefits to all eligible persons. While the experiment was not an unqualified success, it did bring growth into Sikaria, creating jobs for men and women. Arun Sinha, a Delhi journalist described the outcome, saying, "Indeed Sikaria has become symbolic of the changes sweeping through what were once 'the killing fields of central Bihar'. The bloody clashes which left hundreds dead in Jehanabad, Gaya . . . now seem as a thing of the distant past" (Sinha 2011: 269). The *Apki Sarkar Apke Dwar* program was extended over the next four years to 65 other Left-wing extremist affected panchayats. An attempt was thus made to strike at the root of the problem. The promise of delivery of the fruits of development at grass-roots level is still far from being realized, but for the first time, a strategy has been formulated and steps have been taken toward its fulfillment.

FLOODS

While floods do not typically constitute any part of the framework of determinants of growth, they are a regular feature in Bihar and hence do affect growth in the state. Bihar is one of the most flood-prone states in India, and the proportion of area vulnerable to this natural calamity has increased significantly since bifurcation, as all the flood-prone areas have remained in Bihar. These floods are neither new nor unexpected and records going back to the era of British rule indicate a systematic pattern of flooding with regard to the multiple rivers crisscrossing Bihar. These rivers flood during the monsoon season and change their course to wreak havoc, resulting in a significant loss of life and property and affecting the state's income.

Most of Bihar's rivers joining the Ganges from the north are perennial, with their sources in glaciers in the Himalayas, often passing through Nepal. This fact makes flood management and control in Bihar an international matter. Rorabacher (2008) discusses the failure of coordination between Nepal and India in terms of controlling floodwaters that emerge in Nepal and flood the plain in India. Of the rivers emerging from Nepal, the Kosi (the 'River of Sorrow') flows from Nepal into Bihar, after traversing the region to the west of the Kanchenjunga hills. Due to the vast amounts of silt that it brings, the riverbed often rises to levels higher than that of the surrounding areas, causing widespread and unpredictable course deviations. The Kosi waters suddenly inundate areas not usually at risk of flood during periods of heavy rainfall.[13] In recognition of these concerns, the Kosi barrage has been in place since 1963 and has usually worked well, except in 2008 when the Kosi entered a channel it had abandoned over a century ago (i.e., before the barrage was in place). The essential challenge leading to the failure in coordination is in terms of coming up with a viable way to maintain the dam and keep it silt free in perpetuity, considering that the costs are in Nepal and the benefits in Bihar.

While the 2008 Kosi floods led to large-scale devastation, even historically, Bihar has had to routinely deal with floods (see table 10.3).[14] Almost

---

13. See, for instance, N. K. Singh (2009), referred to earlier, for a very lucid examination of the relevant matters.
14. See World Bank and Government of Bihar (2010) for details.

every year, some part of Bihar gets flooded leading to major loss of life and property and requires systematic planning to minimize the damage from the flood (maintenance of barrages, embankments, and de-silting of river beds) as well as soften the impact after it has struck (relief and rehabilitation). Additional complications are quite likely to emerge in the near future as climate change sets in, making it essential to develop flood control and management strategies to counter more frequent and possibly larger shocks in Bihar. Thus, Bihar experiences not only predictable and expected floods on an annual basis but also, every few years, large catastrophic floods occur. In flood-prone districts of Bihar, poverty, lack of human and physical investment, and the incidence of floods are deeply interconnected. A standard regression analysis with controls for household covariates shows that even after accounting for differences in socio-economic and district characteristics, flood-prone districts do poorly by 5–10 percentage points in terms of poverty head-count ratio (Dasgupta 2007). While this analysis is not specific to Bihar, it is indicative of the effect of floods on poverty.

Policy formulation relevant to floods and its implementation are the mandate of the Disaster Management Department of the government of Bihar. The literature on flood control and management in India is rich, with much ground already covered in trying to understand how best to deal with them in Bihar (Ganges Flood Control Commission, GFCC, 2007). Flood-related uncertainty is covariate uncertainty in that it affects everyone in the catchment areas, leading to problems in insurance design. In addition, in view of high population density, large-scale relief operations have to be rolled out once floods occur.

Flood management literature classifies measures against floods as taking (1) structural approaches and (2) non-structural approaches. By and large, all measures under structural approaches are ex ante and seek to build embankments, reservoirs, detention basins, and systems for inter-basin transfer of water. The non-structural approaches are a mixture of ex ante and ex post risk mitigating activities that broadly include flood plain zoning, watershed management, flood forecasting, and disaster mitigation and preparedness. Sinha (2008) argues that both are complementary and not exclusive; however, there are large differences in cost-benefit ratios. While structural defenses are an indispensable tool in controlling flood damage, they also come with prohibitive costs and land-use commitments that are restrictive, and in general, they do not provide complete protection from floods. Flood zoning and watershed management are cheaper to implement, but they work more gradually and are long-run strategies.

The appropriate mix of strategies to pursue is a keenly debated matter in Bihar. There are strong cases made for using structural approaches, such as building embankments to channelizing surplus floodwaters away from

Table 10.3. FLOOD STATISTICS IN BIHAR, 1979–2009

Year	District	Blocks	Panchayats Fully	Panchayats Partly	Panchayats Total	Home (Rs. Lakh)	Public Property (Rs. Lakh)	Human Deaths	Animal Deaths
2009	16	91	150	452	602	528	530	97	2
2008	18	116	341	583	924	8,451	9,772	258	878
2007	22	269	2,235	1,581	3,816	83,145	64,242	1,287	2,423
2006	14	63	10	365	375	1,225	8,456	36	31
2005	12	81	130	432	562	383	305	58	4
2004	20	211	2,015	773	2,788	75,810	103,050	885	3,272
2003	24	172	646	850	1,496	2,032	1,035	251	108
2002	25	6	1,587	917	2,504	52,622	40,892	489	1,450
2001	22	194	838	1,154	1,992	17,358	18,354	231	565
2000	33	213	653	1,674	2,327	20,934	3,781	336	2,568
1999	24	150	820	784	1,604	5,385	5,410	243	136
1998	28	260	1,264	1,475	2,739	5,504	9,284	381	187
1997	26	169	635	1,267	1,902	3,057	2,038	163	151
1996	29	195	1,102	947	2,049	1,495	1,036	222	171
1995	26	177	460	1,441	1,901	7,510	2,184	291	3,742
1994	21	112	490	555	1,045	495	152	91	35
1993	18	124	596	667	1,263	8,814	3,041	105	420
1992	8	19	23	147	170	16	1	4	
1991	24	137	578	758	1,336	614	140	56	84
1990	24	162	475	784	1,259	160	182	36	76
1989	16	74	173	479	652	161	84	26	
1988	23	181	410	1,206	1,616	211	151	52	29
1987	30	382	3,492	2,620	6,112	25,789	681	1,399	5,302
1986	23	189			1,828	647	3,202	134	511
1985	20	162	495	750	1,245	756	205	83	20
1984	23	239	1,325	1,884	3,209	2,292	2,718	143	90
1983	22	138	477	747	1,224	172	258	35	21
1982	15	110		1,112	1,112	687	955	25	14
1981	21	201			2,138	407		18	11
1980	21	193			1,869	561		67	42
1979	13	110				103		14	4

Source: http://disastermgmt.bih.nic.in/Statitics/Statistics.htm.

rivers when they are in flood.[15] On the other hand, with at least eight major breaches in the embankments, a number of scholars argue that prior to the construction of the *bunds*, rivers would gently sweep across the landscape, depositing silt (Sinha 2008; Mishra 2008a). In fact, even as early as 1937, the then Chief Engineer of Bihar came to the conclusion that embankments were harmful and led to excessive flooding.[16] As the rivers were channelized, their velocity increased, allowing the waters to carry sand and gravel and rocks in addition to silt. The river gradients changed and sediment deposition upstream of the barrages increased rapidly. Initially, this excess sediment was deposited in the river channels, as defined by the levees. This led to a rise in the level of riverbed vis-à-vis its banks. Instead of permanently protecting the surrounding area from floods, the embankments thus changed the morphology of the rivers, raising the straitjacketed channels above the surrounding land. As a result, floodwater no longer flows in one or a few clearly defined channels, but instead spreads out across 30–40 square km, filling entire river basins, low-lying lands, and ponds. Somanathan (2011) specifically studies the Kosi basin comparing gross value of output in villages that are regularly flooded and in control villages. The study categorizes villages as those that were regularly flooded, those that were unexpectedly flooded as a result of the breach of the embankment, and those that were not flooded during the period of the study. The last of these served as the control villages. It was found that the regularly flooded villages lying within embankments do no worse on all counts, while "gross output is higher or at least no lower for them" (Somanathan 2011). Thus, learning to live with floods by building suitable infrastructure may in fact be the way ahead.

Quite apart from explicit efforts to control water flow, augmentation of traditional rehabilitation strategies is necessary. It is possible to take advantage of technology to provide a better information base for rehabilitation and improved flood management. A large number of lessons emerge from experiences in Bangladesh and Pakistan, both of which have large flood-prone areas. For example, there is a discussion of a "no village left behind" policy for floods in Pakistan that seeks to combine GIS maps, public supply information, and potential response resources (availability of safe structures) that may be collected using real-time satellite imagery in order to reach people faster and formulate rehabilitation strategies that are better aligned with on-the-ground realities. An excellent implementation of some of these ideas is the Flood MAPS project.[17]

---

15. See, for instance, World Bank (1990); Appu (1973). The latter thought that embankments would provide protection besides allowing extra crop to be grown.
16. Quoted in Mishra (2008b). See also Somanathan (2011).
17. See http://floodmaps.lums.edu.pk/.

AN INFRASTRUCTURE INDEX FOR BIHAR

Access to infrastructure within Bihar differs vastly from place to place, and many districts are easily identifiable as being much worse than the others. To capture diversity in infrastructure in Bihar at the district level, we collected data on 34 different variables using data from the Economic Surveys and the District Level Health Survey from 2007/08. We capture data on different infrastructural dimensions, such as water supply (piped water, toilets, and drainage), health infrastructure (access to the Integrated Child Development Services program, sub-centers, primary health centers, and district hospitals), education infrastructure (primary schools, middle schools, higher secondary schools, and higher education), transport facilities (all-weather roads to health facilities, all-weather roads in general, national, state, and district highways, and distances to railway stations and bus stations), communication (post, computer kiosks, community TVs, and STD booths), energy (percentage of villages electrified), and banking facilities (access to agricultural banks, percentage of households with a member in a self-help group, and per person Kisan Credit Cards distributed). Thus, we have a fairly rich base to use for evaluating district-level infrastructure.

Using a principal component analysis, and subsequent rotation of the factor loadings, we find that three key factors collectively explain over 50% of the variation within the data matrix. The first principle component loads heavily on a range of variables measuring village-level infrastructure, for example, availability of sub-centers in the village and access to a post office, STD booth, bank, private clinic, pharmacy, and computer kiosk. District rankings vary widely on each of these orthogonal dimensions, indicating that there are few districts that perform uniformly well on all dimensions of infrastructure. For ease of discussion, we plot the district ranking on the basis of the first principle component, which explains 25% of the total variation in our data in figure 10.4.[18]

Analysis such as that in figure 10.4 captures the qualitative difference with regard to within-village infrastructure when comparing districts like Patna and Samastipur with others like Araria and Banka. One of the Bihar government's agenda-setting attempts in the infrastructure sector has been to ensure that the road networks are strong enough to enable people to reach Patna in a matter of six hours from anywhere else in Bihar. Similar standards need to be set for a range of other infrastructural variables, such as

---

18. We do not mean for this analysis to be anything more than indicative, since a richer and more balanced set of district-level variables should be used. Ideally, we would have liked to be able to use additional details on power, road infrastructure, mobile penetration, access to agricultural *mandis*, etc. Insofar as the variables we use are correlated with these unavailable variables, we capture infrastructure at the district level; however, a better analysis is possible with richer data.

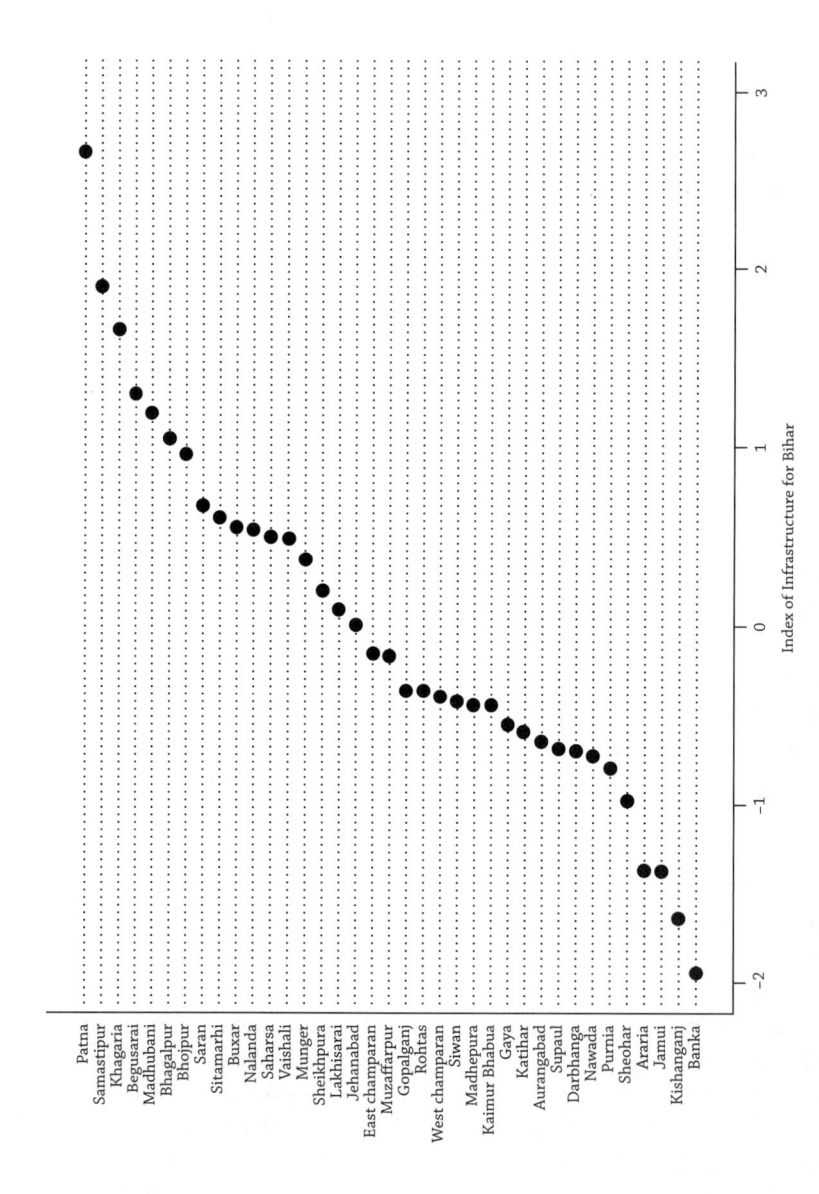

Figure 10.4: District-Level Ranking by Level of Infrastructure Development
Note: We use a set of 34 variables to capture district-level development in Bihar. Above, we plot the ranking of districts for the first principle factor consistent with the largest eigenvalue (7.42).

communication, energy availability, and access to credit and markets. There are vast differences even today across districts on these fronts, which need attention going forward to enable greater and more egalitarian participation in the growth process unfolding in Bihar.

Roads and Bridges

One dimension on which Bihar does well is expansion of roads and bridges. Today, Bihar has on average 90.1 km of roads per 100,000 persons, which is relatively low compared to the national average of 256.7 km per 100,000 persons. This, of course, is not an indicator of the ideal length; in fact, if we look at spatial spread instead of density, Bihar has 50.8 km of roads for every 100 sq. km of area, while the equivalent number for India is 75 km of roads for every 100 sq. km. On the other hand, even today, about half of all villages in Bihar do not have access to all-weather roads and are cut off from nearby urban regions during the rainy season. Thus, there are serious and obvious challenges that the road network in Bihar must meet for better connectivity in terms of both reach and quality. A much higher volume of investment is needed, and the challenge is not only harnessing this investment but also identifying areas and zones that need to be specifically developed on a priority basis.

The Bihar government has initiated a number of projects under its own schemes, such as the Mukhya Mantri Gram Sadak Yojana (Chief Minister's Rural Roads Program), under which some of these issues are tackled. From 2007 to 2010, there has been an increase of almost 25% in the total length of roads making up the state highway network, from 3,021 km to 3,787 km. Most of these gains have been distributed in remote districts such as Nalanda, Madhubani, or Saupal, rather than the more centralized area of Patna, which was already endowed with significant road infrastructure base. There has been limited expansion in the road network with respect to major district roads, the total length of which only increased by about 1.7% over the same period, suggesting that last mile connectivity is still a major issue in Bihar and will need to be targeted to ensure complete road connectivity in the state. Of the various types of roads, the ones nearest to villages are "link roads" that join remote habitations to either national, state, or major district highways; almost 73% of such link roads were unpaved in 2010. Thus, while expansion has taken place, this expansion is incomplete and continues to exclude the majority of villages. Much of this has been possible due to a rapid increase in plan outlay on road construction that went up from 2.36 billion rupees in 2005/06 to 30.45 billion rupees in 2009/10. This reflects the conscious efforts of the government to reallocate expenditure in order to support social sector expenditures.

In terms of building bridges, Bihar's achievement has been very impressive during the 2006 to 2009 period. The Bihar Rajya Pul Nirman Nigam (Bihar

State Bridge Construction Corporation Limited) constructed more bridges during the three years than those constructed during the 30-year period from 1975 to 2005. A total of 518 bridges were completed during the period from 2006/07 up to the end of December 2010. Great support from the state leadership made this possible, with the Chief Minister announcing additional funding for the corporation and personal rewards for engineers who rendered exemplary service. Interestingly, the corporation has now become a source of revenue for the government and is expected to have generated a profit of 915 million rupees in 2009/10, up from 59.6 million rupees in 2005/06.

Also noteworthy is the phenomenal increase in the number of registered vehicles in Bihar. Over the period from 2005/06 to 2009/10, the total number of registered vehicles has increased from 80,000 to 319,000 (i.e., a fourfold jump). This increase has often been attributed to the improved law-and-order situation but surely with better connectivity and greater economic activity, vehicular traffic must have increased as well. This increase in vehicle ownership encompasses the spectrum of vehicle categories, from commercial vehicles such as taxis, trucks, and buses to personal vehicles such as cars, scooters, and motorbikes. The receipts from taxes on registration have gone up as well, from 1.33 billion rupees in 2001/02 to 3.72 billion rupees in 2009/10. Thus, expenditure on roads and bridges has improved the state government's ability to increase its own tax collection in a number of ways, suggesting that these sorts of infrastructure investments have released substantial amounts of pent-up demand in Bihar.

As we have seen earlier, construction of roads and bridges was a high priority for the Nitish Kumar administration's first term, beginning in 2005. The central government scheme Pradhan Mantri Gram Sadak Yojana (PMGSY) scheme (the Prime Minister's Rural Roads Program) from 2000 had been able to complete only 24% of its goal of linking all human settlements. Sinha (2011) documents that a part of this is attributable to the lack of explicit guidelines on accounting for input cost escalation in the PMGSY that completion of projects was so low. The Nitish Kumar government not only allocated 6.6 billion rupees of state money to meet such cost escalation but actively negotiated with the central government to take many of the PMGSY projects under the state schemes, namely, Mukhya Mantri Gram Sadak Yojana (for details, see Sinha 2011: ch. 12). Much of this expansion in the road network took place over 2008 to 2010 and reflects gains that took place near or even after the re-election of Nitish Kumar government.

There were two state agencies involved—the Rural Works Department (RWD) and the Road Construction Department (RCD); the splendid performance of the RCD hid the abysmal performance of the RWD. There were real problems too that impeded improvement of road connectivity; the land acquisition process, which was essential whenever road building or road widening was considered, had to be made to operate more smoothly. A new land acquisition policy was introduced, which considered the market rate to some extent, to make the process of such acquisition appear more reasonable than it had before. Government expenditure on roads rose from 1.33 billion rupees in 2004/05 to almost 25 billion rupees in 2008/09; and against 384 km of roads constructed in 2004/05, almost ten times as much, at 3,474 km were constructed in 2009/10 (Aiyar 2010).

Power

One of the consequences of the bifurcation of erstwhile Bihar, into today's Bihar and Jharkhand, is that while 70% of the power-generating capacity went to Jharkhand, about 70% of the demand comes from Bihar. Since the bifurcation, Bihar has been operating with only two old thermal plants with diminished production capacity; the state needs to purchase 90% of its power needs from central utilities. In 2011/12 the annual per capita power consumption in the state was 100 kilowatt hours, far from the national average of 717 kilowatt hours. Peak demand in 2009/10 was 2,500 MW, while the availability was 1,508 MW, indicating a deficit of 39.7%. The Economic Survey estimated the deficit to be around 44.5% and predicted a rise to 66% in 2011/12. This deficit was as little as 4.6% in 2002/03, suggesting that demand for electricity has grown over time. Over the 2006–09 period, there has been a cumulative growth in demand of 10%; it is anticipated that demand will continue to grow for some years to come.

Quite clearly, electricity consumption is a critical constraint with regard to economic growth. Secure, easily accessible, and cheap electricity is an important catalyst for industrialization. Even for a services-dominated economy such as Bihar, electricity is crucial to initiating and sustaining activities that may not be possible without it, for example, being able to securely run back-end offices that work 24 x 7. One critical problem that is relatively easy to target is the inordinately high transmission and distribution (T&D) losses. In Bihar, this loss has been in the 37.4% to 44.7% range over the 2005–09 period, whereas the national T&D figures are in the range of 25% and international ones are in the 6%–9% range (Economic Census, various rounds). A considerable proportion of the losses is due to obsolete transmission and distribution systems and significant investments are needed to improve the systems. Apart from T&D losses, there are also serious concerns with regard to cost recovery for the Bihar State Electricity Board, with a deficit as great as 47% in 2010/11. Not only are there cost-recovery issues but tariffs have also not kept pace with costs, so that costs have far outstripped revenue collection. While longer term expansion of local supply is inevitable, and plans for this are being implemented with investment in restoring existing plants and developing new ones, stringent management of the power sector may allow for short-run efficiency gains that are sorely needed.

SOCIAL SECTORS

In this section, we discuss the main developments in the social sectors including education and health.

Education

One of the key measures of human capital in the economy is the literacy rate. India's decennial census shows that Bihar's literacy rate increased from 48% in 2001 to 63.8% by 2011; the gap between this and the national average reduced from 17 percentage points in 2001 to 10.2 percentage points in the last decade. Apart from literacy rates, the other variable keenly tracked with regard to education is the enrollment ratio. Bihar made key gains with regard to enrollment ratio between 2006 and 2011; from having 14.5% of all school-age children out of school in 2006, Bihar was able to reduce an out-of-school rate to 4.4% by 2011. This decline has been far more dramatic than the decline seen in rural India, which saw a decline from 8.75% in 2006 to 5.15% by 2011; see various Annual Survey of Education Report (ASER) Center reports (ASER Center 2007, 2012).

This is a very substantial achievement in such a short period of time. Quite interestingly, if one looks at the access to schooling, Bihar has been able to reduce the number of out-of-school children by having a larger and larger fraction of the school-going children attending government schools; over the 2006–11 period, the proportion going to private schools has declined from 13.4% to 5.4%, indicating a large movement of students from private schools to the public school system. This move toward government schools is very interesting and is contrary to the national trend, where we see a sharp increase in the proportion of school-going children attending private school—from 19.6% to 25.2%. Figure 10.5 captures the asymmetric ways in which Bihar has been expanding its enrollment through the public sector.

Thus, Bihar has come a long way toward meeting the target of universal enrollment. In 2004, in an average district in Bihar, the allocation of funds for activities under *Sarva Shiksha Abhiyan* (SSA), the central government program for universalizing elementary education, was around 100 million rupees. By 2008, this figure had risen to 1 billion rupees. According to the Economic Survey of Bihar, in 2007/08, 67% of the state government's social sector expenditure was on elementary education. The survey also highlights Bihar's expenditure of almost 20%–25% of its total state budget on education—possibly the reason enrollment ratios in government schools in Bihar have been rising rather than enrolments in private schools, as is more commonly seen.

While literacy rates in Bihar have been increasing faster than the national average in the last decade, Bihar still remains the state with the lowest literacy

WHAT CHANGED? (*191*)

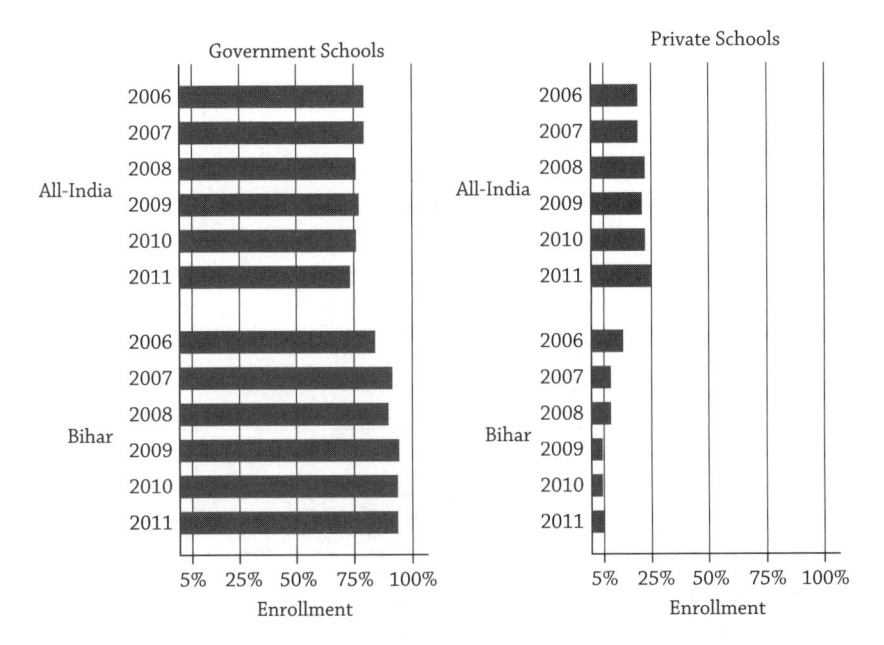

Figure 10.5: Enrollment Ratios across Government and Private Schools, 2006–2011
Source: ASER Data (various rounds).

rates across all states in India. Equally important, what does being literate really mean in the context of human capital? Enrollment, after all, is an intermediate school outcome, and more appropriate measures of learning are needed to capture what students learn in school during the time that they spend there. In terms of learning, perhaps ASER data is the only nationally representative data for India that includes measures for reading and arithmetic learning; here, Bihar's comparative achievements are simultaneously surprising and worrying.

Figure 10.6 captures reading outcomes; these show a rather complex picture. Bihar has had a larger proportion of children who are unable to read anything ("nothing" in figure 10.6) than the national average. Surprisingly, in spite of the increase in enrollment, there appears to be a modest increase in the proportion of people unable to read anything in both India and Bihar; however, this is also accompanied by increases in the proportion of school-age children who are able to recognize letters. Trends with regard to the proportion of school-age children who are able to read words, paragraphs (consistent with Class I level of reading ability) and stories (consistent with Class II level of reading ability) are much more mixed, and there appear to have been no qualitative gains in the last few years. In fact, the trend for stories suggests a very modest decline for the national levels and a sharper one for Bihar.

Outcomes on arithmetic are captured in figure 10.7. As with reading abilities, the proportion of school-going children who have no arithmetic abilities ('nothing') is higher than the national average, and there is a modestly

(192) *Arnab Mukherji and Anjan Mukherji*

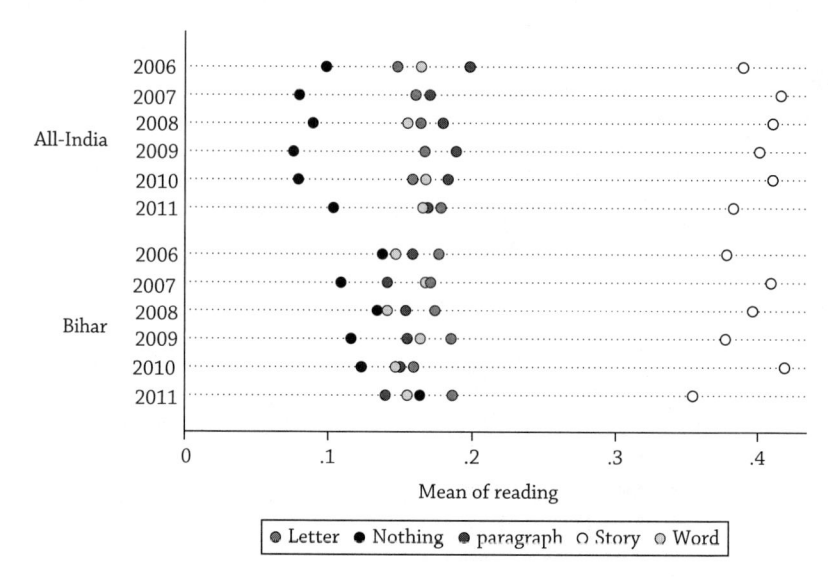

Figure 10.6: Average Reading Abilities in Classes I to VIII in Bihar and India, 2006–2011
Source: ASER Data (various rounds).

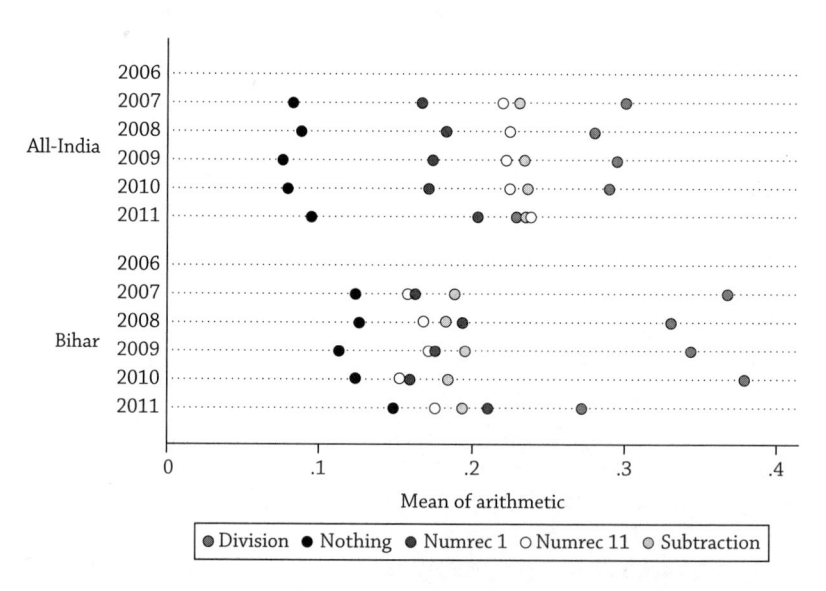

Figure 10.7: Arithmetic Skills in Classes I to VIII in Bihar and India, 2006–2011
Source: ASER Data (various rounds).

increasing trend at both the national level and for Bihar, with Bihar's number being always higher. However, unlike reading abilities, other indicators show key gains in the last few years; thus, there is a modest increase in number recognition ("numrec1," i.e., numbers from 1 to 9 and "numrec11," i.e., numbers from 11 to 99) and the proportion of school-age children who can do subtractions. Quite interestingly, a larger proportion than the national average of school-age children in Bihar can handle division problems, suggesting that numeric abilities are better in Bihar, provided students start learning.

Thus, in spite of increased enrollments, learning within school remains a serious challenge; this is true for not just Bihar but also India at large. Apart from some skills in mathematics, Bihar's learning levels are systematically lower than the national average, raising a number of additional concerns about how soon Bihar's economy will be able to participate in productive and high-skill jobs, both of which are critical for long-term economic growth. Given the high level of structural dependence on the services economy, it also implies that the usually observed relationship between economic growth and growing dependence on the services sector may not work out for Bihar unless there is a rapid and overt drive to improve skills for the job market.

While political will and improvements in educational inputs are evident, data from ASER 2006–11 shows that there has been no systematic increase in school attendance in Bihar, even though enrollment ratios are high; Banerji (2011) reports that Bihar has perhaps one of the lowest attendance to enrollment ratios across states in India. Clearly, delivery of education will be incomplete with low attendance rates, and studies based on five districts in Bihar (Banerji et al. 2008) suggest that only 65% of those enrolled actually attend school. In addition, primary school organization still tends to be around multi-grade classrooms, with almost half of the students in the school studying in multi-grade classrooms. This implies that teaching dynamics vary, with some evidence to suggest that the composition of multi-grade classrooms is unstable (in some years, Class I may sit with Class II and in others, with Class III). Lack of organization is also acute, with few schools making and following timetables, which will perhaps become more meaningful only with reduced teacher absenteeism. Clear evidence of the lack of teacher training and teaching skills is observed in every study that monitors the ability of teachers to teach and explain concepts to primary school students.

Chanda's (2011) work shows that low levels of education have had strong negative implications for economic growth, particularly in Bihar. In addition to this, the literature on the quality and quantity trade-off tells us that as people are able to invest in education for their children, there is a plausibly causal decline in the demand for more children and a consequent decline in fertility ratio. Chanda's (2011) work also shows that quite apart from literacy, declining fertility ratios are also important to growth. Thus, Bihar will need more schools and colleges than most other states, given its age profile.

Interestingly, the government had identified a number of policy responses to counter the dismal state of education in 2005. Some of these are: empowering village education committees to enable active monitoring of schools, increasing the recruitment of primary schoolteachers, expanding the Mid-Day

Meal scheme's reach, and developing the Bihar Education Project as a nodal organization for roll-out of a number of education schemes, such as the SSA. In addition, there have been significant efforts to support professional education, including a Bihar Universities Amendment Act to support the mandate of the existing Bihar State Universities Act. The state government has also worked hard at evolving clear and easy measures to monitor targets for schools, for example, having a teacher–pupil ratio of 1:40 in government schools, improved school infrastructure, and reorganized Mid-Day Meal schemes. A number of reforms relating to syllabuses, examinations, and teacher training institutions have also been discussed. If implemented, these measures will go a long way toward reducing key structural problems by advancing enrollment, converting the enrollment into high attendance, and reducing the dependence on multi-grade classrooms. Improved teacher–pupil ratios and exposure through training institutes can in principle be used to improve school organization and the creation of course plans and timetables to follow. However, implementation and follow-up within the education sector need to be effective, and this will be one of the many responsibilities for the state government to deal with. Apart from the concerns of setting up a fully functional school, there are also concerns about how this education will lead to any employment and what the nature of such employment should be.

Health

Becker (2007) argues that health plays a key role in enhancing human capital through investments made by individuals, hospitals, and the government. In a developing economy context, health is first measured through child and maternal health statistics. On child health statistics Bihar does well. Infant mortality in Bihar has been steadily decreasing; this is confirmed by both NFHS data and the Sample Registration Survey (SRS) data. SRS data estimates suggest a steady decline in infant mortality from 117.8 deaths per 1,000 live births in 1981 to 69 in 1991, 62 in 2001, and 52 in 2008. NFHS data on infant mortality are a little different but support the idea of decline with an estimate of 78 deaths per 1,000 live births in 1998/99 and 62 deaths per 1,000 live births in 2005/06. The rural–urban gradient in infant mortality is relatively small, and in general, follows the national trends. According to NFHS-3, the all-India average in 2005/06 is about 57 deaths per 1,000 live births with estimates ranging from 15 deaths per 1,000 live births (in Kerala) to 73 deaths per 1,000 live births (in Uttar Pradesh). Full immunization against the six key vaccine preventable diseases in Bihar has increased modestly from 22.4% in 1998/99 to 23% in 2002–04; however, within Bihar, there are some districts that have been able to expand coverage wonderfully—some like Patna and Rohtas were able to double or even more than double full immunization coverage.

NFHS-3 data reveal that of women who gave birth in the five years preceding the survey, only 34% received antenatal care from a health professional (29% from a doctor and 5% from other health personnel) for their last childbirth. The majority of women (66%) received no antenatal care. Further, only 17% received three or more antenatal care visits and only 19% received care within the first trimester of pregnancy, as recommended. A half of urban women received antenatal care from a health professional for their last childbirth, compared with 32% of rural women. The percentage of women receiving antenatal care in Bihar is less than half the national average (74%) and is also the lowest of any state in India. These numbers are virtually unchanged over the NFHS-2 and NFHS-3 survey periods. A similar lack of care for women emerges in terms of access to iron and folic supplements and a range of other health inputs to maternal care, all of which are limited. Thus, maternal healthcare had not seen as significant strides as child healthcare at least until 2005/06.

Stepping back from just child and maternal care and looking at the entire disease burden, one can classify the economy according to the ratio of communicable to non-communicable diseases. All economies began with a high incidence of communicable diseases and, with greater maturity of health systems and an increase in prosperity, have transitioned to states in which a larger proportion of the diseases are non-communicable diseases. The Ministry of Health and Family Welfare's 2010 reports state that deaths due to communicable diseases and maternal, perinatal and nutritional disorders account for 38% of all deaths, while non-communicable diseases account for 42% of all deaths in India. The remaining 20% of the disease burden is shared equally between injuries and other ill-defined causes. Official estimates for Bihar's burden of diseases were not available to us; however, the expectation is that Bihar would have a higher than average prevalence of communicable diseases than the national average. Lymphatic filariasis is endemic in Bihar. Japanese encephalitis, leprosy, and HIV/AIDs are also reported in Bihar and while their prevalence is not dangerously high, all of them are close enough to alert levels to cause concern.

The prevalence of non-communicable diseases has been increasing in Bihar. NFHS-3 data show that there are 1,024 diabetes cases per 100,000 women in Bihar, while the national average is 881 cases per 100,000 women. The prevalence of blindness in Bihar is one and a half times the national average at 0.78%. Surprisingly, women in Bihar report a much higher prevalence of asthma, at 1,696 per 100,000, than either men in Bihar (981) or the national average (1,627). A range of other non-communicable diseases such as goiter, cardiovascular diseases, and cancer, represent diseases to which the health system must be prepared to respond.

The health system itself is in dire need of reinvigoration. Ali et al. (2007) report incomplete infrastructure and poorly staffed health facilities at both the preventive levels of the public health system, such as the sub-centers and primary health centers, and at the curative levels, such as the district hospitals. Problems of financial and geographical access abound, and out-of-pocket payments to private providers, for those who can afford them, are the norm. The state government has attempted to respond to these challenges. For example, a new nursing program has been started in the premier Indira Gandhi Institute of Medical Sciences, Patna, and a range of other initiatives are under way to control communicable disease. One area of success has been with regard to efforts aimed at reducing the incidence of new polio cases. However, access to quality healthcare remains a challenge that will need to be addressed to improve statewide health.

MIGRATION AND REMITTANCES

For households in Bihar, migration has long been a strategy to seek better livelihoods outside the state and to support family members left behind. Systematic and large-scale migration from Bihari households has been documented from as far back as the nineteenth century.[19] While much of the pre-independence migration from Bihar was international and frequently permanent in nature, post-independence migration from Bihar has been overwhelmingly seasonal and within India. Before discussing the causes and patterns of migration, it is important to note that migration has played an important role in shaping Bihar's economy.

NSSO estimates that the Net Migration Rate for Bihar, adjusting for in-migrations, was 56 per 1,000 persons in 2007. Among the large states, this is the highest volume of out-migration, immediately followed by Kerala that has an out-migration of 44 per 1,000 persons. In terms of absolute numbers, the 42 crore net migrants from Bihar are second only to the 52 crore from Uttar Pradesh, and Kerala is a distant third with 13 crore migrants. With almost one out of every five out-migrants coming from Bihar, independent of whether they migrate within or outside India, migrants from Bihar form a very large part of the total pool of migrants. The NSSO estimates that almost 584 of every 1,000 Bihari out-migrants is economically active and that 524 of every 1,000 Bihari out-migrants remit income back to their

---

19. Migration from India over the period 1764–1920 took place in large volumes to places such as Natal (South Africa), Mauritius, Fiji, Trinidad-Tobago, Guyana, etc. Tables on migration of labor from different sources inside India to destination abroad are documented on http://www.aapravasighat.org/indenture.htm. Amitava Ghosh acknowledges a large amount of original source material on migration from Bengal and Bihar in his 2008 book *Sea of Poppies*.

families, indicating strong ties with Bihar; again, this number is the highest among all states in India.[20] On average, Bihari out-migrants remit income five times in a year and the average size of their remittance is 13,500 rupees; the size of average remittances is below the average for the country, which is 19,600 rupees. Thus, on average, households that received remittances got an additional 4,500 rupees per month, not an inconsequential figure considering that the monthly per capita consumption expenditure was 695 rupees in rural areas and 1,312 rupees in urban areas in 2007.[21] Thus, for those households that have out-migrants in the family, remittances are an importance source of economic support. The Indian Institute of Planning and Administration (IIPA) study (2010) estimates that remittances may account for as much as 5% of Bihar's Net Domestic Product and this often accrues to poor and marginalized families in extremely backward castes.

Two key studies that have looked at the migration issue in greater depth are the work of Deshingkar et al. (2006) and an IIPA (2010) study led by Girish Kumar and Pranab Banerji. They both conduct independent and original surveys in key districts where migration is a common phenomenon. Migration is almost universal in Bihar and excludes only the poorest of the poor or the very rich, even after accounting for migration for education or due to marriage. While much of the post-independence migration originally tried to serve the wage labor needs of states that had implemented the Green Revolution technologies (e.g., Punjab and Haryana), this has changed over the last decade-and-a-half, toward greater participation in the urban informal sector.[22] Even members of educated and wealthy households began migrating, as local economic prospects remained stagnant through the 1990s. Migration increased substantially in the early part of the last decade, as the Indian economy experienced growth while there was little change in employment prospects in the pre-2005 Bihar economy (Deshingkar et al. 2006).

Caste, clan, and social network ties largely define migration choices, usually with links between the places from which migration took place and the place of work. These are much more important than distance. In fact, social ties facilitate the process of migration and, at the same time, act as a mechanism to keep migrants in the same profession through variously linked contracts across a number of dimensions (Deshingkar et al. 2006). Migration has systemically increased in the post-2000 period so that today,

---

20. In Uttar Pradesh only 246 of every 1,000 out-migrants remit money while 261 of every 1,000 out-migrants from Kerala remit money. Jharkhand is closest at 486 per 1,000 out-migrants.
21. This back of the envelope calculation is quite close to the 4,500 rupees that the IIPA (2010) study observed in the field.
22. Deshingkar et al. (2006) report that work in brick kilns, rickshaw pulling, casual labor in construction and farm wage labor were the four most common professions in 2005 in the six districts they collected data from.

Bihari migrants are spread far and wide, particularly within India. Policies like the National Rural Employment Guarantee Act (NREGA) have played an important role in reducing the very short-run seasonal migration after 2005; however, long-term migration remains. A key concern for many migrants is the lack of access to cheap and easy institutional arrangements for remittances. Informal intermediaries that charge large sums often handle this service. Accessing banking services in order to channelize remittances remains difficult for many migrants as they are unable to provide basic "Know Your Customer" or "KYC" documentation, which is critical to opening bank accounts. Migrant households have systematically worked around such requirements with the help of their social networks that assist with remittance and provide a range of other services, such as help at the time of illness, and other social protection. The lack of remunerative employment options within Bihar has often driven migrants out. As economic conditions within Bihar improve, the impetus for out-migration may reduce and economic development may bring back a group of migrants with skills acquired through experience that may be particularly useful in raising the productivity of work in the already very large services sector in Bihar.

CONCLUDING REMARKS

In this chapter, we identified the steps taken by the government of Bihar since 2005 that helped catalyze faster growth. While the measures were many and diverse, these were all introduced to strengthen governance in Bihar. The chapter also documents how various social indicators improved and provides a discussion of the role of remittances from migrants. We also analyze district-level growth rates with an explicit focus on accounting for variation in growth. Some of the more technical arguments are gathered together in an appendix to Mukherji and Mukherji (2012), referred to earlier in a similar context.

CHAPTER 11

Governance and Reforms Matter

INTRODUCTION

Does governance matter? Olson (1993) argues that the incentive structure for the "ruler" latent in any governance framework is essential to determining the kind of economic outcomes that society enjoys. For example, if the governance system is one that allows frequent and extensive loot of state revenue by multiple competing interests, colorfully called "roving bandits" by Olson, then not only is there no incentive to save and invest in that society, but eventually there is little to loot as well and thus economic failure is inevitable. If one of these looters were to assert control over the state and become a "stationary bandit," then it would be in the "stationary bandit's" interest to enable investment and economic growth, in order to encourage output so that there is more to appropriate. Clearly, the enabling mechanism there is provision of public goods and services within a functional governance structure. Usually, strong institutions to ensure property rights and safety and security are considered essential for growth and development. Whether there exist strong institutions or not depends in large part on the past. For example, a colonial past is difficult to change, and there exists evidence to suggest that depending on the colonizing power and the conditions of colonization, there are differences in the quality of institutions created.[1] So while governance matters, the type of governance that evolves is often itself reflective of the precise history of the place under consideration.[2]

---

[1]. Acemoglu et al. (2001) argue that European colonizers chose a variety of institutions depending on the type of colony they entered. In colonies with high mortalities, they set up extractive institutions, while in others they built institutions that support wealth creation and settled down. The nature of these institutions is associated with long-term growth. Similarly, North (1990) argues that British colonies did better than colonies of other European settlers as they created strong political and legal institutions that are more conducive to long-term growth.

[2]. Acemoglu and Robinson (2012) discuss the telling contrast between living in Nogales, Arizona (USA) and Nogales, Sonora (Mexico); this is explained by different governance, and it also explains more generally why nations may fail.

WHAT IS GOVERNANCE?

Exactly what does the term "governance" mean? The ordinary sense of the word "governance" is the act of governing, and it should hence encompass a wide variety of actions that allow an organization or the government to function smoothly. According to one view, "No theory of governance could be intelligible unless it is seen in the context of its time. India's democratic experience of the past six decades has clearly established that good governance must aim at expansion of social opportunities and removal of poverty" (Singh 2008). Good governance means securing justice, empowerment, employment, and efficient delivery of services. Stated thus, governance is not only absolutely necessary but crucial for any government to bring about betterment in human conditions.

With the advent of the NDA government led by Nitish Kumar in 2005, there was a strong emphasis on good governance. In fact, when asked by the press what the priorities for his government were, the Chief Minister famously replied that the first priority for his government was governance; he went on to list his second and third priorities also as governance. To judge the performance of Nitish Kumar's government, we attempt to identify what constitutes "good governance."

To that end, we start with a reference to Kautilya's *Arthashastra* from the translation by Rangarajan (1992: 108):

> In the interests of the prosperity of the country, a king should be diligent in foreseeing the possibility of calamities, try to avert them before they arise, overcome those that happen, remove all obstructions to economic activity and prevent loss of revenue to the state.

Kautilya continues,

> The pursuit of the people's welfare as well as the maintenance of the philosophic tradition, the Vedas and the economic well-being of the society is dependent on the scepter wielded by the King. The maintenance of law and order by the use of punishment is the science of government.

He finally adds,

> When no punishment is awarded [through misplaced leniency and when no law prevails], then there is only the law of the fish. . . . Unprotected, the small fish will be swallowed up by the big fish. In the presence of a king maintaining just law, the weak can resist the powerful.

According to Kautilya, justice is essential for governance, since it protects the weak. Consequently, it is clear what good governance was for Kautilya: law and order, a just and efficient judiciary, protection from natural and other disasters, and a healthy state of government revenues. Writing almost two thousand years later, in 1755, Adam Smith had an almost identical view, stating, "Little else is required to carry a state to the highest degree of opulence from the lowest barbarism, but peace, easy taxes, and a tolerable administration of justice; all the rest being brought about by the natural course of things." Thus, four things are required: (1) adequate, but not oppressive, taxes to collect adequate revenue; (2) providing public goods of high quality; (3) the rule of law and (4) courts functioning well to provide justice. Besley and Persson (2011) put this succinctly in these words, "State authority, tax systems, court systems and democracy co-evolve in a complex web of interdependent causality." Thus, it seems that the requirements for good governance have long been well understood. However, achieving these conditions must be difficult, since we seldom see the ideal situation in actual fact. One idea subsumed among the requirements is that the state leadership must be sufficiently efficient and competent.

The World Bank in turn has identified the following six key indicators of governance: (1) voice and accountability, (2) political stability and lack of violence, (3) government effectiveness, (4) regulatory quality, (5) rule of law, and (6) control of corruption (Kauffman et al. 2010). As is clear from the quotes from Kautilya and Adam Smith, these six indicators actually overlap, for example, government effectiveness and regulatory quality, on the one hand, and rule of law and control of corruption, on the other. Therefore, without too much further discussion, we can settle on four indicators of good governance: (1) peace and tranquility, (2) adequate revenues, (3) quality of public services, and (4) a just and effective legal system.

AND WHAT DID BIHAR DO?

We proceed to measure the Bihar government's performance against these indicators. Many of the actions taken by the Nitish Kumar government seem to be broadly consistent with improvement in governance along these indicators. As discussed earlier, there was a significant lack of state planning and expenditure throughout much of the 1990s. This in turn led to a retreat of the state from almost each and every activity of governance during that time. Even addressing such omissions and spending the available funds according to the approved state plans would have gone some distance toward improved governance. Under Nitish Kumar, the state government went well beyond this, innovatively restructuring public expenditures to improve the delivery of public services.

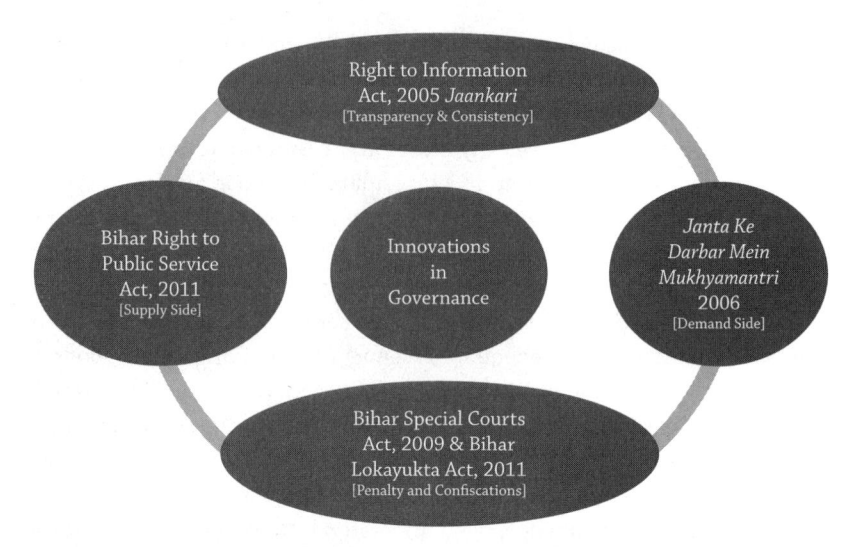

```
                    Right to Information
                    Act, 2005 Jaankari
                   [Transparency & Consistency]


  Bihar Right to                              Janta Ke
  Public Service      Innovations           Darbar Mein
   Act, 2011              in                Mukhyamantri
   [Supply Side]       Governance               2006
                                             [Demand Side]


                    Bihar Special Courts
                    Act, 2009 & Bihar
                    Lokayukta Act, 2011
                   [Penalty and Confiscations]
```

Figure 11.1: Framework for Governance in Bihar
Source: Kumar (2011).

Mukherjee's (2010) interviews with key players in the government in Bihar capture the fact that governance changes in Bihar were driven directly from the office of the Chief Minister. We use figure 11.1 to identify the overarching structure within which many of the initiatives of the government of Bihar may be classified.[3] In an attempt to create trust and faith of citizens in governance, the Bihar administration quickly worked on implementing the Central Government Right to Information Act through the introduction of *Jankari* after coming to power in 2005. The lack of transparency and access to the government under the earlier regime needed to be reversed, and the first step toward this was the creation of this e-governance network through which information could be sought by anyone. Access was significantly improved making it possible for people to file an RTI (Right to Information) request over the phone from anywhere (Kumar 2007). This award-winning e-governance portal not only made it possible for citizens to access information, it also provided an easy mechanism for the state government in Patna to understand the citizens' immediate concerns and follow up on them.[4]

   3. Figure 11.1 was used by Chanchal Kumar, an IAS officer of the Bihar cadre, and Secretary to Chief Minister, Nitish Kumar, at a conference in IIM Bangalore to report on the government of Bihar's attempts to improve state capacity and governance (Kumar 2011).
   4. See http://www.humanrightsinitiative.org/programs/ai/rti/india/states/bihar.htm for more on RTI norms in Bihar. Within the first two years, 22,600 calls were placed through *Jankari*. This e-governance system was the first ever in India and won a Gold Medal in a 2009 competition conducted by the Department of Administrative Reforms, Union Ministry of Personnel, Government of India; *Jankari* won for being the "simplest and the best" (TNN 2009). It has been adopted in other states such as in Karnataka, where it is called *Sakala*.

To ensure that the Chief Minister and his office were apprised of citizen concerns through direct dialogue, a weekly program called *Janata ke Darbar mein Mukhyamantri* (JKDM) was started in 2006. The title of the program loosely translates as "the Chief Minister in the People's Court." The choice of the title is significant: it suggests that the Chief Minister would be answerable for any shortcomings in the state. In the semi-feudal environment that dominates Bihar, the common man associates the holding of *darbars* or courts with the rulers. Therefore, the title of the program signaled who the rulers were: the people of Bihar. The Chief Minister was, thus, portrayed as a mere public servant summoned before the latter. This was powerful imagery. Beginning in 2007, the *darbar* was taken online via a Public Grievance Redressal System, which allowed citizens to file applications electronically and follow the progress. The program went some distance toward building all-important faith in the government process. Above all, it assured both citizens and public service providers that the highest levels of the government were accessible to the citizens.

Given that seeking public services was seen as the last resort prior to 2005, encouraging demand for public services in its citizens was seen to be a necessary strategy for delivering on governance (Kumar 2011). While under the JKDM scheme the Chief Minister would informally allocate a senior officer to follow-up with and commit to a time-line for the applicant, this was formalized into the Bihar Right to Public Service Act in 2011. Over 50 services spread across 10 key departments in the government were brought under this act. In effect, the Bihar government was attempting to ease friction with regard to both demand and supply of public services through greater transparency and effective monitoring from Patna. Clearly, both transparency and monitoring are necessary to ensure that governance remains focused on the needs of citizens and responds when a demand is made.

The final link in this governance framework is the ability of Bihar's legal system and associated policing system to effectively provide peace and security to its citizens. Moving away from the catastrophic failure of security in the past demanded great political will, which was clearly visible, but it also needed legislation to ensure that long trials of well-known criminals with long histories could be concluded quickly. To ensure that due process was followed throughout, prosecution under the Speedy Courts was explicitly legalized under the Constitution of India through the Bihar Special Courts Act of 2009.

To restore faith of the citizens in the system, it was further necessary to ensure that acts of corruption in public office were swiftly punished. Gupta (2011) identifies that leaks from government funds prior to 2004/05 were at the "input stage," that is, before anything was done with the funds as, for example, in the case of the fodder scam. These funds were not invested in the state but were rather spent on acquiring real estate in metropolitan cities or on other items of conspicuous consumption. These diversions of funds became subject to punishment under the Bihar Lokayukta Act of 2011. Rent-seeking activities by bureaucrats were also heavily curtailed by the Bihar Special Courts Act, which enables the government to confiscate property if it was found to be disproportionately large relative to the known sources of the individual's income. The government then reused such confiscated property for appropriate public purpose. In one such highly visible case, the act was used to seize a palatial building built by a senior bureaucrat that was later converted into a school (Ahmad 2011). The Right to Public Service Act also plays an important role in this battle against corruption alongside the Bihar Lokayukta Act of 2011. The Right to Public Service Act explicitly stipulates a time frame within which citizens must receive service; additionally, there are penalty clauses for employees or officers in case the necessary service is not provided within the stipulated time frame. The ability of employees to engage in corruption was, thus, significantly curtailed, first by making it difficult to ask for compensation to perform routine duties and, second, by confiscation of whatever is identified as illegal income from graft.

This complex of governance changes, consisting of legislative action and near continuous monitoring by the Chief Minister's Office (CMO), is one way to ensure delivery of service and combat corruption. While this provides an overarching framework for governance reforms in Bihar, positive steps have also been taken to help the economy grow. Having successfully brought the Maoist insurgency under control, it was necessary to step up spending in social and infrastructure sectors. This required imaginative fiscal management consisting of the use of the existing national schemes for the retirement of the state's debt and accessing funds available under various national schemes. Nitish Kumar and his team of officers set an excellent pace of change and monitored the process closely to ensure success on both fronts.

Two cases illustrate the role of leadership in bringing about improvements in the lives of the people. The first concerns the fight against Maoism in Bihar. Just before the new government came to power in 2005, the Maoists carried out a very well-planned and coordinated attack on the Jehanabad district jail. Some 200 heavily armed Maoists attacked the jail to free some of their leaders. Before launching this attack on the jail and the police barracks in the center of the town, party workers went around telling people to stay indoors because they might otherwise be hurt. The attack allowed the Maoists to escape with 100 of their jailed comrades and brought home the realization to the government how unprepared it was against the Maoist threat (PTI 2005).

Nitish Kumar's stance on dealing with Maoism was very clearly outlined when he said that Maoists are rebels, whereas the people in government are democratically elected and that steps taken by Maoists could not and should not be mimicked by the state. On the contrary what the state needs to do is to take development to them (Express News Service 2010; PTI 2010 a and b.).

This view gave credence to the complaints of Maoists that the fruits of development had passed them by; further, the regions of Maoist influence are also among the poorest in Bihar and indeed the country as a whole. This led the Chief Minister to announce, in a meeting with the Prime Minister, the Home Minister and other Chief Ministers in July 2010, "Bihar has adopted an integrated approach which can be the appropriate strategy for its effective and permanent solution.... Only intensive, holistic development can be the final solution of left wing extremism.... The state government is committed to establish the rule of law by protecting human rights" (Sinha 2011: 260). This was perhaps the only statement from a major political leader that described the Maoists not as "enemies of the state" but as rebels entitled to human rights. Interestingly, on capturing important Maoist leaders, the government did not insist on speedy trials. Whether this was accidental or by design, it was criticized by the media. Some expressed the view that this was aimed at preventing an all-out offensive against Maoists (Sinha 2011: 260–263).

The second example is that of the particularly influential scheme granting 2,500 rupees to every girl studying in Class IX and X to purchase a bicycle that could be ridden to school and providing uniforms to children. This scheme was announced in 2006 and it achieves several objectives at once. To begin with, it targets the extremely poor state of education for the girl child in Bihar (Debroy 2010). Apart from these gender and educational aspects, the scheme also served as an extraordinary litmus test of law and order in the state and has proved to be one of the world's largest and most successful cash transfer programs ever, with over 900,000 cycles purchased over the 2006–10 period. This became so symbolic of the Nitish Kumar administration that Lalu Prasad attacked it in the run-up to the 2010 elections by offering free motorcycles if he were elected. However, he was forced to retract this once Nitish Kumar pointed out that underage schoolgirls would not be given license for driving motorcycles and would be arrested if driving without license.

We have also discussed the increasing role that domestic (within India, but outside Bihar) remittances played in Bihar's economy. Such remittances in principle provide households in Bihar with access to unearned incomes, and much of the existing theoretical and empirical literature argues that access to such unearned income either in the form of aid or remittances is strongly associated with reductions in public goods and spending, and poorer public investment on economic activities.[5] It is to the credit of the leadership in Bihar that, alongside such remittances, the government continued to increase its development expenditures and did so by cutting back on non-development expenditures (see figure 10.2).

---

5. See Ross (2001) for an argument in the context of oil-economies and Ahmed (2012) for a more specific argument in the context of aid and remittances.

Thus, the new government managed to convince the citizens that good things were in the offing and that change was in the air. This was seen to be a major achievement, since the Chief Minister in one of his speeches mentioned that a major barrier to development was the mindset of people who believed that nothing good could happen (or as he said in Hindi, "*kucho nahin hoga*" or the people he described as "*nirasha ke masiha*," literally the prophets of gloom)—the naysayers (Banerji 2011). It is said that the Chief Minister is very sensitive to managing public perceptions to facilitate progress and development. The 2010 elections were fought and won on a pro-economic development plank by the Janata Dal (United) (JD(U)) and Bharatiya Janata Party (BJP) combine; they were triumphant in Bihar where development had hardly seemed possible when Ashish Bose classified it as a BIMARU state as early as the mid-1980s.[6]

THE *BIHAR GAZETTE* NOTIFICATION OF 2010

Once the JD(U)–BJP combine came back to power, it published a very interesting statement of intent in the *Bihar Gazette* (Government of Bihar 2010b). The document set out what the government would like to achieve. The areas picked for special attention were agriculture, infrastructure and urbanization, water resources, human capital, state capabilities, and, of course, governance. Roy (2011) captures some of the salient features of the program:

- Agriculture: One of the objectives was to seek a substantial increase in allocation to agriculture and target a growth rate of 7%, which was well above the national average.
- Infrastructure and Urbanization: The aim was to address the acute power shortages and add more roads, especially rural roads. The target was to travel to Patna from the interior-most part of Bihar in six hours.
- Water Resources: Water resources management (flood control and management and flood forecasting systems) was important; irrigation systems were to be augmented; and groundwater management and irrigation were to be improved.
- Human Capital: It has now been understood that economic growth is sustainable only when human capital is available; to make this human capital effective and healthy, several targets were set. They included cutting malnourishment from the then level of 27% to less than 20%, increasing routine immunization to 90% at least by 2015, making available

---

6. The word BIMARU literally means "sick" in Hindi. But it is also an acronym coined to refer to the four poorest large states in India: Bihar, Madhya Pradesh, Rajasthan and Uttar Pradesh.

round-the-clock healthcare in all healthcare facilities, reducing the infant mortality rate to 28 and maternal mortality rate to 1 per 1,000 live births, and reducing anemia among women and girls by 50%. Apart from health, skill formation has to take place, and on the education front too, several targets were assigned: 100% primary enrollment by 2015, reduction of dropout rates for secondary education to less than 25% and primary to less than 20%, raising the quality of teaching, an increase in capacity and quality of educational institutions, and narrowing the gender gap in educational attainments.
- Migration is an important and noteworthy aspect of the Bihar economy. The economy of Bihar depends heavily on migrant incomes, which accounted for as much as 4%–7% of NSDP in 2007/08 (Rodgers and Rodgers 2011). The objectives in this regard are to provide better training to potential migrants so that they can obtain higher wages in their place of work; to consider some steps to increase employment opportunities at home to reduce out-migration (NREGA has contributed to this, but it is a centrally sponsored scheme); and to emphasize creation of rural livelihoods so that migration does not remain a necessity but gets transformed into an act of choice.
- State Capabilities: The priorities here are rural development (Panchayati Raj and women's participation) and food security (improvements in targeting and delivery by the Public Distribution System).
- Governance: To promote greater transparency, citizens' committees are to be set up wherever there is a public interface, with the assigned task of monitoring development schemes and suggesting improvements. The law and order machinery is being revamped and courts are being exhorted to use novel methods of reducing backlog.

The above list clearly outlines some of the diverse and comprehensive steps the government plans to take. There remain, of course, areas in which progress is likely to be difficult. The functioning of courts and general law and order (see our section on crime) may not respond as desired; for the moment, there does not appear to be any incentive for them to change. Corruption is being targeted but success with limiting corruption has been partial. There also remains the problem of inadequate attention to quality of public service.

Overall, there has been a concerted move to tackle many problems. The government has woken up to the fact that unless there is an integrated move on all fronts, success will not be achieved. There is now better access to justice and public services so that the first interaction for service is no longer the last one. The question one can pose is whether this is enough to make the turn-around we see into a permanent one.

The Nitish Kumar-led government, whether by serendipity or design, appears to have achieved some success and can be expected to continue to mobilize the government for the delivery of services to the people. To keep abreast of the concerns and challenges of ordinary Bihari citizens, the Chief Minister undertakes frequent Sewa Yatras (service travels) that span 38 districts; he stays in each district for a few days, holding meetings with the common people, listening to their complaints, and calling departmental heads when necessary. It is reported that the common people have warmly welcomed these visits, but the bureaucracy is uncomfortable since it is under scrutiny (ET Bureau 2011). In fact, which departmental head will have to accompany the Chief Minister is never divulged beforehand; the surprise element is maintained to keep all personnel alert and ensure that standards are kept up. The objective of these Yatras is to monitor and review issues vital to improving governance. Consequently, the system is being subjected to great regulation and examination. The worrying thing is that the Chief Minister realizes that it is he who must do the regulating. Given this point, one may argue that the system may not be changing after all. In the larger discussion of whether institutions can create development or the leader must create it, Bihar's experience currently is one of the leadership creating the institutions to support growth. Concerns emerge about what would happen in the absence of such tight monitoring and careful overseeing at the top. We have summarized all that was done by the government of Bihar during the period between 2004/05 and 2009/10, the first five years that the government was in power. Looking back at Kautilya, Adam Smith, or Besley and Persson on governance, it would appear that the government is doing everything right. Can it continue to govern consistently in such a manner in the future?

Since governance is the main plank of the current government, it is fair to examine this aspect closely. Clearly, governance in Bihar has been strongly led by Nitish Kumar; this has been its strength, but it is also its weakness once one thinks of long-term growth. It is strength because it has allowed the unrolling of governance in a centralized fashion to deal with the deeply entrenched lack of public service delivery. However, it is also of concern in the long run, since this leadership is not very broad-based; it not only limits growth today, but should Nitish Kumar engage in politics at the central government level, it would be a matter of concern for Bihar's economy. In such a situation, who will support, monitor, and follow up on the logical consequences of existing policies?

A disciplined political party, with a strong organizational structure, that is able to convey issues, capture debates, and provide a sense of citizenship within which disagreements can be resolved is strongly associated with not only improved electoral results but also improved governance outcomes in the long run.[7] Within the context of India, Atul Kohli (1987) argued that a reason for the systematic persistence of poverty, or the failure of good economic outcomes, was poorly utilized state power and incomplete land reforms. Both reasons remain valid in Bihar's context; while the latter's importance has not diminished since independence, it remains an agenda without a political champion within electoral politics, and the former remains critical for long-term growth. A more broad-based political leadership tends to also provide a more supportive environment for private investment and greater industry commitment that the state will necessarily have to seek in order to encourage long-term growth. In this context, it is interesting to return to Olson (1993), who argues that the key difference in incentives between a "stationary bandit" and a democratic system is that in a democratic system, broad-based leadership ensures that political parties can remain engaged in governance and the resulting growth would be "encompassing," while in the former, it is dependent on the individual; growth in such autocracies is most threatened at times of transition.

Finally, it is still true that there are politicians in every party who have a criminal past. What appears to have changed is that when they step out of line now and violate the law, they are hauled up irrespective of the party they belong to. At least this much is clear from past evidence. But so long as such elements are present, it would have to be assumed that they perform some role helpful to the government. It is this aspect of apparent collusion with criminal elements that continues to make people uncomfortable with the governance in Bihar.

WHAT NEXT?

Even if it has begun catching up, Bihar's economy still remains overwhelmingly poor. What further reforms are needed? As discussed, the first five years of the Nitish Kumar government have been focused on improved access. Clearly, something more is required, and that is quality in the delivery of public services. The easiest gains possible through ensuring recruitment and oversight to ensure functionality of different public service mechanisms have already been achieved. However, unless the quality of public service delivery in education, health, and public distribution improves substantially, growth will peter out in the near future. The difficulty is in monitoring the

---

7. See Olson (1986) and Caillaud and Tirole (2002) on better organized parties winning elections more frequently, and Boix (1998) for an articulation of how better organized political parties are better able to build a consensus across interests and deliver better economic outcomes.

quality of service, a process harder to carry out than monitoring existence or creation of services. Apart from these governance challenges, other major economic challenges remain as well. A strategy for robust economic growth for Bihar must take into consideration the following:

- Our analysis shows that much of the unevenness in economic growth in Bihar is due to fluctuation in economic outcomes in a set of key districts. Thought and public service in these districts needs to be oriented toward diversifying economic activity in these districts.
- With significant dependence on agriculture, Bihar must improve its agricultural and factor productivity. Given the long history of low productivity, this is an endemic problem and there are few models that offer an easy path to improved productivity. In this regard, reform in Agricultural Produce Market Committee (APMC) Act, enabling contract farming and high-value produce (horticulture and plantation) may provide some avenues to improved outcomes.
- Closely tied to the issue of improving agricultural productivity is also the issue of the unequal distribution of land in Bihar. Land reform has been and will continue to be strongly needed in Bihar, as would laws for easy and transparent norms for sale, and lease of land.
- Another key shortcoming has been the availability of credit to farmers and programs such as the Kisan Credit Card provide some relief, but more needs to be done since much of rural borrowing in Bihar remains non-institutional and informal (Kamath et al. 2010).
- Development of rural infrastructure, such as irrigation projects, roads, and electrification is important for the economy. While much has been done to improve roads, other areas such electrification and irrigation remain areas where much more can be done.
- Finally, growth in Bihar is centered on services, especially construction, while most of the labor continues to be employed in agriculture. A number of questions arise on the transition of labor from the agricultural to non-agricultural sector: clearly industry today in Bihar does not have the size to absorb a significant fraction of the labor employed in agriculture. The only immediate possible route appears to be the rapid expansion of the food-processing industry. However, the fact that this has been slow to start off does not mean that it cannot expand rapidly in the future. Similarly, the services sector is large in size and can potentially absorb large components of the agricultural labor force. This could in principle lead to significant equity gains as well, but a long-run question that emerges in this context is what kind of a service economy could Bihar become as it considers the service sector as a way forward for growth and development. One of these two strategies will play out and the role of policy will be critical in enabling this transition.

CONCLUDING REMARKS

In this chapter, we began by focusing on the scholarly literature that tries to capture what constitutes good governance. With this as background, we focused on the different innovations in governance that we have seen in Bihar in an attempt to assess whether there have been any obvious omissions. The Bihar government's focus on improved law and order, better public service delivery, and a fair and independent judiciary suggests that its policies are in broad conformity with what scholars on governance consider important for sustained growth that is also inclusive. A negative feature pointed out was that the system itself appeared to have not changed; strict control from the Chief Minister's office was actually necessary to keep everything on the straight and narrow.

CHAPTER 12

Conclusions

The transition in Bihar from a moribund economy to an expanding economy with a state government actively engaging in governance has been remarkable. However, the state remains poor and well below the national average in terms of well-being, productivity, and public investment. The key question for Bihar today is "What next?" Will this be a short-lived expansion—similar to expansion seen in historical Bihar under Sher Shah around A.D. 1500? Or will this be similar to the Chaco Phenomenon, so that after a period of frantic activity, the economy will hit another slump? Either would be a tragic postscript to Bihar's story, and while we believe that this should not happen, there still remain fundamental challenges for the economy to resolve in the near future to sustain growth and include larger and poorer sections of the economy in the expansion process.

We have dwelled on the importance of leadership in the government in the context of both historic notions of governance as well as contemporary academic thought; we also related this to the current functioning of the government of Bihar. A strong leadership that seeks to understand its citizen's demands, provides an appropriate supply of public services, ensures a fair and just law and order mechanism, and manages its revenues to support development has been recognized for centuries as the foundation of a prosperous economy. Such leadership was the key to the success achieved during the Great Mauryan Empire, which flourished under the great emperor Ashoka.

Some peace and healthy commerce have been in evidence in Bihar in the past seven years. Will this continue in the future? And will this alone drive growth in Bihar in the future? A number of challenges remain to be addressed, and these are probably harder challenges to deal with than those that have already been managed.

A key concern with the growth in Bihar has been the effect that this growth has had on the poor. The Planning Commission data released in

2009/10 deepened this concern considerably. In fact these figures showed that poverty levels (using the Tendulkar definition of the poverty line) had stagnated during the period 2004/05 to 2009/10 having moved from 54% to 53.5%. This was quite unexpected as this was also a period of high growth in the state and the general perception is that such rates of growth should lead to poverty being reduced. Initial interpretation of these findings centered on the growth process in Bihar not being inclusive (i.e., the high growth did not benefit the poor); however, recent estimates suggests that the poverty ratio has indeed declined by more than 20 percentage points (table 8.5, last row) over the period 2004/05 to 2011/12. The earlier finding that there was no effect on poverty is now being explained in terms of the temporary effects of the coterminous drought of 2009/10.

According to the Tendulkar methodology, the percentage of people below the poverty line has decreased significantly. Does this mean that poverty is indeed down?[1] To be able to reach this conclusion we need to be sure that the Tendulkar methodology identifies the poor correctly. It is here that the controversy arises and there are many commentators who claim that that people above this poverty line should also be considered poor since according to them, the poverty line according to Tendulkar is set too low.[2] Consequently, to say that growth has been inclusive, namely, the effects of growth have been felt by all the poor, we need to look at many of the people above the Tendulkar poverty line as well; the Planning Commission (2013) document tries to make this calculation for all-India and shows that there is a general decline in poverty levels at a number of different alternative poverty lines. Whether one can attribute this reduction completely or even substantially to the growth process is another question altogether. More important, this presents an all-India picture, and this regularity in reduction of poverty at alternative poverty lines may not necessarily be the case for Bihar either. While this larger question remains an open one, we can say that during a period of rapid economic growth there has been a significant decline in the poverty ratio when poverty is defined by the Tendulkar poverty lines.

The services sector has been leading growth in India since the early 1990s and this is the case for Bihar too, although it started expanding in earnest only after the 2005 elections. Eichengreen and Gupta (2011) estimate that within the services sector, sub-sectors such as communications, business services, financial services, education, health, and hotels account for roughly half the services growth seen in India between 2000 and 2008. Bihar, however, still remains largely rural and substantially informal, and therefore,

1. See Mihir Shah (2013) and N. K. Singh (2013), for example, for some lucid discussion in this connection.
2. See Mihir Shah (2013).

growth in services in it has a narrower base. With sub-sectors such as trade, hotels, and restaurants capturing 27%–28% of NSDP in an economy with very low urbanization rates, it is imperative to engage differently with the services sector at the state level. While India's growth experience deviates from the natural progression seen historically, in Kuznets's work, for instance, even this may not be the right model for Bihar at its current stage and with its present economic structure. It is imperative that the government identifies ways in which employment can be moved from agriculture to other sectors. At the same time, Bihar's existing comparative advantage lies in agriculture: with vast swathes of some of the world's most fertile lands, access to perennial rivers, and the ability to grow a hugely diverse basket of food-grains and horticultural commodities, this sector can produce sustained income growth. However, significant efforts are needed to realize this potential through better inputs for higher productivity and outreach to markets; the entire agricultural value chain is in need of reform.

Apart from a structural transformation of the economy, the other aspect that we would like to re-emphasize is the issue of productivity, the lack of skill generation, the absence of vocational training and the absence of job-ready candidates that can engage in growing sectors and sub-sectors of the economy. Productivity is low in Bihar and there is little that suggests that this can change in the short run. Extensive and creative investment in creating institutions to develop skills with clear links to business is imperative. This process is, however, characterized by long gestation periods and will not immediately ease up skill shortage and boost productivity. The skills, however, are not in short supply in the country; in fact, the large migrant population from Bihar may itself be able to bridge some of the current gaps, provided it finds the right incentives to return to Bihar. The business climate is improving and the state has begun using Bihari pride as a way to reach out to people (TNN 2011). However, to attract migrants back to Bihar's economy and stimulate them to participate productively, the government needs to go beyond pride and appeal to tangible economic motives.

Thus, if one looks only at past policies that hold Bihar at a serious disadvantage today, then one can identify at least four such policies that have had long-lasting impacts on Bihar. These policies are:

- *The Permanent Settlement.* Areas with alternative land tenure system such as the Raiyatwari system have clearly prospered (Banerjee and Iyer 2005). In fact, some of the areas where the Permanent Settlement was institutionalized also prospered but in almost all of them significant land reforms have been carried out (W. Bengal and Bangladesh).
- *Freight Equalization* destroyed any comparative advantage in industry that regions such as Bihar and Jharkhand enjoyed. With the minerals delivered at the same price, industries, which could have otherwise located themselves

in this region, had no reason to do so. And Bihar continued to pay more for commodities not covered by this policy: petroleum, for example. Thus, industrialization was postponed leading to significant losses from forward and backward linkages that could have developed in the absence of this policy.
- *Governance* and specially law and order were an issue, as we have shown above. Raiyatwari areas were better administered: "The raiyatwari provinces, where agricultural output had to be estimated and government benefitted from increases in output needed much more administration than permanent settlement areas" (Kumar 1982: 909). Consequently, law and order were better enforced in these areas. It is of no surprise therefore that Bihar prospered only after 2005 when the law and order received greater emphasis.
- *Designed government failure* was not only a facet of the RJD government but this too had its origins in the long areas of neglect that we have documented. In fact a look at figure 8.2 shows that Bihar has been doing far more poorly than the rest of India since 1980. Matters went really out of hand during the RJD years.

This, of course, does not mean that any of the other issues that we have not highlighted are not important. For example, caste conflicts and the resultant lack of social unity, or the weakness of leadership will continue to bring fresh challenges for Bihar. Two issues that we think will drive much of Bihar in the near future are:

- Bihar is largely rural. At 10.8%, urbanization in 2011 was at the level prevailing in India in 1901. Combined with incomplete demographic transition and bourgeoning population growth rates, public service delivery still is a challenge in Bihar.
- With a very weak industrial sector, the chances of sustaining growth through strengthening industry seem very limited in the current context. In addition, with the power situation being very constrained, there is little ability to support industrialization. While plans are under way to ease this constraint, until this happens, industrialization growth will remain slow. Even land for industrialization may not be easily available; since doing so may be politically infeasible given that the high density of population implies that displacement population would be very high. Thus, only small and niche enterprises are likely to flourish.[3] In this respect,

---

3. In fact there is evidence of one such remarkable establishment in Patna in M. G. Rao (2005), which was converting black and white movies into color for Sony Corporation; the valued added per worker was as high as $4 per second per worker, as mentioned by the author; there were 30–40 Bihari workers involved. Sadly they had relocated to Goa when the author encountered them in 2005. This brings us to the next point of concern, the maintenance of law and order the failure of which must have led to the relocation.

agro- and horticulture-based industries have begun entering Bihar; in this context, the prospects for rapid expansion of food-processing industries appear to be particularly bright.

The framework of governance that the Bihar government has successfully used in the last few years to tackle law-and-order issues, encourage transparency, gave a voice to citizens, and pushed hard to roll-out public programs and public service delivery. Much of what has been achieved has been driven from the Chief Minister's office, with senior bureaucrats working extended hours to monitor and follow-up on service delivery. The importance of such close monitoring will remain undiminished. The state needs to maintain the current tempo and also begin tackling longer term structural issues. How well will it succeed? The current evidence from Bihar gives reason to be cautiously optimistic.[4]

---

4. A discordant note was struck in June 2012 during the funeral of the murdered Ranvir Sena leader in Patna. For a short time, the state had ceased to function! Gupta (2012) describes the incident and cautions the state to ensure that it must "perform its mandated role." Clearly Bihar can ill afford such instances of breakdown of law and order. Investor confidence is notoriously fickle.

PART II REFERENCES

Acemoglu, D., and J. A. Robinson (2012). *Why Nations Fail: The Origins of Power, Prosperity and Poverty*. London: Profile Books Ltd.

Acemoglu, D., S. Johnson, and J. A. Robinson (2001). "The Colonial Origins of Comparative Development: An Empirical Investigation." *American Economic Review* 91(5) (Dec.): 1369–1401.

Adovasio, J. M., with Jake Page (2002). *The First Americans: In Pursuit of Archaeology's Great Mystery*. New York: Random House.

Ahmad, F. (2011). "Bihar Govt. to Turn Corrupt Babu's House into School." *The Times of India*, Patna Edition, Aug. 22. http://timesofindia.indiatimes.com/city/patna/Bihar-govt-to-turn-corrupt-babus-house-into-school/articleshow/9689017.cms.

Ahmed, F. (2012). "The Perils of Unearned Foreign Income: Aid, Remittances, and Government Survival." *American Political Science Review* 106 (Feb.): 146–165.

Aiyar, S. S. A. (2010). "Bihar's Economic Miracle: Real, but Fragile." *The Economic Times*. Feb. 21. http://articles.economictimes.indiatimes.com/2010-02-21/news/27629383_1_bihar-nitish-kumar-state-data.

Aiyar, S., and A. Mody (2011). "The Demographic Dividend: Evidence from the Indian States." IMF Working Papers WP/11. http://www.imf.org/external/pubs/ft/wp/2011/wp1138.pdf.

Ali, A., S. Nayak, and S. Mukhopadhya (2007). *State of Health in Bihar*. New Delhi: Population Foundation of India.

Anonymous (2011). "Bihar's Development Lessons for Nepal." *Republica*. Aug. 2. http://www.myrepublica.com/portal/index.php?action=news_details&news_id=34236.

Appu, P. S. (1973). "Unequal Benefits from the Kosi Development: Cost of Bypassed Institutional Reform." *Economic and Political Weekly* 8(24): 1076–1081.

Arulampalam, W., D. Dasgupta, A. Dhillon, and B. Dutta (2009). "Electoral Goals and Center-State Transfers: A Theoretical Model and Empirical Evidence from India." *Journal of Development Economics* 88(1) (Jan.): 103–119.

ASER Center (2007). "Annual Survey of Education Report (Rural) 2006." Mumbai: Pratham Resource Center. http://images2.asercentre.org/ASER_REPORTS/ASER_2006_Report.pdf.

——. (2012). "Annual Survey of Education Report (Rural) 2011." Mumbai: Pratham Resource Center. http://images2.asercentre.org/aserreports/ASER_2011/aser_2011_report_8.2.12.pdf.

Bagchi, A., and P. Chakraborty (2004). "Towards a Rational System of Centre-State Revenue Transfers in India: An Exploration." *Economic and Political Weekly* 39(26) (June 26–July 2): 2737–2747.

Balchand, K. (2008). "Life Term for Pappu Yadav, Two Others." *The Hindu.* http://www.hindu.com/2008/02/15/stories/2008021560271400.htm.

Banerjee, A. V., and L. Iyer (2005). "History, Institutions, and Economic Performance: The Legacy of Colonial Land Tenure Systems in India." *American Economic Review* 95(4) (Sept.): 1190–1213.

Banerji, R. (2011). "Challenging Bihar on Primary Education." *Economic and Political Weekly* 46(11): 33–39.

Becker, G. (2007). "Health as Human Capital: Synthesis and Extensions." *Oxford Economic Papers* 59: 379–410.

Besley, T., and T. Persson (2011). *Pillars of Prosperity: The Political Economics of Development Clusters.* Princeton, NJ, and Oxford: Princeton University Press.

Bhattacharya, D. (2000). "Bihar after Bifurcation: A Challenging Future." *Economic and Political Weekly* 35(43/44): 3800–3804.

Biswas, R., S. Marjit, and V. Marimoutou (2010). "Fiscal Federalism, State Lobbying at the Center and Discretionary Finance in India." *Economics and Politics* 22(1): 68–91.

Boix, C. (1998). *Political Parties, Growth, and Equality: Conservative and Social Democratic Economic Strategies in the World Economy.* Cambridge: Cambridge University Press.

Caillaud, B., and J. Tirole (2002). "Parties as Political Intermediaries." *Quarterly Journal of Economics* 117(4) (Nov.): 1453–1489.

Chakraborty, P. (2011). "Recommendations of Thirteenth Finance Commission: Implications for Bihar." IGC Working Paper 11/0094. Mar. http://www.theigc.org/sites/default/files/11_0070_wp_bihar_0.pdf.

Chanda, A. (2011). "Accounting for Bihar's Productivity Relative to India's: What Can We Learn from Recent Developments in Growth Theory?" IGC Working Paper 11/0759. Aug. http://www.theigc.org/sites/default/files/11_0579_chanda_bihar_final.pdf.

Chaudhuri, B. (1982). "Eastern India." In Dharma Kumar (ed.), *The Cambridge Economic History of India*, vol. 2: *c. 1757–1970*, 86–175. Cambridge: Cambridge University Press.

Chaudhuri, S., and N. Gupta (2009). "Levels of Living and Poverty Patterns: A District-wise Analysis for India." *Economic and Political Weekly* 44(9): 94–110.

Das, A. N. (1992). *The Republic of Bihar.* Delhi: Penguin Books India.

Dasgupta, A. (2007). "Floods and Poverty Traps: Evidence from Bangladesh." *Economic and Political Weekly* 42(30) (July 28–Aug. 3): 3166–3171.

Das Gupta, C. (2010). "Unraveling Bihar's 'Growth Miracle.'" *Economic and Political Weekly* 45(52): 50–62.

Das Gupta, C., and K. P. N. Haridas (2012). "Role of ICT in Improving the Quality of School Education in Bihar." IGC Working Paper 12/0169. Mar. http://www.theigc.org/sites/default/files/das_gupta_and_haridas_kpn_final_1.pdf.

Debroy, B. (2010). "A Bicycle Built for Many." *The Indian Express.* Dec. 8. http://www.indianexpress.com/story-print/721798/.

Deshingkar, P., S. Kumar, H. K. Chobey, and D. Kumar (2006). *The Role of Migration and Remittances in Promoting Livelihoods in Bihar.* London: Overseas Development Institute.

Dhaliwal, R. (2010). "Batala Foundries in a Shambles." *The Tribune.* July 10. http://www.tribuneindia.com/2010/20100711/jal.htm#1.

Dutt, S. (1962). *Buddhist Monks and Monasteries of India: Their History and Contribution to Indian Culture*. London: George Allen and Unwin Ltd.

Easterly, W., M. Kremer, L. Pritchett, and L. W. Summers (1993). "Good Policy or Good Luck? Country Growth Performance and Temporary Shocks." *Journal of Monetary Economics* 32(3) (Dec.): 459–483.

Eichengreen, B., and P. Gupta (2011). "The Service Sector: India's Road to Economic Growth?" NBER Working Paper No. 16757. http://www.nber.org/papers/w16757.

Eshwaran, M., A. Kotwal, B. Ramaswami, and W. Wadhwa (2009). "Sectoral Labor Flows and Agricultural Wages in India, 1983–2004: Has Growth Trickled Down?" *Economic and Political Weekly* 44(2) (Jan. 10): 46–55.

ET Bureau (2011). "Nitish Kumar Commences Sewa Yatra, Inspects Development Projects." *The Economic Times*. Nov. 10. http://articles.economictimes.indiatimes.com/2011-11-10/news/30382166_1_nitish-kumar-sugar-mill-lauriya.

Express News Service (2010). "Nitish's Nuanced Line on Maoists Faces Its First Test." *The Indian Express*. Sept. 3. http://www.indianexpress.com/story-print/676568/.

Friedman, R. A., J. R. Stein, and T. Blackhorse, Jr. (2003). "A Study of a Pre-Columbian Irrigation System at Newcomb, New Mexico." *Journal of GIS in Archaeology* 1 (Apr.): 4–10.

GFCC (2007). "Annual Report of the Ganga Flood Control Commission." Technical Report of the Ministry of Water Resources. Patna: Government of India. http://gfcc.bih.nic.in/Docs/Annual%20Report%202006-07.pdf.

Ghosh, P. P. (2007). "Change from the Middle? The Paradox that is Bihar: A Symposium on the State's Efforts at Overcoming a Troubled Past." Seminar 580. Dec. http://www.india-seminar.com/2007/580.htm.

Ghosh, P. P., and S. Gupta (2010). "Economic Growth and Human Development in Bihar." In Shovon Ray (ed.), *Backwaters of Development: Six Deprived States of India*, 37–72. New Delhi: Oxford University Press.

Glaeser, E. L., and A. Shleifer (2005). "The Curley Effect: The Economics of Shaping the Electorate." *Journal of Law, Economics, & Organization* 21(1): 1–19.

Government of Bihar (2005). "The Bihar Right to Information Rules, 2005." Patna: Government of Bihar. http://bipard.bih.nic.in/rti/Bihar%20RTI%20Rules_eng.pdf.

———. (2007). *Bihar Economic Survey 2006–2007*. Patna: Ministry of Finance, Government of Bihar.

———. (2008). *Bihar Economic Survey 2007–2008*. Patna: Ministry of Finance, Government of Bihar.

———. (2009). *Bihar Economic Survey 2008–2009*. Patna: Ministry of Finance, Government of Bihar.

———. (2010a). *Bihar Economic Survey 2009–2010*. Patna: Ministry of Finance, Government of Bihar.

———. (2010b). Program for Sushashan (2010–2015). *The Bihar Gazette*. Dec. 16. Serial No. 05/2010-1717. Sachivalaya, Patna. http://egazette.bih.nic.in. Note: *Sushashan* is a Hindi word. Translated into English it is "good governance." The entire announcement in the *Gazette* is in Hindi.

———. (2011). *Bihar Economic Survey 2010–2011*. Patna: Ministry of Finance, Government of Bihar.

Gupta, S. (2011). "The Buccaneering in Bihar." *The Indian Express*. Oct. 14. http://www.indianexpress.com/news/the-buccaneering-in-bihar/859591/.

Gupta, Shaibal (2012). "The Day They Laid a Wreath of Wrath." *GovernanceNow*, June 16–30, 56–58.

Guruswamy, M. (2007). "Centrally Planned Inequality. The Paradox that is Bihar: A Symposium on the State's Efforts at Overcoming a Troubled Past." Seminar 580. Dec. http://www.india-seminar.com/2007/580.htm.

Hirschman, A. O. (1958). *The Strategy of Economic Development*. New Haven, CT: Yale University Press.

IHD and ADRI (2010). "International Seminar on Poverty in Bihar: Pattern Dimension and Eradication Strategies." Apr. 18–20. http://www.ihdindia.org/pdf/Poverty_Seminar_Report.pdf.

IIPA (2010). "A Study of Bihari Migrant Labourers: Incidence, Causes and Remedies." Technical Report. New Delhi: Indian Institute of Public Administration.

Kamath, R., A. Mukherji, and M. Sandstrom (2010). "Accessing Institutional Finance: A Demand Side Story for Rural India." Special Article. *Economic and Political Weekly* 45(37) (Sept. 11): 56–62.

Kauffman, D., A. Kraay, and M. Mastruzzi (2010). "The Worldwide Governance Indicators: Methodology and Analytical Issues." *Hague Journal on the Rule of Law* 3: 220–246. Kingdon, G., R. Banerji, and P. Chaudhary (2008). "School TELLS Survey of Rural Primary Schools in Bihar and Uttar Pradesh, 2007–08." London: Institute of Education, University of London.

Kishore, A. (2004). "Understanding Agrarian Impasse in Bihar." *Economic and Political Weekly* 39(31) (July 31–Aug. 6): 3484–3491.

Kletzer, K., and N. Singh (1997). "The Political Economy of Indian Fiscal Federalism." In Sudipto Mundle (ed.), *Public Finance: Policy Issues for India*, 259–298. New Delhi: Oxford University Press.

Kohli, A. (1987). *The State and Poverty in India: The Politics of Reforms in Rural India*. Cambridge: Cambridge University Press. Reprinted 2006.

Kumar, A. (1996). *Chaos, Fractals and Self-organization*. New Delhi: National Book Trust.

Kumar, C. (2007). "Project Report on 'JANKAARI': ICT-Based Facilitation Center under RTI Act. A Government of Bihar Initiative." http://cic.gov.in/CIC-Articles/JAANKARI-pdf-26-03-07.pdf.

——. (2011). "Governance Issues & Reforms in Bihar." Presented at the 6th Conference on Public Policy and Management, IIM Bangalore, Dec. 29.

Kumar, D. (1982). "The Fiscal System." In Dharma Kumar (ed.), *The Cambridge Economic History of India*, vol. 2: *c. 1757–1970*, 905–912. Cambridge: Cambridge University Press.

Kumar, N. (2007). "Mission Impossible, the Paradox that is Bihar: A Symposium on the State's Efforts at Overcoming a Troubled Past." Seminar 580. Dec. http://www.india-seminar.com/2007/580.htm.

Kuznets, S. (1971). "Modern Economic Growth: Findings and Reflections." Nobel Prize Lecture. http://www.nobelprize.org/nobel_prizes/economics/laureates/1971/kuznets-lecture.html.

Lahiri, A., and K. Yi (2009). "A Tale of Two States: Maharashtra and West Bengal." *Review of Economic Dynamics* 12: 523–542.

Lekson, S. H. (1986). *Great Pueblo Architecture of the Chaco Canyon, New Mexico*. Albuquerque: University of New Mexico Press.

Lewin, S. (1993). *Complexity: Life on the Edge of Chaos*. London: Phoenix.

Mathew, S., and M. Moore (2011). "State Incapacity by Design: Understanding the Bihar Story." IDS Working Paper No. 366. May. http://www.ids.ac.uk/files/dmfile/Wp366.pdf.

Mishra, D. K. (2008a). "Bihar Floods: The Inevitable Has Happened." *Economic & Political Weekly* 43(36) (Sept. 6): 8–12.

———. (2008b), *Trapped! Between the Devil and Deep Waters*. Dehradun and Delhi: People's Science Institute and South Asia Network on Dams, Rivers and People.

Mookerji, R. (1959). *The Gupta Empire*. Reprinted (2007) New Delhi: Motilal Banarsidass Publishers.

Mukherjee, R. (2009). Interview with Mr. Abhayanand, IPS Officer from the Bihar Cadre. Series: Governance Traps, Interview B-1, Oral History Program. Princeton University's Innovations for Successful Societies. http://www.princeton.edu/successfulsocieties/content/data/oral_history/B1_PL_PP_CE_RT_ME__Abhayanand_id93/_Abhayanand.pdf.

———. (2010). "Reviving the Administration: Bihar State, India 2005–2009." Princeton University's Innovations for Successful Societies. http://www.princeton.edu/successfulsocieties.

Mukherji, Arnab, and Anjan Mukherji (2012). "Bihar: What Went Wrong? And What Changed?" National Institute of Public Finance and Policy Working Paper 12/107. http://www.nipfp.org.in/media/medialibrary/2013/04/WP_2012_107.pdf.

Mukim, M., and A. Panagariya (forthcoming). "A Comprehensive Look at Poverty Measures in India," Columbia University.

Muralidharan, Karthik and Venkatesh Sundararaman (2011). "Teacher Performance Pay: Experimental Evidence from India," *Journal of Political Economy*, 2011, Vol. 119, No. 1, pp. 39–77

Nagaraj, R., and A. Rahman (2010). "Booming Bihar: Fact or Fiction." *Economic and Political Weekly*, Feb. 20.

Nardulli, P. F., B. Peyton, and J. W. Bajjaleih (2011). "Measuring Cross-National and Inter-Temporal Differences in Law-Based Orders: 1946–2010." The American Political Science Association Annual Meetings, Sept. 1–4. http://papers.ssrn.com/sol3/papers.cfm?abstract_id=1903307.

North, Doughlas (1990). Institutions, *Institutional Change and Economic Performance*, Cambridge, UK: Cambridge University Press.

NSSO (2011). "Employment and Unemployment Situation in India 2009–10." NSS Report No. 537(66/10/1). New Delhi: National Statistical Organisation, Ministry of Statistics & Program Implementation, Government of India.

Olson, M. (1986). "A Theory of the Incentives Facing Political Organizations: Neo-Corporatism and the Hegemonic State." *International Political Science Review* 7: 165–189.

———. (1993). "Dictatorship, Democracy, and Development." *American Political Science Review* 87(3) (Sept.): 567–576.

Panagariya, A., P. Chakraborty, and M. G. Rao (2014). *State Level Reforms, Growth and Development in Indian States*. New York: Oxford University Press.

Planning Commission (1997). "A Background Note on Gadgil Formula for Distribution of Central Assistance for State Plans." http://pbplanning.gov.in/pdf/gadgil.pdf.

———. (2002). "National Human Development Report." Technical report. New Delhi: Government of India.

———. (2012). "State-Specific Poverty Lines, Number and Percentage of Population below the Poverty Line by States-2004-5-2009-10." Data Sheet. http://planningcommission.nic.in/data/datatable/0814/table_99.pdf; accessed 20 October 2014.

———. (2013). Press Note on Poverty Estimates 2011–12, issued on July 22, 2013.
Polgreen, Lydia (2010). "Turnaround in India's State Could Serve as a Model." *New York Times*, Apr. 10. http://www.nytimes.com/2010/04/11/world/asia/11bihar.html.
Prakash, A. (2001). *Jharkhand: Politics of Development and Identity*. New Delhi: Sangam Books Ltd.
Prasad, K. N. (1997). *Bihar Economy: Through the Plans (in Comparison with All-India and Other States)*. New Delhi: Northern Book Center.
PTI (2005). "HC Seeks Report on Jehanabad Jail-Break Case." *The Times of India*, Dec. 5. http://articles.timesofindia.indiatimes.com/2005-12-05/india/27853672_1_naxalite-attack-pil-jehanabad.
———. (2007). "Speedy Trial Soon for Criminal-Politicians in Bihar." *The Times of India*, Oct. 5. http://articles.timesofindia.indiatimes.com/2007-10-05/india/27970089_1_speedy-trial-special-courts-swift-trial.
———. (2010a). "86 Policemen Killed by Naxals in Bihar since 2005: Statistics." *The Times of India*, Sept. 5. http://articles.economictimes.indiatimes.com/2010-09-05/news/27599267_1_gaya-district-lucas-tete-sheohar-district.
———. (2010b). "Nitish Kumar Attacks Chidambaram's Strategy to Tackle Maoists." *The Hindustan Times*, Apr. 16. http://www.hindustantimes.com/India-news/NewDelhi/Nitish-Kumar-attacks-Chidambaram-s-strategy-to-tackle-Maoists/Article1-532189.aspx.
Quah, D. (1993). "Empirical Cross-Section Dynamics in Economic Growth." *European Economic Review* 37: 426–434.
Rao, M. G. (2005). "Unleashing the Creative Power." *Business Standard*, June 6.
———. (2009). "Reform of Intergovernmental Fiscal Arrangements of Balanced Regional Development in a Globalizing Environment." In M. G. Rao and A. Shah (eds.), *States' Fiscal Management and Regional Equity: An Overview*, 143–170. New Delhi: Oxford University Press.
Rao, M. G., and S. Mandal (2009). "Resource Endowments, Fiscal Flows, and Regional Equity in Indian Federalism." In M. G. Rao and A. Shah (eds.), *States' Fiscal Management and Regional Equity: An Overview*, 171–186. New Delhi: Oxford University Press.
Rao, M. G., and N. Singh (2005). *Political Economy of Federalism in India*. New Delhi: Oxford University Press.
Rangarajan, L. N. (1992). *Kautilya: The Arthashastra*. New Delhi: Penguin Classics, India.
Rodgers, G., and J. Rodgers (2011). "Inclusive Development? Migration, Governance and Social Change in Rural Bihar." *Economic and Political Weekly* 46(23) (June 4): 43–50.
Rorabacher, J. A. (2008). "Gerrymandering, Poverty and Flooding: A Perennial Story of Bihar." *Economic and Political Weekly* 43(7) (Feb. 16): 45–53.
Ross, M. (2001). "Does Oil Hinder Democracy?" *World Politics* 53 (Apr.): 325–361.
Roy, A. (2011). "Development Priorities for the State of Bihar and Consequent Research Possibilities for the IGC India State of Bihar." Report presented at the Growth Week, London School of Economics, Sept.
Scharfe, H. (2002). *Education in Ancient India*. Leiden; Boston; Koln: Brill.
Shah, M. (2013). "Understanding the Poverty Line." *The Hindu*, Aug. 5.
Sharma, A. N. (1995). "Political Economy of Poverty in Bihar." *Economic and Political Weekly* 30(41/42) (Oct. 14–21): 2587–2589, 2591–2595, 2597–2602.

———. (2005). "Agrarian Relations and Socio-Economic Change in Bihar." *Economic and Political Weekly* 43(46) (Nov. 15): 40–42.
Sharma, K. L. (1976). "Jharkhand Movement in Bihar." *Economic and Political Weekly* 11(1/1) (Jan.): 37–43.
Singh, B. P. (2008). "The Challenge of Good Governance in India: Need for Innovative Approaches." Ash Institute for Democratic Governance and Innovation. http://www.innovations.harvard.edu/cache/documents/1034/103461.pdf.
Singh, N., and G. Vasishta (2004). "Some Patterns in Center–State Fiscal Transfers in India: An Illustrative Analysis." Santa Cruz Center for International Economics, Working Paper Series qt1r02k470. Santa Cruz, CA: Center for International Economics, UC Santa Cruz.
Singh, N. K. (2009). *Not by Reason Alone*. Delhi: Viking Penguin.
———. (2013). "Not Soulless Statistics." *Hindustan Times*, Aug. 8.
Singh, S. (2011). "For Bihar IAS, IPS Cadre, 11 Days to Declare Assets or Go Without Pay." *The Indian Express*, Feb. 17. http://www.indianexpress.com/news/for-bihar-ias-ips-cadre-11-days-to-declare-assets-or-go-without-pay/750991/0.
Sinha, A. (2011). *Nitish Kumar and the Rise of Bihar*. Delhi: Penguin Viking.
Sinha, C. P. (2008). "Management of Floods in India." *Economic and Political Weekly* 43(46) (Nov.): 40–42.
Somanathan, E. (2011). "Are Embankments a Good Flood Control Strategy? A Case Study of the Kosi River." Presented at the Bihar Growth Conference, International Growth Centre's India-Bihar program, Dec.
Sundberg, M., M. Kaul, T. Vishwanath, A. Narayan, R. Nayak, N. Yoshida, S. Guimbert, M. Nagarajan, M. Prasad, R. S. Deshpande, M. Kida, D. B. Gupta, P. Clarke, and P. Sundaram (2005). "Bihar: Towards a Development Strategy." World Bank. http://siteresources.worldbank.org/INTINDIA/Resources/Bihar_report_final_June2005.pdf.
Thapar, R. (1966). *A History of India*, vol. 1. London: Penguin Books. Reprinted in 1990 Delhi: Penguin India.
Thirteenth Finance Commission (2009). "Thirteenth Finance Commission 2010–2015, vol. 1: Report, December, Government of India." http://fincomindia.nic.in/ShowContentOne.aspx?id=28&Section=1.
TNN (2009). "Bihar's 'Janakari' Model Found Simplest and Best." *The Times of India*, Jan. 30. Patna Edition. http://articles.timesofindia.indiatimes.com/2009-01-30/patna/28035432_1_second-appeals-rti-act-applications.
———. (2011). "We Want to Celebrate Bihari Pride." *The Times of India*, Mar. 23. Patna Edition. http://articles.timesofindia.indiatimes.com/2011-03-23/patna/29177979_1_bihar-diwas-bihari-pride-artistes.
Tripathy, R. (2007). "The Problem, the Paradox that is Bihar: A Symposium on the State's Efforts at Overcoming a Troubled Past." Seminar 580. Dec. http://www.india-seminar.com/2007/580.htm.
Vivian, R. G. (1990). *The Chacoan Prehistory of the San Juan Basin*. San Diego, CA: Academic Press.
Vyas, V. S., A. N. Sharma, R. S. Srivastava, and A. K. Sinha (2012). "Towards Accelerated Agricultural Development in Bihar: Report of the Steering Group on Vision of Agriculture Development in Bihar." Patna: Government of Bihar.
Waldauer, C., W. J. Zahka, and S. Pal (1996). "Kautilya's Arthashastra: A Neglected Precursor to Classical Economics." *Indian Economic Review* 31(1): 101–108.

World Bank (1990). "Flood Control in Bangladesh: A Plan for Action." May. World Bank technical paper; no. WTP 119. Washington, D.C.: The World Bank. http://documents.worldbank.org/curated/en/1990/05/440463/flood-control-bangladesh-plan-action.

——. (1994). *World Bank Report 1994: Infrastructure for Development.* New York: Oxford University Press.

World Bank and the Government of Bihar (2010). "Bihar Kosi Flood (2008) Needs Assessment Report." https://www.gfdrr.org/sites/gfdrr/files/publication/GFDRR_India_PDNA_2010_EN.pdf.

PART III

Gujarat

ARCHANA DHOLAKIA AND RAVINDRA DHOLAKIA

CHAPTER 13

Growth and Development in Gujarat

An Overview

Today, Gujarat is economically one of the most dynamic states of India. It accounts for 5% of the national population and 6% of the geographical area but 8% of the national income. Since 2007/08, the state has the third highest real per capita income (Net State Domestic Product at constant prices) among the largest 15 states, behind only Maharashtra and Haryana. This rank represented a movement up by two notches from the ranking in 1993/94 when Kerala and Punjab additionally enjoyed higher per capita incomes than Gujarat.[1]

Commentators often refer to Gujarat as a land of entrepreneurs with a sharp business sense. Gujaratis have distinguished themselves as a leading trading community around the world. They are known to travel long distances to unfamiliar foreign territories and even settle there if necessary

---

We would like to thank Professor Arvind Panagariya for his painstakingly detailed constructive comments and editorial improvements in our earlier drafts. We also record our appreciation of the frank feedback and a few suggestion made by Professor M. Govinda Rao. We express our gratitude to Professor Bibek Debroy and three anonymous reviewers of the Oxford University Press for their useful comments. We are also thankful to Mr. Mannish Pandya and several other officials of the Government of Gujarat for fruitful discussion and sharing data on the economy. Moreover, we acknowledge the support by the Columbia University's Program on Indian Economic Policies, funded by a grant from the John Templeton Foundation. The opinions expressed in the book are those of the authors and do not necessarily reflect the views of the John Templeton Foundation. We are also grateful to Mr. Amey Sapre for assistance in computations, charts, and material collection.

1. This obviously contradicts the argument of Nagaraj and Pandey (2013) that the ranking of Gujarat has remained almost the same during the last two decades and hence cannot be said to have outperformed other states. They consider all states and union territories for comparison, but in our view, we should take only large states for valid comparison.

to achieve their commercial goals (KPMG and CII 2007; Shah 2011). While recognition of these factors is useful for understanding the evolution of the state's economy, it is far from sufficient for explaining its outstanding performance in recent years. Whereas the superior performance of the state relative to other states in terms of growth and development is of a more recent origin, these cultural and institutional advantages were always there. Therefore, deeper analysis is required to explain the state's turnaround. This is the task we undertake in the present study.

In this introductory chapter, we begin with a brief review of the performance of the state's economy, its structure, progress toward urbanization, and the status of poverty, inequality, education, and health. This broad-brush discussion would serve as the essential background for more detailed analysis in the remaining chapters of the book. In the next section, we summarize the economic growth history of Gujarat since its inception in May 1960. In the third section, we consider the structure of the economy in terms of different sectors and sub-sectors to give the reader an idea of the leading and lagging sectors of the economy. In the fourth section, we consider the progress achieved in urbanization. In the fifth and sixth sections, we discuss poverty and inequality, respectively. In the seventh section, we summarize the progress in health and education. In the last section, we conclude the chapter.

GROWTH

Gujarat is one of the 10 most populous states in India. With a population of 60 million in 2011, it is larger than South Korea and South Africa, which have populations of 50 and 51 million, respectively. The state has 1,659 km or 27.6% of the national coastline. Historically, this has provided Gujarat a natural link to the world markets both in terms of trade and migration. In the year 2010/11, 24.6% of the national exports originated in Gujarat (Government of India 2012: 171). It implies that exports were a gigantic 54.9% of the domestic production in the state. This proportion is the highest among all Indian states, making Gujarat the most globalized state of India.[2] Trade has played an important role in the state's economy leading to the early development of several financial products and institutions (Varadarajan 2011). All these factors along with locational advantages and a mineral

---

2. Gujarat had the highest share in exports in India in 2010/11, followed by Maharashtra (21.4%) and Tamil Nadu (9.3%). Exports were 24% of the domestic production in Maharashtra and 19.9% in Tamil Nadu during this year (GoI 2012: 171 and A-12).

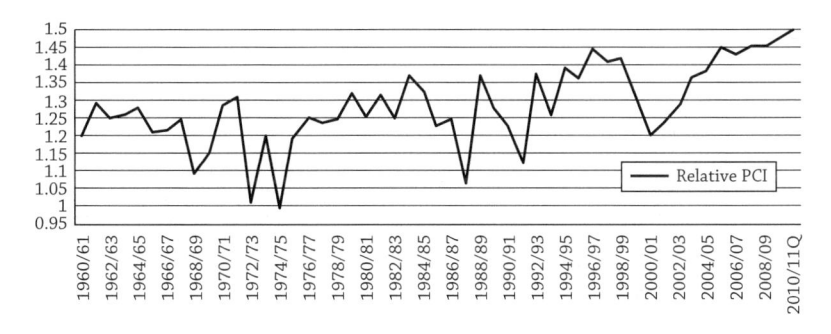

Figure 13.1: Per Capita Income of Gujarat Relative to All-India Average at 2004/05 Constant Prices
Source: Authors' construction based on data from the GoI (2012) and Department of Economics & Statistics (DE&S), Government of Gujarat.

resource base made the state relatively rich compared to the national average from its inception in 1960.

In considering the performance of the economy, it is useful to begin by placing the state in the national context. This is done in figure 13.1, where we depict per capita Gross State Domestic Product (GSDP) in Gujarat as a ratio of per capita Gross Domestic Product (GDP) in India. In 1960/61, Gujarat began with a per capita income 20% higher than the national average. But it performed relatively poorly in the early years, dropping to almost the national average in 1972/73 and 1974/75. The state then had a decade of steady progress relative to the national average, followed by a decade of wild fluctuations. Beginning in the early 1990s, the state picked up momentum in a big way, achieving a per capita income 45% higher than the national average in 1996/97. But the state then suffered a series of shocks including the East Asian currency crisis and a major earthquake. As a result, in 2000/01, the state dropped relative to the national average to the level it had begun at inception. Luckily, high growth resumed soon with the state reaching a per capita income 50% higher than the nation average in 2010/11.[3]

The relative performance of Gujarat in figure 13.1 partially reflects the performance of the Indian economy. To get a fuller understanding of the performance of the Gujarat economy, we must also consider the absolute performance of its GSDP. To this end, we present in figure 13.2, the evolution of the

---

3. High volatility of relative per capita income from year to year was a feature of the state economy till 2000/01. Comparison of relative performance of the state at a point of time could, therefore, be very misleading unless proper care is taken to adjust for the fluctuations. However, during the last decade, the state's relative performance in terms of per capita income is steadily improving with per capita GSDP as a proportion of the national per capita GDP rising from 1.2 in 2000/01 to 1.5 in 2010/11 and 1.64 in 2013/14.

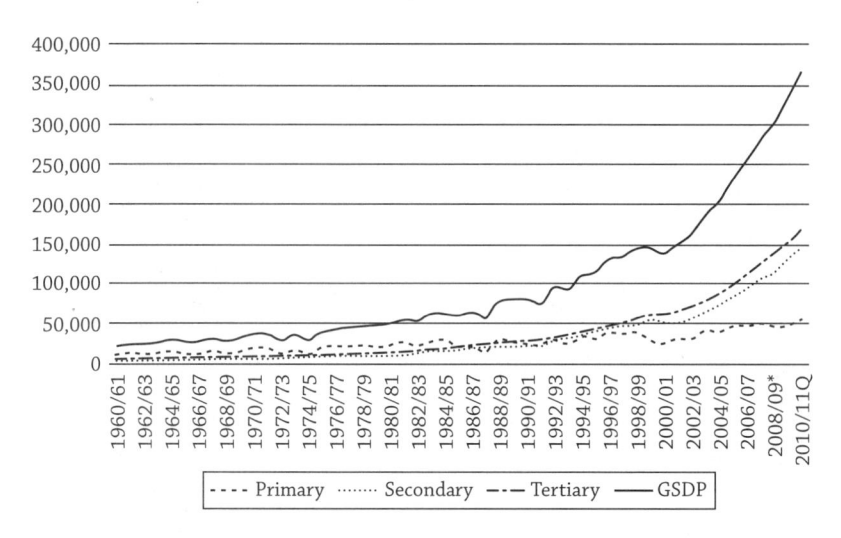

Figure 13.2: Time Paths of Real GSDP and Three Broad Sectors in Gujarat (in 10 million rupees)
* Provisional Estimates Q: Quick Estimates
Source: Department of Economics & Statistics (DE&S), Government of Gujarat.

GSDP and its major components at constant 2004/05 prices in Gujarat. In conformity with the government of India (GoI 2012: A-5), we define the primary sector to include agriculture, forestry and logging, fishing, and mining and quarrying. The secondary sector consists of manufacturing, construction, and electricity, gas, and water supply. Finally, the tertiary sector comprises all service sectors other than construction, namely, trade, hotels and restaurants, storage, communications, transport, banking and insurance, real estate, dwellings, and business services, public administration, social services, and other services.

Figure 13.2 underlines more forcefully the slow progress until mid-1970s, some pick up in the following one and a half decades until 1988/89 and then sharp decline during 1989/90 and 1990/91 due to severe draught. Beginning in the early 1990s, following the economic reforms at the national level that considerably freed up entrepreneurs from the license-permit raj, there was significant acceleration in the economy. Although the economy suffered a temporary setback during the last two to three years of the 1990s, it took off in a major way thereafter, growing at a double-digit rate during the 2000s.

Figure 13.3 depicts the growth rates of the GSDP and the primary sector. It brings into sharp focus the close link between the performance of the GSDP and that of the primary sector until 2000/01. The primary sector was the dominant sector in the state till about 1985/86 (figure 13.2). From 1985/86 to 1994/95, the three sectors contributed almost equally. After 1994/95, however, the services and industrial sectors started contributing substantially more than the agriculture sector to the state product. After 2000/01, total

GSDP in the state became almost immune from agricultural fluctuations (figure 13.3) and has started moving in tandem with industries and services in the state (figure 13.4). Over the last two decades, the secondary sector has been a major driver of the economy registering negative growth only for three years: during 1991/92 due to import compression, during 1997/98 on account of East Asian currency crises and during 2000/01 due to the earthquake in

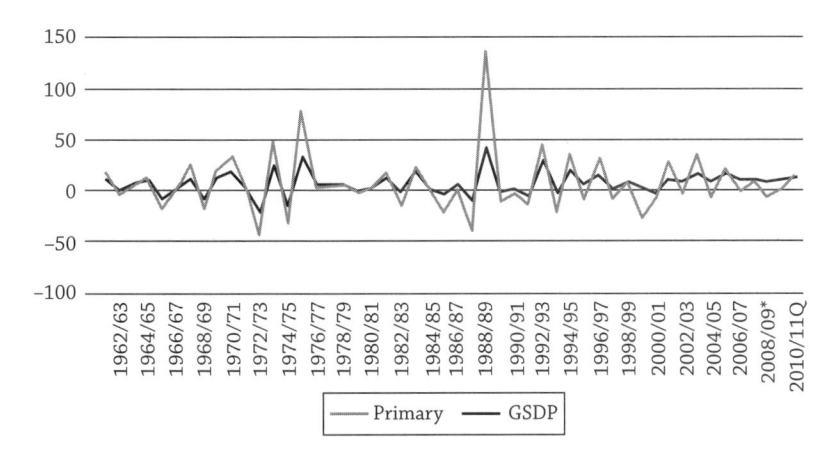

Figure 13.3: Time Paths of Annual Growth Rates of GSDP and Primary Sector Incomes in Gujarat (in %)
* Provisional Estimates Q: Quick Estimates
Source: Department of Economics & Statistics (DE&S), Government of Gujarat.

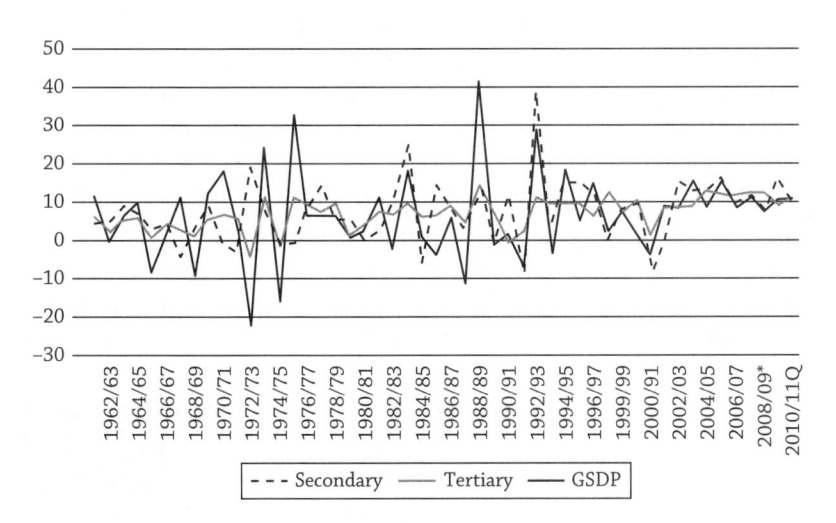

Figure 13.4: Time Paths of Annual Growth Rates of GSDP, Secondary Sector Incomes, and Tertiary Sector Incomes in Gujarat (in %)
*Provisional Estimates Q: Quick Estimates.
Source: Department of Economics & Statistics (DE&S), Government of Gujarat.

Table 13.1. COMPOUNDED ANNUAL TREND GROWTH RATES IN GUJARAT AND INDIA (IN %)

Period	Primary	Secondary	Tertiary	GSDP/GDP
Gujarat				
1960/61 to 1970/71	3.0	3.7	3.1	3.3
1970/71 to 1980/81	3.6*	5.6	5.6	4.5
1980/81 to 1990/91	0.0*	7.8	7.3	4.6
1990/91 to 2000/01	2.1*	9.3	8.5	7.1
2000/01 to 2010/11	6.4	11.8	10.8	10.4
India				
1960/61 to 1970/71	2.1	5.5	4.1	3.5
1970/71 to 1980/81	2.0	4.3	4.5	3.4
1980/81 to 1990/91	3.5	5.7	6.6	5.3
1990/91 to 2000/01	3.3	6.4	7.7	6.1
2000/01 to 2010/11	3.3	8.8	9.3	7.9

* Statistically not different from zero percent.
Source: Authors' construction based on data from the GoI (2012) and Department of Economics & Statistics (DE&S), Government of Gujarat.

the state.[4] The tertiary sector has had a smooth run throughout the period, though there are fluctuations in its annual growth (figure 13.4).

In table 13.1, we provide the trend growth rates of the GSDP and its major components by decades.[5] As we have already seen, the state's growth performance was not very impressive and was actually less than the all-India average during the 1960s. During 1970s, the state economy started looking up in all sectors though the growth in the primary sector was marred by considerable fluctuations. The tertiary sector and secondary sector registered considerable acceleration because the oil from Bombay High helped petrochemical production with auxiliary and ancillary units coming up in Gujarat during the decade (Vyas 2002), and the state performed better than the all-India average.

The decade of the 1980s saw Gujarat maintaining its average annual growth of around 4.5% in spite of severe drought years and highly fluctuating agriculture. This was because further acceleration of growth in the secondary and

4. Currency crises in Southeast Asian countries led to considerable depreciation of their currencies against the Indian rupee. As a result, India's exports suffered and so did exports from Gujarat, because of its high degree of openness. It led to a fall in the industrial output in Gujarat (Parekh 2004). To appreciate the extent of the devastation caused by the earthquake in 2001, see Appendix 3.

5. To minimize the biases that may arise due to large fluctuations in the annual growth rate, we do not use the simple average of the annual growth rates. Instead, we rely on the trend growth rate obtained by fitting semi-logarithmic regressions against time.

tertiary sectors compensated for weak agriculture. However, with the initiation of some measures of liberalization and expansionary fiscal policy at the center, the country as a whole experienced a sharp acceleration in its annual growth from 3.4% during the 1970s to 5.3% during the 1980s. Although Gujarat's industry and service sectors benefited from it, the overall growth fell short of the national level due to the poor agricultural performance.

During the 1990s, the secondary sector in Gujarat continued with further acceleration followed closely by the tertiary sector. Since agriculture also started growing positively though with wide fluctuations, the overall growth of the state accelerated to more than 7% per annum against 6% at the national level. It was during the 1990s that Gujarat could achieve almost 2.5 percentage points of acceleration in growth. It translated into about a quarter of national acceleration in growth during the same period.

In the 2000s, Gujarat has continued to accelerate its growth and has emerged among a handful of investment magnets in the country. The state achieved relative stability in its agricultural performance and clocked a very high positive and statistically significant growth in the otherwise precarious and fluctuating sector. Simultaneously, the growth continued to accelerate substantially in the secondary and tertiary sectors resulting in a double-digit overall growth. The acceleration achieved during the decade in the growth was about 33% higher than the one achieved in the previous decade. Further, Gujarat achieved almost 2.5 percentage points lead over the national growth rate, with all broad sectors performing better than their national counterparts during 2000–2011. But during the 1990s, its lead over the national growth rate was only 1.0 percentage point.[6]

The most distinguishing feature of the growth performance of Gujarat is its consistently better growth in the industry and service sectors over the last four decades. It was the indifferent and highly fluctuating agriculture that made the state's performance in relation to the national average as unstable as depicted in figure 13.1. During the last decade, when the agricultural growth in the state stabilized relatively at a higher level, its overall growth crossed double digits.

STRUCTURE OF THE ECONOMY

Economic Survey 2012/13 (GoI 2013a: ch. 2) has analyzed trends in the GDP and employment shares of agriculture, industry, and services in India, China, Indonesia, and Korea. It compares the sectoral output and employment

---

6. Ghatak and Roy (2014) argue by taking difference-in-difference of the annual growth rates that "there is no evidence of any differential acceleration in 2000s ... relative to the 1990s." Taking trend rates of growth, which is more appropriate, in place of simple annual growth our table 13.1 clearly contradicts their argument (see n. 5).

Table 13.2. PERCENTAGE OF SHARES OF THE MAJOR SECTORS IN THE GSDP AT 2004/05 PRICES

Triennial Average	Primary Sector	Secondary Sector	Tertiary Sector	Total GSDP
1979–82	46.91	22.91	30.18	100
1989–92	32.81	29.05	38.14	100
1999–2002	20.16	35.79	44.05	100
2008–11	14.87	39.05	46.08	100

Source: Authors' calculations using the data from the Department of Economics & Statistics (DE&S), Government of Gujarat.

trajectories of the countries following the takeoff date.[7] It finds that the employment and GDP shares of agriculture in India have fallen at a similar pace as in other Asian economies. While the employment shares of industry and services in India have increased at a pace similar to those in other Asian economies, the movement of GDP shares of these sectors in India is very different. The increase in GDP share of industry is substantially lower and of services higher than in those countries.

A similar analysis for Gujarat (with the takeoff date around 1991) shows that its experience is closer to the one in China, Korea, and Indonesia in the movement of both employment and output shares of the three sectors. The fall in the output share of agriculture in Gujarat has been sharp after 1980, though the absolute rate of decline has fallen considerably during the last decade (table 13.2). The secondary and tertiary sectors have picked up steadily and are now at a level comparable to the levels reached in China. The primary sector in Gujarat contributes marginally more than it contributes in China, because agriculture in Gujarat has been growing at more than double the rate it grew in China over the last decade.

Finer disaggregation of sectors in table 13.3 shows that agriculture, forestry and logging, fishing, mining and quarrying, railways, storage, and real estate and dwellings have proportionately declined almost continuously from 1980/81 to 2010/11. The clearly rising sectors in the state, on the other hand, are registered manufacturing, construction, trade-hotels-restaurants, communications, and banking and insurance. Thus, the revealed comparative advantage of the state is in formal-sector (registered) manufacturing, construction, trade, and modern financial services including communications. Traditional sectors such as unregistered manufacturing (which largely consists of small enterprises), electricity, gas, and water supply, transport by

---

7. The takeoff dates for these economies are taken as 1967 for Korea, 1973 for Indonesia, 1979 for China, and 1991 for India.

Table 13.3. SHARES OF SECTORS IN GSDP AT 2004/05 PRICES IN SELECTED TRIENNIUMS (IN %)

Sector	1980–83	1989–92	1999–2002	2007–10
Agriculture	29.96	20.22	12.86	11.43
Forestry and logging	5.39	3.57	2.36	1.51
Fishing	1.05	1.52	1.09	0.60
Mining and quarrying	6.03	7.10	4.11	2.30
Registered manufacturing	12.18	16.02	19.68	21.6
Un-registered manufacturing	4.33	5.09	7.03	5.87
Electricity, gas, and water supply	1.64	2.55	3.58	2.76
Construction	4.52	4.43	5.15	7.70
Trade, hotels, and restaurants	11.86	12.86	13.94	18.82
Railways	1.21	1.05	0.77	0.57
Transport by other means	2.44	3.97	5.06	4.48
Storage	0.07	0.05	0.03	0.02
Communication	0.31	0.37	1.02	2.66
Banking and insurance	2.07	4.51	6.00	6.72
Real estate and ownership of dwellings	9.27	8.16	6.79	5.67
Public administration	3.23	3.61	4.25	2.84
Other services	4.45	4.92	6.26	4.44
Total GSDP sum	100	100	100	100

Source: Authors' calculations using the data from the Department of Economics & Statistics (DE&S), Government of Gujarat.

other means, and other services sectors have been proportionately shrinking during the 2000s.

Gujarat attracted a very large proportion of industrial investment following the reforms and liberalization initiated at the center in 1991/92 (Parekh 2004). Like much of India, this was in the capital-intensive rather than labor-intensive manufacturing. However, during 2005–10, the compound annual growth of employment in the factory sector in the state was 6.2% (GoG 2012) and more labor-intensive industries started coming up. This is seen in table 13.4, which reports the percent shares of different industries in the factory sector in net value added in 1991/92, 2000/01, and 2009/10 and in employment in 2009/10 using the Annual Survey of Industries data. While metals and alloys, chemicals, and machinery are capital-intensive, the rest of the industries are labor-intensive.

Share of capital-intensive industries increased and of labor-intensive industries declined in the 1990s, but the trend reversed in the 2000s. Capital-intensive industries like chemicals and machinery and traditional labor-intensive industries like textiles and plastics declined in the last decade. But new labor-intensive industries such as non-metallic minerals and food processing and capital-intensive fabricated metal products, watches, and motor vehicles are coming up recently. Thus, the experience of the state in the 2000s does not corroborate the general belief that reforms would result in growth of only capital-intensive industries.

Data on the composition of employment across sectors reinforce the suggestive evidence from table 13.4. Gujarat has a larger proportion of its workforce in manufacturing and industry than all-India. As table 13.5 shows,

Table 13.4. PERCENT NET VALUE ADDED AND EMPLOYMENT IN SELECTED INDUSTRIES IN GUJARAT, 1991/92 TO 2009/10

Industry Groups	Share of Net Value Added			Share of Employment
	1991/92	2000/01	2009/10	2009/10
1. Metals and alloys	7.1	5.1	18.8	12.5
2. Chemicals	35.4	48.7	30.6	15.8
3. Machinery	13.1	13.0	10.2	9.5
Capital-intensive industries (1 + 2 + 3)	55.6	66.8	59.6	37.8
4. Textiles	13.8	8.0	5.1	17.4
5. Food processing	7.4	4.3	4.9	7.6
6. Plastics and petroleum	3.5	6.0	4.2	4.5
7. Non-metallic minerals	*	4.4	5.6	7.7
8. Other	19.7	10.5	20.6	25.0
Labor-intensive industries (4 + 5 + 6 + 7 + 8)	44.4	33.2	40.4	62.2
All industries	100	100	100	100

* Included in "Other."
Source: CSO (Annual): Annual Survey of Industries—Factory Sector, 1991/92 to 2009/10.

Table 13.5. EMPLOYMENT SHARES OF USUALLY WORKING PERSONS IN THE PRINCIPAL STATUS AND SECONDARY STATUS IN RURAL AND URBAN REGIONS COMBINED, 1999/2000 AND 2011/12 (IN %)

State/Country	Agriculture	Industry	Services	Manufacturing	Construction	Total
1999/2000						
Gujarat	59.6	12.4	28.0	12.1	4.2	100
India	60.8	11.4	27.8	11.0	4.4	100
2011/12						
Gujarat	49.4	21.1	29.5	19.7	4.8	100
India	48.6	13.4	38.0	12.8	10.6	100

Source: The NSSO reports on employment-unemployment survey of 1999/2000 and 2011/12 with interpolated and extrapolated population from Census years.

the employment shares of different sectors in Gujarat were remarkably similar to that in India in 1999/2000. Although the extent of transition of the workforce out of agriculture to non-agricultural sectors remained similar in the state and the nation, the shift was largely to industry and manufacturing in Gujarat while it was toward services and construction in the country as a whole.

URBANIZATION

An important aspect of transformation from a primarily traditional agrarian economy into a modern industrial and service-oriented one is urbanization. As modernization proceeds, more and more regions turn urban. Therefore, it is important to consider urbanization as a part of the study of transformation to modern economy in its own right.

The proportion of the state population living in the urban areas is the conventional indicator of urbanization. Gujarat is currently the sixth most urbanized state in the country after Goa, Mizoram, Tamil Nadu, Kerala, and Maharashtra. According to the 2011 census, 42.6% of its population lives in urban areas. However, only 3.8% of its geographical area is considered urban.

Gujarat has been more urbanized than the country as a whole from the very inception of the state in 1960. As shown in table 13.6, the state maintained a consistently faster tempo of urbanization than the nation through the decades. The difference in the degree of urbanization in Gujarat and the nation was 7.7 percentage points in the 1961 census, which increased to 11.4 in the 2011 census.

Table 13.6. URBAN POPULATION AND DEGREE OF URBANIZATION, GUJARAT AND INDIA

Census Years	Gujarat		All-India	
	Urban Population (in millions)	Share of Urban Population (%)	Urban Population (in millions)	Share of Urban Population (%)
1961	5.31	25.74	78.90	18.00
1971	7.49	28.06	109.10	19.91
1981	10.60	31.10	159.50	23.70
1991	14.24	34.47	217.20	25.71
2001	18.93	37.36	285.40	27.78
2011	25.71	42.58	377.10	31.16

Source: Decennial Census Reports.

Table 13.7. SIZE CLASS-WISE URBAN POPULATION IN GUJARAT FROM 1961 TO 2011 (IN THOUSANDS)

Classes		1961	1971	1981	1991	2001	2011
Class I	Population	2,363	3,702	6,313	9,496	14,413	19,851
	% growth		56.6	70.6	50.4	51.8	37.7
Class II	Population	758	1,172	1,453	1,799	1,836	1,987
	% growth		54.8	24	23.8	2.1	8.2
Class III	Population	1,098	1,181	1,416	1,437	1,857	2,287
	% growth		7.5	20	1.5	29.2	23.2
Class IV	Population	636	944	1,063	1,177	676	1,193
	% growth		48.4	12.7	10.7	−42.6	76.5
Class V	Population	427	481	340	309	121	356
	% growth		12.6	−29.2	−9.2	−60.8	194.2
Class VI	Population	35	17	15	27	27	38
	% growth		−50.9	−13.9	82.4	−2.1	45

Source: Census of India for respective years.

Some further insight into the nature of urbanization can be obtained by considering the composition of urban areas in terms of six size-classes of towns that are identified in India: (1) Class I having population of 100,000 and above; (2) Class II having population between 50,000 and 99,999; (3) Class III having population between 20,000 and 49,999; (4) Class IV having population between 10,000 and 19,999; (5) Class V having population between 5,000 and 9,999; and (6) Class VI having population less than 5,000. Table 13.7 provides the breakdown of urban areas in Gujarat by the size-class of towns from 1961 to 2011.

Urbanization in Gujarat was essentially a phenomenon of the Class I city growth till 2001. These cities grew by more than 50% per decade from 1961 to 2001. During the 1960s, Class II and Class IV towns also grew rapidly, but thereafter their growth sharply fell. During the 1990s, Class IV, V, and VI towns sharply declined with Class III towns picking up in growth. However, during the last decade (2001–11), smaller towns have started contributing significantly to the rapid growth of urban areas. All towns and cities with 20,000 or more population (Class I, II, and III) have grown at 33%, but towns with less than 20,000 populations grew at 93% pulling the average growth of all urban areas to 36% during 2001–11. Thus, urbanization has started acquiring "extensive" character of late.

POVERTY

After initiation of economic policy reforms at the national level around 1991, the government of Gujarat operated on the principle of promoting a

Table 13.8. PERCENTAGE OF POPULATION BELOW POVERTY LINE (TENDULKAR METHODOLOGY)

Year	Gujarat			All India		
	Rural	Urban	Total	Rural	Urban	Total
1993/94	43.10	28.00	37.80	50.10	31.80	45.30
2004/05	39.10	20.10	31.60	42.00	25.50	37.20
2009/10	26.70	17.90	23.00	33.80	20.90	29.80
2011/12	21.54	10.14	16.63	25.70	13.70	21.92

Source: Ahluwalia (2011); and Bandyopadhyay (2010) for 1993/94 estimates; and GoI (2011a) for 2004/05 and 2009/10 estimates; and GoI (2013b) for 2011/12 estimates.

growth-friendly environment to generate employment and thereby alleviate poverty both through rising wages and the use of enhanced revenue resources to finance social spending. The result has been a steady decline in poverty.

The Planning Commission of India has temporarily accepted the definition and measurement of poverty suggested by the Tendulkar Committee.[8] As table 13.8 shows, poverty in both rural and urban Gujarat is considerably lower than the corresponding all-India averages and is consistently declining during the last two decades. The rate of decline in the rural poverty in Gujarat during 1993–2004 was half the rate for the national average, but it was 1.5 times during 2004–09. This may be related to the growth of agriculture in the state and the nation during those periods. As table 13.1 above reveals, annual growth of agriculture in the state during 1990s was 2.1% with wide fluctuations when the national average was 3.3%, but Gujarat's agriculture grew steadily at twice the national average during the last decade. Although the latest estimates for the year 2011/12 show a further fall in the poverty ratio in rural areas of both the state and the nation, convincing explanation of the extent of decline is difficult.

INEQUALITY

The household expenditure surveys done by the National Sample Survey Office (NSSO) allow us to measure consumer expenditure inequality at the state level. Table 13.9 reports the Gini coefficient of these expenditures in rural and urban areas in Gujarat, India, and five additional states with comparable per capita incomes during 1983, 1993/94, 2004/05, and 2009/10. The value of the Gini coefficient as a measure of inequality varies between 0 and 1

---

8. There still exists a genuine difference of opinion among experts on the measurement of poverty and the poverty line in the country (see Rath 2011; GoI 2013b).

Table 13.9. GINI COEFFICIENT IN SELECTED STATES AND INDIA FROM 1983 TO 2009/10

State/Country	1983	1993/94	1999/2000	2004/05	2009/10
Rural					
Gujarat	0.252	0.236	0.234	0.269	0.253
Haryana	0.271	0.301	0.239	0.322	0.301
Kerala	0.330	0.288	0.270	0.341	0.417
Maharashtra	0.283	0.302	0.258	0.308	0.268
Punjab	0.279	0.265	0.239	0.279	0.288
Tamil Nadu	0.324	0.307	0.279	0.316	0.264
India	0.297	0.282	0.260	0.300	0.291
Urban					
Gujarat	0.264	0.287	0.286	0.305	0.328
Haryana	0.304	0.280	0.287	0.360	0.360
Kerala	0.371	0.338	0.321	0.400	0.498
Maharashtra	0.329	0.351	0.348	0.372	0.410
Punjab	0.321	0.276	0.290	0.393	0.371
Tamil Nadu	0.347	0.344	0.381	0.356	0.332
India	0.325	0.340	0.342	0.371	0.382

Source: Planning Commission (2013: 74).

with the former representing perfect equality and the latter representing the most unequal distribution. A rising value of the Gini coefficient represents rising inequality.[9]

Two observations follow from the table. First, consumption inequality has been consistently lower in Gujarat than comparable states and India in both rural and urban areas. Kerala shows the highest levels of inequality in both rural and urban areas with a major jump in it during the last decade. Indeed, for a relatively rich state, Gujarat shows remarkably low values of the Gini coefficient. Second, the rural Gini coefficient shows no clear long-term trend in Gujarat, but declined during 2004–10 when agriculture did well. Urban Gini has seen some upward movement, which is approximately the same in magnitude as that in the national Gini.

Inequality can also be measured regionally. For this, we need estimates of per capita income at the district level. While the Department of Economics and Statistics of the government of Gujarat has prepared the estimates of District Domestic Product (DDP) from 1999/2000 onward, it has not made

---

9. Such an interpretation is strictly not valid if the underlying Lorenz curves are intersecting. However, Gini coefficients are often calculated by statistical curve fitting to avoid intersecting Lorenz curves.

Table 13.10. COEFFICIENT OF VARIATION IN
PER CAPITA DDP IN GUJARAT (IN %)

Years	1999/2000	2000/01	2001/02	2002/03	2003/04	2004/05	2005/06
Coefficient of variation	49.6	51.9	47.9	53.2	48.4	50.9	54.3

Source: Department of Economics & Statistics, Government of Gujarat.

them public. Luckily, we have been able to obtain the estimated coefficient of variation of per capita DDP across districts from 1999/2000 to 2005/06. This coefficient varies from 0 to 100 with the rising value showing larger inequality. We report the values of the coefficients in table 13.10.

Although the coefficient of variation shows a small net increase between the beginning and ending years, it exhibits no consistent trend. In part, the fluctuations are likely to be associated with fluctuations in agricultural output, because the poorer districts are more dependent on agriculture. The industry and services outputs tend to be steadier and so the better off districts dependent on them would experience smaller fluctuations in their income. As a result, when agricultural income fluctuates, the fortune of the poorer districts relative to the richer districts also moves in the same direction.

ADDITIONAL DEVELOPMENT INDICATORS

There is a growing view that inequalities in a society are better reflected through access to inputs determining the quality of life than mere income. Conventionally, indicators of education, health, and household amenities are used for this purpose. A more comprehensive measure is of Human Development Index (HDI). Estimates of HDI for Gujarat based largely on the data of the 1990s (Hirway and Mahadevia 2005) and using the data up to the mid-2000s (Planning Commission 2011) show the state not performing satisfactorily on this count. The situation in this regard has significantly improved in the last few years (Debroy 2012). Literacy rates of males and females in Gujarat have been higher than the corresponding all-India averages since the state's inception (table 13.11). The literacy rates in Gujarat have also been improving at a faster rate than the all-India average during the last three decades. More important, the female literacy rate that determines several other socioeconomic indicators has risen faster than the male literacy rate and the absolute gap is rapidly narrowing both in Gujarat and in the country. Interestingly, in Gujarat the rate of increase in the literacy rate was higher in all categories during the 2000s than during the 1990s, whereas in the nation it was the other way round.

Table 13.11. LITERACY RATES BY GENDER IN GUJARAT AND ALL-INDIA, 1961 TO 2011 (IN %)

Years	Gujarat			All-India		
	Persons	Males	Females	Persons	Males	Females
1961	31.5	42.5	19.7	28.3	40.4	15.4
1971	37.0	47.6	25.6	34.5	46.0	22.0
1981	44.9	56.0	33.2	43.6	56.4	29.8
1991	61.3	73.1	48.6	52.2	64.1	39.3
2001	69.1	79.7	57.8	64.8	75.8	54.2
2011	79.3	87.2	70.7	74.0	82.1	65.5

Note: Literacy rates for 1961 to 1971 exclude children aged 0–4 years; and for 1981 to 2011 exclude children aged 0–6 years.
Source: Census of India, 1961 to 2011, Government of India.

Table 13.12. INFANT MORTALITY RATE AND CRUDE DEATH RATE IN GUJARAT AND INDIA

Year	Gujarat						India					
	IMR			CDR			IMR			CDR		
	Total	Rural	Urban	Total	Rural	Urban	Total	Rural	Urban	Total	Rural	Urban
1971	145	155	110	14.9	18.1	13.1	129	138	82	14.9	16.4	9.7
1981	116	123	89	12.0	12.4	10.7	110	119	62	12.5	13.7	7.8
1990	72	79	54	8.9	9.6	7.2	80	87	53	9.8	10.6	7.1
1995	62	68	47	7.6	8.3	6.2	74	80	48	9.0	9.8	6.6
2001	60	67	42	7.8	8.8	5.6	68	72	42	8.4	9.0	8.4
2005	54	63	37	7.1	8.0	5.8	58	64	40	7.6	8.1	6.0
2009	48	55	33	6.9	7.7	5.6	50	55	34	7.3	7.8	5.8
2012	38	45	24	6.6	7.3	5.6	42	46	28	7.0	7.6	5.6

Note: IMR is defined as infant deaths per 1,000 live births and CDR as deaths per 1,000 persons.
Source: Sample Registration System, Registrar General of India.

For health, two outcome indicators: infant mortality rates (IMR) and crude death rates (CDR) are relevant. Gujarat was considerably lagging behind the all-India average not only in rural areas but also urban areas in both the above indicators during the 1960s and 1970s (table 13.12). It was only during the 1980s that the IMR in the rural Gujarat fell below the all-India rural average. IMR and CDR in urban Gujarat continued to be higher than the national urban average even during the early 1990s. Better health sector performance in Gujarat than the national average is, thus, a phenomenon after the mid-1980s for rural areas and mid-1990s for urban areas. The health sector performance in terms of IMR and CDR in Gujarat came closer to the national average by the year 2009, but again improved at faster rate by 2012.

In other health indicators like life expectancy, percentage of institutional deliveries, and maternal mortality, Gujarat's performance has been better than all-India average in the recent past as shown in chapter 18.

MINORITIES AND WEAKER SECTIONS

In this section, we review the conditions of weaker sections of the society conventionally identified in terms of castes and religious minority groups. Among the weaker sections, we have Scheduled Tribes (ST), Scheduled Castes (SC), and Muslims. Here we report on several socioeconomic indicators relating to them (table 13.13). Being a snapshot at a point in time, the table admittedly does not tell us anything about the progression of these indicators through time. It nevertheless allows us to assess the total sum of progress the state has achieved to date.

Table 13.13 reveals that, by and large, the quality of life of these vulnerable groups as compared to the total population in the state is inferior. Two key points may be gleaned from these indicators. First, the SC and Muslims fare better than their national average in all 10 indicators shown. The remaining group, ST, also does better than their national average in 7 out of the 10 indicators. There are just three indicators in which the Scheduled Tribes do worse in Gujarat than their national average: child immunization, under-5 mortality rate, and children with anemia.

The second point to note concerns the performance of the disadvantaged groups in Gujarat relative to the total population of the country. Compared to the total population of India, Muslims in Gujarat perform better in 8 out of 10 indicators, SC in 5 out of 10 indicators, and ST in only 3 out of 10 indicators of the quality of life. In terms of two aspects: unemployment rate and electricity for domestic use, all the three disadvantaged groups in Gujarat fare better than the total population of the country. As Debroy (2012) argues, none of the tribal districts in Gujarat face the problems of extremist violence, unlike most of the tribal districts in other states.

CONCLUDING REMARKS

In this chapter, we have provided an overview of the achievements of Gujarat in the economic and social spheres since its inception in May 1960. Our review shows that the performance of Gujarat was at best moderate relative to the average of the country during the first three decades. The state has done far better during the last two decades. The relative growth performance of Gujarat compared to the nation is significantly higher in the 2000s than in the 1990s. From fifth rank in 1993/94, Gujarat now enjoys the third highest per capita income among the largest 15 states of India.

Table 13.13. SELECTED SOCIOECONOMIC INDICATORS BY SOCIAL GROUPS, GUJARAT AND INDIA

Indicators	Year	Entity	ST	SC	Muslims	All Population
Percentage households with pucca houses	2007/08	Gujarat	63.9	45.0	87.5**	75.7
		India	57.9	38.3	63.8	66.1
Percentage households with electricity for domestic use	2007/08	Gujarat	92.1**	85.5**	95.1**	93.4
		India	66.4	61.2	67.5	75.0
Percentage children immunized	2007/08	Gujarat	44.2*	58.7**	58.7**	54.8
		India	45.5	52.6	44.5	53.5
Under-5 mortality rate per 1,000 children	2005/06	Gujarat	115.8*	86.6	48.0**	60.9
		India	95.7	88.1	70.0	74.3
Percentage children with any anemia	2005/06	Gujarat	83.3*	69.6	67.1**	69.7
		India	77.2	72.4	69.7	69.5
Percentage children (5–14 years) working	2004/05	Gujarat	4.1	2.3**	2.0**	2.5
		India	3.8	2.8	3.5	3.3
Rural unemployment rates current daily status (%)	2007/08	Gujarat	3.5**	3.6**	4.6**	3.4
		India	7.5	11.9	8.8	8.4
Urban unemployment rate current daily status (%)	2007/08	Gujarat	6.2**	6.9**	5.0**	3.9
		India	10.0	10.1	7.3	7.1
Rural literacy rate	2007/08	Gujarat	60.8	66.4	65.7	68.1
		India	58.8	60.5	63.5	67.0
Urban literacy rate	2007/08	Gujarat	80.4	79.9	81.1	86.5
		India	78.0	74.9	75.1	84.3

* Indicates poorer performance in Gujarat than India-wide average in absolute terms. All other indicators reflect superior performance in Gujarat.
** Indicates better performance than the all-India average for total population.
Source: Planning Commission (2011).

Gujarat has also moved farther along than India on the path to economic transformation. It shows significantly higher shares of manufacturing and industry in the GSDP than the corresponding India-wide measures. The state has also achieved a much greater degree of urbanization than India as a whole. In these aspects, Gujarat looks more like China than the average of India. During the last several years, employment in manufacturing has increased rapidly.

The performance of Gujarat in the social sectors has been more controversial in the media. Our review shows, however, that while there are specific areas in which Gujarat has not done as well as it could, its performance overall in terms of other development indicators is consistent with its economic performance. Poverty has come down steadily throughout the past two decades in both rural and urban areas. Importantly, rapid growth in Gujarat has been achieved without increased inequality and the level of inequality in the state has stayed well below those in India and the comparable states.

In terms of literacy rates, Gujarat started with a lead of 3 percentage points over India as a whole and currently shows a lead of about 5 percentage points. The performance has varied over time, however. During the 1980s, the state made unprecedented gains of 16 percentage points in the literacy rate but only 5 percentage points during the 1990s. But it showed recovery in the 2000s adding 10 percentage points, one of the highest gains during the decade.

Turning to health, Gujarat performs better than the India-wide average in infant mortality, crude mortality, life expectancy, and maternal mortality. Its lead in institutional deliveries and maternal mortality over the average of India is particularly large. Although media has been highly critical of Gujarat in the area of malnourishment of children a recent report by the Comptroller and Auditor General of India (CAG 2013) shows that Gujarat made the greatest progress in bringing down child malnutrition between 2007 and 2011.

In the penultimate section of the chapter we also discuss the progress in Gujarat toward improving the status of the disadvantaged groups, the Scheduled Castes, Scheduled Tribes, and Muslims. We find that the Scheduled Castes and Muslims in Gujarat do uniformly better than their counterparts in India as a whole. The performance of the Scheduled Tribes is more mixed: they do worse in Gujarat in indicators relating to children. We also compare the performance of these three groups with the total population of the nation. Muslims in Gujarat perform better than the national population on 80% of the indicators. Scheduled Castes perform better on 50%, and Scheduled Tribes on only 30% of the indicators. However, unlike other tribal-dominated districts in the country, the ones in Gujarat do not face problems of extremist violence.

CHAPTER 14

Policy Reform in Economic Sectors

Gujarat performed poorly during the 1980s relative to the nation as a whole. Not only was growth rate lower, it also fluctuated wildly. The state saw a turnaround, however, following the economic reforms that ended the central control over the scale, location of industry and investment, foreign trade, and foreign investment. It grew faster than the average of India in both the 1990s and 2000s. During the 1990s, the state's growth rate was about one and a half times that in the preceding decade. By 2000, it began to attract the attention of national policymakers (Ahluwalia 2000) and private investors. During the 2000s, the growth rate further accelerated by 3.3 percentage points over that in the 1990s with fluctuations in the growth rate dramatically declining.

The connection of the upward shifts in the growth rate at the national level to economic reforms has been widely discussed (IMF 2006; Balakrishnan 2011; Bhagwati and Panagariya 2013). But policy changes and initiatives of state governments also influence the performance at the state level. The global competitiveness index considers efficiency in production, physical and social infrastructure, and public institutions as components (Schwab 2013). In this chapter, we review the policy changes by the Gujarat government in different production and various infrastructural sectors of the economy. Urban infrastructure, education, health, and public institutions are taken up in the subsequent chapters.

POLICY INITIATIVES IN AGRICULTURE

Three consecutive decades—the 1970s, 1980s, and 1990s—failed to yield sustained growth in agricultural output in Gujarat with the compound annual growth rate turning out to be statistically no different than zero.

Gujarat agriculture presented the case of "high risk and low return" activity. It was, however, during the last decade (2000–11) that the annual agricultural growth in the state increased sharply to 6.4% with fluctuations much reduced. For the first time, this decade saw the state agriculture turn into an attractive business proposition with significantly higher returns and lower fluctuations. This transformation was achieved through all the three factors determining the total agricultural output, namely, (1) gross cropped area, (2) cropping pattern, and (3) yield rates of crops.

Gross cropped area remained almost constant at 10.7 million hectares during the 1990s, but increased by 3% during the 2000s. The cropping pattern shows a dramatic shift away from cereals with the area declining from the peak of 44.5% in the early 1970s to the trough of 28.4% in the early 2000s with slight recovery to 30.4% during 2005–08. Almost the entire decline in the area under the cereals was on account of the reduction in the coarse grains like Jowar and Bajra. Interestingly, however, area under wheat has expanded in the 2000s rising from 4% in 2000–03 to 9.7% in 2005–08. The crops making gains in the last two decades are cotton, fruits, vegetables, spices, and flowers. Incidentally, such a cropping pattern substantially differs from the one at the all-India level (for details, see Pathak and Shah 2010).

Yield rates of wheat, cotton, and horticultural crops increased remarkably in the last decade leading to phenomenal increase in their production with 12% to 15% annual compound rate of growth in the state. Moreover, the annual fluctuations in their yield rates also declined. Diversification to such high-value crops has emerged as a safe and lucrative direction for future agricultural growth in the state.

As we will see, several scholars have attempted to explain the success of Gujarat agriculture in the last decade. It follows from these studies that the government of Gujarat gave a strategic push in seven major areas. These include water conservation and management, systematic extension effort on a massive scale, assured electricity supply to agriculture, emphasis on non-food crops like BT Cotton and horticulture, marketing and information networks to help farmers, emphasis on supporting the livestock sector, and facilitation of agricultural exports by creating reliable infrastructure. In the following, we elaborate on each of these items.

Water Conservation and Management

Gujarat is a semi-arid, drought-prone, and water-scarce region. The state government has focused on efficient conservation and management of water resources by harnessing rainwater and completing the long pending multipurpose mega project on the Narmada River, the Sardar Sarovar Project

(SSP).[1] Although considerable progress has been made on SSP, it is not yet complete. By the year 2010, the maximum area irrigated (including the illegal draw of water for irrigation by farmers) was still less than a quarter of the 1.8 million hectares of potential command area of the project. While the project has contributed to the growth acceleration of the state agriculture during the 2000s, it is not the principal driver of it (Aiyer 2009).

The state government substantially scaled up the watershed development program after the Planning Commission took up the program on a much larger scale around the early 1990s. The state started adding more than 100,000 hectares per year from the early 2000s. By the year 2009, almost 2 million hectares were covered under the program. Additional 900,000 hectares remained to be covered under the program. Similarly, the state took up projects for building check-dams, recharging wells, and reviving village ponds and minor tanks on war-footing (Pathak and Shah 2010). In addition, the micro-irrigation systems like drips and sprinklers were taken up during 2006–10 covering 200,000 hectares under the Gujarat Green Revolution Company, specifically created for the purpose. All these efforts enhanced the availability and efficiency of water for irrigation. Percentage of irrigated area in the gross cropped area increased from 32% in 2000/01 to 45% in 2006/07 (GoG-SER 2011).

Agricultural Extension

On the agricultural extension front, a program was launched in 2002/03 to issue soil health cards and kisan credit cards to each farmer in the state. After due tests of the farmer's soil, the soil health card was issued to help the farmer decide an appropriate cropping pattern, precise type and quantity of fertilizers needed, and crop rotation. It was supported by another program using a mobile van with agricultural exhibition and soil testing facilities (Pathak and Shah 2010). The government started organizing annually a "Krushi Mahotsav" or "Festival of Agriculture" for one full month during May–June, when officials and experts from agricultural universities also directly interact with farmers at the village level and advise them on area and crop-specific issues. This was helpful in effecting changes in cropping patterns.

Assured Electricity Supply to Agriculture

A program was launched by the state to supply three-phase electric connection to every village and a daily eight hours full voltage power to farmers on a pre-announced schedule. Since all villages were electrified under the

1. Appendix 2 provides some relevant details about the Sardar Sarovar Project on the Narmada River.

rural electrification program, it helped to mitigate unauthorized agricultural usage and power thefts. It also reduced overdraw of groundwater and helped farmers plan their activities in advance (Shah et al. 2009).

BT Cotton and Horticulture

Gujarat was an early and successful adopter of BT Cotton seeds in the country. The adoption of BT Cotton in Gujarat increased from 10,000 hectares in 2002 to 2.13 million hectares or 81% of the total cotton area in the state in 2010. The extent of adoption of BT Cotton was even more in Maharashtra (92%) and Andhra Pradesh (98%) by the year 2009/10. However, the yield rate in Gujarat was 650 kilograms per hectare in 2009/10 and was far greater than in Andhra Pradesh (583) and in Maharashtra (330).[2] Gujarat turned out to be a success story because the government of Gujarat played an important supporting role in the spread of BT Cotton technology, promotion of rainwater harvesting, and the creation of necessary infrastructure for both irrigation and marketing system (Gandhi and Namboodiri 2010).

Datta (2010) argues that the horticultural crops are not so much export-dependent unlike the traditional commercial crops, because they are more income elastic and could be domestically demanded in large quantity due to high growth in income. The state provided marketing and related infrastructural support for the growth of these crops. He also sees a greater potential for such diversification-led growth in agriculture occurring in a geographically well spread manner.

Marketing Networks

All villages were covered under broadband connectivity to facilitate the flow of information to farmers. The state has amended the Agricultural Produce Marketing Committee (APMC) Act in 2005 and 2007 to allow competition through spot markets, private markets, or direct marketing and contract farming. However, several limitations still remain. The state government needs to further strengthen the value chain for high-value commercial crops, which can be achieved by improving the functioning of the open regulated markets, setting up more private markets, mandatory adoption of the open auction system, and promoting contract farming (Singh 2010). Allowing foreign direct investment in the multi-brand retail sector would further lead to savings in the wastage and costs involved in the entire supply chain and thereby strengthen the value chain.

---

2. The source of this information is ISAAA (2009) coupled with recent data from Cotton Corporation of India.

Livestock Products

The high growth of income in Gujarat and the nation during the last two decades has led to a high demand for livestock products. Sharma and Thaker (2010) find that annual growth of livestock production was 12% during 1999/2000 to 2008/09 and the share of milk produced by cooperatives increased to 39% in Gujarat against the national average of 8%. Over the last decade, similarly meat production in Gujarat increased annually by 11% against national average of 4%.

The role played by the state government in this sector is very important. On the supply side, it incentivized improved technology, encouraged processing units, provided better and timely care to animals, spent for the disease control, incentivized better breeds, and created better infrastructure. The state government increased its expenditure on this sector by 4.7 times during 2004/05 to 2008/09 (Sharma and Thaker 2010).

Facilitation of Agricultural Exports

The agricultural success of Gujarat is generally attributed to political stability, timely and perceptive policy measures by the state government relating to water management, roads, power, and financial management, and institutional reforms (Aiyer 2009; Gulati et al. 2009; Balakrishna 2010). However, a substantial increase in agricultural exports from the state also played an important role. Within a period of four years from 2000/01 to 2004/05, the agri-exports increased 10 times. Among them the non-traditional items like fresh fruits and vegetables, flowers, poultry, and dairy products grew much faster (Rastogi and Dholakia 2010).

The state government provided necessary support for exports by investing in infrastructure that has brought a stream of riches to villages and rural areas of Gujarat, a subject we take up later in the chapter.

POLICIES IN THE INDUSTRIAL SECTOR

The development strategy of the state government that emphasized industrial development from the very beginning was clear and shared by all political parties that came to power (Parekh 2004).[3] Here we review some of the policy initiatives taken by the state beginning from the early 1990s. As a general practice, the state always had a separate industrial policy in place to provide the

---

3. We are grateful to Mr. Pratik Anand for assistance in collecting and compiling material for this sub-section.

basic framework and direction for industrial development. There have been five distinct industrial policy announcements during the last two decades in years 1990, 1995, 2000, 2003, and 2009. We briefly discuss them here.

Industrial Policy: 1990 to 2003

There have been three distinct policies during this period in the state, namely, 1990, 1995, and 2000. These three policies were traditional and focused largely on interest subsidies and incentives for small and tiny manufacturing sectors. Industries that were employment-intensive, export-oriented, using modern technology, ready to locate in backward regions, and set up by social groups like Scheduled Castes and Tribes and other backward castes were given incentives. Assistance was also available for quality certification and patent registration (GoG 1990, 1995, 2000).

Under these three policies covering the short period of 13 years, the state undertook several initiatives that ensured geographical spread of industries. The impact of these traditional policies is also seen on the acceleration in the growth of unregistered manufacturing in the state in 1990s over the 1980s. Figure 14.1 reveals 1.7 percentage points acceleration in the unregistered manufacturing compared to 0.7 in the registered manufacturing. While economic reforms and liberalization at the national level did play an important role, the state industrial policies and changes made therein have also contributed in stepping up the growth in both the sub-sectors during the 1990s.

The registered manufacturing in the state continued to experience further acceleration in its annual growth from 9.2% during the 1990s to 11.7% during the 2000s (figure 14.1). The unregistered manufacturing, on the other

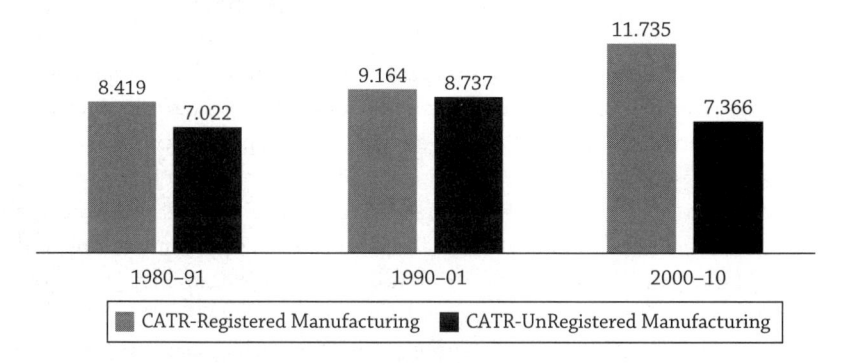

Figure 14.1: Compound Annual Trend-Based Growth Rates of Registered and Unregistered Manufacturing in Gujarat
Source: Authors' construction based on data from the GoI (2012) and Department of Economics & Statistics (DE&S), Government of Gujarat.

hand, slowed down from annual growth of 8.7% to 7.4%. As we will see in the following paragraphs, the state industrial policies of 2003 and 2009, and policies to attract mega investment projects to the state are addressing larger issues impacting the location and expansion decisions of large industries.

Industrial Policy of 2003

Industrial policy of 2003 was designed and implemented under the leadership of the Chief Minister, Narendra Modi. It marked a significant departure from the traditional sector-specific policy to a comprehensive development policy encompassing not only the industries but also all infrastructural sectors including marketing and distribution (GoG 2003). Among other things, it specifically stated as its objective the achievement of global competitiveness for the industries of the state and provided an environment conducive to production and distribution. It also spelled out steps to integrate various ministries and departments, and for coordinating their tasks. This helped the state machinery to determine the strategy, thrust areas, and action plans that touched upon the reforms relating to land, labor, energy, administration, infrastructure, and management of resources.

Implementation of the 2003 policy also called for labor reforms to the extent permissible at the state level. Inspections carried out under the labor department substantially reduced in numbers and so also the harassment to the industries. Hirway and Shah (2011) pointed out that the number of sanctioned posts in the labor department was reduced to two-thirds of the ILO norms and 30% of the posts were kept vacant for a year or more. In our perception, this would imply mitigation of corruption, state control, and compliance costs to industries. These measures were reinforced by the extension of the authorization period for individual industries from one to five years and the provision of a self-certification facility with severe punishment for false certification.

Similarly, a large number of industries were exempted from obtaining No-Objection Certificate (NOC) from Pollution Control Board and several industries were given a Gold-Pass depending on their past record.

Relatively easy and quick possession of land through the "urgency" clause, simplification of administrative processes to release agricultural land for industrial use, liberal land pricing strategy for unused government land and efficient land acquisition policy were all fall out of the 2003 policy attracting large number of entrepreneurs to the state.

Efforts were made to ease the supply of inputs such as natural gas, electricity, non-conventional energy, and water through price and tax reductions leading to cost-savings. Power reforms in Gujarat, discussed later in the chapter, also played an important role in this regard.

In order to gear up the administrative machinery for reforms, training was provided to different levels of officials and was made mandatory. E-governance through the use of Internet and Intranet increased efficiency and answerability of officials. Not only the state machinery but also the district and taluka headquarters were provided with the broadband connectivity. Several administrative processes were fully computerized and the files were tracked and cleared on a regular basis.

The roles and jurisdiction of different institutions were clearly defined with respect to the size of the project and powers were delegated at the regional level to expedite decision-making. For instance, relatively small and medium projects were handled by committees headed by the Industries Commissioner, but large and mega projects would be the responsibility of the Gujarat Industrial Promotion Board (GIPB), headed by the Chief Minister, who would ensure the fastest possible clearance.

The 2003 industrial policy of Gujarat laid down the long-term policy framework in the state. Stability in the policy regime helped the state to attract investments for industries and infrastructure.

The compound annual growth of industries in the state during the last decade was 11.8% compared to 8.8% for the nation. With a large and diversified industrial base and despite considerable global slowdown toward the end of the decade, this represents excellent growth performance. Moreover, exports originating from Gujarat touched US$40.3 billion or 21.7% of the national exports in 2008/09 (GoI 2011b). Thus, the principal objective of making Gujarat globally competitive as envisaged in the 2003 industrial policy was broadly achieved.

Industrial Policy of 2009

The logical step following the success of the 2003 policy was to aim at turning the state into a global hub for selected industries and global investment destination. Achieving global leadership in selected areas was one of the explicitly stated objectives in Gujarat's industrial policy of 2009. This policy essentially continued the thrust and several policy measures of the previous policy. It added emphasis on large and mega projects[4] in the manufacturing and infrastructural sectors by creating specific investment regions, zones, corridors, and cities.

Since 2009, several mega investment projects have come to Gujarat. Tata motors with the Nano car project, and subsequently, Peugeot and

---

4. The definition of mega projects is based on the investment of 10 billion rupees or more for industrial projects and 50 billion rupees or more for infrastructure projects (GoG 2009).

Ford have made the entry. Domestic auto-giants like Maruti and Hero have also started shopping for land in the state (*Economic Times*, June 6, 2011). Similarly, in the ship-making industry, the state now accounts for more than 60% capacity in the country (GoG-SER 2011). Moreover, maintenance, repair, and overhaul for the auto sector, ship, and aircraft are also focused for development in the state. As per the policy, varying types and extent of concessions and incentives are offered to such mega projects because by their very nature, they would have substantial forward and backward linkages in terms of ancillary and auxiliary industrial and service sector development, and considerable income and employment multiplier effects also resulting in raising the tax revenues of the government.[5]

In certain critical areas, central policies hampered progress in the state. A specific instance in which the state suffered on this count include temporary bans on onion exports and cotton exports (*Times of India*, Sept. 3, 2011); critical decisions on gas-grid and supply of gas to industries (*Economic Times*, Mar. 9, 2011); coal and gas pricing and utilization policies (*Economic Times*, March 16, 2011); and mining and environment clearances (*Economic Times*, Apr. 4, 2011). The absence of facilitating policies at the center can potentially undermine the investment-friendly actions at the state level as has been the case in these instances.

Special Economic Zones

The idea of Special Economic Zone (SEZ) as a policy instrument was introduced by the government of India in March 2000 but was enacted into law only five years later in 2005. Using the flexibility provided by the Indian constitution, however, Gujarat had already enacted its own SEZ Act in 2004 (GoG-SER 2012). An SEZ is a deemed foreign territory for tariff and trade operations with clear guidelines regarding the management, power supply, environmental clearance, water supply, labor regulations, taxation, and law and order (see Desai 2002). The economic rationale is that when political and other constraints forbid the introduction of the set of reforms over the entire country, they may be first tried in a limited geographical area. Once their efficacy is demonstrated, the way to their wider implementation may be paved. They can expand rapidly partially because they provide tax breaks and single window clearances not available outside the zones and governments find them a useful vehicle to showcase industrialization.

---

5. Incentives include lower price of land on lease or on sale, tax concessions, interest subsidies, stamp duty reduction, reduction in electricity duty subject to export commitment, and special benefits available for investment in Kutchh district.

The first SEZ in the country was approved in Gujarat, and by June 2010, the government of India gave approval to 60 SEZs in Gujarat covering an area of 31,967 hectares with investment requirement of 2.64 trillion rupees and expected employment generation for 2 million workers (Government of Gujarat-Industries Commissionerate 2010; *Economic Times*, Mar. 26, 2011). Information technology, information technology enabled services, and multi-product SEZs are relatively in greater numbers in Gujarat (GoG-Industries Commissionerate 2010).

Just two districts, Ahmedabad (17) and Kutch (14), account for more than half of the existing SEZs in the state. Bharuch (8), Gandhinagar (6), and Vadodara (5) account for another third. Unfortunately, however, the government of India abruptly halted further approvals to SEZs in 2011 and ordered a review of those already approved by the Board of Approvals (*Business Standard*, Mar. 17, 2011). This is one more illustration of the central government actions leading to adverse implications for the state.

POLICIES FOR INFRASTRUCTURE

The state government set up Gujarat Infrastructure Development Board (GIDB) in 1995 to provide facilitation services to the private sector for their active participation and investments in infrastructural projects in the state. It tries to achieve coordination among various government agencies for the purpose. The state enacted the Gujarat Infrastructure Development Act, 1999 specifying a framework for private sector participation to augment the resource flow to this critical sector.

Infrastructure can be classified into four broad categories: transport (ports and roads), support (water and electricity), distribution (storage and marketing), and information (Internet and mobile phones). We discuss each of these components in turn.

Transport: Ports and Roads

Gujarat has a long coastline of about 1,659 km. It can provide natural access to the world markets for the vast northern and central Indian hinterland contributing about 35% of the national exports. The state has 41 minor and intermediate ports with south Gujarat accounting for 14 ports, Saurashtra 23 ports, and Kutch 4 ports. Kandla is a major port under the central government and has been handling the highest cargo in the country among all major government ports for the last four years (GoG-SER 2012; Deloitte 2009).

Gujarat was the first state in the country to formulate an independent port policy in 1995 to facilitate the growing demand for international trade.

Gujarat Maritime Board (GMB) under this policy identified 10 greenfield sites for port development. Although six sites were earmarked for development through exclusive private sector development, only two ports of Pipavav and Mundra could be developed on Build-Own-Operate-Transfer (BOOT) basis. The country's first two LNG terminals and the only chemical port in the country have also been developed in Gujarat through private investment.

Figure 14.2 shows the total cargo handled by ports in Gujarat from 1980/81 to 2009/10. The impact of the port policy can be seen on the rate of increase in the annual cargo handled by the intermediate and minor ports with a clear break in 1998/99. From 1990/91 to 1998/99, annual cargo of these ports increased from 7.6 million tons to 25.1 million tones, or by three times; but the increase was eight times between 1998/99 and 2009/10 from 25.1 million tons to 205.5 million tons (GoG-SER 2011). During this entire period, the annual cargo handled by centrally operated Kandla port did not show any significant break in the time trend. The port policy of the state succeeded because it responded quickly to the increased demand for international trade by systematically linking industrial and agricultural development, power generation, and infrastructural linkages through roads. Involvement of the private sector with clear property rights and well-defined incentives ensured that ports developed by them have all necessary connectivity to be fully used commercially (Deloitte and CII 2009; Aiyer 2008).

Airports are another major transport link, and Gujarat has a total of 14 government airports, out of which 3 are non-operational, 3 are for air force, and 8 are operational having scheduled flights (GoG-iNDEXTb 2011). There are also two private airports at Mundra and Mithapur (*Times of India*,

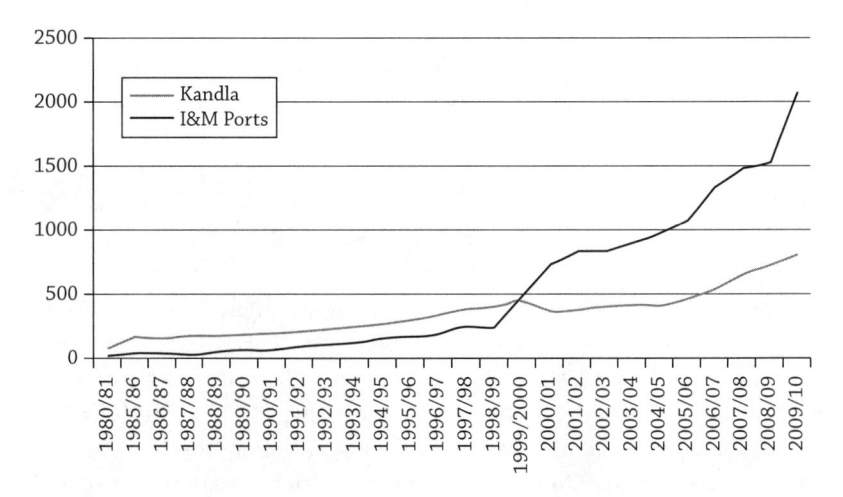

Figure 14.2: Time Path of Total Cargo (in metric tons) Handled by Ports in Gujarat
Note: Kandla is a major port that is centrally administered. Intermediate and Minor (I&M) ports are under the state-run Gujarat Maritime Board.
Source: GoG-Socio Economic Review (2011).

Mar. 8, 2011). As we have seen above, the 2009 industrial policy of the state has identified aviation sector and ship-building and ship-repairing as the major opportunities and thrust areas.

The road sector was accorded the foremost priority and Gujarat State Road Development Corporation Limited (GSRDC) was created to implement all the plans for creating and managing high-quality road infrastructure in the state. A recent World Bank (2010) study finds the currently planned road network of 74,111 km as "among the best managed networks." The road network in Gujarat is among the highest in network density per square kilometer in India. The report identifies private sector involvement as a crucial factor in the reforms in the highway sector in Gujarat. Investment in new roads in the state increased six times compared to pre-reform period.

With GSRDC in place, the role of the existing Roads and Building (R&B) department changed from provider to the manager of roads. It started paying more attention to maintenance and repairs and could perform the task more effectively. The department uses the computer-based Gujarat Roads Management System (GRMS) that covers about 20,000 km of the highest priority major roads. This system helped the R&B department to obtain the maintenance funding (World Bank 2011).

The World Bank (2010) observes, "Gujarat was one of the first states in India to develop a strategic or core road network by applying the 80/20 rule, i.e. 20% of the road network, which carries 80% of the traffic, should be prioritized for further development and asset management" (p. 5). This was implemented for the World Bank funded highway projects in Gujarat. Various categories of state roads were built using this concept leading to efficient use of such investments. The report also noted that there were no contract disputes unlike most highway development projects in India.

The impact of infrastructure investment like roads and ports on the income of a state and the nation is generally felt through various rounds of multiplier effects. However, the first round effects of such investment projects are invariably on the local economy through an increase in income from the sector concerned. For investments in roads and ports, the relevant sectors of first round impact are trade and transport (other than railways). Figure 14.3 shows that the growth of income from these sectors substantially picked up after 1999/2000. This may be partially attributed to the policy changes relating to ports and roads.

Support: Water and Electricity

Except south Gujarat, most other areas in the state are drought-prone, and availability of both rainwater and groundwater is severely limited (Goswami 2011). The water resource management in the state aims at augmenting the

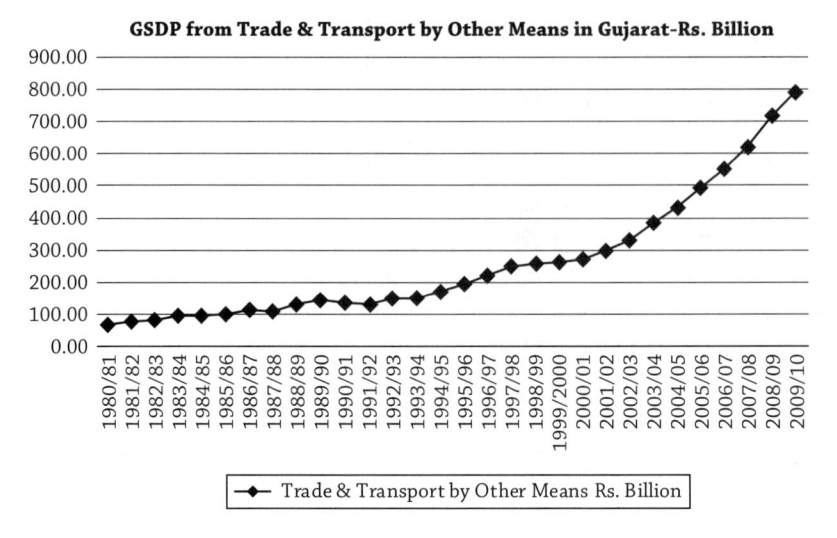

GSDP from Trade & Transport by Other Means in Gujarat-Rs. Billion

Figure 14.3: Time Path of GSDP Originating in Trade and Transport (Other than Railways) at 2004/5 Prices in Gujarat
Source: Department of Economics and Statistics, Government of Gujarat.

supply and providing water efficiently, equitably, and sustainably. By June 2010, the overall irrigation potential in the state was raised to 3.9 million hectares of surface irrigation and 2.6 million hectares of groundwater (GoG-SER 2011).

This includes 1.8 million hectares of irrigation potential of the Narmada project, most of which is not utilized so far because it is yet not built to the full height and though the main canal is completed, the network of distributaries faces multiple bottlenecks. The major challenge in the area of water resource management in Gujarat is to complete the Narmada project. Participatory irrigation management and computerized canal operations and management are some of the initiatives the state government is experimenting with to address the problem.[6]

The SSP would also generate substantial benefits for drinking water and municipal and industrial uses (Alagh et al. 1995). In 2003/04, the government of India had identified 9,628 habitations with inadequate quantity of water and 7,675 habitations suffering from inadequate quality of drinking water in the state. About 4,000 villages were depending on the water-tankers around 2002/03. By 2009/10, the state could cover all these habitations and villages with potable drinking water facilities. The percentage of households having tap-connection increased from 27% in 2002 to 72% by 2011. The number of deep tube wells also fell from 1,146 in 2001 to only 47 by 2009. Some villages are re-emerging as problem villages in this respect.

6. For further details, see Parthasarathy and Dholakia (2011: vol. 3).

POLICY REFORM IN ECONOMIC SECTORS (259)

The power sector in Gujarat represents one of the most dynamic sectors in terms of reforms and private sector participation. It has substantial impact on production and consumption in the economy with all implied forward and backward linkages and multiplier effects.

In 1998, the Central Electricity Act was amended to allow private participation in transmission of power. The act also provided for setting up of an independent Electricity Regulatory Commission for determining the tariffs. However, this act had many shortcomings leading to a major overhaul of laws through the Electricity Act of 2003. This made the power reforms possible and successful in Gujarat. The 2003 Act led to: (1) creation of a regulatory body for the power sector for determining tariffs, giving distribution licenses, and developing performance standards; (2) unbundling of the Gujarat State Electricity Board into generation, transmission, and distribution companies but with a single buyer model; and (3) powers given to the state government to give policy direction to GERC regarding subsidies (Sankar and Mondal 2010; Shah and Mehta 2012).

Further, under the reforms triggered by the Electricity Act of 2003, generation was exempted from licenses; captive generation became free from controls; generation through non-conventional sources and co-generation were promoted; open access to transmission lines was provided to the distribution licensees and generating companies; metering was made obligatory; open access in distribution was allowed; and trading with licenses and regulations was permitted. These reforms were further strengthened with amendments to the act in 2004, 2005, and 2007 (Sankar and Mondal 2010). This led to a significant increase in private sector participation. Its share in the installed capacity increased from 11.2% in 1997 to 13.3% in 2003 to 41.6% in 2013 (GoG-SER 2014).

The power policy in the state also encourages the non-conventional and green sources of energy like solar, wind, tidal, and nuclear power. Under the Gujarat Energy Development Agency, renewable energy development in the state is proceeding at a fast pace. Asia's first Solar Park in 2,000 hectares of arid land in Patan district has been set up to generate 500 MW through public–private partnership. This would also reduce emission of carbon (GoG-SER 2011).

Table 14.1 shows a remarkable turnaround of the power sector in the last decade. Gujarat turned into a power surplus state with an increase in revenues and profitability and substantial decline in transmission and distribution losses.

Distribution: Storage and Marketing

Storage facilities for raw materials, semi-finished goods, intermediate goods, and finished goods are critical links in the supply chain. Available data on storage facilities pertain to public sector facilities only and show that state sector

Table 14.1. THE TURNAROUND OF THE ELECTRICITY SECTOR IN GUJARAT, 2000/01 AND 2010/11

Item	Year 2000/01	Year 2010/11
Supply–demand gap	−500 mega watts	2,114 mega watts
Profit	−Rs. 22.46 billion	Rs. 5.33 billion
Revenues	Rs. 62.80 billion	Rs. 218.95 billion
Transmission and distribution losses	35.30%	20.10%
Plant load factor	66.70%	79.00%
Average cost per unit	Rs. 3.51	Rs. 4.41
Average realization per unit	Rs. 2.70	Rs. 4.52
Collection efficiency	96%	100%

Source: Sankar and Mondal (2010); and Shah and Mehta (2012).

storage is shrinking while central warehousing is expanding at 5% annually (GoG-SA 2008). It is possible that private sector storage is replacing the state sector storage. The developments after 2003 industrial policy of encouraging industrial clusters might have resulted in storage facilities as a part of infrastructure facilities within the clusters. Moreover, organized retail stores in the urban and semi-urban areas, which have grown, also have their own storage facilities. Reliable data are, however, not available to verify these hypotheses.

The Agricultural Produce and Marketing Committee (APMC) yards provide a vast network for rural marketing. As noted earlier, the APMC Act was amended in the years 2005 and 2007 allowing competition through spot markets, private markets or direct marketing, and contract farming. However, several critical areas of suggested reforms are not adopted in the amended act in the state. For instance, facilities like single registration and single fee for more than one market has not yet been adopted. Suggestions regarding market extension cells, removal of commission agents, and transfer of rights and ownership in contract farming have also not been adopted.

It is important to note that agriculture and allied activities now contribute only 14% of state income and marketing infrastructure is required for the remaining sectors as well. The industrial policies of 2003 and 2009 have focused on such critical marketing infrastructure by specifically encouraging development of spaces for marketing fairs, convention centers, and exhibitions; allowing organized multi-product retailing resulting in number of malls, supermarkets, and multiplexes; and marketing development efforts abroad.

Information: Internet and Mobile Phones

Information and communication are critical to efficient operation of markets. Rural tele-density in Gujarat was 29.4% higher and urban tele-density was 10.6% lower than the corresponding national averages in December 2012 (GoG-SER 2014).

Gujarat's e-Village scheme of 2003/04 has become very effective and a successful tool to empower every village panchayat with broadband connectivity. This has enabled all villages to be connected to the latest information. Similarly, radios and television sets are available in every village, thanks to full rural electrification and round-the-clock supply of electricity.

This has served two purposes: (1) connecting each village panchayat with the taluka, district, and state capital establishing a direct eye-to-eye contact for citizens to government (C to G); and (2) providing channels of communication and contact for business to consumers (B to C). This project was implemented in all villages on the PPP model involving well-known private sector companies. It has resulted in several benefits like efficient price discovery, expert technical advice to farmers, timely supply of weather information, issuance of several documents by village panchayats (like birth and death certificates and landownership certificates), payment of electricity bills, telephone bills, visa applications, and e-postal service (Newsletter 2009).

All these developments on the information-infrastructure front in the state along with other developments at national level taking place in the information technology sector are reflected in the GSDP originating in the communication sub-sector. From 1994/95, the series shows rapid growth perhaps on account of the national reforms in the sector. The growth got accelerated in Gujarat from 2003/04 perhaps due to further liberalization in the sector at the national level, and the e-Village scheme coupled with electricity reforms in the state (figure 14.4).

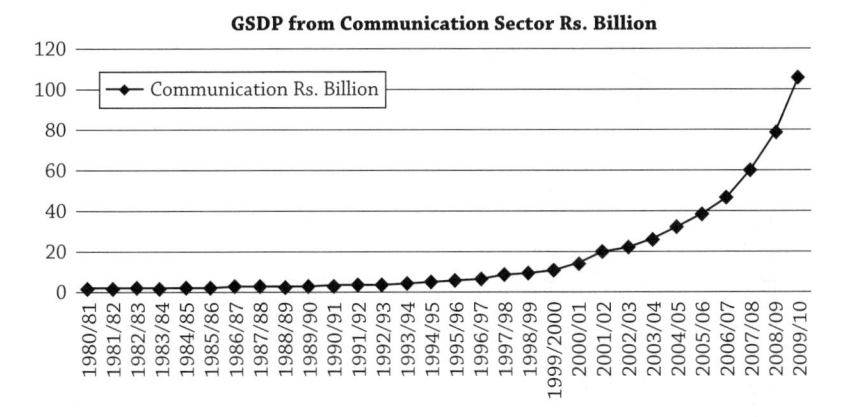

Figure 14.4: Time Path of Real GSDP Originating in Communication Sub-Sector in Gujarat
Source: Department of Economics and Statistics and the Government of Gujarat.

VIBRANT GUJARAT INVESTORS' SUMMIT

A unique feature of Gujarat widely discussed is its biennial investors' summit, called Vibrant Gujarat Summit (VGS) that started in 2003. VGS is held for three days by inviting industrialists, business houses, banks, financial institutions, and individuals from within and outside the country to invest in the state. At the summit, participants interact with one another and the state's top bureaucrats have the opportunity to inform potential investors on the attractiveness of the state as an investment destination. The summit results in the signing of many Memorandums of Understanding (MoUs) between the appropriate state government departments and investors pledging interest in investing specified volume of resources in well-specified projects with time-lines.

Since 2003, it has been held every two years with increasing fanfare, because the idea has clicked and investors' interest in Gujarat has grown exponentially with time. The quantum of the MoUs signed during the summit provides some indication of the investors' interest. The 2011 summit had an explicit objective of building the brand of Gujarat and of showcasing the state as a potential global hub for several products, besides attracting large private sector investments.

The number of proposed projects has significantly increased from summit to summit and now stands at 5,549 (table 14.2). The proposed investments as per the MoUs have also been increasing rapidly at each successive summit

Table 14.2. VIBRANT GUJARAT INVESTORS' SUMMITS—PROPOSALS AND PERFORMANCE TO DATE

Year	Projects Proposed — Number	Projects Proposed — Investment in Billion Rupees	Proposals Still Active — Number	Proposals Still Active — Investment in Billion Rupees	Actual Investment — As percentage of proposed	Actual Investment — Billion Rupees	Actual Investment — As percentage of proposed
2003	80	660.7	47	484.6	73.3	329.4	49.9
2005	227	1,061.6	138	658.7	62.0	341.0	32.1
2007	454	4,653.1	351	4,003.4	86.0	1,053.6	22.6
2009-Large	1,653	12,253.6	1,547	11,803.2	96.3	842.2	6.9
2009-MSME	921	95.4	1,834	93.8	98.3	68.3	71.6
2011-Large	4,319	24,081.0	4,296	24,042.9	100.0	85.9	0.4
2011-MSME	1,230	30.9	1,213	30.6	99.0	6.4	20.8

Source: Industries Commissionerate, GoG (data provided as at end of Sept. 2011).

promising the staggering investment of 24 trillion rupees. The strategy of VGS, thus, seems to have received a good response.

The success rate as measured by the investments of the proposals not dropped so far to the originally proposed total investment turns out to be in excess of 60% even after four to eight years in the case of the first three summits (table 14.2). Big and mega investment projects require a long time for planning, for obtaining numerous clearances and approvals from the central government, and for implementation. Six to seven years for such purposes may not be considered as unusual delay. Therefore, the success rate for the last two summits of 2009 and 2011 should be ideally measured only after an appropriate lag.

As per table 14.2, the conversion rate of the investment is ranging from 20% to 50% for the first three summits. For the last two summits the smaller projects or Micro, Small, Medium Enterprise (MSME) type projects have been converting at the rate of 70% in two and a half years and 20% in less than one year. This strategy ensures that the state economy is likely to experience high growth in income not only over next five to six years but even longer period of time.

CONCLUDING REMARKS

In this chapter, we have discussed the state-level policies and initiatives in agriculture, industry, and infrastructure that help explain the superior performance of Gujarat relative to other states during the 1990s and 2000s. After the low and highly variable annual growth during 1970–2000, agriculture experienced sustained growth of 6.4% during the decade 2000–2011. This growth was also characterized by significantly reduced annual fluctuations. This performance coincided with several policy initiatives taken by the state government such as water conservation, massive extension effort, assured electricity supply to agriculture, emphasis on high-value crops, marketing and information networking to help farmers, support to the livestock sector, and promotion of agricultural exports by creating reliable infrastructure. While the Sardar Sarovar Project on the Narmada River made considerable progress during the decade, it is still incomplete and irrigates less than a quarter of the 1.8 million hectares of its potential command area (Appendix 2).

The state had five specific policies for the industrial development in 1990, 1995, 2000, 2003, and 2009. While the first three policies had the emphasis on various incentives and subsidies for capital investment, sales tax, and geographical coverage of units, the last two policies differed in terms of their vision, scope, and reform measures. Their objectives have been to make Gujarat industries globally competitive, create a global brand image of the state, and attract mega investment projects into it. Special Economic Zones (SEZs) and several such special regions and large-scale investments therein have been encouraged. The annual industrial growth in the state during the last decade has been 11.8% compared to 8.8% nationally. Exports originating from the state have also risen to 24.6% of the national exports in 2010/11.

We have also discussed policy initiatives by the state in infrastructural sectors such as ports and roads, water and power, storage and marketing, and Internet and mobile phones. Private sector participation in almost all these infrastructure sectors has made the state stand out in terms of quantity and quality of the services. Salient features of development in these sectors in the state include privately owned ports, application of 80/20 rule for strategic road networks, participatory irrigation management, substantial reforms in the electricity sector since 2003, non-agricultural marketing infrastructure development, and e-connectivity from each village panchayat to taluka to district to state capital through public–private partnership. All this not only facilitated free flow of information so critical to the efficient operation of markets but also improved transparency and effective governance.

The biennial Vibrant Gujarat Investors' summits from 2003 onward as a strategy to invite the global investors and showcase the progress and progressive outlook of the government has received an ever-increasing response from the investors. Out of the investment proposals received during these summits aggregating to trillions of rupees, significant proportions have been realized and most of the commitments remain active.

CHAPTER 15

Urban Development

The operational definition of urban areas adopted by the censuses in India is to consider the statutory towns as urban areas because of the presence of public administrative infrastructure and manpower. Among the non-statutory areas, urban areas are those meeting all three of the following conditions: (1) density of population exceeding 400 per sq km; (2) more than 75% of male working force engaged in the non-agricultural activities; and (3) minimally, a population of 5,000. Areas having nagar panchayats, municipalities, municipal corporations, or a Cantonment Board, and outgrowth of cities and towns are also treated as urban areas. Every decadal census carefully examines different spatial units for these criteria and identifies new urban areas or de-recognizes existing urban areas if they fail to meet any of these criteria.

The present chapter begins with an examination of the role of migration and other factors in the relative growth of urban areas in Gujarat. It then discusses the extent of slums and some critical urban public services like drinking water, disposal of solid waste, and urban roads in cities in Gujarat. Finally, it considers urban financing and policy changes influencing the urban development in the state including innovative financing mechanisms and municipal bond issues.

URBAN GROWTH

Growth of urban population may occur due to natural increase in population, absorption of peripheral rural areas by expanding urban centers known

---

We are thankful to Ms. Shivika Mittal for useful assistance in collecting material and data for this chapter.

Table 15.1. URBAN AND RURAL POPULATION, AREA, AND DENSITY

Years	Population ('000) Urban	Population ('000) Rural	Area (sq km) Urban	Area (sq km) Rural	Density (pop/sq km) Urban	Density (pop/sq km) Rural	Urban Area as Percentage of the Total
1981	10,602	23,484	4,764.6	191,259.4	2,225.1	122.8	2.43
1991	14,246	27,064	5,137.4	190,886.6	2,773.0	141.8	2.62
2001	18,930	31,741	5,227.5	190,796.5	3,621.3	166.4	2.66
2011	25,713	34,671	7,406.8	188,617.2	3,471.5	183.8	3.78

Source: Census of India for respective years.

as urban sprawl, migration from rural to urban areas, and reclassification of previously rural agglomerations as urban.

Rural density has been increasing continuously in Gujarat over the last 30 years due to rising population (table 15.1). Urban density also rose from 1981 to 2001, but during the last decade (2001–2011), the average urban density in Gujarat declined. This was perhaps because of the steep increase in the geographical land covered under urban areas in the 2011 census. It signifies extensive nature of urbanization not only in terms of the usual phenomenon of urban sprawl but also because of formation of smaller new towns out of the villages, which have much lower density of population than big towns and cities.

There is 42% increase in the urban geographical area during 2001 to 2011 (table 15.1). During 1981–91, the growth was 8% and from 1991 to 2001, the growth was only 2%. A major distinguishing feature of the last decade is that urban land increased by a rate 20 times that experienced during the preceding decade.

In order to derive the contribution of net immigration to the growth of urban areas in the state, crude birth and death rates in the urban areas are used.[1] Natural growth of population in the urban Gujarat works out at 23.16%, 18.34%, and 15.86%, respectively during 1981–91, 1991–2001, and 2001–11. The contribution of urban sprawl is worked out on the assumption that the new or additional geographical area getting converted into urban area during a census year has the density of 400 persons per sq km.[2] The estimates of contribution of urban sprawl are, therefore: 1.41%, 0.24%, and 4.29%, respectively for the three decades. As against these, the observed growth rates of urban population in Gujarat during the same periods are respectively 34.34%, 32.94%, and 35.82%. Thus, the contribution of net immigration to urban Gujarat during these decades would be 9.77%, 14.36%, and 15.67%, respectively.

1. Obtained from various Bulletins of Sample Registration System (SRS).
2. This is the minimum qualifying density as per the definition of an urban area.

These findings clearly show that urban Gujarat is attracting accelerating proportions of immigrants over the last three decades. Migrants accounted for approximately 44% of urban population growth during 2001–11. As we discussed in chapter 13, since Class IV, V, and VI towns with population less than 20,000 grew by 93% with the growth of major cities sharply declining from 51% to 37% during 2001–11, it may imply that several of these new immigrants would be getting located in the smaller towns and semi-urban areas. Thus, these smaller towns and semi-urban areas have likely emerged as new centers of attraction of economic activities and hence immigrants. Very substantial structural changes in the Gujarat economy are indicated by these findings.

Gujarat is among the few net in-migrant states in the country that receive large inflows of migrant labor from several states. On a net basis, migrants from outside states amount to 16 per 1,000 of population, which is higher than most other states (NSSO 2008a). The issue of migration both from within and outside the state is often linked to unplanned growth of cities, undue pressure on urban infrastructure, civic services, and particularly to creation and proliferation of slums to which we turn next.

SLUMS IN GUJARAT

At the all-India level, the proportion of slum population in total urban population has remained almost constant at 22%–23% over the 20 years from 1981 to 2001 (table 15.2). Gujarat shows this proportion almost constant around 20%. From the available results of the 2011 census, it is seen that the coverage has shifted from population to the households living in slums. In 2011, the

Table 15.2. URBAN AND SLUM POPULATION (IN 100,000) AND ITS PROPORTION (IN %) IN SELECTED STATES

Selected States	1981			1991			2001		
	Urban	Slum	% Slum	Urban	Slum	% Slum	Urban	Slum	% Slum
Andhra Pradesh	79.1	19.1	24.2	119.8	27.3	22.8	171.3	38.9	22.7
Bihar	48.2	15.0	31.0	59.6	18.4	30.9	79.3	24.8	31.2
Gujarat	67.6	13.9	20.6	94.8	18.7	19.7	131.0	25.9	19.8
Maharashtra	166.9	46.0	10.5	237.7	65.0	27.3	325.6	88.5	27.2
Tamil Nadu	104.8	22.1	21.0	127.0	24.2	19.1	157.8	30.4	19.3
West Bengal	120.3	36.2	30.1	153.0	45.3	29.6	190.5	55.7	29.2
All-India	1,023.9	242.9	23.7	1400.8	314.3	22.4	1900.5	424.5	22.3

Source: Ministry of Urban Affairs and Census for respective years.

proportion of households living in slums at the national level is 17.4% and for Gujarat it is 6.7% (Chandramouli 2013). Since the average size of households may be higher in slums than in non-slums, the proportion of urban population as opposed to households in slums may be larger. However, this difference is too small to explain a fall from 19.8% to 6.7% in Gujarat during 2001–11. Although one has to wait for more data and information to fully understand the phenomenon, we may note several specific efforts made by the state government and municipal authorities to reduce the slums during the last decade.

As per the census data, slums in Gujarat are more a phenomenon of smaller cities and towns than big cities. Three big cities, Ahmedabad, Surat, and Vadodara accounted for 37% of slum population in Gujarat in 2001 and have the proportion of slum population less than the state average (see table 15.3).

In these three big cities and elsewhere, slums exist on the encroached government land in prime locations. Urban development projects such as widening of roads, flyovers, bridges, bus rapid transit system (BRTS), riverfront development, lake area development, and metro-rail automatically lead to slum clearance. Gujarat has the record of being a high performer in implementing such urban development projects during the last decade including the ones under the Jawaharlal Nehru National Urban Renewal Mission (JNNURM). As of 2012, it was the only state in the country to implement all reforms required by the Mission (jnnurm.nic.in, accessed on June 21, 2013).

Moreover, the state government and municipal authorities also regularly undertake slum resettlement programs and by merging Slum Cell with the Housing Development Board have relocated a large number of slum dwellers to either within the city or on periphery. In this regard, the state has passed regulations for rehabilitation of slums in 2010. The government has also incentivized private developers by offering the land where slums exist with increased Floor Space Index (FSI) provided they in return offer free housing

Table 15.3. SLUM POPULATION IN CITIES WITH MORE THAN MILLION PEOPLE IN GUJARAT AND INDIA AND ITS PROPORTION TO TOTAL POPULATION, 2001

Name of the City	Total Population (in 100,000)	Slum Population (in 100,000)	% Slum Population
Surat (12)	24.34	4.06	16.68
Ahmedabad (19)	35.15	4.40	12.51
Vadodara (23)	13.06	1.07	8.21
All India—total of 26 big cities	708.00	166.00	23.00

Note: Figures in parentheses are ranks of cities in All India.
Source: Census of India 2001.

to the slum dwellers (Pandit 2011). While concrete data on the impact of these efforts on the overall reduction in the slum population in Gujarat are not available, it is likely that they are partially responsible for the large decline in slum population in Gujarat reflected in the census data between 2001 and 2011.

URBAN LAND

Planned urban development based on the concerns of equity and efficiency requires sound policies on urban land supply. The government of India repealed the Urban Land Ceiling and Regulation Act (ULCRA) of 1976 in 1999. The government of Gujarat acted almost simultaneously, repealing the state-level act within months of the decision at the center.

The act had been a major source of corruption, unnecessary litigation, and restricted urban land market in major cities in India. Therefore, the repeal of ULCRA was an important step toward increasing the supply of urban land. Unfortunately, however, the benefit from it has not been maximized because a formal clearance for the property from the urban development authority with respect to the land ceiling criteria is still required. This has continued to remain a source of inefficiency and corruption. It is essential that the government drop this requirement in the interest of transparency.

Anticipating rapid urban growth, the state government had already enacted the Gujarat Town Planning and Urban Development (GTPUD) Act in 1976 to empower the government to use land for development purposes without actual transfer of the landownership. This was done to enable the government to provide critical urban public goods like water supply, drainage, and public transportation. This act has been modified from time to time but the approach is transparent involving private developers. The GTPUD Act essentially pools the group of landowners together to get adequate size of the aggregate land plot. On that plot, appropriate town planning norms for social amenities and roads are applied and the corresponding area is deducted for infrastructure development. The remaining land area is then redistributed among the original landowners in proportion to the size of the original plot (World Bank 2008).

SERVICE DELIVERY

The Ministry of Urban Development (MUD) has prescribed the benchmarks for basic service norms for cities, which are available on their official website. The MUD norms for provision of water supply in cities are: (1) 100% individual piped water supply for all households including informal settlements for all cities; (2) 24 x 7 water supply; and (3) consumption norm of 135 liters

Table 15.4. AVAILABILITY OF WATER SUPPLY IN FOUR METROPOLITAN CITIES, 2005

Cities	Water Consumption (lcpd)	% Population with Water Supply Available
1. Ahmedabad	142	95
2. Surat	195	95
3. Vadodara	183	75
4. Rajkot	110	73

Source: City Development Plans of respective cities.

per capita per day (lpcd) for all cities. Against this, the performance of the four metropolitan cities of Gujarat is given in table 15.4.

Three of the four cities meet the MUD norm for the volume of water consumption. More disconcertingly, none of the cities meets the MUD norms of continuous 24 x 7 water supply and 100% coverage of households by piped water supply. Installation of water meters and user charges linked to water usage within municipal corporations recommended by ADB (1999) have been under consideration for a long time but little progress in this direction has been made. This, in part, is the reason for unsatisfactory progress in achieving the MUD norms.

Segregation of municipal solid waste and its scientific disposal are considered very important urban services. As the City Development Plan (CDP) of Ahmedabad (2006) observed, more than 70% of the solid waste consisted of organic and bio-degradable matters. However, the lack of both segregation at collection points and effective scientific technique for disposal rendered the service in metropolitan cities inefficient and unsatisfactory. Involvement of private companies in solid waste collection in Surat and Ahmedabad yielded results and their collection efficiency improved to about 98% by 2005 (CDP for Surat 2006; and CDP for Ahmedabad 2006), which is very close to the MUD norm. The remaining two cities—Vadodara and Rajkot—have also started involving the private sector in the activity to improve their efficiency as per their CDPs.

On the front of urban roads, their density in kilometer per 1,000 persons has increased rapidly in Gujarat from 0.78 in 2005 to 0.86 in 2008. This might be due to focused policy intervention by the government. Similarly, the quality of roads in Gujarat is far better than the national average because more than 90% of the roads in Gujarat are surfaced against hardly 55% at the national level (GoG-SER 2011). In Ahmedabad, the municipal corporation has also successfully introduced an extensive bus rapid transit system (BRTS) based on public–private partnership (for details, see National Institute of Urban Affairs 2011). It is a highly successful project covering more than 70 km of operational corridor, 300,000 passengers per day, and commercial speed in excess of 24 km/hour. It has won three national and three international awards for its performance during 2008–11 (see http://gujaratindia.com/media/news.htm?enc=KIN4q/jNm90+toii5qZl5EPC7kzGIsfoo/Golnrswj7pk9fBjT+kzGKHUj17F4hnIZ1uHAK4cV1euMVzD3X7kO7fIn2R/nobyduKhGbKNgsWd9MPRYhXNd0PuAhM9OuiOnkJb7CYgVWZ5YxtsD5xkQ, accessed on Mar. 2, 2014). Surat and Rajkot have already started implementing this project to ease their transportation problem.

URBAN FINANCES

The third tier of government in the federal democracy of India consists of local bodies. In urban Gujarat, these bodies are regularly elected by residents and are very active. They are governed by Bombay Provincial Municipal Corporation (BPMC) Act of 1949 and by Gujarat Municipalities Act of 1963. Under BPMC Act, taxes on property, vehicles, boats, and animals are obligatory for municipal corporations, whereas octroi and several other minor taxes and fees are discretionary. In the case of municipalities governed by the Gujarat Municipalities Act, all taxes are discretionary and most of them are levied in practice in Gujarat.

Budgets of major corporations (Surat, Ahmedabad, and Vadodara) exhibit revenue surplus over time. Overall, the urban local bodies of Gujarat have a very high revenue collection implying a strong economic base. Their "own revenue" as percentage of the GSDP is on an average 0.98% during 2002–09 compared to 0.42% for the all-India average (MUD 2011). The problem still remains in Class III and IV municipalities, since they continue to depend heavily on the grant-in-aid.

Octroi

The State Public Finance Reform Committee (SPFRC 2000) in Gujarat clearly recommended unconditional abolition of octroi from the state in its report. Subsequently, it was abolished in May 2001 for all local bodies (numbering more than 1,200) except seven municipal corporations. It was the main source of revenue for all these local bodies, but the decision to abolish the octroi was taken to promote efficiency and trade. However, it continued in the seven municipal corporations accounting for almost 80% of the total octroi revenue in the state. It was difficult to abolish octroi from these corporations because it contributed 50–60% of their revenues and there was no agreement on the alternative.

In 2007, octroi was finally abolished from the remaining seven municipal corporations without effectively finding an alternative. The corporations were compensated through the grants in lieu of octroi. At the aggregate level, share of grants in total expenditure, often termed as "dependency ratio," rose sharply from 8% in 2003/04 to 35% in 2009/10 for municipal corporations in Gujarat (CDP 2006; and Budgets of all Municipal Corporations in Gujarat, for respective years).

Property Tax

Mathur (2009) argues that increasing the collection efficiency of property tax alone in all cities could generate sufficient revenues to compensate for the loss from octroi. In order to increase collection efficiency, it is essential that coverage of all properties through proper registration is ensured for assessment of the tax. Ahmedabad Municipal Corporation has built strong database of properties by mapping through Geographic Information System (GIS) and other corporations are following the suit because it has resulted in improved collection efficiency.

A major reform in the property tax is carried out by replacing the basis of assessment and taxation from annual ratable value (ARV) to area-based system of per square meter tax rate. Now the property tax rate depends on four factors: location, age, type of the building and use or occupancy of the property. In order to promote greater transparency, the government of Gujarat is encouraging tools like e-governance for self-assessment of property tax. It has resulted in enhanced collection efficiency and reduced litigation (World Bank 2008).

Municipal Bonds

The issue of specific bonds is a new measure to tap the capital market to raise additional resources for infrastructure development by municipal bodies. Ahmedabad Municipal Corporation (AMC) was the first in the country to use this instrument in 1998 and issue 1 billion rupees worth of bonds at 14% interest for seven years (Vaidya and Johnson 2001; Mathur 2006). AMC could successfully raise the resources from the capital market because of its "excellent" credit rating by rating agencies such as CRISIL, ICRA, and CARE. Incidentally, these bonds were not backed by the state government security.

The key to the success of the bond issue, apart from the excellent credit rating from the three highly regarded agencies, was the confidence enhancing mechanism put in place by the AMC and clarity on specific funding need for the Ahmedabad water supply and sewerage project. The specific measures

AMC put in place were: earmarked account where a fixed proportion of revenues from taxes would go; debt reserve account for repayment of principal amount to reduce investors' risk; revenues from 10 octroi collection centers earmarked for debt service payment; and creation of an escrow account to be managed by an independent trustee until the final redemption of the bonds. Subsequently, encouraged by the success of AMC, other corporations such as Ludhiana, Bangalore, Nashik, Nagpur, Madurai, Hyderabad, and Indore also raised resources through the same route (Bagchi and Kundu 2003).

AMC was also the first municipal corporation in the country to issue tax-free bonds of 1 billion rupees in 2002. The central government providing the tax benefits on such bonds with certain conditionality was a great help for urban local bodies to reduce interest cost. So far, all these issues are placed privately. With better fiscal discipline and prudence, it is possible to go public as well.

CONCLUDING REMARKS

The extent of urbanization as measured by the proportion of population that is urban has always been higher in Gujarat than the national average. During the last decade (2001–11), average urban density in the state declined due to extensive nature of urbanization. The contribution of net migration to urban growth in Gujarat is increasing continuously and stands at 44% during the last decade. In addition to its own rural residents, urban Gujarat also attracts migrants from other states due to employment opportunities and a generally welcoming environment.

Proportion of the slum population in the state has been less than the national average. Going by the 2001 census data, it appears that slums in Gujarat are a phenomenon of smaller cities and towns than the bigger ones. Preliminary data from the 2011 census indicate a sharp fall in the proportion of slum population in the nation and more so in Gujarat. A careful analysis suggests that specific efforts by the state government and municipal authorities in this direction have yielded results.

Gujarat repealed the Urban Land Ceiling Act of 1976 almost simultaneously with the center in April 1999 to bring surplus land back on the market, but the processes are yet not simplified enough. There is further scope for improvements in this area.

The performance of big cities in the state on water supply is far from satisfactory perhaps because suggested reforms in this regard have not been implemented for a long time. However, in the disposal of solid waste, reforms have been introduced with private participation and, as a result the collection efficiency is fast improving in the big cities of the state. Focused state intervention has not only improved the urban road density but has also raised their quality remarkably above the national average. In Ahmadabad, the government has successfully implemented the bus rapid transit system through PPP, reducing congestion and pollution. Other cities in the country are now emulating this success.

Municipal finances in Gujarat show significantly higher revenue collection than the national average and major municipal corporations on average show revenue surplus. Octroi, a highly distorting and economically inefficient tax, was completely abolished by 2007. Several reforms directed to increase collection efficiency and reduce litigation have been undertaken in area of property tax in the state. Ahmedabad Municipal Corporation successfully demonstrated twice (1998 and 2002) that with strict fiscal discipline, it is possible to tap the capital market through bonds to finance infrastructure projects for urban development.

Gujarat's experience in management of urban development shows that focused government interventions with reforms to encourage private participation can be highly productive and beneficial.

CHAPTER 16

Fiscal Reforms and Performance

In the present chapter, we provide an analysis of the fiscal performance and fiscal reform measures in Gujarat during the last two decades and show how the fiscal situation compares with prior decades. India is a federation with inter-state transfers as its integral feature. Such transfers are made through the instrumentality of the Finance Commission and the Planning Commission. Whether the transfers ensure "adequate" finances for the states has been a contentious issue.[1] But for the purpose of this chapter, we treat them as exogenously given without going into their pros and cons.

Basic objectives of the state's fiscal policy include: (1) provision of public goods without compromising efficiency and sustained rapid growth; and (2) reduction in disparities among different regions and social groups through appropriate fiscal instruments. Sector-specific policies discussed in chapter 14 interact with fiscal policy in an essential way. During the post-reform years, a third objective has been explicitly added to the list, namely, fiscal discipline and fiscal consolidation for reducing various deficits and debt of the state government.

FISCAL REFORM MEASURES DURING 1991–2001

Historically, Gujarat had enjoyed revenue surplus for a very long period after its formation in 1960[2] (GoG 2009). However, from 1986/87 to 2004/05, the

---

1. A large body of literature exists on this issue. See, for instance, Rangarajan and Srivastava 2008; Bagchi and Chakrabarti 2004; Godbole 2001; Kumar and Vemuri 2002; Anand, Bagchi, and Sen 2002.
2. Revenue Deficit is measured as the excess of current expenditures minus current revenues of the government. Fiscal Deficit is measured as excess of total expenditure over revenue receipts and other non-debt receipts of the government. Primary Deficit is measured as Fiscal Deficit minus interest payments. Negative Deficits indicate Surplus.

situation had reversed with the state running a deficit on its revenue account during almost all years. All fiscal parameters, namely Revenue Deficit, Fiscal Deficit, Primary Deficit, and Debt-GSDP ratio showed considerable deterioration in the state finances (table 16.1). This phenomenon was not confined to Gujarat but occurred simultaneously in the majority of the Indian states and at the center as well (Finance Commission 1994).

In the early 1990s, the fiscal deficit and the burden of total debt in the state crossed the prudent levels of 3% and 28% of the GSDP, respectively. Fiscal performance improved during 1993–95 but began deteriorating again thereafter due to various factors including the burden imposed by the implementation of the Fifth Pay Commission recommendations. This period saw a buildup of pressures for fiscal reforms in the state (ADB 1999).

Reforms were required to reduce unproductive and wasteful expenditures, on one hand, and enhance the revenue receipts through tax, non-tax, and public-sector reforms, on the other hand. Since the government of Gujarat had also committed to carry out overall economic reforms, for which additional resources were needed, it had to explore various possibilities to enhance resources also through Public-Private Partnership (PPP).

The state government also tried to get inputs from the experts to determine the direction, pace, and sequencing of fiscal reforms. In 1994 it set up a committee to study the finances of the state, which submitted its report containing suggestions regarding tax and non-tax reforms, and potential of disinvestment and restructuring of the state public-sector undertakings (GoG 1994).

Subsequently, in December 1996, the state government obtained a loan of $250 million from the Asian Development Bank (ADB) for financial restructuring of Public Sector Enterprises (PSEs) and government departments. The ADB had put conditionality in terms of improving certain fiscal parameters, and the successive tranche of the loan was released to the state only on meeting the laid down targets achieved through structural reforms (ADB 2007).

The ADB team of consultants looked at aspects of finances of the state, resource generation through private sector participation, and computerization. They also worked out the implications of replacing sales tax by value added tax (VAT) on the potential taxpayers and finances of the state government. Moreover, the reform proposals for minor taxes, non-tax revenue, subsidies, and municipal finances along with their possible implications on the exchequer and taxpayers were prepared by the consultants. The enactment of laws for regulating the private sector participation and formulation of GIDB were also the results of ADB assignments.

As a follow-up of the ADB reports, the state government set up a "State Public Finance Reform Committee" (SPFRC), which studied the above reports in detail and came up with a concrete action plan for fiscal reforms (SPFRC 2000). It submitted its report in December 2000, but unfortunately

Table 16.1. BROAD FISCAL INDICATORS AS PERCENTAGE OF THE GSDP AT CURRENT PRICES, 1980/81 TO 2011/12

Year	Fiscal Deficit	Revenue Deficit*	Interest Payment	Primary Deficit	Total Expenditure	Capital Outlay	Public Debt	Outstanding Liabilities	Interest Rate IP/OL
1980/81	2.82	−1.39	0.78	2.04	17.14	5.44	20.30		
1986/87	4.70	1.61	1.27	3.42	19.82	5.75	18.41		
1991/92	4.91	1.58	1.96	2.96	21.37	3.83	19.01	28.80	8.83
1996/97	2.53	0.63	1.72	0.81	13.95	2.58	13.43	20.70	10.77
2000/01	6.66	5.27	2.61	4.05	26.06	3.27	17.84	31.10	9.13
2001/02	4.88	5.05	3.15	1.73	32.44	1.49	23.04	38.50	9.82
2003/04	5.05	2.05	3.20	1.85	22.17	3.11	26.78	39.00	10.49
2005/06	2.56	0.16	2.51	0.06	14.00	3.13	28.48	37.70	8.60
2006/07	1.99	−0.62	2.43	−0.44	13.83	2.90	27.56	33.90	8.30
2011/12 (RE)	2.41	−0.07	1.81	0.59	13.36	2.53	21.54	26.70	7.66

RE = Revised Estimate. * A negative sign indicates surplus.
Source: Various volumes of Budget in Brief, GoG (Annual) and RBI (Annual–2013).

on January 26, 2001, there was a major earthquake in which more than 13,800 lives were lost and assets worth millions of rupees were destroyed (see Appendix 3). The SPFRC and ADB reports were temporarily shelved by the government to pay attention to the emergent needs of the earthquake affected population and area (ADB 2007). The pace of fiscal reforms in Gujarat during 1991–2001, thus, remained relatively slow.

Nevertheless, some steps were taken for reforming the taxes such as: input tax was phased out to almost zero; sales tax incentives were withdrawn; rationalization of tax structure, rates, and administration started; and computerization of processes initiated. As a part of the non-tax reforms selected public-sector units were restructured and user charges of a few selected public services were revised upward though not to the required extent.

FISCAL REFORM 2001–2011

In May 2000, the state government prepared a fiscal consolidation plan, since it offered high dividends in terms of access to larger market borrowings at lower interest rates than those paid on the central loans. Moreover, the Eleventh Finance Commission (2000–2005) had also recommended linking the devolution of the funds to the fiscal discipline of the states (Finance Commission 2000). This link offered an additional dividend to fiscal consolidation.

As a response to the incentive scheme of the Eleventh Finance Commission, the government of Gujarat signed the Memorandum of Understanding (MoU) with the center to design and implement a Mid-Term Fiscal Reform Program. This was also necessary to avail the "Fiscal Reform Facility Fund." In the MoU, the state government committed to bringing the fiscal deficit down to 3% of the GSDP, revenue deficit to zero, and public debt to 30% of the GSDP by March 2008.

During the last quarter of the fiscal year 2001/02 and the following two years, 2002–04, however, the efforts of the state government on fiscal consolidation got derailed by the major earthquake and communal violence in Gujarat. The expenditure of the state increased substantially and reached 32% of GSDP in 2001/02 from an average of around 16% in earlier years. Total liabilities touched 39% of the GSDP in 2003/04 (see table 16.1).

This fiscal deterioration made fiscal reforms and consolidation essential to restore the credibility of the state government and for sustaining growth. Hence, after 2003/04, the state resumed its focus on bringing down the deficits. A key element in this process was the passage of the Fiscal Responsibility Legislation (FRL) in 2005.

Reform measures include elimination of input taxes and octroi, transfer of profession tax to local bodies, cap on state guarantees and creation of a redemption fund for the same, use of the debt-swap facility to reduce interest burden, creation of a sinking fund to redeem the debt, an amnesty scheme for recovery of taxes and mitigating litigation, increased market borrowing, introduction of a new pension scheme, cap on state subsidies, and, most important, the replacement of sales tax by VAT in 2006.

Reforms relating to minor taxes like entertainment tax, stamp duty, electricity duty, and motor-vehicle tax, suggested by the earlier committees were implemented selectively and gradually by the state government during 2003–11. Several other proposals regarding improvement in the non-tax revenues and cost recovery rates, however, were not satisfactorily implemented. The recommendations for increasing the user charges for water, education, and health were implemented but only in bits and pieces (Budget Speeches of the Finance Minister of Gujarat, 2001–2012; ADB 2007).

On the expenditure side, the reforms include a freeze on new appointments, abolition of vacant posts, redeployment of existing staff, appointments on a contract basis, and a new pension scheme reducing the burden on the exchequer. Further, performance-linked grants to local bodies, e-tenders, and zero-based budgeting principles improved the efficiency of expenditures.

In respect of all three deficits, namely, revenue deficit that measures fiscal discipline, fiscal deficit that reflects fiscal prudence, and primary deficit that helps to determine the debt sustainability, Gujarat's performance improved following the enactment of the FRL. Minor slippage occurred in 2009/10 and 2010/11 in the wake of the global financial crisis and subsequent slow-down, but by 2011/12 the state was back on track for meeting the deficit targets (table 16.1).

In terms of the narrow definition of "public debt," the long-term FRL target of 25% has already been achieved by the state (GoG 2012). Also the yearly rolling targets set by the Thirteenth Finance Commission using the Reserve Bank of India (2006) definition of outstanding liabilities are comfortably met by Gujarat (table 16.1). The state had already put in place the systems to control its total liabilities and the corresponding interest costs to take advantage of the incentive package offered by the Twelfth Finance Commission (Finance Commission 2004). As a result, official liabilities as a proportion of the GSDP have been consistently declining since 2005/06 with the effective weighted interest rate declining since 2003/04 as well (table 16.1).

The FRL for the state also caps the outstanding guarantees given by the state to attract investments and economic activities in its territory. The limit of 200 billion rupees in absolute amount was set in the year 2001 and has not been revised so far (RBI, Annual–2011, GoG 2012). This was necessary to monitor the contingent liabilities of the state government. The state government has not only adhered to the prescribed limit but has also reduced the amount of guarantees in absolute terms over the years (figure 16.1).

It is important to note, however, that fiscal consolidation is achieved partially by cutting the capital outlay as a proportion of the GSDP from 3.83% in

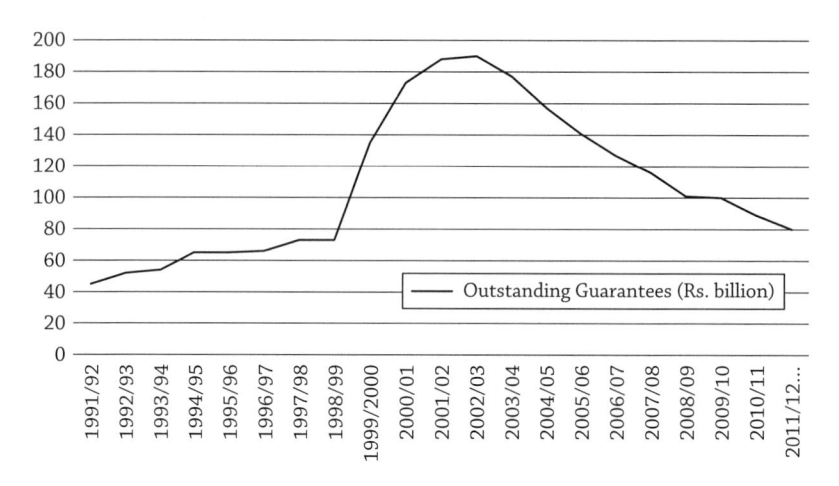

Figure 16.1: Outstanding Guarantees of Government of Gujarat, 1991/92 to 2011/12
Source: RBI (Annual–2011) and GoG (2012).

1991/92 to 2.53% in 2011/12 (table 16.1). Thus, the state's direct role in capital formation has been declining over the years. It is likely that this fall in the ratio could have been more than compensated by continuous increase in the private capital formation through the "enabling" role of the state government.[3]

Fall in the total expenditure as a proportion of the GSDP to 13% in recent years from the pre-reform figure of 16%–17% range could be viewed as an important and visible impact of fiscal reform in Gujarat. This is also relevant from the perspective of future economic growth because the experts have shown that there is an inverted U-shaped relationship between the growth and size of government as measured by the percentage of government expenditure (Grossman 1987; Scully 1989; and Peden and Bradley 1989).

In the next section we present some statistics to show how these changes in the size and structure of expenditures as well as revenues are brought about. This would not only reflect the efforts of the government but also changes in its priorities over the years.

REVENUES AND EXPENDITURES

The state's aggregate revenue comes from the central transfers, tax, and non-tax sources. The financial independence of a state can be judged by the proportion of its "own revenue" to its aggregate revenue receipts (table 16.2). By and large, in Gujarat, this proportion has exceeded 75%, which also implies

---

3. In the absence of any credible estimates of state-level capital formation by the private sector, it is difficult to provide conclusive evidence on this issue.

Table 16.2. VARIOUS RECEIPTS AS PERCENTAGE OF AGGREGATE REVENUE RECEIPTS

Year	Central Transfers (Taxes + Grants)	Sales Tax or VAT	Minor Taxes	Total Tax Revenue	Non-Tax Revenue	Total Own Revenue	Tax–GSDP Ratio
1	2	3	4	5 = 3 + 4	6	7 = 5 + 6	8
1980/81	30.09	34.52	17.29	51.81	18.10	69.91	6.70
1986/87	15.67	40.03	18.51	58.54	25.79	84.33	6.59
1990/91	17.05	51.49	19.53	71.02	11.94	82.96	7.23
1995/96	18.51	42.06	20.24	62.30	18.30	81.49	6.82
2001/02	18.66	36.64	21.17	57.81	23.53	81.34	6.94
2002/03	24.34	34.98	18.33	53.31	22.35	75.66	6.26
2006/07	24.48	41.34	18.22	59.56	15.96	75.52	6.51
2009/10	22.75	43.67	20.49	64.16	13.08	77.25	6.23
2010/11 (RE)	23.72	45.75	20.35	66.10	9.55	74.41	6.74
2011/12 (BE)	24.75	43.42	21.78	65.20	10.04	75.24	6.58

Note: RE is Revised Estimates. BE is Budget Estimates
Source: Calculated on the basis of the data from GoG (annual): "Budget In Brief."

that its dependence on the central transfers has generally remained less than 25% of its revenue resources.

Interestingly, the Compound Annual Trend Rate (CATR) of State's Own Revenue decelerated from 16% in 1978–91 to 13% during 1991–2002, but again accelerated to 15% during 2002–12, largely on account of introduction of VAT. In 2001/02 the sales tax contributed about 37% of revenue, but comparable figures for the VAT after 2006 rose to 43% to 45%. Like most other states, sales tax or VAT has remained the dominant source of revenue in Gujarat (table 16.2).

The share of minor taxes like land revenue, profession tax, electricity duty, state-excise, entertainment, and motor-vehicle tax together has remained low around 20% to 21% of the state's total revenue (table 16.2). Each one of these so-called "minor taxes" has the potential to generate much more revenue than it does if the tax structure and administration are simplified (ADB 1999). It is believed that the proposed GST (Goods and Service Tax) is likely to subsume a majority of these minor taxes so that the problems relating to their high compliance and administration costs would hopefully be mitigated (ECSFM 2008).

It is the non-tax revenue that is a matter of greater concern. Its share, growth, and buoyancy all declined during the 2000s. The factors generally discussed in the literature such as poor cost recovery rates on publicly provided goods and services implying high magnitude of implicit subsidies, low profitability, and often negative profits of public-sector enterprises and unrevised/low royalty rates for minerals, lignite, and gas, all seem responsible for low and declining growth of non-tax revenues in Gujarat (ADB 1999; Purohit and Purohit 2010).

As noted earlier, fiscal consolidation measures in Gujarat have caused an observable decline in the total expenditure as a proportion of the GSDP in the post-2003/04 period (table 16.1). CATR of aggregate spending in Gujarat during 2003–12 was also less in comparison to 1991–2002. This deceleration has been brought about largely through cutting the non-development expenditure, which consists of items like interest, subsidies, salaries, and pension payments. The CATR of non-development expenditure, declined from 28% during 1991–2002 to -minus 7% during 2002–12 implying a high deceleration of 35 percentage points. Growth of development spending, on the other hand, declined from 14% to 13% only during the same period.

Historically, in Gujarat, the development expenditure has always been around two-thirds of the total spending barring the exceptional years (figure 16.2). Since the development expenditure consists of spending on social services like health, sanitation, education, and housing and economic services like industry, minerals, agriculture and allied services, water, energy, transport, and communication, its larger share is consistent with the state's objectives (figure 16.2).

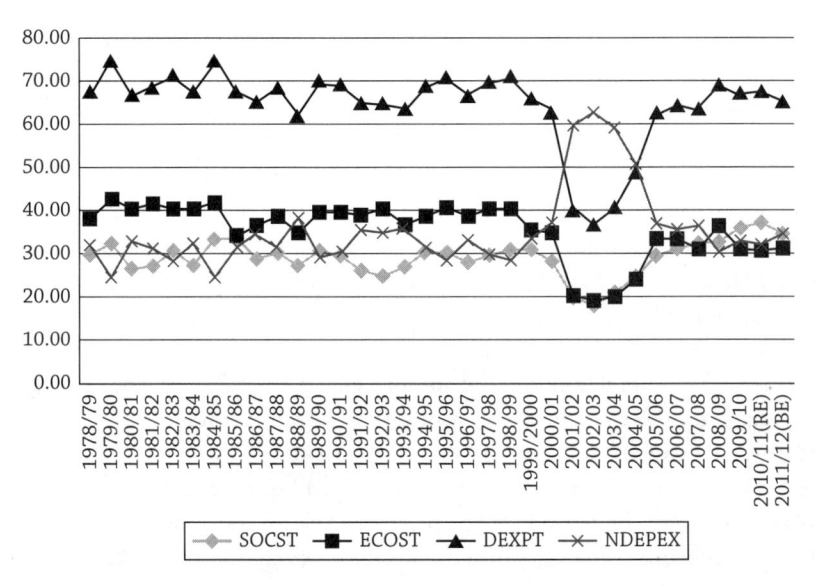

Figure 16.2: Share of Different Types of Government Expenditures in Gujarat, 1978/79 to 2011/12
Note: SOCST = Social Sectors Total; ECOST = Economic Sectors Total; DEXPT = Development Expenditure Total; and NDEPEX = Non-Development Expenditure.
Source: Various volumes of Budget in Brief, GoG (Annual) and RBI (Annual–2013).

Considering the sector-specific spending, we find that the share of social sector as a percentage of total spending dropped during and after the earthquake, but recovered quickly and has surpassed the previous peak in recent years as clearly brought out in figure 16.2. Similar behavior is observed in economic expenditures also.

While both revenue and capital components of economic sectors show marginal decline in growth over the reform years, capital spending in the social sector actually accelerated from a mere annual 8% during 1991–2002 to 20% during 2002–12. It indicates the changing priority of the state government during the last decade in favor of building human capital rather than physical capital. Moreover, a rising proportion of these expenditures are spent on the welfare and upliftment of tribal population, which constitutes 23% of the rural population and 15% of the total population of the state. Expenditures on Tribal Sub-Plans and Scheduled Castes Sub-Plans are more sincerely adhered to in Gujarat compared to other states (see Debroy 2012). Given the concern for the welfare of the weaker sections, it seems to be an appropriate strategy.

Within the social sectors, education is given priority followed by health. Their respective shares in the total expenditure of the state increased from 8% and 2% to 15% and 4% during 2001–12. Within the economic sector, priorities have shifted from agriculture and irrigation to sectors such as energy and transport during the post-reform years (GoG-Budget in Brief, different years).

CONCLUDING REMARKS

In this chapter, we have reviewed fiscal performance and fiscal reforms in the state during the last two decades. In the early 1990s, the fiscal position of the state had raised serious concerns about sustainability because various deficits and interest payments had crossed prudent limits. The state had to design and carry out fiscal reforms under tremendous pressure by the late 1990s. The state started making all preparations to follow a rigorous fiscal reforms program including divestment of selected state public-sector units, but on January 26, 2001, a major earthquake taking toll of about fourteen thousand lives and destroying buildings, roads, and bridges worth billions of rupees in the state derailed the efforts (details in Appendix 3). The entire state machinery and funds had to be diverted to meet the emergent needs of the affected population and infrastructure and hence the reform agenda had to take the back seat. Several reforms in sales tax, public-private partnership, and public-sector restructuring were nevertheless undertaken during 1990s.

During the last decade, fiscal reforms particularly on the revenue side with simplification and rationalization of taxes started moving fast. In 2005, the state passed the Fiscal Responsibility Legislation and in 2006, the VAT replaced sales tax. Power sector reforms were also carried out to improve state finances. The state has been comfortably achieving almost all FRL targets including the absolute cap on the outstanding guarantees of the state government. Philosophically, the government of Gujarat has adopted the enabling role and not the predominantly controlling role. The fiscal reforms have, therefore, led to a sharp decline in the total government expenditure to GSDP ratio from 17% to around 13%, one of the lowest in the country.

Dependence of the state on the central transfers has generally been less than 25% of its revenue resources. The share of development expenditures is around 65% and non-development expenditures around 35% barring the exceptional 3–4 years post-earthquake. A clear strategic shift in expenditure allocation in favor of the social sector is visible during the last decade vis-à-vis the previous decade. Within the social sectors the priority has clearly shifted in favor of education followed by healthcare during 2001–12. Our analysis shows that with resolve, the state government could implement most of the fiscal reform agenda.

CHAPTER 17

Elementary and Higher Education

Given the broad concept of education and its role in the society, almost all governments accept at least elementary education as a merit good. Therefore, it is imperative for them to ensure provision of the educational facilities and services in the society in adequate proportion and at affordable cost. As per the Indian constitution, primary and secondary education are predominantly state subjects. The central government has a small role, a role that it has expanded aggressively in the last decade through the Sarva Shikhsha Abhiyan, which culminated in the passage of Right to Education Act, 2009.

We have already reviewed some broad indicators relating to literacy in the introductory chapter of the study. Here we examine trends in indicators of educational spread and performance in Gujarat over recent years. Quality of education in the state is examined by considering the physical infrastructure, availability of human resources, and quality of output measured through some specific national surveys carried out in the sector. Finally, we discuss the problems and prospects of higher education in the state.

PERFORMANCE INDICATORS

We begin by reporting the gross and net enrollment ratios (GER and NER) in Gujarat in recent years. The GER is defined as the total enrollment regardless of age in the given grades as a percentage of the total number of children in the age group that normally corresponds to those grades. For example, age group 6 and above but below 14 is normally associated with grades one to eight. Therefore, the GER for these grades is the total number of children regardless of age enrolled as percentage of the population aged 6 or above but below 14. If overage children

---

We are grateful to Ms. Aparajita Singh for assistance in collecting material for this chapter.

Table 17.1. THE GROSS ENROLLMENT RATIO (GER), NET ENROLLMENT RATIO (NER), AND DROPOUT RATES IN GRADES I TO VII

Year	GER Boys	GER Girls	GER Total	NER Boys	NER Girls	NER Total
2004/05	109.7	109.4	109.5	96.1	95.2	95.7
2006/07	111.8	111.5	111.6	97.8	96.2	97.0
2009/10	104.7	102.3	103.5	98.8	98.0	98.3

Drop Out Rates in Primary Education

Year	Standards I to V Boys	Girls	Total	Standards I to VII Boys	Girls	Total
1999/2000	23.8	20.8	22.3	42.8	39.9	41.5
2003/04	17.8	17.8	17.8	36.6	31.5	33.7
2009/10	2.2	2.2	2.2	8.3	9.0	8.7

Source: GoG-SER (2011).

enroll in those grades, the GER can exceed one hundred.[1] The NER is defined as the enrollment in the given grades of children within the age group normally associated with those grades as a percentage of the total children in that age group. By definition, the NER cannot exceed one hundred while the GER may.

Table 17.1 shows NER of 98.3% in 2009/10 implying that most of the children in the school age group are actually attending the schools in Gujarat. The children not enrolled in the schools are less than 2%—1.2% among boys and 2% among girls. The sex ratio in enrollment is also steadily improving in the state. The improvement in the NER along with reduction in GER implies that the proportion of overage children in the primary schools is declining.

New enrollment in the right age group and focus on increasing the retention ratio are the elements in the government strategy. GoG has launched several specific programs and taken some initiatives to reduce the dropout rates among children.[2] There is a remarkable success in achieving a significant reduction in the dropout rate from 22% to 2% in the primary schools, and from 41% to 9% in the elementary schools during the last decade (table 17.1).

---

1. As per the existing rules, underage children are not allowed to register in the primary school.
2. Various schemes started such as a bond scheme to incentivize parents to complete education of the girl child; an insurance scheme to cover accidental death of students; computer-aided learning; joyful learning; and community participation for enrollment and provision of free uniform, school bags, slates, and books. For details, see GoG-SER (2011) and Debroy (2012: ch. 6).

Table 17.2. PERCENTAGE DISTRIBUTION OF DROPOUTS (AGES 5–29) BY CAUSES, 2007/08

Reasons for Dropping Out	Males Gujarat	Males India	Females Gujarat	Females India
1. Parents not interested	4.4	4.0	12.9	14.5
2. Has to work on a wage/salary	8.7	9.0	1.5	1.8
3. Has to participate in other economic activities	10.1	10.1	1.8	1.7
4. Financial constraints	19.8	24.2	16.5	18.1
5. Helping in household enterprises	7.1	5.0	1.3	1.0
6. Child not interested in studies	24.1	22.9	23.5	16.4
7. Unable to cope or failure in studies	14.2	11.1	10.3	9.4
8. Completed desired level of schooling	6.6	8.3	14.3	12.2
9. School is far off	1.1	1.1	5.5	4.4
10. Attend other domestic chores	1.4	1.3	11.8	10.2
11. Miscellaneous	2.4	3.0	6.5	10.5
TOTAL (All Reasons)	100	100	100	100

Source: NSSO (2008b) Report No. 532 on Education in India, 2007–08.

Major reasons for the dropout are different for Gujarat and the country as a whole (see table 17.2). The most important cause for dropout in Gujarat is a child's lack of interest in studies, but in the country, it is financial constraints of the family. Failure in studies is a more important cause in Gujarat than in the country. Moreover, in both the cases, the percentage of parents "not interested in educating the child" was 8 to 10 percentage points higher for girls than for boys. The state government is making efforts to overcome these limitations. It is increasing the geographic spread of upper primary and secondary schools in the state and trying to eliminate hurdles of stressful examinations detaining children in the same standard. Similarly special incentives are given to families to educate girls (GoG-SER 2012).

QUALITY OF EDUCATION, PHYSICAL INFRASTRUCTURE, AND HUMAN RESOURCES

The quality of education in a society depends on availability of qualified human resources and the state of physical infrastructure, besides many subjective factors. We begin by considering results of an evaluation-oriented sample survey of schools and students carried out annually in all major states of the country by a nongovernment organization (NGO), called Pratham since 2005.

Pratham surveys found the proportion of out-of-school children in Gujarat in 2005 at 3.6% and 2.7% in 2011 (table 17.3), broadly supporting the state government's claim of bringing it down to around 2%. The overall quality of primary education in the state was very poor in 2005 as about 20% children could not read even a word and more than 40% could not do even a subtraction in elementary school. However, by 2011, the situation had improved, though there was deterioration in specific grades. In school attendance of students and teachers, Gujarat's performance is substantially higher than the nation and is improving over the years. Private sector schools offer a relatively better quality of education than the government schools in both Gujarat and the country, though their absolute quality is far from satisfactory (table 17.3).

Next, consider the role of private versus public schools at various levels of education. According to the data provided in NEUPA (2005, 2010), the government dominates the primary and primary with upper primary schools, whereas the private sector dominates all other categories of schools such as upper primary, secondary, and higher secondary schools in the state. The total number of schools, teachers, and enrollment has increased respectively by 12.4%, 29.6%, and 16.9% in the state over 2003–09 as expected on account of (1) the emphasis placed by the state on education as discussed in the previous chapter and (2) rising incomes leading to a considerable

Table 17.3. PERFORMANCE IN PERCENTAGES ALONG DIFFERENT CHARACTERISTICS IN GUJARAT AND INDIA, GRADES I TO VIII

Characteristics	2005		2011	
	Gujarat	India	Gujarat	India
Proportion children: out-of-school children	3.6	6.6	2.7	3.3
Children who cannot read even a word	19.6	25.4	17.1	16.6
Children who cannot do even a subtraction	43.5	45.4	26.2	23.4
Proportion of Teachers attending	83.5	74.6	95.6	87.2
Proportion of Students attending	80.5	72.5	85.0	70.9

Source: Pratham: Annual Status of Education Report (ASER), 2005 and 2011.

Table 17.4. SELECTED PARAMETERS AFFECTING QUALITY OF SCHOOL PERFORMANCE IN GUJARAT, 2003/04 AND 2008/09

Indicators	Primary Only	Primary with Upper Primary	Primary with Upper Primary Secondary/ Higher Secondary	Upper Primary Only	Upper Primary with Secondary/ Higher Secondary
2003/04					
Single-room schools as percentage of total	14.7	2.4	2.7	2.5	2.6
Single-teacher-schools as percentage of total	10.0	2.5	2.0	5.6	4.6
Percentage of schools with pre-primary	7.9	8.3	35.7	0	0
Pupil–teacher ratio	31.0	38.0	40.0	40.0	38.0
Student–classroom ratio	34.0	41.0	40.0	37.0	30.0
Teachers per school	3.0	7.0	8.0	5.0	4.0
2008/09					
Single-room schools as percentage of total	6.4	0.8	0.4	0.6	2.4
Single-teacher-schools as percentage of total	5.5	0.6	0.5	2.8	2.4
Percentage of schools with pre-primary	22.2	24.6	57.6	11.6	22.2
Pupil–teacher ratio	28.0	33.0	35.0	35.0	32.0
Student–classroom ratio	29.0	35.0	36.0	34.0	31.0
Teachers per school	3.0	7.3	11.3	5.3	7.0

Source: State Report Card 2003–04 and 2008–09 (NUEPA 2005, 2010).

increase in the proportion of private schools as well as enrollments in all relevant categories.[3] Over 2003–09, there has been very large shift toward the private sector from 8.7% to 15.2% in number of schools, from 11.2% to 20.9% in number of teachers, and 11.1% to 22.1% in terms of enrollment.

The government policy of targeting improvements in single-classroom and single-teacher schools seems to have worked in the state (table 17.4). Emphasis on starting pre-primary schools in all types of schools has also

---

3. The state government first ensured that a primary school exists within one-kilometer radius from each settlement. It then planned to upgrade or provide separate upper primary and secondary schools within the distance of two kilometers from all settlements. This explains marginal reduction in the number of only primary schools and only upper primary schools between 2003/04 and 2008/09 in the state.

yielded results. Moreover, there is a substantial decline in the average pupil-teacher ratio (PTR) and in the average number of students in a class indicating better learning conditions. Finally, the table also shows that the average number of teachers per school has increased in the state. All these input parameters affecting the quality of education in the state have shown significant improvement over the last decade.

Decent physical infrastructure in the school is important for the mental comfort and convenience of the students and teachers. While teacher and parent involvement are perhaps the most crucial elements determining learning outcomes, the absence of proper classrooms, toilets, or drinking water facilities can be sources of distraction as well.

Essential infrastructure like drinking water availability in the school premises was far from satisfactory in almost all categories in 2003/04, but by 2008/09, the drinking water availability in the school premises increased substantially in all categories. However, there are still a large number of primary and primary plus upper primary schools without the drinking water facility in the state. Similarly, non-availability of the toilet facility in the schools in Gujarat is a major infrastructural limitation. Separate toilet for girls is not the feature of the majority of schools in Gujarat. There is some improvement during the last decade in these dimensions (NUEPA 2005, 2010), but much more improvement is required before the condition can be termed satisfactory.

National University of Educational Planning and Administration (NUEPA) reports (2005, 2010) further reveal that the number of teachers in the primary and secondary schools in Gujarat has increased at about 5.5% compounded annual rate during 2003/04 to 2008/09. This increase is, however, not through para-teachers because their proportion in the total teachers has actually fallen.[4] In any case, para-teachers account for only 1% of the total teachers in Gujarat. NUEPA (2005, 2010) also finds the quality of these para-teachers not significantly different from the regular teachers as revealed by their qualifications. The qualification profile of both the regular and para-teachers shows a marked improvement over time. New recruits were by and large more qualified and increasing proportion of teachers received in-service training in all categories of schools in the state over the last decade. This augurs well for improving the quality of elementary and secondary education in the state as measured by teacher qualifications.[5]

4. Para-teachers are teachers employed on short to medium-term contract on a lump-sum salary as opposed to regular employees appointed on a scale of pay and perks. The cost of para-teachers is one-third to one-fourth of the cost of a regular teacher. This distinction is relevant in government and aided private schools.

5. A novel scheme called "Gunotsav" to improve the quality of primary education in government schools started in 2009/10. Ministers and senior bureaucrats spend a day in the field visiting various schools to evaluate students, teachers, and amenities independently. This is besides the evaluation from teachers. This is akin to accrediting the schools.

HIGHER EDUCATION

Higher education in the state has remained the weakest link in the development and growth of the state for a long time. The policies of the state government in this regard are equally if not more responsible for the situation than the policies of the central government. It is a widely held perception that Gujaratis are more interested in entrepreneurial activity and neglect education in favor of business, stock market, and trade. If the latter perception indeed reflects reality, it raises serious questions about the quality, content, relevance, and returns of education in the state. An enterprising and entrepreneurial population by definition cannot ignore education that is useful, relevant, and productive. They may not be its enthusiastic consumers, but they would certainly be investing in education as human capital. If it is not happening, it must be because what is available is not sufficiently valuable, relevant, and useful to them.

The problem of higher education in the state is thus largely of right quality and right intensity. In this context, we find that high schools, higher secondary schools, or intermediate/pre-degree/junior colleges in Gujarat account only for 4.8% of the countrywide total against its population share of 5% and income share of 7.5%. Similarly, the share of Gujarat in degree colleges for general education is also lower at 4.7%. However, Gujarat's share of universities and academic institutions is 6.5% and in professional education institutes is about 7.9% (GoG-SER 2011).

This has happened because, of late, the state government and the central government have allowed private sector to start both universities and professional education institutes in the state. However, the feeder category, namely, higher secondary schools/colleges remains in lower proportion in the state. This peculiar existing structure of high schools, universities, and professional education institutions suggests that there is no systematic vision, consistent policies, and genuine concern for the higher educational sector and its output and quality in the state. This is not the result of the involvement of the private sector, but of the policies restricting and prohibiting their participation.

Even after five Vibrant Gujarat investors' summits, only partial privatization in selected domains of education is allowed. There still exist many administrative, academic and procedural constraints that discourage private-sector investors including a large number with foreign direct investment (FDI). If the sector is genuinely and fully opened up for the private sector with accreditation agencies providing rankings based on transparent evaluation criteria, such anomalies would be ironed out and would lead to improvement in the quality of entire education sector.

To see how the technical education was ignored prior to 1999/2000 in the state by the central government, we need to look at the number of seats

Table 17.5. NUMBER OF SANCTIONED SEATS AND ACTUAL ADMISSIONS IN TECHNICAL EDUCATION IN GUJARAT, 1980/81 TO 2010/11

Year	Sanctioned Seats Degree	Sanctioned Seats Diploma	Actual Admissions Degree	Actual Admissions Diploma
1980/81	2,339	4,549	2,508	5,041
1990/91	3,555	7,076	3,845	6,778
1997/98	6,136	10,250	6,365	10,594
2000/01	9,430	13,368	8,840	11,088
2005/06	16,228	22,523	15,289	18,493
2010/11	46,569	48,967	42,272	46,880

Source: Directorate of Technical Education, Gujarat state.

sanctioned by the central government and the actual admissions granted to the degree and diploma courses.[6]

Table 17.5 shows that the number of seats sanctioned by the central government for technical education in Gujarat was much lower than the demand as reflected in the actual admissions granted until 1999/2000 for the degree courses and until 1997/98 for diploma courses. During this period from 1980/81, the sanctioned seats (i.e., supply) increased at the annual rate of 6.5% for degree courses and 4.9% for the diploma courses in the state. During the same period, the non-agricultural sector in Gujarat grew at the annual rate of about 9%, which can be seen as an indicator of the demand for technical education in the state.

After 2000/01, the central regulatory bodies started granting expansion in the number of seats in the technical education regularly in such a manner that the annual growth rate became 17.7% in degree courses and 12.8% in diploma courses. During the same period the annual growth of the non-agricultural sector was around 11% to 12%. Therefore, the demand and supply came to be better balanced. Indeed, all seats granted were actually not filled.

During 2004/05 to 2009/10, the number of institutions of higher learning in the state grew at the annual rate of 13.5%, but the number of teachers grew at 12%. This led to the number of teachers per institution declining

---

6. Two streams exist in higher education: technical and general. The former is under direct control and supervision of the central government's regulatory bodies for recognizing institutions and courses, and sanctioning seats for both the private and government institutions. It includes courses on management, computer science, pharmacy, and all branches of engineering. The general education is under the university system governed by the state and the University Grants Commission of the government of India. Until recently, the private sector participated in the field of technical education only.

from 15.3 in 2004/05 to 14.3 in 2009/10 (GoG-SER 2011). This implies that the newer institutions of higher learning in the state are starved of faculty and have to either go without teachers or depend on ad hoc visiting teachers. Moreover, it also indicates the problems with the quality of teachers.

The quality of teachers in the institutions of higher learning in Gujarat becomes a problem because the institutional needs of good quality teachers cannot be met by migration of qualified teachers from outside due to a significant language barrier created in the state through its policy of Gujarati medium even in higher education (Bhatt 2002). The quality of education and research has deteriorated because only local teachers with Gujarati medium could be hired, restricting the competition and compromising the quality. Vested interests through textbooks in Gujarati also made things worse and gave rise to a downward spiraling vicious circle to drag the university academic standards below all acceptable limits. This is also reflected in lower success rates in national level examinations and jobs (Bhatt 2002).

The report of the Comptroller & Auditor General of India (CAG 2010) on Gujarat made specific observations on the quality of higher education in the state. In particular, it points to acute shortage of teachers, lack of accreditation in more than 60% of institutions, absence of teachers' training institutes in spite of earmarking the funds, adverse student–teacher ratio in non-technical courses and absence of e-journals and e-books in a large number of technical institutions.

The problems of shortage of teachers and quality of higher education in the state are likely to reduce in the next 5 to 10 years because the state government has also liberalized the feeder institutions like higher secondary, secondary, and elementary schools to allow better quality English-medium schools in the private sector. Response from the private sector has been encouraging. This will ensure quality students and subsequently quality teachers in the higher education sector in the state over time.

CONCLUDING REMARKS

In this chapter, we have reviewed the trends in educational spread, qualitative aspects of primary education and problems and prospects of higher education in the state. During the last decade, the state has made substantial progress by raising the net enrollment ratios to more than 98% and by bringing down the dropout rate from 22% in 1999/2000 to 2% in 2009/10 in the primary schools. Moreover, both these indicators are very similar for boys and girls.

Evaluation studies conducted by NGO Pratham reveal that the overall quality of primary education has improved albeit gradually in Gujarat over the last decade. Attendance of teachers and students has improved considerably over time. Private sector schools deliver a better quality of primary education than the government schools and partially encouraged by the government's liberal policies have proportionately grown rapidly over the last decade.

All input parameters considered relevant to the quality of education such as teachers per school, proportion of single classroom schools, pupil–teacher ratio, and average number of students in a class have shown improvement over the last decade in Gujarat. The experiment of employing para-teachers at lower cost from local areas without compromising the qualifications in the government schools seems to be successful.

The physical infrastructural facilities in the primary and upper primary schools in the state are far from satisfactory even though some progress has been made during the last decade. There are still a large number of schools in the state without drinking water and toilets—particularly girls' toilet—facilities.

Higher education has remained one of the weakest links in the development of the state economy. The problem is of both quality and quantity of education. Of late both the state and the central governments have allowed the private sector to start universities and professional education institutes, but their feeder institutions were not sufficiently liberalized. Only partial privatization in selected domains of education was allowed till recently. There still exist many administrative, academic, and procedural constraints to discourage private and foreign direct investments in the sector. The central government policies and central regulatory bodies have also contributed to such a state of affairs.

State policy of Gujarati medium even in the higher education over the years has resulted in poor quality of teachers and library resources in the institutions of higher education in the state. Things are likely to change over the next 5 to 10 years because recently the state government has liberalized private sector entry to the feeder institutions like higher secondary, secondary, and primary schools with English medium.

While the state has performed well on the primary education front, its performance on the higher education front has been far from satisfactory. It is because of the lack of vision, consistent policies, and commitment to quality on the part of the state government.

CHAPTER 18

Primary Healthcare and Medical Education

At a personal level, health is an integral part of wealth, and according to a Gujarati saying, it is a primary indicator of happiness. At the community and state level, health is not only an important source of wealth creation in the society but also an essential ingredient in human development and social welfare. As an input, health has intrinsic economic value, and as an output, it is a source of empowerment of individuals.

In the present chapter, we discuss the performance of the Gujarat state in the health sector over time, and recent policy changes by the government to improve the health outcomes in the state. It is important to recognize at the outset that the government can affect the health outcome not only by the interventions in the health sector alone, but also by considering several interrelated sectors like food and nutrition particularly for children and mothers, family welfare, water, sanitation, education, roads, pollution control, and pharmaceuticals. However, here we confine our discussion largely to the health sector.

The present chapter briefly reviews the performance of the state in the domain of health over the years by considering various indicators of health outcomes, health output, and health-related infrastructure and manpower inputs. It also discusses the problem of meeting the acute shortage of manpower through expansion of medical and paramedical education in the state.

We are grateful to Mr. Hem Dholakia and Mr. Shreekant Iyengar for help in collecting and compiling material for this chapter.

(295)

HEALTH INDICATORS

There are three categories of health indicators: outcomes, outputs, and inputs. A brief explanation of each may be given at the outset:

- Outcomes would include life expectancy, birth rate, death rate, maternal mortality, child mortality, infant mortality, neonatal mortality, malnutrition, and morbidity (incidence of ill-health or specific disease). They measure the concerns of the society in terms of what is ultimately expected out of the health system or provision of healthcare in the society.
- Outputs of the health system include hospitalization, out-patients treated, immunization, ante-natal care (ANC), post-natal care (PNC), institutional delivery, and delivery attended by qualified birth attendant (QBA). These outputs of the health system show the extent and intensity of the healthcare reach in the society.
- Inputs in the health system measure availability of the healthcare facilities like Community Health Centers (CHC), Primary Health Centers (PHC), Sub-Centers (SC), hospitals, dispensaries, blood banks, general doctors, specialist doctors, staff nurses, paramedics, and households with electricity connections, safe drinking water, and toilet facility. These are essential inputs in the healthcare system to deliver extensive and intensive healthcare services to the society.

An efficient and productive organization of the health system should have a strong causal link from the health input indicators to the health output indicators; and from the health output indicators to the health outcome indicators. However, these relationships are not simple and bivariate, but depend on several socio-cultural and economic factors like income, education, caste composition, and quality of governance. Although such factors are important to explain variations in the health outcomes and health outputs across states, availability of health infrastructure, manpower, and other inputs are equally, if not more, relevant determinants.

A comparison between the performance of Gujarat and the nation on broad health outcomes like Infant Mortality Rate (IMR) and Crude Death Rate (CDR) was considered in the overview chapter earlier. Here we present a more comprehensive picture by considering most of the available indicators for health outcomes, health outputs, and health inputs for the selected years over the period 1990–2009.[1]

We consider 12 different outcome indicators relating to infant, child, and maternal mortality, birth outcomes, and child nutrition (table 18.1). There is a

---

1. In order to capture the trend in these indicators, we have reported the data from the same source to avoid non-comparability issues.

Table 18.1. HEALTH-OUTCOME-RELATED INDICATORS FOR GUJARAT AND INDIA, 1990–2009

Indicators	Gujarat 1990–93	India 1990–93	Gujarat 1998–2001	India 1998–2001	Gujarat 2010–12	India 2010–12
Vital Health Statistics[(i)]						
Male life expectancy at birth	60.2	59.7	62.4	61.6	64.9	64.6
Female life expectancy at birth	62.0	60.9	64.4	63.3	69.0	67.7
Neonatal mortality (NN)	40.4	47.2	42.0	44.0	33.5#	39.0#
Infant mortality rate (IMR)	78.0	77.0	60.0	66.0	38.0	42.0
Maternal mortality ratio (MMR)	300.0	400.0	202.0	327.0	122.0	
Birth rate	28.4	29.6	25.0	25.4	21.1	21.6
Death rate	8.5	9.8	7.5	8.5	6.6	7.0
Total fertility rate	3.1	3.6	2.9	3.2	2.3	2.5
Undernourishment Related (percent of children below 3 years of age classified as)[*(ii)]	1990–93	1990–93	1998–2001	1998–2001	2006–09	2006–09
Stunted (too short for age)	48.2	52.0	43.6	45.5	42.0	38.0
Wasted (too thin for height)	18.9	17.5	16.2	15.5	17.0	19.0
Underweight (too thin for age)	50.1	53.4	45.1	47.0	47.4	46.0
Percent children under 2.5 kg at birth	—	—	—	—	22	21.5

* For the period 1990–93, age group 0–4 years is considered.
# Figures pertain to 2006–09.
Sources: (i) SRS: Sample Registration System, Ministry of Health and Family Welfare; (ii) NFHS: National Family Health Survey—1, 2, and 3.

consistent trend in the direction of improvement in all these outcome indicators except those relating to child nutrition over the last two decades. During the 1990s, the state's performance was better than the national average in all outcome indicators except "children too thin for height." However, by 2006–09, the state slipped below the national average in "children too short for age" and "too thin for age." It is surprising that the same source of data shows better performance of the state than the nation in 2006–09 for "children too thin for height." It is difficult to reconcile these findings with credible explanation.[2]

Health output indicators for maternal care show consistent improvement, but the ones for childcare and vaccinations show fluctuations (see table 18.2). In particular, the percentage of children vaccinated for DPT, Polio, and "all vaccinations" increased during the 1990s, but declined in 2006–09. Gujarat's performance has been better than the national average in all years except in the case of Polio vaccination during 2006–09. One of the reasons for the numbers on vaccination deteriorating in the last decade could be a relative fall in the government expenditure on health in the post-earthquake years. However, Debroy (2012) argues that by 2011–12, there were spectacular improvements achieved by Gujarat on immunization and institutional deliveries.

Turning to input indicators, we find deterioration in several of them during 1990/91 to 2008/09 (see table 18.3). In some indicators, like the availability of specialists, general doctors, staff nurses, and ANMs in PHCs and CHCs, there is a sharp decline in the availability. This could be one of the reasons for slowing down the rate of improvement of the outcome and output indicators in Gujarat for that period. Shortage of qualified manpower in the public sector would bring down the credibility, reliability, and quality of services; and hence, performance would seriously suffer especially in rural areas.

It is interesting to note from table 18.3 that availability of total allopathic doctors has increased with a corresponding decline in the AYUSH (Ayurveda, Yoga, Unani, Siddha, and Homeopathic) doctors, dispensaries, and hospitals in the state over the last two decades. The shortage of doctors and specialists is more severe in the public sector health facilities than in the private sector. Surprisingly, however, the availability of total nurses has gone down sharply during the last decade in the state against almost a fivefold increase in the

2. An alternative source of data on proportion of malnourished children collected by the Ministry for Women and Child Welfare under its nation-wide program on Integrated Child Development Services (ICDS) reveals that between March 2007 and March 2011 it declined from 70.7% to 38.8% in Gujarat, from 45.5% to 23.3% in Maharashtra, from 38.8% to 36.9% in Kerala, 39.1% to 35.2% in Tamil Nadu, and from 50.1% to 41.2% in the country as a whole (CAG 2013). Percentage point decline in Gujarat was largest among all states. While this does reflect very positively on the emphasis and efforts put out by the state government in the post-2007 period, it also points to problems in reconciling two alternate data sources—NFHS and ICDS.

Table 18.2. HEALTH-OUTPUT-RELATED INDICATORS FOR GUJARAT AND INDIA, 1990–2009

Indicators	1990–93 Gujarat	1990–93 India	1998–2001 Gujarat	1998–2001 India	2006–09 Gujarat	2006–09 India
Immunization Related (percent of children 13–23 months receiving)						
BCG	77.1	62.2	84.7	71.6	86.4	78.1
DPT	63.8	51.7	64.1	55.1	61.4	55.3
Polio	62.9	53.4	68.6	62.8	65.3	78.2
Measles	55.9	42.2	63.6	50.7	65.7	58.8
No vaccinations	18.9	30.0	6.6	14.4	4.5	5.1
Percent with vaccination card	32.0	30.6	31.8	33.7	36.4	37.5
All vaccinations	49.8	35.4	53.0	42.0	45.2	43.5
Maternal Care						
% Pregnant women received ANC	75.4	44.0	86.4	65.4	87.4	77.0
% Of pregnancies with PNC	—	—	—	—	61.4	41.2
% Deliveries in health facilities	35.6	26.0	46.3	33.6	52.7	38.7
% Deliveries assisted by health personnel	42.7	34.2	53.5	42.3	63.0	46.6

Sources: NFHS: National Family Health Survey—1, 2, and 3.

Table 18.3. HEALTH-INPUTS-RELATED INDICATORS FOR GUJARAT AND INDIA, 1990–2009

Indicators	Gujarat	India	Gujarat	India	Gujarat	India
	1990–93		1998–2001		2006–09	
Infrastructure Related (per 100,000 rural population)[(ii)]						
Sub-centers (SC)	26.84	20.90	22.95	18.51	20.98	16.86
Primary health center (PHC)	3.36	3.25	3.16	3.08	3.13	2.68
Community health centers (CHC)	0.59	0.35	0.76	0.41	0.81	0.51
Government hospitals	—	—	0.62	0.40	0.60	1.00
Beds in government hospitals	—	—	43.93	38.76	48.00	44.60
Private hospitals	—	—	4.38	1.37	4.39[#]	3.29[#]
Beds in private hospitals	—	—	81.40	28.50	88.90[#]	32.80[#]
AYUSH hospitals	0.13	0.36	0.12	0.34	0.10	0.28
Beds in AYUSH hospitals	6.00	7.16	5.18	5.93	1.53	2.00
AYUSH dispensaries	1.41	2.72	2.07	2.30	1.22	1.84
Manpower Related (per 100,000 population)[*(ii)]						
Accredited social health activist (ASHA) (per 1,000 rural population)	—	—	—	—	0.86	0.98
Multi-purpose worker (MPW)	16.00	9.63	11.44	9.60	12.90	7.20
Auxiliary nurse midwife	—	—	22.22	18.1	18.50	22.20
Health assistant (HA)	3.48	2.73	2.10	2.70	2.19	1.97
Lady health visitor (LHV)	3.58	2.87	2.70	2.70	2.52	2.23
Staff nurse at PHC and CHC	—	—	—	—	4.01	2.40
General doctors at PHC	3.25	4.41	2.99	3.47	2.94	2.94
Specialist doctors at CHC	—	—	3.43	4.02	0.22	0.71
Total doctors (allopathic)	52.20	44.74	66.51	56.05	76.91	67.50
Total AYUSH doctors	—	—	78.93	92.45	57.69	62.20
Total nurses	—	—	220.80	18.10	145.00	86.20
Household Amenities Related (percentage of households)[(i)]						
With electricity	76.60	50.90	84.30	60.10	93.40	75.00
With improved source of drinking water	75.10	68.20	84.50	77.90	94.80	92.50
With toilet facility	35.80	30.30	44.90	35.90	56.40	50.80

* Population for Census 1991, 2001, and Estimated Population for 2011 is considered. Rural populations for respective years have been considered for ASHA, SC, PHC, CHC, ANM, HA, LHV, MPW, general doctors, staff nurses, and specialist doctors. Total population is considered for total government and private hospitals, beds, Ayurved-Yoga-Unani-Siddha-Homeopath (AYUSH) doctors, AYUSH hospitals and dispensaries, and total nurses.
# Estimated on the basis of the proportion of private hospitals to government hospitals during 1998–2001.
Sources: (i) NFHS: National Family Health Survey—1, 2, and 3; and (ii) MoHFW: Ministry of Health and Family Welfare.

nation.[3] Given the high growth in demand for healthcare services in the state (also from the foreign sector due to health tourism), the demand for medical and paramedical personnel totally outstrips their supply in the state. Manpower availability is a serious constraint in the healthcare sector in Gujarat.

On all other general inputs (such as drinking water, electricity, and toilet facilities) and availability of amenities and income, the state has been consistently performing better than the national average over the last two decades.

HEALTHCARE INFRASTRUCTURE

Healthcare infrastructure consists of all medical and paramedical personnel; institutions like dispensary, hospitals, and healthcare facilities; and arrangements like mobile vans; besides laboratories, blood banks, and medical stores.

The central government of India launched the National Rural Health Mission (NRHM) in the year 2005 and the National Urban Health Mission (NUHM) in 2010 to target definite improvements in respectively rural and urban health facility infrastructure and thereby in health outcomes. All states including Gujarat are involved in implementing NRHM and NUHM by suitably modifying its design and elements as per their specific requirements.

Health-Related Infrastructure in Rural Areas

It is clear from table 18.4 that substantial expansion of the rural healthcare infrastructure took place in Gujarat during the seventh plan period (1985–90) at all levels. The growth slowed down considerably during the eighth plan period (1992–97) and practically stopped during 2002–09. This indicates a conscious shift in the state policy in the sector. This could be one of the reasons why Infant Mortality Rate (IMR) in rural Gujarat fell below the national rural average during the 1980s but came back to the national average by 2009 (see table 13.12 in chapter 13). If the Gujarat government faces criticism of ignoring the health sector after the economic reforms initiated from 1991, table 18.4 provides some clear evidence.

Table 18.5 shows that Sub-Centers (SCs) at village panchayat level are in surplus but Primary Health Centers (PHCs) and Community Health Centers (CHCs) are in 7.5% and 4% short supply in Gujarat as per the norms given by the Indian Public Health System (IPHS). Thus, the shift away from the

---

3. While migration of nurses and doctors from other states can considerably mitigate the problem, these migrants generally get better salaries and perks in the private sector and in the urban areas and do not prefer to go to rural areas because of language and dialect problems, cultural differences, and poor quality infrastructure.

Table 18.4. PUBLIC HEALTHCARE INFRASTRUCTURE IN RURAL GUJARAT, EXISTING AT THE END OF DIFFERENT FIVE YEAR PLANS

Health Facilities	Sixth Plan (1981–85)	Seventh Plan (1985–90)	Eighth Plan (1992–97)	Ninth Plan (1997–2002)	Tenth Plan (2002–07)	Eleventh Plan (2007–09)
SC*	4,869	6,834	7,472	7,472	7,472	7,472
PHC*	310	842	960	1,032	1,073	1,084
CHC*	22	143	185	252	273	281

* SC stands for sub-center, PHC for primary health center, and CHC for community health center.
Source: Rural Health Statistics by Ministry of Health & Family Welfare (2009), Government of India.

Table 18.5. HEALTH FACILITIES IN GUJARAT—REQUIRED NUMBER AND SHORTFALL AS OF MARCH 31, 2009

Health Facilities	Required*	Existing	Shortfall
SC	7,263	7,274	(Surplus)
PHC	1,172	1,084	88
CHC	293	281	12

* Based on Indian Public Health System (IPHS) norms.
Source: Rural Health Statistics by Ministry of Health & Family Welfare (2009), Government of India.

needed expansion of the healthcare facilities in the block and taluka level by the government during the last decade is not justified.

It may be argued, however, that mere presence of physical infrastructure does not necessarily indicate adequate functioning of the healthcare system. Efficiency and efficacy of the system also depend on other factors such as accessibility, availability, and affordability of services. These things in turn depend on having required human resources along with other factors. Figures from Ministry of Health and Family Welfare (2009) show that there is a large shortfall of both medical and paramedical manpower at all the three levels of facilities compared to the IPHS norms. Thus, the existing healthcare facilities are not only quantitatively inadequate as per the IPHS norms but also qualitatively weak and ineffective because of lack of human resources in all categories in rural Gujarat.

Regarding the manpower shortage, fewer positions are sanctioned than the required number in most of the categories in the state, implying that even if all posts are filled, there would still be a shortfall in those categories. However, a more important cause for the shortfall is that all the sanctioned posts are not filled. This could be due to either the state government's explicit policy of not filling the vacant posts to meet fiscal targets, or the genuine shortage of the skilled manpower to take up the jobs in rural Gujarat.

To some extent, both these reasons operated, though for the skilled category of doctors, specialists, nurses, technicians, and pharmacists, the government's policy of employment freeze is less responsible than the genuine shortage of such skilled manpower. Lack of soft infrastructural facilities, such as English-medium schools, colleges, a network for cooking gas cylinders, efficient transport to commute from city to villages, branded eateries, and entertainment facilities in rural areas, becomes barrier to mobility of skilled manpower to rural areas. However, significant shortfall of pediatricians, gynecologists, and obstetricians at the CHC level would have very detrimental effects on the maternal and child health outcomes in rural Gujarat.

Health-Related Infrastructure in Urban Areas

Gujarat had initiated an urban healthcare project (see GoG 2003) aiming to provide primary healthcare to the urban slum population under the public–private partnership (PPP) in 143 municipal areas out of 242 towns in the state. In order to address the problems of access and affordability of healthcare services for the urban poor and slum-dwellers, the central government of India proposed the National Urban Health Mission (NUHM 2010). Since the private healthcare providers are available in a large number in urban areas of Gujarat, the NUHM's three-tier structure is expected to address the specific problem of the urban poor and slum-dwellers regarding their access to affordable healthcare.

The health hazards due to pollution are serious concerns for urban areas. The state government has taken several steps to control pollution. A separate department of Climate Change was created in 2009 to transform the economy into a low carbon region. Almost all three wheelers were converted to CNG and so also the municipal buses supplying major municipal corporations. It helped to improve the air quality of Ahmedabad, Surat, and Vadodara. Clean Development Mechanism (CDM) projects are encouraged resulting in 40% of the national share for its market in Gujarat. Processes of Gujarat Pollution Control Board have been fully computerized. Despite high degree of industrialization, area under forest has increased by 60% over the last decade (GoG-SER 2014).

HEALTHCARE POLICIES OF THE STATE GOVERNMENT

In this section, we consider a few innovative policies of the state government that aim to improve the health outcome indicators included in the Human Development Index (HDI) and the Millennium Development Goals (MDGs). They principally relate to the maternal and child health and mortality. (For other schemes in this sector, see GoG-SER 2011; and Debroy 2012: ch. 7).

Maternal Health

There are three direct schemes introduced by the state government to improve the health outcomes for mothers and newborn babies, around the year 2005 when the NRHM was launched in the country.

Chiranjivi Scheme

In order to promote institutional deliveries among the poor in rural areas, the Chiranjivi Scheme introduced by the government of Gujarat identified private obstetricians from different localities offering a fixed sum to carry out 100 deliveries and multiples thereof. The sum included charges of medicines and hospital stay also till the mother and the baby are discharged. Thus, for the beneficiary mothers the delivery (normal or complicated) becomes free of direct costs if it is done in the designated private maternity homes. The scheme was meant for the mothers living below poverty line (BPL). A sum of 179,500 rupees per 100 deliveries was fixed by considering the average cost of normal and complicated deliveries with associated probabilities of such deliveries based on the experience of some renowned NGOs in the field.

Institutional deliveries under the scheme increased 15 times by the third year of the scheme; and 20 times by the fifth year (table 18.6). By now, the scheme covers almost one-third of the total deliveries annually and more than 40% of the available gynecologists are empanelled in the scheme in Gujarat. Although the scheme could satisfactorily target the poor households (Bhat et al. 2007), there are a few concerns in this unique PPP model in the health sector introduced by the state government that require some minor modifications (see Singh 2009).

Singh (2009) also points out some disturbing unintended consequences of the scheme. For instance, the sex ratio in such deliveries is found to be significantly less than the non-Chiranjivi scheme deliveries. In view of the declining sex-ratio in the state, this finding about the scheme is a cause for concern.

Table 18.6. PERFORMANCE OF THE CHIRANJIVI SCHEME

Year	Normal Deliveries	Lower Segment Cesarean Section (LSCS)	Other Complications	Total Deliveries	LSCS Percentage	Doctors Enrolled
2005/06	6,809	417	567	7,793	5.4	163
2006/07	40,828	2,913	3,965	47,706	6.1	742
2007/08	106,080	7,651	7,312	121,043	6.3	865
2008/09	77,213	5,133	3,728	86,072	6.0	824
2009/10	140,132	9,425	6,164	155,721	6.1	721

Source: Health Statistics of Gujarat—Annual Reports, Government of Gujarat.

Janani Suraksha Yojana (JSY)

Under this standard safe motherhood NRHM scheme, the only innovative element introduced in Gujarat is to link it to the Chiranjivi scheme by making the cash incentives available to both the mother and the Accredited Social Health Activist (ASHA) for the delivery at the private health facility of an empanelled doctor. Beneficiaries under this scheme increased from 12.6 thousand in 2005/6 to 342 thousand in 2011/12.

"108" Emergency Response Services

This scheme launched in 2007 provides integrated medical, fire, and police emergency services round the clock free of cost available on call all over the state and is highly successful PPP (Debroy 2012). It has a team of 2,600 committed personnel and 525 high-tech ambulances with the state of art headquarter at Ahmedabad. It responds to about 70,000 emergencies per month including deliveries, accidents, heart attacks, crime victims, and serious patients. By 2013, it had attended more than 4 million emergencies including about 41,057 deliveries and saved about 290,000 lives (gujhealth.gov.in/108-services.htm, accessed on March 2, 2014).

Child Health

There are universally acceptable, low-cost remedies readily available for preventing child deaths caused by under-nutrition, diarrhea, and pneumonia. Among preventive interventions, breastfeeding, complementary feeding, clean delivery, water and sanitation, and zinc supplements together can prevent 31% of deaths. Similarly, among treatment interventions, oral rehydration therapy and antibiotics can prevent another 27% of deaths (Jones et al. 2003). By making these interventions effective for all mothers and children, it would be possible to prevent about 60% of all child deaths. The state government has adopted various central schemes to address the child morbidity and mortality along these well-researched lines during the last five to seven years. These include: (1) integrated management of neo-natal and childhood illness; (2) addressing malnutrition; and (3) improving immunization (for details, see GoG-SER 2011).

Public Finances in Healthcare

Total public health spending in Gujarat, revealed by annual budget documents, has increased at a compound annual growth rate of 15.7% during the last decade. From 2007/08 to 2010/11, capital expenditure on health has gone up by 87% compounded annually. The capital expenditure on health relative to the capital expenditure on all social sectors increased from 1.6% in 2002/03 to 21.5% in 2010/11. As a result, the state has built 74 new PHCs and 37 CHCs almost wiping out the deficit developed on this count.

Relative public spending on health and other social sectors is fairly stable as a proportion of GSDP over the last decade (figure 18.1). At the national level, policy makers have explicitly recognized now for over a decade that total health spending in the economy should be well above 6% of GDP, and that public spending should be at least 40%–50% of it or about 3% of GDP (see GoI 2002; NRHM 2005; and S. Rao et al. 2005). Individual states including Gujarat do not have such specific targets, though states do allocate higher spending on healthcare depending on their priorities.

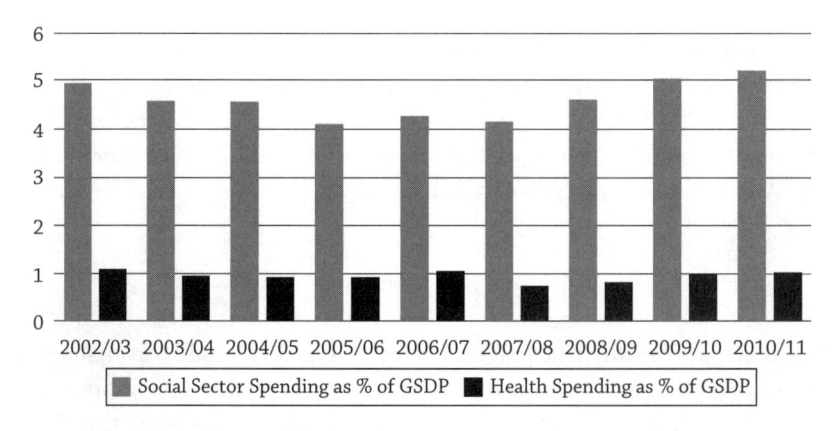

Figure 18.1: Public Spending on Health and Social Sectors as Percentage of State Income (GSDP)
Source: GoG-Budget in Brief, for different years.

According to the estimates of National Health Accounts (MoHFW 2004), the proportion of public spending in total health spending in Gujarat is 21% against 10% in Kerala, 19% in Punjab, 17% in Maharashtra, and 18% in Tamil Nadu. Of late Gujarat has become more conscious about public spending on healthcare as discussed above. In order to meet such additional public expenditures on healthcare, the state can use several mechanisms. It can increase user fees, apply levy on excise, or depend on buoyancy of its revenues due to high growth. Gujarat has tapped all these sources, besides insisting on corporate social responsibility spending at least from the profit-making state public sector undertakings and facilitating the private sector to provide affordable healthcare and by aiming at PPP in the sector through schemes like Chiranjivi.

MEDICAL AND PARAMEDICAL EDUCATION

At the outset, we must note that medical education is not fully under the purview of the state government. Various medical councils at the central government level are controlling the medical education in the country. Table 18.7 shows that the number of medical and paramedical colleges existing in Gujarat in 1999/2000 was meager compared to the population, income level, and the need of the state. Their admission capacity was also very low, and the students allowed admissions were very close to the capacity.

During the last decade, things started changing rapidly. While the number of Allopathic medical colleges and Ayurvedic colleges increased marginally, all other colleges—Dental, Pharmacy, Homeopathic, and Physiotherapy colleges increased many fold. Admission capacities of all these institutions also increased significantly—twice in Allopathic, six times in Pharmacy, seven times in Dental, two-thirds in Ayurvedic, thrice in Homeopathic, and 20 times in Physiotherapy (table 18.7). This was due to the state government policy of allowing participation of the private sector in this field.

Table 18.7 also shows the progress on actual number of students allowed admission in those institutions. In Allopathic medical colleges the number of students allowed admission actually fell over the decade, leaving more than 50% capacity already created in the state unutilized. Very similar was the case with both Dental and Physiotherapy colleges. Actually during the same years, there were about 3,000 students from the state seeking admissions to medical institutions elsewhere in and outside the country paying substantial capitation fees as per a Gujarati Daily (see *Divya Bhaskar*, May 19, 2011).

This happened because the medical councils of the central government effectively prevented those admissions to the Gujarat institutions disqualifying them and not allowing seat expansion. There are several court cases pending on this count, because such decisions of the medical council were

Table 18.7. NUMBER OF MEDICAL AND PARAMEDICAL EDUCATIONAL INSTITUTIONS AND THEIR STUDENT STRENGTH IN GUJARAT, 1999–2010

Colleges	1999/2000	2000/01	2001/02	2002/03	2003/04	2004/05	2005/06	2006/07	2007/08	2008/09	2009/10
Number of Colleges											
Allopathic	8	8	10	10	13	13	13	13	13	13	14
Pharmacy	12	12	13	13	37	25	37	50	64	NA	NA
Dental	2	2	2	4	5	5	5	9	9	9	11
Ayurvedic	9	9	9	9	9	9	9	9	11	11	11
Homeopathic	8	8	11	12	13	14	13	13	16	16	16
Physiotherapy	2	2	2	2	10	10	10	17	16	16	22
Admission Capacity											
Allopathic	1,025	1,275	1,275	1,375	1,375	1,525	1,525	1,755	1,755	1,755	1,905
Pharmacy	683	743	685	765	825	1,485	2,205	2,925	3,825	NA	NA
Dental	140	140	280	280	280	320	320	620	670	780	980
Ayurvedic	303	305	369	375	375	375	375	375	475	495	490
Homeopathic	525	609	1,050	1,300	1,300	1,375	1,275	1,375	1,375	1,525	1,525
Physiotherapy	70	70	80	220	220	320	320	775	765	900	1,305
Number of Students Allowed Admission											
Allopathic	1,019	1,075	1,073	1,073	1,270	1,087	1,087	1,069	955	953	955
Pharmacy	553	708	693	760	817	1,394	1,852	2,495	3,781*	NA	NA
Dental	139	140	140	138	236	223	223	205	144	133	200
Ayurvedic	303	359	369	374	375	374	375	375	475	495	490
Homeopathic	375	609	952	1,279	1,012	779	948	367**	NA	NA	1,525
Physiotherapy	69	70	70	78	170	190	190	133	198	198	230

* Provisional.
** Only Government Institutions.
Source: Health Statistics Gujarat 2003/04 to 2009/10 (GoG 2004, 2010).

seen as acts of politically motivated discrimination. The case becomes stronger because for Pharmacy, Ayurvedic, and Homeopathic colleges where the admissions are within the control of the state councils, the students allowed admission are as per the capacity created in the state (table 18.7).

In this context, it is interesting to observe some recent developments. In June 2011, the Medical Council of India (MCI) gave approval only to two medical colleges and rejected applications of eight other medical colleges in the state. As a result, the state government acted within a week to give powers to the state medical council for starting and recognizing special courses of two-year diploma and three-year fellowship in the government and private sector medical colleges to mitigate the shortage of qualified medical personnel in the state (*Divya Bhaskar*, June 14, 2011). These doctors would be recognized to practice in the state and such other states that recognize those qualifications. This model was already in operation in Maharashtra. It will end the undue monopoly of the Central Medical Council of India and expand medical education in the state that may alleviate the shortage of medical personnel.

In terms of the education and training of a paramedical nature like nursing, multipurpose health workers, X-ray technicians, and laboratory technicians and assistants, the number of their training institutes, colleges, and schools has increased significantly in the state during the last decade. From only one nursing college in the state until 2004/05, now there are 20, and Nursing Schools have increased from 17 in 2004/05 to 47 in 2009/10 (GoG-SER 2011). Thus, the state government has made substantial efforts in the last decade to create necessary health infrastructure for addressing the pressing problem of the shortage of manpower in the health sector.

CONCLUDING REMARKS

In this chapter, we have discussed the performance of the state in health outcomes, health output, and health-related inputs of infrastructure and manpower along with recent policy changes. We have also highlighted the problem of meeting the acute shortage of manpower through expansion of medical and paramedical education in the state.

Most of the health outcome indicators except child nutrition show consistent improvement in Gujarat. Recent data from the central government show that the state has significantly improved its performance even in child nutrition during 2007–11. Health outputs except those related to childcare show improvement over time as well. But input indicators, particularly availability of medical and paramedical manpower, show a sharp decline over time. Shortage of qualified manpower is a serious constraint adversely affecting the performance of healthcare in Gujarat.

Although health-related general amenities have been improving, physical infrastructure of health centers grew very slowly during the eighth Plan (1992–97) and practically stagnated during 2002–09 in the state. Poorer performance of Gujarat in the health indicators than in the country up to mid-2000s can be attributed to such conscious policy shifts as the neglect of public health infrastructure by the state.

The state government has adopted and implemented several central government schemes addressing maternal and child health, nutrition, and mortality. Particular mention may be made of the Chiranjivi scheme and "108" emergency services, both of which are based on the PPP model achieving remarkable success in Gujarat.

Medical education is not fully under the purview of the state government, but various medical councils under the central government are effectively controlling it. It is perceived that this has created the problem of acute shortage of qualified manpower in the state. The state government has recently made substantial efforts to create medical educational infrastructure and introduced new courses to produce doctors recognized within the state for addressing the shortage of qualified manpower in the health sector.

The state's relative performance is showing improvements. Of late, the state government has become more conscious about creating healthcare infrastructure. From 2007/08 to 2010/11, capital expenditure on healthcare has increased by 87% compounded annually allowing the state to wipe out deficit in physical infrastructure in the sector developed over many years. The state simultaneously encourages the public and private sector corporations to use their corporate social responsibility funds for the social sectors, particularly health. It has taken several initiatives on the environmental front, too. All these recent efforts have started showing improvements in the health performance of the state.

CHAPTER 19

Governance, Efficiency, and Effectiveness

Role of government in promoting economic growth and development and thereby achieving social welfare has always been considered a very important but highly debatable issue in the literature. Classical economists had explicitly addressed this issue and held vastly differing opinions on it. Following the success of the East Asian tigers and the oil shocks of the 1970s and early 1980s that forced many developing countries to rethink the interventionism of the government in their development process, the question about the role of the government in promoting growth and development returned to center stage.

Many authors argued that big government was not conducive to high economic growth in the long run (Scully 1989; Peden and Bradley 1989). Promoting private sector participation in the activities previously reserved for the government sector gained traction. On the one hand, economic development and social welfare came to be increasingly linked to the economic freedom and liberty (Beach and Kane 2008; Messick 1996); while, on the other, the questions of how to make governments more effective to improve the delivery of public goods and services to enhance social welfare gained currency (World Bank 2004). As of now, all this has converged to the way the government conducts itself and provides critical services to its population.[1]

---

1. During the last few years, an empirical exercise along this line was carried out and a report is annually published on "Economic Freedom of the States of India" (see Debroy et al. 2013). The authors argue that better performance and faster improvement in economic freedom are associated with higher economic growth and cite Andhra Pradesh, Tamil Nadu, and Gujarat as examples supporting this view.

To be operationally meaningful, the concept of governance requires more explicit definition, however. In our view, good governance consists of democratic, transparent, non-discriminating, and non-intruding provision and delivery of the relevant government services in the required quantity and quality. It presupposes answerability and accountability of the government. If there are formal structures, processes, and norms established to ensure these things, the government may be considered more efficient, performing, and effective. Some authors also explicitly consider all these aspects to measure corruption that serves as a component of index of economic freedom (see Debroy et al. 2013).

In the present chapter, we briefly review the nature and type of governance in Gujarat during the last decade when the growth of the state's economy has been historically the highest on record. We begin with a discussion of the role of modern technology to improve governance and delivery of government services. Then we briefly review judiciary reforms to reduce the burden of pending cases and expedite efficient delivery of justice. We then consider some specific measures taken by the state government to enhance transparency and efficiency. Steps to increase answerability and interdepartmental coordination too are briefly covered. We also raise a few issues of conflicts and contradictions in governance at the central and state levels. Finally, we try to correlate the role of political leadership at the state with Gujarat's success. The chapter ends with concluding remarks.

APPLICATION OF TECHNOLOGY FOR BETTER GOVERNANCE

Gujarat is one of the leading states in terms of the use of e-governance. Land records, licensing, approvals, registration of properties, title clearance, pension, provident funds, and other treasury functions were computerized as early as 1998/99 (SPFRC 2000). Subsequently, almost all departments have been computerized. The state has already implemented an Integrated Work-Flow and Document Management System and Integrated Financial Management System to make the working more automated at all levels of administration in the government.

According to a report by the World Bank (2010: 33), "Gujarat has been a pioneer in strengthening governmental policies, institutions and procedures for better governance. . . . Gujarat also ranks first in the country to have made E-Governance functional in all its municipalities and municipal corporations." Taking advantage of the connectivity among all district, taluka, and even village panchayats via the Internet and Intranet infrastructure (chapter 14 above), the government introduced in 2004/05 an innovative grievance redress program giving direct access to each citizen to the Chief Minister (GoG-SER 2011).

The program is known as SWAGAT (State Wide Attention on Grievance with Application of Technology), in which the Chief Minister and his office directly handle complaints of individual citizens with video conferencing at the taluka headquarters. This has now been expanded to cover even the village panchayats. On average, about 4,000 grievances are heard annually and most of them are resolved through online instructions to the relevant officials. Satisfactory disposal rate of such grievances is estimated at about 92%–96% (*Economic Times*, Feb. 12, 2011; World Bank 2010). The e-governance has increased efficiency, transparency, accountability, and effectiveness in the provision of government services in the state.

Another area of application of technology is in water management and public health. Remote sensing and Geographic Information System (GIS) is applied for watershed management in the state. Even the Narmada (SSP) project canal network is being operated with state of art digital technology (Joshi and Acharya 2011). Similarly, GIS is also used for providing emergency medical services and managing disasters, natural calamities, and public health hazards. Like "911" emergency service in the United States, Gujarat has instituted "108" emergency service. It has become very popular in the state because of its prompt response, affordability, and geographical reach.

The state government has generally preferred private-sector participation in providing public (or merit) goods not only in the economic sectors but also in the social sectors whenever feasible. It almost automatically ensures use of state of the art technology because all these PPP projects are based on transparent bidding or selection processes to increase competition and minimize the cost to the government without sacrificing quality. Such applications of technology have resulted in cost-savings, rule-based non-discriminating and non-intruding provision of services by the government.[2]

JUDICIARY REFORM

A serious backlog of judicial cases in the courts all over the country is threatening to make the judicial system inefficient and ineffective because "justice delayed is justice denied." There is no dearth of suggestions from commissions and committees to reduce the backlog by increasing the disposal rate of the cases in the court but acceptance and implementation leaves much to be desired. The judicial reforms within the purview of the state are largely confined to the operational level in improving the effectiveness and efficiency in case disposals.

In this context, Gujarat has already implemented several measures to increase the case disposals. Establishment of fast-track courts has had a

---

2. For an illustration of this in road projects in Gujarat, see World Bank (2010, 2011).

remarkable impact though it is currently functioning only at the session court level (Gujarat National Law University (GNLU) 2010). It is recommended by GNLU (2010) that it should become a permanent feature of the state judiciary and extended at the magisterial level, since more than a million cases are pending at that level. Similarly evening courts are also introduced but are not very efficient everywhere, particularly in rural areas (GNLU 2010).

Lok Adalats or courts of the people for the poor and the needy were first started in Gujarat in 1982 and subsequently spread throughout the country to relieve the regular courts from the heavy burden of cases with the jurisdiction to deal with all matters except non-compoundable offenses (GNLU 2010). Mobile courts are also operational in Gujarat to reach out to the remote rural areas with low frequency connectivity mainly for the *Lok Adalats*. GNLU (2010) recommended extending such arrangements even for regular courts.

MEASURES TO IMPROVE TRANSPARENCY AND EFFICIENCY

In our policy discussion in the previous chapters, we have reviewed several reform measures introduced during the last decade to increase transparency and efficiency of the government programs, policies, and actions. For instance, an Anti-Theft law for electricity was enacted and rigorously implemented to reduce transmission and distribution losses. In order to reduce transaction costs, self-assessment in several matters relating to labor laws, factories act, pollution control measures, and value added tax with severe punishment for false declaration helped reduce bureaucracy, and inspector visits to business premises. Single-window and priority clearances were given to new projects including mega projects with pre-announced criteria for investment magnitude and location.[3]

Other areas of reforms relate to procedures and mechanisms to operationalize the PPP model, e-procurement provisions to reduce corruption and complaints, and simplification of administrative processes in various departments. Stringent adherence to fiscal targets and hard budget constraints,

---

3. There have been some political debates and questions raised about the transparency of special incentive packages offered by the state government to attract some selected mega investment projects. These figures are available now either as answers to specific Legislative Assembly Questions or through press releases. Honest differences of opinion can exist on the measurement of the extent and magnitude of such incentives and on whether they are justified on the basis of the social cost-benefit analysis of the action, since these mega projects have substantial impacts not only on the local area but the whole state and national economies through multiplier effects including secondary and tertiary effects on tax revenues.

including significant reduction in state guarantees for businesses, has been the hallmark of functioning of the government. A host of information regarding the above is regularly uploaded on the government portal. Gujarat topped 10 major states surveyed on transparency on budget-related matters based on 8 different criteria carried out by the Centre for Budget and Governance Accountability (CBGA) (*Business Standard*, Feb. 24, 2011).

SPECIFIC MEASURES FOR ANSWERABILITY AND EFFECTIVENESS

In order to improve the governance, the state government has decentralized powers and devolved funds at lower levels of government to encourage them to take appropriate democratic decisions with full responsibility and accountability. Abolition of Octroi from the state was one such bold move encouraging the local bodies to efficiently use their fiscal powers and explore alternative avenues for raising required resources. The state government has also transferred certain tax powers like profession tax[4] to them to help. Reforms in property tax, PPP in waste management, municipal bonds with clear commitments, and similar reforms are the consequences of such policies. Autonomy makes the local bodies more efficient and answerable.

Similarly, in order to encourage regional integration and reduce any feelings of neglect on the part of distant district places from the state capital, the state government has been consciously following the policy of giving prominence to different district headquarters for numerous programs including official state level celebrations like the Independence Day and the Republic Day by rotation.

Another unique initiative was to hold regularly interdepartmental and inter-ministerial seminars and workshops, where departmental heads (secretaries) present detailed SWOT (Strength-Weaknesses-Opportunities-Threats) analysis of their departments before the senior policymaking group consisting of the whole cabinet and the senior most bureaucrats pointing out the complicated issues, bottlenecks, and interdepartmental disputes. It has often resulted in sensitization and appreciation of the problems if not immediate solutions.

Moreover, the political leadership of the state decided to reduce political interference from the management of the state Public Sector Undertakings (PSUs). The Managing Directors and Chairmen of various state PSUs were traditionally political appointees by the party in power. This was changed

---

4. It is an annual tax on selected professions like doctors, lawyers, photographers, professors, traders, and so on. It is imposed by a state or a local government with an absolute cap on the amount per assessee.

in 2003/4 and competent civil servants with adequate experience and background were appointed for long tenure but with clear performance targets and reasonable autonomy. This increased accountability and the performance of most of the state PSUs substantially improved within one to two years.[5]

ADVERSE EFFECTS OF UNCERTAINTIES AND REVERSALS OF DECISIONS BY THE CENTRAL GOVERNMENT

There are several areas in which central regulations and procedures hamper progress at the level of the state. These roadblocks impact asymmetrically states such as Gujarat that have been trying to move forward at a rapid pace. Such contradictions may arise when the political party in power at the center and the state are different. While we have pointed to some of them in our detailed discussions in various areas above, here we briefly recount and summarize some of them:

1. General policy paralysis, indecision, and policy reversal at the center adversely impact the prospect and the plans of the state to attract investment, mega projects, and partnerships.
2. Sudden export bans and duties imposed by the central government on cotton, onions, pulses, sugar, and wheat and their equally sudden withdrawal create an environment of uncertainty.
3. Revocation of approvals granted for Special Economic Zones by the center in a non-transparent manner likewise hampers decision-making at the level of the state.
4. Uncertainty created by the central government through retrospective review of policies and contracts involving land transfers provides a disincentive to industries desirous of investing in states.
5. Non-transparency and inconsistency in granting and withdrawing approvals to medical and technical institutions of the state by the central bodies have been very damaging to progress in the area of higher education with consequent detrimental effects on the availability of medical and engineering personnel.
6. Imposition and revision of Minimum Alternate Tax by the central government after the grant of a tax holiday for infrastructure projects and Special Economic Zones has had an asymmetrically large adverse impact on a state like Gujarat, which had taken the lead in these areas.

---

5. In 2004, the state government appointed a High Level Expert Committee for Restructuring of Public Sector Undertakings with 12 loss-making undertakings referred to it. Within less than one year most of them turned around and started making profits. One of the probable reasons for this was the change in the top management.

7. Sudden imposition of gas price regulation and introduction of Gas Utilization Policy that denies gas to user industries connected by gas-grid in which the state had taken a lead long back has had harmful effects on Gujarat.

POLITICAL LEADERSHIP AND GUJARAT'S SUCCESS

The quality of governance, efficiency, and effectiveness of the state government is reflected in the confidence put by the private sector businesses and investments committed in the state (see table 14.3 on Vibrant Gujarat Investors' Summits). If the share of Gujarat in the nation for any economic activity is substantially higher than its share in aggregate income (8%), the state has a revealed comparative advantage[6] over other states in that activity. Since the number of such activities is very large and in diverse fields in Gujarat,[7] it indicates that the revealed advantage is largely on account of the competitive advantage of the state in terms of its overall economic environment and governance rather than any specific resource base.[8]

The role of the top leadership is always crucial in creating impact. Gujarat has been fortunate in having dynamic and forward-looking political leadership for the better part of its existence. Mr. Chimanbhai Patel during the early 1990s and Mr. Keshubhai Patel during the late 1990s as the Chief Ministers of the state had made important contributions to the Narmada Project and in carrying out early reforms. The Chief Minister, Mr. Narendra Modi, who held the office from 2001 to 2014, had a very different style from his predecessors. Without worrying about the immediate political fall-outs, he took faster, bolder, and more innovative decisions keeping a longer term perspective of 15 to 20 years in mind.

His leadership was established with his strategy to simultaneously attack all sectors like water, power, transport, agriculture, industry, and construction. He streamlined the administration and reduced effective political interference in such sectors. This started bringing results due to which he was re-elected twice in 2007 and 2012. During his tenure, the state achieved several milestones such as 100% electrification, fastest rehabilitation and

---

6. For details on the concept, see Balassa (1965).

7. To illustrate, Gujarat's share in the nation is substantial in exports originating (24%), sale of surplus electric power (38%), cargo handled by non-major ports (70%), ship breaking yard (100%), ship building capacity (60%), LNG terminals (67%), gas consumption (33%), diamond processing (80%), ceramic (80%), coal imports (60%), stock market capitalization (30%), and in production of petrochemicals (65%), agrochemicals (40%), total industrial output (17%), cotton (31%), groundnut (37%), lignite (31%) and marine fish (23%). (Source: GoG-SER 2010, 2011, 2012; GoG-iNDEXTb 2011; GoI 2012).

8. For the concept of competitive advantage of nation (state), see Porter (1990).

reconstruction of an earthquake-affected region, full computerization of administration, innovative e-governance, and the attraction of investments on a large scale, for which it received several awards and acclaim (for details, see Debroy 2012; Kamath and Randeri 2009). His strategy and implementation of reforms have direct bearing on bringing Gujarat to the top of the list of 20 Indian states ranked on the Index of Economic Freedom (IEF).[9] In 2005, the state ranked at number five with a score of 0.46. It achieved number one position by 2009 and for the last three consecutive years, it has maintained at the top position with a score of around 0.65.[10] The difference between the scores of Gujarat and states at the second rank in these years has been of the order of 15% to 20% (Debroy et al. 2013).

A US Congressional Research Service (CRS) report stated, "Perhaps India's best example of effective governance and impressive development is found in Gujarat, where controversial Chief Minister Narendra Modi has streamlined economic processes, removing red tape and curtailing corruption in ways that have made the state a key driver of national economic growth" (CRS 2011: 47).

CONCLUDING REMARKS

Gujarat has received much attention from national and international development agencies and hence in the media for its superior governance and achievements in recent years. In this chapter, we have shown that the use of modern technology and management principles in delivery of public services and several reforms including judicial reforms have improved transparency, accountability, and interdepartmental coordination up to the highest level of administration. Various illustrations suggest how the state's efficiency is hampered by the center's unilateral policies, particularly when a different political party rules the latter.

From rankings based on the performance of the state in several fields, one can conclude that, on the whole, the state government has performed well in terms of quality of governance, efficiency, and effectiveness to win the confidence of the domestic and global private sector. The revealed comparative advantage enjoyed by the state in several diverse economic activities would indicate that such an advantage is more on account of the economic environment created by good governance rather than any specific resource base.

9. IEF is constructed out of 20 different indicators relating to size of government, legal system and property rights, and regulation of labor and business.
10. Out of the three major components of IEF, in "regulation of labor and business" the state has been consistently at the top; in "size of the government" it generally remained at the second position; and in "legal structure and property rights" its rank fluctuated between 4 and 12 during 2005–13.

The role of the political leadership in this context cannot be overemphasized. Progress and achievements of the state on different fronts especially after 2003 establishes the role of effective leadership provided by the Chief Minister Narendra Modi. After his elevation to the position of Prime Minister of the country in May 2014 a senior Minister in his cabinet for the last 13 years, Ms. Anandiben Patel has taken over as the Chief Minister of the state. She is likely to continue with the process of development and reforms on similar lines. The process will be smoother since now the same political party rules both the state and the center reducing the probability for conflicts.

CHAPTER 20

Lessons from the Gujarat Experience

From our discussion so far, we can draw several lessons that may be useful for other states in the country or for regional economies within other countries with a federal structure. At the outset, we may note that there are several distinguishing features of Gujarat state both in terms of geophysical and human factors, including entrepreneurship, that may not be directly comparable with other regional economies. We have, therefore, attempted to draw lessons such that the possible impacts of those factors are minimized.

The growth story of Gujarat during the 1990s demonstrated how a state government by cooperating with the central policy reforms like liberalization, privatization, and globalization can achieve better overall performance. Unlike many states, Gujarat did not contradict the central reforms by its own policies, but wholeheartedly adopted and implemented most of them with efficiency (Ahluwalia 2000). Continuing with the reform agenda, however, the subsequent decade in Gujarat saw a comprehensive change in the role of the state putting it on a higher growth trajectory.

The widely discussed growth story of Gujarat during the 2000s on account of further acceleration and its higher lead over national growth compared to the 1990s is based on several replicable initiatives, interventions, and policy actions by the state government. We can divide all such lessons into three broad categories: development strategy, governance, and fiscal discipline, which form the crux of what has come to be known as Modi's Gujarat Model.

DEVELOPMENT STRATEGY

Development strategy of the state was based on providing freedom and encouragement to individuals and businesses so that they can flourish in legitimate economic activities of their choice in all sectors. On its own, this would ensure that activities with comparative cost advantage expand in the economy. Gujarat's experience during the 2000s suggests that the state would derive more mileage by focusing on removing the bottlenecks in the way of productive activities rather than distributing wasteful subsidies. A major learning from the model is that reforming simultaneously all of the crucial sectors, like roads, power, and water, yields higher economic and social returns.

Gujarat's experience also shows that farmers are willing to pay for a regular and adequate supply of electricity and water, which in turn can stabilize agriculture and thereby the state income. Providing connectivity, storage, and linkages with industries can incentivize the farm sector to achieve higher yields and diversify cropping patterns in favor of high-value crops. Higher growth in agriculture thus achieved would also lead to a sharp decline in rural poverty and regional disparity.

For the industrial sector, reaping agglomeration economies through the cluster approach and encouraging larger scale of operation is likely to go a long way toward bringing cost advantage to industries in the state. Increasing the connectivity to markets and improving infrastructure proved to be a better strategy to attract investments than providing subsidies on inputs.

Fostering private-sector participation in all possible spheres is a distinguishing feature of the development strategy of the state during the last decade. Its involvement in the provision of public and merit goods such as water, power, education, and health has several advantages including reduction in fiscal burden, use of modern technology, timely completion of projects, and better quality of services.

GOVERNANCE

"Small government and more governance" is the philosophy behind the Gujarat model. Effective use of e-governance through computerization of administration, processes, and records in all departments at all levels makes the system more transparent, democratic, and cost-effective, apart from reducing corruption and delays. Labor and land market reforms, single window approvals, and rapid clearances helped to reduce transaction costs to the industries and business. Moreover, a commitment to long-term direction of policies attracted investments in industries, infrastructure, and several other businesses by reducing policy risks.

Gujarat's experience clearly brings out a strong case for reducing political interference in administration and state-owned public sector units to improve the efficiency and viability of the activities. It was achieved by creating specific laws and norms for such things. A notable feature of governance in Gujarat has been the bureaucracy's willing participation encouraged by granting a reasonable degree of autonomy accompanied by accountability.

FISCAL DISCIPLINE

Reduction in the size of the government by cutting wasteful and unproductive public expenditure has made it possible to meet all targets under fiscal responsibility legislation (FRL) without imposing an additional tax burden. This has created space for expanding the productive activities in the private sector. The FRL targets ensure fiscal prudence and prevent the state from slipping into a debt-trap. This along with an absolute cap on state guarantees enhanced the credibility of the state among investors and facilitated market borrowing at competitive rates.

An important feature of the state's fiscal policy is improvement in the quality and efficiency of public expenditure through various processes and measures. The PPP model has also helped in releasing fiscal resources for social sectors to create the essential infrastructure that directly impacts the outcomes.

Finally, we may note that success of all these policies and initiatives would critically depend on two factors: political stability with a clear mandate over the longer span and top political leadership. The translation of the policies into effective outcomes requires the backing of strong political will, sustained action, and dynamic bureaucracy.

APPENDIX 2
Sardar Sarovar Project (SSP) on the River Narmada

Narmada is 1,312-km-long westward flowing perennial river with 27 million acre feet annual flow of water. In Gujarat, it flows only for the last 161 km before meeting the Arabian Sea. SSP is the terminal project among the series of projects in the river valley. Since the project involved four states—Madhya Pradesh (MP), Gujarat, Maharashtra, and Rajasthan, it was referred in 1969 to the Narmada Water Disputes Tribunal, which gave its award in 1978. The tribunal award allocated 16% of the power benefits to Gujarat and the rest to MP (52%) and Maharashtra (32%); and one-third of the water-flow benefits to Gujarat with two-thirds allocated to MP, Maharashtra, and Rajasthan.

Initial cost estimation of the project was at 50 billion rupees at 1981 prices, which was equivalent to the cost of all major and medium irrigation projects of the central and state governments taken together during the Seventh Five Year Plan (1985–90) in the country. It is a multi-purpose mega project with direct tangible benefits in terms of irrigation, hydro-power, and municipal and industrial water availability besides the indirect benefits like employment and income generation, public health, environment, entertainment, and poverty reduction.

There have been more than five formal economic appraisals carried out by different organizations over the past 30 years and each one of them without exception found the project economically highly viable in spite of missing out some important benefits of the project. Their estimates of economic (real) rate of return under all plausible sensitivity analyses range from 11% to 19%. It can be argued that once SSP is completed, it may lead to acceleration of economic growth in the state and the country. However, the project has run into unprecedented delays on account of litigation concerning rehabilitation and environmental issues.

Although the project was formally commissioned in 2004, it is likely to be completed only in 2014–15. The project's command area is 1.8 million hectares, but by now hardly 0.4 to 0.5 million hectares get irrigation benefits. Thus, more than 70% to 80% of irrigation benefits of the project are yet to be realized. As and when they are realized, it will certainly lead to higher agricultural growth in the state and the nation. However, at most, a small proportion of the recent agricultural and overall growth acceleration in Gujarat during the last decade can be attributed to SSP.

In three edited volumes, Parthasarathy and Dholakia (2011) provide further details on SSP and its current and future impact on the state economy.

APPENDIX 3

The Earthquake and Its Impact on the Kutchh District

Kutchh is the largest district of India with 45,652 sq km of area. Most of the sub-district-level units of Kutchh were highly backward till 2001, when a devastating earthquake struck Gujarat with its epicenter in the district. Almost 85% to 90% of total deaths and destruction in the state occurred in the single district of Kutchh. It caused deaths of 12,221 people, injuries to 167,000 persons, loss of livelihood for 19,000 artisans, destruction of assets worth 99 billion rupees, output worth 106 billion rupees, and large proportion of public infrastructure in the district (GoG-Cowlagi Committee 2005). A huge amount of revenue and capital funds had to be rushed for rehabilitation and reconstruction, which also shows up in the fiscal aggregates for the state during 2000–2004 (table 16.1 and figure 16.2).

Reconstruction and repair for the houses was based on the PPP model with the owners involved in decision-making and customization of designs and construction of residences and shops to cater to modern needs and avoid limitations of earlier designs. The entrepreneurs were encouraged to take the benefits of excise concessions given by the center, and sales tax and stamp duty relief given by the state government. It spurred economic development in the regional economy.

Disaster management and development of the region thereafter has attracted international attention and bagged three awards from the United Nations in 2003, Commonwealth Association in 2004, and the World Bank in 2004. A survey of more than 10,000 beneficiaries of the state government schemes by KPMG revealed that the quality of life of the people was higher by 20% after the earthquake than before (GoG-Cowlagi Committee 2005).

A recent review of Kutchh (*Economic Times*, 2011) mentions that the district has better quantity as well as quality of valuable property assets, houses, roads, shops, shopping malls, industries, multiplexes, food chains, banks, and entertainment centers. The district is emerging as a hub for power generation. Since the earthquake, about 296 major industrial projects have been completed in the region. Investment commitments of 2.04 trillion rupees have already been made since 2001.

PART III REFERENCES

ADB (1999). "Gujarat's Reforms of Public Finances (TA No. 2668-IND)—Final Report on Gujarat Finances: Reforms of Budgetary Management, Minor Taxes and Non-Tax Revenue." Authored by Atul Sarma and Archana Dholakia. Manila: The Asian Development Bank & ORG.

———. (2007). "Performance Evaluation Report: India—Gujarat Public Sector Resource Management Program (TA. No. PPE: IND 29458)." Authored by Bruce Murray. Manila: Asian Development Bank.

Ahluwalia, Montek Singh (2000). "Economic Performance of States in the Post-Reform Period." *Economic and Political Weekly* 35(19) (May 6): 1637–1648.

———. (2011). "Prospects and Policy Challenges in the Twelfth Plan." *Economic and Political Weekly* 46(21) (May 21): 88–105.

Aiyar, Swaminathan S. A. (2008). "Benefits of Port Liberalisation." *Economic Times*, Dec. 11.

———. (2009). "Agriculture: Secret of Modi's Success." *Economic Times*, July 22.

Alagh, Y. K., R. D. Desai, G. S. Guha, and S. P. Kashyap (1995). *Economic Dimensions of the Sardar Sarovar Project*. Ahmedabad: HarAnand Publications, SPICER.

Anand, M., Amaresh Bagchi, and Tapas Sen (2002). *Fiscal Discipline at the State Level: Perverse Incentives and Paths to Reform*. New Delhi: NIPFP.

Bagchi, Amaresh, and Pinaki Chakrabarti (2004). "Towards a Rational System of Centre–State Revenue Transfers in India: An Exploration." NIPFP Working Paper. http://www.nipfp.org.

Bagchi, S., and A. Kundu (2003). "Development of Municipal Bond Market in India—Issues Concerning Financing of Urban Infrastructure." *Economic and Political Weekly* 38(8) (Feb. 22): 789–798.

Balakrishna, V. N. (2010). "With Vision & Determination, Growth Follows." In Commissioner of Information (ed.), *Agriculture Miracle of Gujarat*, 51–54. Gandhinagar: Government of Gujarat.

Balakrishnan, Pulapre (2011). *Economic Reforms & Growth in India—Essays from Economic and Political Weekly*. New Delhi: Orient Blackswan.

Balassa, Bela (1965). "Trade Liberalization and Revealed Comparative Advantage." *Manchester School* 33: 99–123.

Bandyopadhyay, K. R. (2010). *Poverty in India—A Chronological Review of Measurement and Identification*. http://mpra.ub-uni-muenchen.de.

Beach, W. W., and Tim Kane (2008). "Methodology: Measuring the 10 Economic Freedoms." In *2008 Index of Economic Freedom*, 39–54. Washington, DC: Heritage Foundation.

Bhagwati, Jagdish, and Arvind Panagariya (2013). *Why Growth Matters*. New York: Public Affairs.

Bhat, R., D. Mavalankar, P. V. Singh, and N. Singh (2007). "Maternal Health Financing in Gujarat: Preliminary Results from a Household Survey of Beneficiaries under the Chiranjivi Scheme." IIMA Working Paper Series, Ahmedabad, Oct.
CAG (Comptroller and Auditor General of India) (2010). "Report of the CAG India on Gujarat." Government of India. http://www.myengg.com.
———. (2013). "Report on Integrated Child Development Scheme (ICDS)." Report number 22 of 2012–13, tabled in the Parliament on Mar. 24, New Delhi.
CDP (City Development Plan) (2006). City Development Plans for Ahmedabad, Surat, Vadodara, and Rajkot, respective Municipal Corporations, submitted under Jawaharlal Nehru National Urban Renewal Mission. http://jnnurm.nic.in/.
Census of India (2011). *Provisional Population Totals—Urban Agglomerations and Cities*. Registrar General of India, Government of India.
Chandramouli, C. (2013). "Housing Stock, Amenities and Assets in Slums—Census 2011." PPT prepared for the Office of the Registrar General and Census Commissioner of India. http://tinyurl.com/o2rrsnt.
Commissioner of Information (ed.) (2010). *Agriculture Miracle of Gujarat*. Gandhinagar: Government of Gujarat.
CRS (Congressional Research Services) (2011). "India: Domestic Issues, Strategic Dynamics and U.S. Relations." Authored by K. Alan Kronstadt, Paul K. Kerr, Michael F. Martin, and Bruce Vaughn. Congressional Research Service, USA, Sept.
CSO (Central Statistical Organization) (Annual). "Annual Survey of Industries—Factory Sector, 1990–1 to 2009–10." Kolkata: Ministry of Statistics and Program Implementation, Government of India.
Datta, Samar K. (2010). "Examining Gujarat's 'Success Story' in Fruits and Vegetables." In Ravindra H. Dholakia and Samar K. Datta (eds.), *High Growth Trajectory and Structural Changes in Gujarat Agriculture*, 69–94. Delhi: Macmillan.
Debroy, Bibek (2012). *Gujarat—Governance for Growth and Development*. New Delhi: Academic Foundation.
Debroy, Bibek, L. Bhandari, and S. Aiyer (2013). *Economic Freedom of the States of India, 2013*.New Delhi: Academic Foundation in association with Friedrich Naumann Foundation, Cato Institute and Indicus Analytics.
Deloitte and CII (2009). "Background Paper on Port Connectivity in Gujarat." Deloitte Touche Tohmatsu India Private Limited. http://www.deloitte.com/assets.dcomindia.
Desai, S. (2002). "Policy Regarding Establishment of Special Economic Zones in Gujarat." July 19. http://www.gujaratindustry.gov.in/gr-sez.html.
Dholakia, Ravindra H., and Samar K. Datta (eds.) (2010). *High Growth Trajectory and Structural Changes in Gujarat Agriculture*. Delhi: Macmillan.
ECSFM (Empowered Committee of States' Finance Ministers) (2008). "A Model and Road Map for Goods & Service Tax in India." Apr. 30. New Delhi: Government of India.
Finance Commission (1994). "Report of the 10th Finance Commission." New Delhi: Government of India.
———. (2000). "Report of the 11th Finance Commission." New Delhi: Government of India.
———. (2004). "Report of the 12th Finance Commission." New Delhi: Government of India.
Gandhi, Vasant P., and N. V. Namboodiri (2010). "The Economics and Contribution of Cotton Biotechnology in the Agricultural Growth of Gujarat." In Ravindra

H. Dholakia and Samar K. Datta (eds.), *High Growth Trajectory and Structural Changes in Gujarat Agriculture*, 29–50. Delhi: Macmillan.

Ghatak, M., and S. Roy (2014). "Did Gujarat Growth Rate Accelerate under Modi?" *Economic and Political Weekly* 49(15) (Apr. 12): 12–15.

GNLU (Gujarat National Law University) (2010). "Report of the Swarnim Gujarat Committee on Legal Reforms." Gandhinagar: Gujarat National Law University.

GoG (Annual). "Speech of Finance Minister on Budget Estimates, Part A and Part-B." Gandhinagar.

———. (Annual). "Budget in Brief—Gujarat State: An Analytical Summary." Budget Publication No. 33. Gandhinagar: Directorate of Economics and Statistics.

———. (1990, 1995, 2000, 2003, and 2009). "Industrial Policy of Gujarat State." Gandhinagar: Government of Gujarat.

———. (1994). "Report of the Gujarat State Finance Commission." Gandhinagar: Government of Gujarat.

———. (2004). "Health Statistics Gujarat 2003–04." Gandhinagar: Commissionerate of Health, Government of Gujarat.

———. (2009). "An Analytical Summary of Budget Statistics—Gujarat State, 1960–61 to 2007–08." Gandhinagar: Directorate of Economics and Statistics.

———. (2012). "Statements under the Gujarat Fiscal Responsibility Act, 2005." Budget Publication No. 30. Gandhinagar: Government of Gujarat.

———. Cowlagi Committee (2005). *Report of the Committee to Study Backwardness of Talukas of Gujarat*. Vols. 1–5. June. Gandhinagar: Government of Gujarat.

———. Industries Commissionerate (2010). "Industries in Gujarat—Statistical Information." Mimeo. Gandhinagar: Government of Gujarat.

GoG-SER (Annual). "Socio-Economic Review (Year)—Gujarat State." Budget Publication No. 34. Gandhinagar: Directorate of Economics and Statistics, Government of Gujarat.

GoI (1961, 1971, 1981, 1991, 2001, 2011). Census of India.

———. (2002). "National Health Policy—2002." New Delhi: MoHFW, Government of India.

———. (2011a). "Press Note on Poverty Estimates, 2009–10." Planning Commission of India.

———. (2011b). "Economic Survey 2010–11." Feb. New Delhi.

———. (2012). "Economic Survey 2011–12." Mar. New Delhi.

———. (2013a). "Economic Survey 2012–13. Feb. New Delhi.

———. (2013b). "Press Note on Poverty Estimates, 2011–12." Planning Commission of India.

Godbole, Madhav (2001). "Finance Commissions in a Cul-de-sac." *Economic and Political Weekly*, 36(01), Jan. 6, 29–34.

Goswami, S. (2011). "Revisiting Sardar Sarovar Canal Based Drinking Water Project in Gujarat." In R. Parthasarathy and Ravindra H. Dholakia (eds.), *Sardar Sarovar Project on the River Narmada*, vol. 3: *Impacts So Far and Ways Forward*, 693–726. New Delhi: Concept Publishing Company.

Grossman, P. J. (1987). "The Optimal Size of Government." *Public Choice* 59(2): 131–147.

Gulati A., T. Shah, and G. Shreedhar (2009). *Agriculture Performance in Gujarat since 2000: Can Gujarat Be a "Divadandi" (Lighthouse) for Other States?* New Delhi: IWMI and IFPRI.

Hirway, I., and D. Mahadevia (2005). "Gujarat Human Development Report 2004." Ahmedabad: Mahatma Gandhi Labour Institute.

Hirway, I., and N. Shah (2011). "Labor and Employment under Globalization: The Case of Gujarat." *Economic and Political Weekly* 46(22) (May 28): 57–65.

IMF (2006). "Asia Rising: Patterns of Economic Development and Growth." World Economic Outlook, Washington DC: International Monetary Fund, chapter 3.

ISAAA (2009). "Biotech Crops in India: The Dawn of a New Era." ISAAA Brief No. 39. New Delhi: International Service for the Acquisition of Agri-biotech Applications (ISAAA) South Asia Office.

Jones, G., R. Steketee, R. Black, Z. Bhutta, and S. Morris (2003). "How Many Child Deaths Can We Prevent This Year?" *The Lancet*, 65–71.

Joshi, M. B., and K. D. Acharya (2011). "Challenges Involved in Operation of SSP Canal Conveyance System and Use of State-of-Art Technology." In R. Parthasarathy and Ravindra H. Dholakia (eds.), *Sardar Sarovar Project on the River Narmada*, vol. 3: *Impacts So Far and Ways Forward*, 869–891. New Delhi: Concept Publishing Company.

Kamath, M. V., and K. Randeri (2009). *Narendra Modi—The Architect of a Modern State*. -New Delhi: Rupa & Company.

KPMG and CII (Confederation of Indian Industries) (2007). "Accelerating Growth in Gujarat—A Discussion Note." KPMG Publication, India.

Kumar, Ravi T., and Murlidhar Vemuri (2002). "Centre–State Transfer of Resources—The Population Factor." *Economic and Political Weekly*, 37(33), Aug. 17, 3406–3409.

Mathur, O. P. (2006). *Financing Municipal Services: Reaching Out to Capital Markets*. New Delhi: NIFPFP.

——. (2009). *Urban Property Tax Potential in India*. New Delhi: NIPFP.

Messick, R. E. (1996). *World Survey of Economic Freedom, 1995–96*. New Brunswick, NJ: Transaction Publishers.

MOHFW (Ministry of Health and Family Welfare) (2004). "National Health Accounts." Government of India.

——. (2009). "Rural Health Statistics." New Delhi: Ministry of Health and Family Welfare, Government of India.

MUD (Ministry of Urban Development) (2011). "Report on Indian Urban Infrastructure and Services." High Powered Expert Committee for Estimating the Investment Requirements for Urban Infrastructure Services, Government of India.

Nagaraj, R., and S. Pandey (2013). "Have Gujarat and Bihar Outperformed the Rest of India?" *Economic and Political Weekly* 48(39) (Sept. 28): 39–41.

National Institute of Urban Affairs (2011). "Ahmedabad Bus Rapid Transit System." In Urban Transport Initiatives in India: Best Practices in PPP. http://www.niua.org/projects/tpt/AHMEDABAD BRTS.pdf.

Newsletter (2009). "Launch of e-Gram Vishwa-Gram in Gujarat." *Information Technology in Developing Countries* 19(1) (Feb.). Published by IFIP Working Group 9.4 and IIMA Centre for E-Governance.

NRHM (2005). "National Rural Health Mission: Framework for Implementation." New Delhi: MoHFW, Government of India.

NSSO (National Sample Survey Organization) (2008a). "Migration in India, 2007–08." NSS Report No. 533 (64/10.2/2). New Delhi: Ministry of Statistics and Programme Implementation, Government of India.

——. (2008b). "Education in India—Participation and Expenditure, 2007–08." NSS Report No. 532 (64/10.2/3). New Delhi: Ministry of Statistics and Programme Implementation, Government of India.

———. (various years). 55th and 68th rounds on "Employment and Unemployment Survey in India."

NUEPA (National University of Educational Planning and Administration) (Annual). "Elementary Education in India—State Report Card" (Year). New Delhi: Government of India.

NUHM (2010). "National Urban Health Mission: Framework for Implementation." New Delhi: Ministry of Health & Family Welfare, Government of India.

Pandit, Virendra (2011). "Free Flats for Gujarat Slum Dwellers." *Business Line*, Oct. 8, article 2521139.

Parekh, Sunil (2004). "Gujarat's Industrial Development—A Perspective." Presented to the Workshop on Selected Aspects of Development of Gujarat, Indian Institute of Management, Ahmedabad, Sept. 25.

Parthasarathy, R., and Ravindra H. Dholakia (eds.) (2011). *Sardar Sarovar Project on the River Narmada*, vol. 1: *History of Design, Planning and Appraisal*; vol. 2: *History of Rehabilitation and Implementation*; and vol. 3: *Impacts So Far and Ways Forward*. New Delhi: Concept Publishing Company.

Pathak, Mahesh, and V. D. Shah (2010). "Five Decades of Gujarat Agriculture: Some Reflections." In Ravindra H. Dholakia and Samar K. Datta (eds.), *High Growth Trajectory and Structural Changes in Gujarat Agriculture*, 15–28. Delhi: Macmillan.

Peden, E. A., and M. D. Bradley (1989). "Government Size, Productivity and Economic Growth: Post-war Experience." *Public Choice* 61(3): 229–245.

Planning Commission (2002). "National Human Development Report 2001." New Delhi: Government of India.

———. (2011). "India Human Development Report 2011—Towards Social Inclusion." New Delhi: Government of India.

———. (2013). "Data Book for DCH, Unofficial Estimates." New Delhi: Government of India.

Porter, Michael E. (1990). "The Competitive Advantage of Nations." *Harvard Business Review*, Mar.–Apr., 73–91.

Pratham Foundation (2005). "Annual Status of Education Report (Rural) (ASER) 2005." New Delhi.

——— (2012). "Annual Status of Education Report (Rural) (ASER) 2011." New Delhi.

Purohit, M. C., and V. K. Purohit (2010). *Non-Tax Sources in India—Issues in Pricing and Delivery of Services*. New Delhi: Foundation for Public Economics and Policy Research.

Rangarajan, C., and D. K. Srivastava (2008). "Reforming India's Fiscal Transfer System: Resolving Vertical and Horizontal Imbalances." *Economic and Political Weekly*, 43(23), June 7, 47–60.

Rao, S., S. Selvaraju, S. Nagpal, and S. Sakthivel (2005). *Financing of Health in India*. New Delhi: National Commission on Macroeconomics and Health, Government of India.

Rastogi, Siddhartha K., and Ravindra H. Dholakia (2010). "Linkages of Agricultural Exports and Infrastructure Development in Gujarat." In Ravindra H. Dholakia and Samar K. Datta (eds.), *High Growth Trajectory and Structural Changes in Gujarat Agriculture*, 136–151. Delhi: Macmillan.

Rath, Nilakantha (2011). "Poverty in Retrospect and Prospect." Keynote paper in the seminar on Poverty in Contemporary World—Malady and Remedy at Acharya Nagarjun University, Guntur, Aug. 18.

RBI (2006). "Report of the Working Group on Compilation of State Government Liabilities." Mumbai: Reserve Bank of India.

RBI (2006). (Annual). "State Finances—A Study of Budgets" (Year). Mumbai: Reserve Bank of India.

Sankar, Gopi, and Shankar Mondal (2010). "A Study on Organization Restructuring of Gujarat Electricity Board, Anand, India." Anand: International Water Management Institute.

Schwab, K. (2013). *The Global Competitiveness Report 2013–14*. Geneva: World Economic Forum.

Scully, G. W. (1989). "Size of the State, Economic Growth and Efficient Utilization of National Resources." *Public Choice* 61(2): 149–164.

Shah, Hasmukh (2011). "Preface." In Lotika Varadarajan (ed.), *Gujarat and the Sea*, xiii–xv. Ahmedabad: Darshak Itihas Nidhi.

Shah, T., A. Gulati, P. Hemant, G. Shreedhar, and R. C. Jain (2009). "Secret of Gujarat's Agrarian Miracle after 2000." *Economic and Political Weekly* 44(52): 45–55.

Shah, Tushaar, and Madhavi Mehta (2012). "Magical Transformation of Gujarat's Electricity Utility." Institute of Water Management India—Tata Policy Research Program.

Sharma, Vijay Paul, and Hrima Thaker (2010). "Livestock Development in Gujarat in 2000s: An Assessment." In Ravindra H. Dholakia and Samar K. Datta (eds.), *High Growth Trajectory and Structural Changes in Gujarat Agriculture*, 95–113. Delhi: Macmillan.

Singh, Prabal (2009). "Managing Maternal health Care through Public Private Partnership: Policy Issues and Implications: A Case Study of Chiranjivi Scheme in Panchmahals District of Gujarat, India." Ph.D. dissertation, IIM Ahmedabad.

Singh, Sukhpal (2010). "High Value Crops and Gujarat's Agricultural Growth: Cases of Castor and Psyllium (Isabgol)." In Ravindra H. Dholakia and Samar K. Datta (eds.), *High Growth Trajectory and Structural Changes in Gujarat Agriculture*, 51–68. Delhi: Macmillan.

SPFRC (2000). "Report of the State Public Finance Reform Committee on Medium Term Fiscal Consolidation." Gandhinagar: Government of Gujarat.

SRS (Sample Registration System) (Annual). *Bulletin*. Ministry of Health and Family Welfare, Government of India.

Vaidya, C., and B. Johnson (2001). "Ahmedabad Municipal Bond—Lessons and Pointers." *Economic and Political Weekly* 36(30) (July 28): 2884–2891.

Varadarajan, Lotika (2011). "Introduction." In Lotika Varadarajan (ed.), *Gujarat and the Sea*, 1–10. Ahmedabad: Darshak Itihas Nidhi.

Vyas, Jaynarayan (2002). "Industrial Gujarat—Today and Tomorrow" (in Gujarati). In Digant Oza and Sudarshan Iyengar (eds.), *Gujarat—a Balance-Sheet*, 118–130. Mumbai: Navbharat Sahitya Mandir.

World Bank (2004). *World Development Report—Making Services Work for Poor People*. -Washington DC: World Bank and Oxford University Press.

———. (2008). *The Town Planning Mechanism in Gujarat, India*. Authored by S. Balleney. Washington, DC: World Bank Institute and IBRD.

———. (2010). *Institutional Development and Good Governance in Highway Sector: Learning from Gujarat*. Authored by A. Bandyopadhyay and N. Stanaevich. Washington DC: Transport Research Support Program, World Bank.

———. (2011). *Maintaining Road Assets: A Fresh Look at the World Bank's 1988 Policy Paper—Road Deterioration in Developing Countries*. Authored by C. Harral, G. Smith, and W. Paterson. Washington DC: World Bank.

CHAPTER 21

Lessons from the States and Looking Ahead

ARVIND PANAGARIYA AND M. GOVINDA RAO

Our three case studies provide a wide range of insights into the process of development that Indian states can offer. Ultimately, it is the state governments that are closer to the people where action takes place. Good national policies are no doubt essential, but they may not translate into significant improvement in well-being if the state-level administration is weak. This is particularly true in India, where once we are past the central government all remaining power is largely concentrated at the level of the state. Having undertaken these studies, it is our firm belief that more state-level studies are essential to identify the bottlenecks that impede growth and development in some states while others flourish within the same set of national polices.

We have already provided a summary of the three case studies in the introduction and will not repeat that effort here. Instead, we undertake three tasks in this concluding chapter. First, we offer some lessons that emerge from the studies. Second, we discuss the changes that have occurred in the three states since the terminal year, 2010/11, of the studies and speculate on what may lie ahead in view of these developments. Finally, we discuss the implications of the policy changes likely to take place at the center for the states.

LESSONS FROM ANDHRA PRADESH, GUJARAT, AND BIHAR

Despite the differences that we have highlighted in the introduction, some common threads tie the experiences of the three states together so that we may glean lessons that may be applicable to most states. First, policies to accelerate economic growth are important, particularly in states with large concentrations of poverty. All of the three states have shown significant acceleration in growth rates during the last decade. Commensurately, there has been a sharp acceleration in the growth of development expenditures in the states in the last decade, which has helped improve connectivity to markets and social outcomes. More important, acceleration in growth and increase in public spending has led to appreciable reduction in poverty.

Second, the composition of growth is important as well. Focus on agriculture in general and high-value commodities, such as fruits and vegetables, commercial crops, dairy, and animal husbandry, in particular in Andhra Pradesh and Gujarat, has led to much faster reduction in rural poverty in these states. On the other hand, due to labor market rigidities, labor-intensive industry has failed to grow in all three states leading to much slower migration out of agriculture into industry. Even in a state such as Gujarat, which has the largest share of output in industry and a high degree of urbanization, the share of workforce in agriculture remains high.

Third, history and institutions play an important role in determining economic outcomes. The long history of successive kingdoms in Bihar strengthened the caste system with all its rigidities and exploitative characteristics. The zamindari system of land tenure under which landownership rights got transferred to the revenue-collection agent of the government called the zamindar created perverse incentives in farm production. Given the social relations, the much-touted land reform was bound to fail and the production relationships in land have continued to be exploitative. In contrast, in Gujarat and large parts of Andhra Pradesh, the ryotwari system of land tenure under which taxes were collected directly from the tiller has been more conducive to acceleration in agricultural growth in these states. Gujarat also has had a history of manufacturing and trade and commerce and an entrepreneurial class willing to take risks. Historically there was a culture of manufacturing and trade with the city of Surat serving as a major port during the British rule before the latter acquired Bombay. The entire Bombay–Ahmedabad belt was known for its manufacturing activity with Ahmedabad called the "Manchester" of India.

Fourth, given the historical legacy, the most important factor contributing to growth is the quality of leadership and governance. The acceleration in growth in all the three states is directly associated with visionary leadership. Bihar was considered a basket case until Nitish Kumar assumed office in 2005. His initiative of ensuring law and order in Bihar, improving connectivity to the villages, appointing teachers and health workers to improve human development, and improving the infrastructure by enhancing development expenditures was an important factor contributing to growth acceleration.

In a similar vein, one of the first things that Chandrababu Naidu did when he assumed power in Andhra Pradesh was work toward turning the state into an important investment destination. His focus on the creation of an enabling environment to attract investments, particularly in modern technology industries and application of modern technology in administration to impart effectiveness to service delivery and targeting of beneficiaries in Andhra Pradesh, helped to create a more market-friendly environment in the state. YSR, who succeeded Naidu as the chief minister, even as he refocused attention toward the agricultural sector, continued to provide market-friendly climate and infrastructure to manufacturing and service sectors.

Finally, the visionary leadership of Narendra Modi in creating a market-friendly, corruption-free, development-oriented governance in Gujarat played an important role in attracting investments, as documented in the study by Dholakia and Dholakia. An investor-friendly environment and fast clearances were important factors in attracting investments to the state. Interestingly, the state leadership also focused on expanding irrigation and water harvesting and the use of modern technology in the cultivation of cash crops like cotton.

Fifth, the three case studies also bring out the importance of reforms aimed at development of markets and use of modern technology in different sectors of the economy including the government. Nitish Kumar's emphasis on the importance of building the network of roads and his focus on reducing the travel time from anywhere in Bihar to Patna to six hours or less were attempts to improve mobility and open up the markets. Andhra Pradesh's attempts to upgrade the infrastructure and use information technology in administration to provide fast clearances and fully utilize central assistance are some of the examples. Similarly, Gujarat was able to create a favorable environment for land acquisition, fast track all clearances through a single-window scheme, ensure efficient infrastructure by facilitating special economic zones and perhaps implement labor laws in the most market-friendly manner possible within the overall framework of Union government's labor laws.

Finally, the three studies show that good economics can also be good politics and the policies aimed at long-term growth can help a government get re-elected. There is considerable discussion on whether the short-run populist policies or the long-term growth-oriented policies deliver superior electoral outcomes. The three case studies provide important insights into this issue. The Bihar case study shows the importance of ensuring law and order, particularly when life and properties of the people are threatened by anarchy. The re-election of Nitish Kumar on a developmental plank even in a traditional feudal society riddled with caste prejudices shows that focusing on good economic policies aimed at development can help a government get re-elected.

Andhra Pradesh seemingly presents a contrasting picture as the Telugu Desam Party led by Chandrababu Naidu failed to win the re-election in spite of its focus on modernizing governance and attracting investments into the state. A closer analysis shows, however, that this is not due to the policies per se, but partially because Naidu failed to balance investment in industry with that in agriculture and faced a formidable campaigner in YSR. After the latter came to power in 2004, he continued to advance the vision of the previous government in industry and services while incorporating policies to promote agriculture and won his bid for re-election in 2009.

The experience under Narendra Modi in Gujarat was no different. After the rehabilitation work following the devastating earthquake in 2001, he too embarked upon a policy that promoted industrial and agricultural growth, which got him re-elected in 2007 and again in 2012. Indeed, on the strength of his achievements in Gujarat, he has been able to mount a highly successful national campaign for the office of the Prime Minister of India.

Before we conclude this section, we wish to underline yet again the critical importance of a leader able to deliver good governance at the level of the state. While states have some leeway to bring about policy change, the bulk of the policies are given to them by the central government. The vast majority of the important policy subjects in the Indian Constitution are listed in the Central and Concurrent Lists. The former list is the exclusive preserve of the center. In the areas covered by the latter, both center and states can legislate but the latter cannot override a central legislation without the permission of the central government. In the past, the central government has rarely given such permission. Therefore, much of the legislative activity of the state is limited to the State List, which is limited in scope.

This means that the ability to govern becomes crucial at the level of the state. The state government must be able to use the flexibility available in the central laws effectively to attract investors. Because the laws are largely uniform across states, the state that provides good administration can become a magnet for investors. Likewise, states capable of good administration can also build and maintain within-state infrastructure better than states that are poorly run. Once again, this can translate in a large advantage.

LOOKING AHEAD: RECENT DEVELOPMENTS AND WHAT THEY MAY MEAN

All three states discussed in this volume have seen major changes since the completion of the studies. There had been a long-standing movement in Andhra Pradesh for a separate state of Telangana consisting of 10 of the 23 districts that had belonged to the State of Hyderabad under the British.

On June 1, 2014, this state formally came into existence. The remaining 13 districts of which nine belong to the coastal Andhra Pradesh and four to Rayalaseema came to form the new Andhra Pradesh state. Hyderabad, which is in Telangana, is to serve as the capital of both states for 10 years during which time a new capital is to be built for Andhra Pradesh. Chandra Babu Naidu returned as the Chief Minister of the new Andhra Pradesh.

Agriculture accounts for a far greater share of the GSDP in Andhra Pradesh than Telangana. On the other hand, Hyderabad, which is the second most important center of the information technology industry in India, being in Telangana, services dominate the economy of the latter. Andhra Pradesh has the second largest coastal line after Gujarat in India. In contrast, Telangana is landlocked but more urban than Andhra Pradesh. With these differences, economies of the two states offer much scope for inter-state trade.

But in certain areas, they are also likely to be healthy competitors. Already, signs of this competition can be seen. According to reports at the time of writing, Hero MotoCorp was looking for land for a manufacturing plant for its southern Indian market in the region. Chief Ministers of both states hold the key industry portfolio themselves and are promising major concessions to Hero for setting up the plant to manufacture 2 million motorbikes in their respective states.

What impact will the bifurcation have on the future growth of the two states? At least going by the experience of three other states that were bifurcated in 2000, it stands to reason that both component parts of the original larger state may see their progress improve. For example, Bihar had been bifurcated in 2000 into the current state of Bihar and Jharkhand. Both of these states have grown significantly faster than the original Bihar. The loss of mine-rich areas to Jharkhand has not hampered the ability of the dynamic Nitish Kumar to achieve unprecedented growth in the state. If Andhra Pradesh gets the promised status of a Special Category state for the first five years, it would also be the beneficiary of significantly increased transfers from the center.

Two important issues with a bearing on the growth of successor states may be noted in this context. First, even before the bifurcation is complete in terms of division of staff, assets, and liabilities between the two states, signs of rising protectionism can be seen, especially in Telangana. For example, according to a parental education clause introduced by Telangana government, Andhra-origin students in the state will only be eligible for fee reimbursement if their parents have also studied in Telangana. The provision would effectively raise fee liability of the students whose origin can be traced to Andhra Pradesh.

Second, special category status, which would allow Andhra Pradesh to introduce tax concessions for industry, could result in significant diversion of investments and migration of capital from not just Telangana but also other neighboring states such as Karnataka, Maharashtra, and Tamil Nadu. This would have implications for investment and growth both in the new states as well as their neighbors.

In Bihar, the political drama featuring Nitish Kumar and Lalu Yadav seems to have come full circle. As Mukherji and Mukherji discuss in their study, these two politicians had begun their political careers simultaneously and on the same side of the fence. But they eventually became archrivals with each successively serving as Chief Minister of Bihar while the other sat in the opposition. Nitish Kumar, who became Chief Minister in 2005 and scored a second successive victory in 2010, had presided over a coalition consisting of his own party, JD(U), and BJP.

As the politics of the 2014 parliamentary elections began to take shape, Gujarat Chief Minister Narendra Modi emerged as the BJP prime ministerial candidate. Being entirely opposed to Modi, Nitish Kumar went on to break the alliance with the BJP. Because his other ally, Lok Janshakti Party or LJP, chose to ally with the BJP, he lost yet more members in the state assembly to the opposition. Eventually, Modi emerged as a highly popular leader on the national stage and JD(U) could only win 2 out of the 40 parliamentary seats in Bihar. This outcome dramatically weakened Nitish Kumar and led him resign as Chief Minister in favor of another member of his party. With the BJP and LJP surging in the state, there is now an existential threat to Nitish Kumar as well as Lalu Yadav, who are both opposed to the BJP, in the assembly elections due in 2015. As the saying goes, enemy's enemy is a friend. So there has been a rapprochement between these two archenemies and one can no longer rule out the possibility that they might contest the 2015 election as allies. As American politician William Clay has said, "This is quite a game, politics. There are no permanent enemies, no permanent friends, only permanent interests."

These developments suggest that the state and national politics can sometimes interact in unpredictable ways. Nitish Kumar, whose political standing in Bihar had seemed beyond challenge until even a year ago on account of his stellar performance, has been so weakened politically due to the changes resulting from the national politics that it now appears doubtful that his party would be returned to power even with the support of Lalu Yadav in the 2015 election.

Whatever the result of the 2015 election, it stands to reason that the next government will have an enormous pressure to deliver good governance and policies. If either Nitish or Lalu Yadav comes to the helm, he would need to work hard to win the trust of the people back. And if a BJP-led government comes to power, it will have the burden of delivering on its promises already made in the national election by Prime Minister Modi. There is reason to be optimistic about the future of the state.

Finally, Gujarat shows signs of greater continuity. Its Chief Minister during 2001–2014 has now become the Prime Minister of India, but he has been succeeded by his protégé Anandiben Patel, who is expected to govern the state in a similar spirit as him. She exhibits a high level of energy and promises to uphold the tradition of clean governance in the state. With a friendlier government installed at the center, the government is also likely to have more headroom to promote development in the state. Therefore, there are good reasons for optimism for Gujarat as well.

A NEW GOVERNMENT AT THE CENTER AND WHAT IT MAY IMPLY

In May 2014, a new national government came to the helm in India. For the first time, the country has a prime minister who built his entire political career in a state. Having served as the Chief Minister of Gujarat for more than 12 years, Prime Minister Narendra Modi has a great appreciation of the constraints under which states must function. Insofar as these constraints result from the central government policies, he is sympathetic to find ways to relax them.

During the first month of taking office, Prime Minister Modi has also successfully ended the inertia, indeed paralysis, which had characterized the previous government at the center. Various central clearances, especially those relating to the environment and forests, are now being processed swiftly. The new government is also keen to forge partnerships with states and give greater fiscal and legislative space to the states.

Increased fiscal space may translate into more fiscal resources as well as greater flexibility in spending the available resources. For example, currently, states cannot shift funds from one centrally sponsored scheme to another, which has the implication that if it has an abundance of funds under one scheme and scarcity in another it will simply have to return the leftover funds from the former despite unfulfilled needs in the latter. This may change.

Likewise, increased legislative space would impart to the states power to change laws that they did not previously have. In particular, in the past, the laws relating to the subjects on the Concurrent List of the Constitution, which include such important subjects as labor, property, education, and health, have been largely governed by the central government. This is because the Constitution gives central laws primacy over the state laws. Only if the central government authorizes a state can the latter amend the central law falling under the Concurrent List. But the past central governments have rarely given such authorization.

Prime Minister Modi has shown much greater inclination to give states permission to amend the central laws. Encouraged by this, the state of Rajasthan has recently initiated the process of changing some key labor laws.

If the central government indeed makes good on its promise, India may witness a truly major intensification of laboratory federalism. Insofar as different states may take different approaches to changing the central laws, we would witness a degree of experimentation not experienced before.

CONCLUDING REMARKS

In this concluding chapter, we have drawn the common lessons from the three case studies, discussed the latest developments in the states and their likely implications, and speculated on how the promise of changed central government policies toward states under Prime Minister Modi's new central government may enhance the role of the states. It is our view that scholars need to give greater attention to the study of states to understand the process of development. This is particularly important in a large country like India in which many states house more people than most countries. Ten Indian states are as large as or larger than the United Kingdom according to population. The state of Uttar Pradesh by itself would be the fifth largest country in the world. Through two book volumes, we have initiated this process in a systematic manner. We hope that other scholars of India will follow suit.

INDEX

Figures and tables are indicated by "f" and "t" following page numbers.

Aarogyasri (health insurance), 91–94, 106
Abhayanand (Additional Director General of Police, Bihar), 179
Acemoglu, D., 2, 199n1
Aghion, P., 47, 50
Agricultural Produce Market Committee (APMC) Acts
   Bihar (1960), 210
   Gujarat (2005, 2007), 249, 260
Agriculture sector
   agricultural credit program, 44
   agricultural extension programs, 43, 248
   agricultural outputs, factors determining, 247
   in Andhra Pradesh, 32, 33t, 37–42, 57, 70, 71t, 76, 105
   animal husbandry services, 41
   in Bihar, 133, 134, 139, 141, 146, 150f, 210, 214
   in Coastal Andhra Pradesh, 112–113
   crop insurance program, 43
   dairy products, 38, 39f, 40, 41, 250, 334
   demand and supply-side effects on, 40
   eggs, production of, 38, 39f
   food grains, land devoted to, 38
   food-processing industry, 210, 216
   fruits and vegetables, 37, 38, 40, 41, 57, 103, 247, 250
   grain crops, 247
   growth rates, 33t
   in Gujarat, 14, 32, 230–234, 246–250, 263
   in Gujarat Model, 321
   high-value commodities, 37–42, 75, 103, 247, 249
   irrigation, 42–43, 62–63, 248, 258, 263
   Kumar government's goals for, 206
   livestock, 38, 41, 250
   loans, to Bihar farmers, 210
   marketing networks, 249
   meat, production of, 38, 39f, 250
   onion exports, 254
   output shares, 34t
   power subsidies to, 47–48, 49
   rural poverty rates and, 62
   in Ryalseema, 112–113
   social group employment in, 65
   subsidies to, 42
   supply-side effects on, 40–41
   in Telangana, 112–113
   workforce share in, 36
   yield rates for crops, 247
Ahluwalia, Rahul, 3, 8, 9, 19
Ahmedabad city (Gujarat)
   bus rapid transit system in, 270–271, 274
   City Development Plan, on solid waste, 270
   as "Manchester" of India, 334
   slum population of, 268
   water supply in, 270t
Ahmedabad district (Gujarat) special economic zones in, 255
Ahmedabad Municipal Corporation (AMC), 272–273, 274
Airports, 256–257
Ajatashatru (Magadha ruler), 126
Alexander the Great, 127
Ali, A., 196

Anarchy, economic effects of, 11n6
Ancient Greeks, in India, 127
Andhra Pradesh state. *See also* Naidu, Chandrababu; Reddy, Y. S. Rajshekhar; *following headings starting with "Andhra Pradesh"*
  average growth rate in, 104
  bifurcation of, 4n2, 16, 109–111, 336–337
  BT Cotton in, 249
  conclusions on, 102–108
  economic growth of, 29–58, 111–114. *See also* Andhra Pradesh, economic transformation and growth
  economic vision of, 21–22
  education in, 94–101. *See also* Andhra Pradesh, education in
  employment, 59–76, 81–87. *See also* Andhra Pradesh, poverty and employment in
  growth in, 6
  health outcomes, 88–94, 100–101
  leadership of, 25–27
  microfinance in, 77–81, 86–87
  MNREGA in, 81–86, 87
  overview, 8–10, 21–28
  per capita development expenditures by, 76
  per capita GSDP, 22–24
  poverty and employment in, 59–76. *See also* Andhra Pradesh, poverty and employment in
  poverty rates in, 24–25
  regional poverty trends, 114–115
  as research object, choice of, 5
  total fertility rate in, 149
  urban and slum population of, 267
Andhra Pradesh, economic transformation and growth, 29–58
  agriculture, performance of, 32, 33t, 37–44, 57
  conclusions on, 56–58
  growth, 30–31
  industrial policies, 44–46
  IT sector, role of, 51–56
  key elements of, 31–37
  overview of, 29–30
  power sector, role of, 46–51
  region-wise analysis, 111–114
Andhra Pradesh, education in, 94–101
  access and enrollment, 95–96
  conclusions on, 100, 101
  literacy rates, 94–95
  overview, 94
  public vs. private schooling, 97–98
  Right to Education Act, 99–100
  teacher performance pay, 98–99
Andhra Pradesh, poverty and employment in, 59–76. *See also* Mahatma Gandhi National Rural Employment Guarantee Act; Microfinance
  conclusions on, 75–76
  employment, 69–75
  poverty, overall trends, 59–63
  poverty in, vs. Uttar Pradesh, 8, 24–25
  poverty reduction among social groups, 63–69
  regional poverty trends, 114–115
  rural areas, employment guarantees in, 81–87
Andhra Pradesh Electricity Reforms Act (1998), 49
Andhra Pradesh Electricity Regulatory Commission (APERC), 49
Andhra Pradesh Industrial Single Window Clearance Act (Single Window Act, 2002), 45, 46, 57, 103–104
Andhra Pradesh Livestock Development Agency, 41
Andhra Pradesh Microfinance Institutions (Regulation of Money Lending) Ordinance (2010), 80
Andhra Pradesh NGO Alliance (APNA), 86
Andhra Pradesh Pollution Control Act, 54
Andhra Pradesh Power Generation Corporation Limited (APGENCO), 49
Andhra Pradesh Socio-Economic Survey, 38–39, 40–41, 43–44, 46, 95
Andhra Pradesh State Electricity Board (APSEB), 47–49
Annual Survey of Education Report (ASER) Center reports, 190, 191, 193
Annual Survey of Industries (ASI), 50

Apki Sarkar Apke Dwar ("your government at your doorstep") strategy, 180–181
APTransco (Transmission Corporation of Andhra Pradesh Limited), 49
Arms Act (1959), 176, 178*t*
Arthashastra (Chanakya), 127–128, 200–201
Arulampalam, W. D., 160
Asian Development Bank (ADB), 276
Assam state
   per capita government health expenditures in, 158
   separation from Bengal Presidency, 153n2

Bagchi, Amaresh, 162, 163
Banerjee, Abhijit, 6, 81, 155, 156n5
Banerji, Pranab, 197
Bangalore (Bengaluru), as outsourcing location, 51
Bangladesh, flood control in, 184
Banking and insurance sector, 35. *See also* Finance and fiscal policies
   remittances from out migrants, 198
Becker, G., 194
"A Bend in the River" (Singh), 160n8
Bengal Presidency, 153–155, 157–158
Besley, T., 47, 201
Bharatiya Janata Party (BJP), 16, 131, 171, 206, 338
Bharuch district (Gujarat), special economic zones in, 255
Bicycles for schoolgirls scheme (Bihar), 205
Bifurcation of states
   Andhra Pradesh, 4n2, 16, 109–111, 336–337
   Bihar, 12, 138–142, 189, 337
Bihar state. See also *following headings starting with "Bihar"*
   Bengal Presidency, separation from, 153n2
   bifurcation of, 12, 138–142, 189, 337
   caste system, influence of, 167–168, 334
   conclusions on, 212–216
   economy, 3, 123–151. *See also* Bihar, economy in
   governance and reforms in, 199–211. *See also* Bihar, governance and reforms in
   growth determinants, 167–198. *See also* Bihar, growth determinants in
   historical past, loss of, 124
   Jharkhand, comparison with, 109
   Kumar government's goals for, 207
   overview, 6, 10–12
   policy impacts, 152–166. *See also* Bihar, policy impacts in
   as research object, choice of, 5
   urban and slum population of, 267
Bihar, economy in, 123–151
   conclusions on, 150–151
   district level poverty, 142–143, 144*t*
   economy, overview, 130–131
   economy, phase I (1980–2000), 131–138
   economy, phase II (2000–2005), 138–145
   economy (post-2005), 145–150
   historical sketch of, 125–130
   overview, 123–125
Bihar, governance and reforms in, 199–211
   Bihar Gazette notification (2010), 206–209
   conclusions on, 211
   future of, 209–210
   governance, description of, 200–201
   governance performance, 201–206
   overview, 199
Bihar, growth determinants in, 167–198
   conclusions on, 198
   fiscal reform, 173–175
   floods, 181–184
   infrastructure, 185–189
   law and order, 175–181
   migration and remittances, 196–198
   overview, 167
   political leaders, 167–172
   public service delivery, 172–173
   social sectors, 190–196
Bihar, policy impacts in, 152–166
   conclusions on, 165–166
   Freight Equalization Policy, 163–164
   governance failure, deliberate, 164–165, 215
   overview, 152–153

Bihar, policy impacts in (*Cont.*)
  permanent settlement, history of, 153–156
  state finances, 156–163
Bihar Gazette notification (2010), 206–209
Bihar Lokayukta Act (2011), 204
Bihar Police Academy, 179
Bihar Rajya Pul Nirman Nigam (Bihar State Bridge Construction Corporation Limited), 187–188
Bihar Reorganization Act (2000), 130, 141, 171
Bihar Right to Public Service Act (2011), 203, 204
Bihar Special Courts Act (2009), 179, 203, 204
Bihar State Electricity Board, 189
Bihar Universities Amendment Act (2007), 194
BIMARU states, 206
Bimbisara (Magadha ruler), 126
Biswas, R., 160
BJP. *See* Bharatiya Janata Party
Bombay Presidency, 156–158
Bombay Provincial Municipal Corporation (BPMC) Act (1949), 271
Bonds, municipal, 272–273
Bose, Ashish, 206
Boston, Massachusetts, economic policies under Curly, 164
Boys. *See* Education; Males and boys
British East India Company, 153–154
BT Cotton, 249
Buddhism, 10, 126–127, 128
Burgess, R., 47
Business Process Outsourcing (BPO) sector, 52–53

Capital expenditures (Gujarat), 279–280, 306–307
Capital-intensive industries, 235–236
Castes. *See also* Scheduled Castes
  in Andhra Pradesh, 83
  in Bihar, 167–168, 334
CBGA (Centre for Budget and Governance Accountability), 315
Central Bureau of Investigation (CBI), 170
Central Electricity Act amendment (1998), 259

Central Government Right to Information Act (Bihar), 202
Central List (Indian Constitution), 336
Central Provinces, per capita government health expenditures in, 158
Central Statistical Office (CSO), 23
Centre for Budget and Governance Accountability (CBGA), 315
Chaco Canyon civilization (Chaco Phenomenon), 129–130, 212
Chakraborty, Pinaki, 3, 7, 162, 163
Chanakya (Kautilya, advisor to Maurya), 10, 127, 128, 201–202
Chanda, A., 193
Chandrashekar Rao, K., 108
Chaudhuri, B., 154
Chaudhuri, S., 142, 143
Chhattisgarh state, growth of, 109
"Chief Minister in the People's Court" (*Janata ke Darbar mein Mukhyamantri*, JKDM), 203
Chief Minister's Rural Roads Program (Mukhya Mantri Gram Sadak Yojana), 187, 188
Children, 286, 297t, 298, 305–306. *See also* Education; Females and girls; Health and healthcare; Males and boys
China, urbanization in, 31–32
Chiranjivi Scheme, 304, 305t, 310
City Development Plan (CDP) of Ahmedabad (2006), 270
Clay, William, 338
Clean Development Mechanism (CDM) projects, 303
Climate Change Department (Gujarat), 303
Coastal Andhra Pradesh
  as constituent of new Andhra Pradesh, 16, 337
  growth rate, 111–114
  literacy levels in, 95
  poverty in, 114–115
Colonial era, 11, 157–158, 166, 199. *See also* Bengal Presidency
Communications sector, 35, 52, 260–261. *See also* Telecommunications
  emergency services, integrated phone number for, 305, 310, 313

Community Health Centers (CHCs), 301, 302t
Comptroller and Auditor General of India, 13–14, 245, 293
Computer software, sales tax on, 54
Concurrent List (Indian Constitution), 2, 336, 339
Congressional Research Service (CRS, US), on Gujarat, 318
Congress Party, 26, 167–168, 169, 172
Constitution
  Central List, 336
  Concurrent List, 2, 336, 339
  State List, 336
  union-state relationships under, 158–159
Construction sector
  in Andhra Pradesh, 65–66
  in Bihar, 133, 139, 146, 150f
  casual workforce in, 74
Cornwallis, Charles, 154, 155
Corruption, 170, 203–204, 207, 269
Cotton, 249, 254
Courts, 179, 313–314. See also Judiciary
Courts of the people (Lok Adalats), 314
Credit, Andhra Pradesh agricultural credit program, 44
Crime (Bihar)
  burglary rates, 175–176, 177t
  jail system, 180
  kidnapping rates, 175–176, 177t
  murder rates, 175–176, 177t
  robbery rates, 175–176, 177t
  theft rates, 175–176, 177t
Crude death rates (CRD, Gujarat), 242, 245
Curly, James Michael, 164
Currency crises, East Asian, 231, 232n4
Cyberabad. See Hyderabad

Dacoity rates (Bihar), 175–176, 177t
Das Gupta, C., 140
Datt, G., 62, 76
Datta, Samar K., 249
Debroy, Bibek, 243, 298
Debt-GSDP ratio (Gujarat), 276, 277t
Deficits, 163, 275, 278–279, 283
Delhi, total fertility rate in, 149
Deloitte, outsourcing by, 53
Demand and supply side factors, 40
Democracy
  economic effects of, 11n6
  good governance and, 100, 201
  local governance and, 271
  representative democracies, 100, 102, 104, 107
  stationary bandits vs., 209
Democracy in America (Tocqueville), 1
Department of Economics and Statistics
  Andhra Pradesh, 111
  Gujarat, 240–241
Deshingkar, P., 197
Devi, Rabri, 170, 171
Dhaliwal, R., 164n12
Dholakia, Archana, 13, 15, 225, 335
Dholakia, Ravindra, 13, 15, 225, 323, 335
Disadvantaged groups. See Muslims; Scheduled Castes; Scheduled Tribes
Disaster Management Department (Bihar), 182
Diseases. See Health and healthcare
District domestic products (DDP, Bihar), 145–146
District Industries Centers (Andhra Pradesh), 46
Doctors, availability of (Andhra Pradesh), 89–90
Duflo, E., 81
Dutta, P., 81–82, 83
Dynamic processes, nonlinearity of, 152

Earthquakes, 278, 283, 325–326
East Asian currency crises, 231, 232n4
East India Company, 153–154
EBC (Extremely Backward Classes), 168
Economic development. See also Bihar, growth determinants; Growth miracles; Gujarat, growth and development in
  in Andhra Pradesh, 21–22, 30–31, 111–114
  in Bihar, 132–133, 145–146
  composition of, 334
  expenditures for, 174–175, 282, 282f, 283, 284, 334
  factors enhancing, 9
  in Gujarat, 228–233, 320–321
  industry sector growth rates, 33t
  mega investment projects, 14, 54, 253–254, 314n3
  per capita development expenditures, in Bihar vs. in India, 174

Economic development(*Cont.*)
  productivity (Bihar), 214
  prosperity (Andhra Pradesh), 8, 25, 26, 56, 104, 106
  socioeconomic developments, relationship to, 107
"Economic Freedom of the States of India" (Debroy, Bhandari, & Aiyer), 311n1
Economic Survey 2012/13, 232–233
Economic Survey of Bihar, 190
Economy. *See also* Andhra Pradesh, economic transformation and growth; Bihar, economy; Economic development; Gujarat, economic sectors, policy reform in; *specific sectors*
  Asia vs. India, 233–234
  of Gujarat, structure of, 233–237
Education. *See also* Andhra Pradesh, education in; Gujarat, education in; Literacy rates; Private schools and universities
  Andhra Pradesh teachers, 97–99
  arithmetic skills, in Bihar vs. India, 191–193
  as Bihar growth determinant, 190–194
  dropout rates, 286–287
  enrollment rates, 95–96, 96f, 190, 191f, 285–286
  fertility rate, relationship to, 150, 193
  general higher education, 292n6
  government schools, 99, 190, 191f, 288
  in Gujarat, 287–294
  higher education, 291–294, 316
  infrastructure for, 289–290, 294
  language barriers in higher education, 293, 294
  multi-grade classrooms in, 193
  para-teachers, 290, 294
  performance indicators, 285–287
  pre-primary schools, 289–290
  primary schools, 95, 96f, 97, 190, 288
  public vs. private schooling, 97–98
  school choice programs, 97, 99, 100, 106
  secondary schools, 95, 97, 289
  single-classroom schools, 289, 289t, 294
  single-teacher schools, 289, 289t, 294
  teacher-pupil ratios, 99, 194, 289t, 290, 294
  technical education, 291–292
  upper primary schools, 95, 96, 97, 289
EFMS (electronic Fund Management System), 85
E-governance
  for Aarogyasri health insurance, 92
  in Andhra Pradesh, 54, 55
  in Gujarat, 253, 312–313, 321
  Jankari, 202
Eichengreen, B., 213
Electricity. *See* Energy
Electricity Act (2003), 49, 259
Electricity Laws (Amendment) Act (1991/1998), 48
Electricity Regulatory Commission, 259
Electricity Regulatory Commission Act (1998), 48
Electronic Fund Management System (eFMS), 85
Electronic Muster and Measurement System (eMMS), 85
Eleventh Finance Commission, 278
Emergency services, integrated phone number for, 305, 310, 313
Employment. *See also* Worker migration
  in Andhra Pradesh, 27–28, 69–76, 81–87
  in Bihar, 134
  casual labor workforce, 66, 72–74
  in Gujarat, 236–237, 302–303
  job cards, 74
  labor laws, 14, 47, 76, 105
  labor market rigidities and, 334
  private sector employment, 72
  public sector employment, 72
  regular wage workforce, 72, 73
  salaried workforce, 72, 73
  self-employed workforce, 72–73
  size of workforce, 69–70
  unemployment and underemployment, 74–75
  work culture, 155
  workforce participation rate (WPR), 69, 148, 149f, 150

Energy
  in Andhra Pradesh, role in economic growth, 46–51, 57
  as Bihar growth determinant, 189
  control of, 48
  in Gujarat, 248–249, 252, 259, 260t
  own-generated electricity, 50–51
  transmission and distribution (T&D) losses (for electricity), 189
E-procurement, 55, 56
E-Village scheme (Gujarat), 261
Exports, 228, 253, 264
Extremely Backward Classes (EBC), 168

Fa-Hien (Buddhist traveler to Magadha), 129
Farmer Empowerment Program (Rythu Chaitanya Yatra), 43
Farmer markets (Rythu Bazars), 40–41, 103
Federalism, 1–2, 159, 340
Females and girls
  bicycles for schoolgirls, 205
  employment by industry divisions (Andhra Pradesh), 71t
  employment categories for, 72t, 73
  life expectancy rates, 136–137
  literacy rates, 62, 95, 135–136, 241, 242t
  MNREGA participation, 83, 84f
  rural unemployment and underemployment of, 75t
  school enrollment rates, 95–96, 286
Fernandes, George, 169
Festival of Agriculture (Krushi Mahotsav, Gujarat), 248
Finance and fiscal policies. *See also* Gujarat, fiscal reforms and performance
  Bihar, fiscal reform in, 173–175
  dependency ratio (of grants in urban finances), 272
  financial inclusion, 77
  fiscal deficits, definition of, 275n2
  fiscal federalism, 159
  microfinance, 77–81, 86–87
  municipal bonds, 272–273
Finance Commission, 159
Fiscal Responsibility and Budget Management (FRBM) Acts, 173

Fiscal Responsibility Legislation (FRL, 2005, Gujarat), 278–279, 283, 322
Fish production (Andhra Pradesh), 39, 40f, 41
Flood MAPS project, 184
Floods (Bihar), 140, 181–184
Fodder scam (Bihar), 170
Ford Motor Company, 254
Forests (Gujarat), 303
Freedom (individual), government policies and, 107
Freight Equalization Policy (FEP, 1948), 11, 163–164, 214–215

Gandhi, Indira, 167
Gandhi, Rajiv, 168
Gandhi, Sonia, 172
Gandhinagar district (Gujarat), special economic zones in, 255
Gender gaps and biases. *See also* Females and girls; Males and boys
  in life expectancy rates, 136–137
  in literacy rates, 135–136
  school enrollment rates, 95–96, 286
General Electric, 53
Genpact, 53
Geographic Information Systems (GISs), 272, 313
Ghatak, M., 233n6
Ghosh, Amitava, 196n19
Ghosh, P. P., 132, 134, 157
Gini coefficient, 143, 144t, 239–240
Girls. *See* Females and girls
Glaeser, E. L., 164
Glennerster, R., 81
Goods and Services Tax (GST), 175, 281
Governance. *See also* Bihar, governance and reforms in; E-governance; Gujarat, governance in; Leadership
  deliberate failures of, 164–165, 215
  description of, 200–201
  dictatorships, economic effects of, 11n6
  effectiveness and answerability, 315–316
  importance of, 334
  individual freedom, government policies and, 107
  interdepartmental coordination, 315
  justice and, 201

Governance (*Cont.*)
  Kumar government's goals for, 207
  law and order (Bihar), 12, 175–181, 215, 335
  local bodies (urban governments), 271
  mismanagement (Bihar), 169–170
  overview of, 311–312
  police forces, sizes of, 157
  policy experimentation and reforms, importance of, 103, 104, 105, 106, 107
  political will, 322
  principal component of, 11
  role of government in representative democracies, 100
  smart governance, 103
  unproductive expenditures (Gujarat), 276, 322
Govinda Rao, M., 1, 3, 7, 333
Gowda, Deve, 169
Greeks (ancient), 127
Green energy, 259
Gross State Domestic Product (GSDP). *See also* Per capita GSDP
  in Andhra Pradesh and Uttar Pradesh, 22–24
  in Bihar, 6
  data on, 7
  in Gujarat, 6, 13, 229–235, 257, 258f, 261
Growth. *See* Economic development
Growth miracles. *See also* Andhra Pradesh state; Bihar state; Gujarat state
  Andhra Pradesh, overview of, 8–10
  Bihar, overview of, 10–12
  conclusions on, 15–16, 333–340
  Gujarat, overview of, 13–15
  overview of, 1–2
  state choices, reasons for, 4–6
  state features, 6–7
  state-level analysis, need for, 2–4
GSDP. *See* Gross State Domestic Product
Gujarat state. *See also following headings starting with "Gujarat"*
  cities in, size-classes of, 238
  conclusions on, 320–322
  economic growth and development in, 227–245. *See also* Gujarat, growth and development in
  economic sectors in, 246–264. *See also* Gujarat, economic sectors, policy reform in
  education in, 285–294. *See also* Gujarat, education in
  fiscal reforms and performance, 275–284. *See also* Gujarat, fiscal reforms and performance in
  governance, 311–319. *See also* Gujarat, governance in
  healthcare and medical education, 295–310. *See also* Gujarat, health and medical education in
  Kutchh District earthquake, 325–326
  overview, 6, 13–15, 227–228
  as research object, choice of, 5
  Sardar Sarovar Project, 323–324
  urban development in, 265–274. *See also* Gujarat, urban development in
Gujarat, economic sectors, policy reform in, 246–264
  agriculture, 246–250
  conclusions on, 263–264
  industrial sector, 250–255
  infrastructure, 255–261
  investment policies, 235
  overview, 246
  Vibrant Gujarat Summit, 262–263
Gujarat, education in, 285–294
  higher education, 291–294
  human resources for, 290
  infrastructure for, 289–290
  overview of, 15, 285
  performance indicators, 285–287
  quality of, 287–289
Gujarat, fiscal reforms and performance in, 275–284
  conclusions on, 283–284
  fiscal reforms (1991–2001), 275–278
  fiscal reforms (2001–2011), 278–280
  investment policies, 262–263
  overview of, 275
  revenues and expenditures, 15, 276, 280–283, 284, 322
Gujarat, governance in, 311–319
  answerability and effectiveness in, 315–316
  central government's effects on, 316–317
  conclusions on, 317–318
  judicial reform, 313–314

overview of, 15, 311–312, 321–322
political leadership and, 317–318
technology for improving, 312–313
transparency and efficiency improvements in, 314–315
Gujarat, growth and development in, 227–245
  conclusions on, 243–245
  development indicators, additional, 241–243
  economy, structure of, 233–237
  growth in, 228–233
  inequality in, 239–241
  minorities and weaker sections in, 243
  overview, 227–228
  poverty in, 238–239
  urbanization of, 237–238
Gujarat, healthcare and medical education in, 295–310
  conclusions on, 309–310
  healthcare infrastructure, 301–303
  healthcare policies, 304–307
  health indicators, 296–301
  medical and paramedical education, 307–309
  overview, 13, 15, 295
Gujarat, urban development in, 265–274
  conclusions on, 273–274
  overview of, 265
  service delivery and, 267–271
  slums, 267–269
  urban finances and, 271–273
  urban growth, 265–267
  urban land, 267
Gujarat Energy Development Agency, 259
Gujarat Green Revolution Company, 248
Gujarat Industrial Promotion Board (GIPB), 253
Gujarat Infrastructure Development Act (1999), 255
Gujarat Infrastructure Development Board (GIDB), 255
Gujarat Maritime Board (GMB), 256
Gujarat Model, 320–322
Gujarat Municipalities Act (1963), 271
Gujarat National Law University (GNLU), 314
Gujarat Pollution Control Board, 303

Gujarat public debt, 279
Gujarat Roads Management System (GRMS), 257
Gujarat State Road Development Corporation Limited (GSRDC), 257
Gujarat Town Planning and Urban Development (GTPUD) Act (1976), 269
Gujral, Inder, 170
Gunotsav (government primary school evaluation scheme), 290n5
Gupta, N., 142, 143
Gupta, P., 46–47, 213
Gupta, Shaibal, 132, 134, 203, 216n4
Gupta dynasty, 128–129
Guruswamy, M., 160

Hanumantha Rao, C. H., 109
Haryana state, consumer expenditure inequality in, 240
Hasan, R., 46–47
Hayek, Friedrich, 107
Health and Family Welfare Ministry, 195, 302
Health and healthcare. *See also* Gujarat, healthcare and medical education; Infant mortality rates; Life expectancy rates
  in Andhra Pradesh, 88–94, 100–101
  antenatal care, 195
  as Bihar growth determinant, 194–196
  births, medical attendance at delivery, 91
  blindness, 195
  diseases, 195
  economic value of, 295
  healthcare indicators, 296–301, 309
  health insurance, 91–94, 101, 106
  HIV/AIDS, 195
  hospital beds, availability of, 90
  household amenities, as Gujarat healthcare indicators, 299t
  immunization rates, 194–195, 298, 299t
  infrastructure, as Gujarat healthcare indicator, 299t, 301–303, 310
  malnourishment of children, 297t, 298
  manpower, as Gujarat healthcare indicator, 298, 299t, 301–303

Health and healthcare (*Cont.*)
  maternal care, 298, 304–305
  maternal mortality, 243, 245
  medical education, 307–309, 310, 316
  nurses, availability of, 298
  paramedical education, 307–309
  private healthcare providers, 90–91, 92, 93, 105–106
  public health infrastructure, 89–90, 172–173
  public health insurance schemes, 94
  suicides, 80
Hero (auto manufacturing company), 254
Hero MotoCorp, 337
High Level Expert Committee for Restructuring of Public Sector Undertakings, 316n5
Himachal Pradesh state, total fertility rate in, 149
Hindus, poverty rates and ratios, 66, 67–68*t*, 67*f*
Hirschman, A. O., 167
Hirway, I., 252
History, impact on states' economic outcomes, 6–7, 11
Horticulture, land devoted to (Andhra Pradesh), 38, 39*f*
HSBC, 53
Human capital, Kumar government's goals for, 206–207
Human Development Index (HDI), 132, 241
Human Development Indicator (HDI), 137–138
Hyderabad (city)
  as investment destination, 9
  IT entrepreneurs in, 52
  Naidu's vision for, 9
  role in state economic development, 26
  software technological park in, 52
  as state capital, 4n2, 337
Hyderabad state, as Andhra Pradesh component, 8
Hysteresis, 152

IMRs. *See* Infant mortality rates
Incentives
  for information technology sector, 54
  for mega projects, 254

Independent judiciary, 201, 211
Index of Economic Freedom (IEF), 318
India. *See also* Andhra Pradesh state; Bihar state; Gujarat state; *entries beginning "National"*; *names of other individual states*
  actions by, with adverse state implications, 255, 316–317
  agricultural workforce share, 36. *See also* Agriculture sector
  Bihar, lack of support for, 153
  consumer expenditure inequality in, 240
  crime rates in, 174–175
  government structure, 1–2, 271
  GSDP, major sectors of, 233–234
  Gujarat, central transfers to, 281*t*, 284
  infant mortality rates in, 88, 89*f*, 137
  inter-state financial transfers, 275
  life expectancy rates in, 89, 90*f*
  literacy rates in, 135–136
  malnourishment of children, 298n2
  migration from, 196n19
  new national government (2014), implications of, 339–340
  output shares, by sector, 34*t*
  poverty levels, 60, 61*f*, 62*f*, 64*t*, 213. *See also* Poverty
  pre-independence revenue sharing, 157–158
  revenue transfer channels, 159–160
  sector growth rates in, 33*t*. *See also* Industry sector and industrialization
  state-level analysis on, need for, 2–4
  urban and slum population of, 267–268
  urbanization in, 37. *See also* Urbanization (urban development)
  workforce participation rates in, 69, 70*t*
India, statistical comparisons with states
  Andhra Pradesh vs., infant mortality rate, 84*f*
  Andhra Pradesh vs., literacy rates, 94*t*
  Andhra Pradesh vs., religious group poverty, 67*t*

Andhra Pradesh vs., workforce participation rates, 70t
Bihar vs., arithmetic skills, 191–193
Bihar vs., Human Development Indicator, 137–138
Bihar vs., infant mortality rates, 194
Bihar vs., per capita development expenditures, 174
Bihar vs., population growth rates, 138
Bihar vs., reading abilities, 191, 192f
Gujarat vs., crude death rates, 242
Gujarat vs., employment by sectors, 236–237
Gujarat vs., health-outcome-related indicators, 297t, 299t, 300t
Gujarat vs., infant mortality rates, 242
Gujarat vs., per capita income, 229
Gujarat vs., urbanization, 237
various states vs., MGNREGA participation, 82f, 84f
various states vs., rationing rate, 84f
various states vs., targeting differential in, 83f
Indian Institute of Information Technology (IIIT, later International Institute of Information Technology), 53, 54
Indian Institute of Planning and Administration (IIPA), 197
Indian Penal Code (IPC), 176, 178t
Indian Public Health System (IPHS), 301, 302
Indian states. *See* India, statistical comparisons with states; *names of individual states*
Indian Statutory Commission, 157
Indira Gandhi Institute of Medical Sciences, 196
Industrial Infrastructure Development Fund (IIDF, Andhra Pradesh), 45
Industrial Investment Promotion Policy 2010–15 (Andhra Pradesh), 46
Industry sector and industrialization
in Andhra Pradesh, 32, 44–46, 70, 71t
in Bihar, 133–134, 139, 141, 146, 150f, 215–216
in Coastal Andhra Pradesh, 112–113

growth rates, 33t
in Gujarat, 14, 230–234, 245, 250–255, 263–264
in Gujarat Model, 321
in India, vs. other Asian countries, 234
output shares, 34t
in Rayalseema, 112–113
in Telangana, 112–113
Inequality, 239–241. *See also* Gender gaps and biases; Poverty
Infant mortality rates (IMRs)
in Andhra Pradesh, 62, 88–89, 105
in Bihar vs. India, 137, 194
in Gujarat, 242, 245, 301
Information technology
Aarogyasri health insurance and, 92
in Hyderabad, 26
importance of, 335
MNREGA implementation, use in (Andhra Pradesh), 84–86, 87
Information Technology Enabled Services (ITES) sector, 51–56, 57, 103
Infrastructure
in Bihar, 185–189, 210
Gujarat policies supporting, 255–261, 264
Kumar government's goals for, 206
Integrated Financial Management System (Gujarat), 312
Integrated Work-Flow and Document Management System (Gujarat), 312
Interdepartmental coordination, 315
International Institute of Information Technology (formerly Indian Institute of Information Technology (IIIT)), 53, 54
Internet, Gujarat policies supporting, 260–261
Irrigation, 42–43, 62–63, 248, 258, 263
Iyer, Lakshmi, 6, 155, 156n5

Jainism, 10, 126–127
Janani Suraksha Yojana (JSY, safe motherhood scheme), 305
Janata Dal (JD) and successor parties (JD (George), JD (United)), 131, 168, 169, 170, 171, 206, 338

Janata ke Darbar mein Mukhyamantri (JKDM, "Chief Minister in the People's Court"), 203
Jankari (Bihar government information phone access center), 202
Jawaharlal Nehru National Urban Renewal Mission (JNNURM), 268
Jharkhand state
    Bihar, differences from, 130–131, 337
    growth of, 109
    impact of creation of, 171
Jobs. *See* Employment
Judiciary
    fast-track courts, 313–314
    independent judiciary, 201, 211
    mobile courts, 314
    reforms of, in Gujarat, 313–314
    Speedy Trial Courts (Bihar), 179

Kandla, Gujarat, port of, 255–256
Kapoor, Mudit, 8, 9, 19
Karnataka state, total fertility rate in, 149
Kashi, kingdom of, 126
Kautilya (Chanakya, advisor to Maurya), 10, 127, 128, 201–202
Kerala state
    consumer expenditure inequality in, 240
    infant mortality rates in, 89, 194
    life expectancy rates in, 90*f*
    malnourishment of children in, 298n2
    Net Migration Rate, 196
    per capita income in, 227
    public health spending in, 307
    total fertility rate in, 149
Khandker, S., 81
Kingdon, G., 97
Kinnan, C., 81
Kishore, A., 134, 135
Kletzer, K., 159
Kohli, Atul, 209
Kosala, kingdom of, 126
Kosi River, 12, 160n8, 181
Krushi Mahotsav (Festival of Agriculture), 248
Kumar, Chanchal, 202n3
Kumar, D., 157
Kumar, Girish, 197
Kumar, Nitish
    change under, 204
    election, 131, 132, 335
    government of, statement of intent for, 206–207
    improvements under, 12, 188, 334, 335
    leadership of, 7
    political career, 16, 169–172
    problems faced by, 173
    state governance under, 200, 201–202
    Yadav, relationship with, 168–170, 338
Kumar, U., 46–47
Kurmis (Hindu agricultural community), 169
Kurnool district (Andhra Pradesh), health care claims per poor person, 92
Kutchh district (Gujarat)
    earthquakes in, 278, 283, 325–326
    ports in, 255
    special economic zones in, 255
Kuznets, Simon, 142, 214

Labor. *See* Employment
Laboratory federalism, 1–2
Labor-intensive industries, 235–236, 334
Lakdawala methodology (for poverty determination), 59, 142, 143
Land market
    land reforms, 209, 210, 252, 334
    land revenue system, 153–156, 166
    land tenure systems, 6, 154–156, 334
    urban land (Gujarat), 267
Large states
    poverty declines in, 60*f*
    rural poverty in, 60, 65*f*, 67*f*, 68*t*
    urban poverty in, 60, 61*f*, 65, 68*t*, 69*f*
Laws, limitations on local amendment of, 336, 339
Leadership. *See also* Politics and politicians
    importance of, 204–205, 212, 334, 336
    institutional creation by, 208
Liberalized State Incentive Scheme (LSIS, Andhra Pradesh), 44

License raj, 52. *See also* Single-window systems
Life expectancy rates, 89–90, 105, 136–137, 245
Literacy rates
 in Andhra Pradesh, 94–95, 105
 in Bihar, 135–136, 190–191
 of females, 62, 95, 135–136, 241, 242*t*
 in Gujarat, 13, 241, 242*t*
 of males, 135–136, 241, 242*t*
 reading abilities, in Bihar vs. India, 191, 192*f*
Lobbying, impact on inter-state finances, 160, 162*t*
Lok Adalats (courts of the people), 314
Lok Dal party, 168
Lok Janashakti Party (LJP), 338
LSIS (Liberalized State Incentive Scheme, Andhra Pradesh), 44

Madhya Pradesh (Indian state)
 growth of, 109
 Sardar Sarovar Project and, 323
Madras Presidency
 per capita government expenditures in, 157, 158
 Ryotwari system in, 156
Magadha, kingdom of, 126–129
Maharashtra state
 BT Cotton in, 249
 consumer expenditure inequality in, 240
 exports, 228n2
 malnourishment of children in, 298n2
 medical education in, 309
 per capita income in, 227
 public health spending in, 307
 Sardar Sarovar Project and, 323
 total fertility rate in, 149
 urban and slum population of, 267
Mahatma Gandhi National Rural Employment Guarantee Act (MNREGA, 2009, formerly National Rural Employment Guarantee Act), 61–62, 73, 74, 81–86, 87, 198
Malegam committee, 80

Males and boys
 category of employment, 72*t*, 73
 employment by industry divisions, 71*t*
 life expectancy rates, 136–137
 literacy rates, 135–136, 241, 242*t*
 rural unemployment and underemployment of, 75*t*
 school enrollment rates, 95–96, 286
Mandal, B. P., 167
Mandal, S., 160n9
Mandal Commission (Second Backward Classes Commission), 167, 168
Manufacturing sector, 33*t*, 34*t*, 46–47, 245, 251–252
 in Gujarat, 235
 registered manufacturing, 46, 47–48, 50–51, 71–72, 251
 unregistered manufacturing, 251–252
Maoist insurgency (Bihar), 180, 204–205
Maruti car company, 254
Mathew, S., 164, 165
Mathur, O.P., 272
Maurya, Ashoka, 128
Maurya, Bindusara, 128
Maurya, Chandragupta, 10, 127, 128
McKinsey (consulting company), 52
Medical Council of India (MCI), 309
Micro, Small, Medium Enterprise (MSME) projects, 263
Microfinance, 77–81, 86–87
Microfinance Institutions (MFIs), 77–80
Mid-Term Fiscal Reform Program (Gujarat), 278
Migration
 as Bihar growth determinant, 196–198
 to Gujarat, 267, 273, 301n3
 Kumar government's goals for, 207
 Net Migration Rate (Bihar), 196
 worker migration, 27, 31–32, 37, 57, 142
Minimum Alternate Tax, 316
Ministry for ___.
 See *name of specific ministry*
Mithapur, Gujarat,
 airport at, 256

Modi, Narendra. *See also* Gujarat model
   BJP, control of, 16
   flamboyance, 5
   Gujarat Model of, 320–322
   industrial policies under, 252
   leadership of, 7, 15, 317–318, 319, 335–336
   political career, 338
   as prime minister, 339–340
   on states' rights, 2
Mookerji, R., 128
Moore, M., 164, 165
Morduch, J., 81
Mukherji, Anjan and Arnab, 10, 12, 121, 141, 338
Mukhya Mantri Gram Sadak Yojana (Chief Minister's Rural Roads Program), 187, 188
Mundra, Gujarat, 256
Muralidharan, K., 98
Muslims
   in large states, poverty declines, 68*t*, 69*f*
   poverty ratios, rural and urban, 66, 67*t*, 68
   socioeconomic indicators for, 243, 244*t*, 245

Nagaraj, R., 227n1
Naidu, Chandrababu
   economic vision of, 8n5, 22, 102–103, 335
   focus of, 9
   growth, recognition of virtues of, 107
   growth under, 31
   IT industry, focus on, 35, 52–53, 55
   leadership of, 7, 8–10, 25–26, 102, 106
   political career, 25
   position in new Andhra Pradesh, 16
   re-election failure, 336
   reforms by, 29–30, 79, 105, 108
Nanda, Mahapadma, and Nanda dynasty, 127
Nano car project, 253
Narmada River, Sardar Sarovar Project, 247–248, 258, 263, 313, 323–324
Narmada Water Disputes Tribunal, 323
National Association of Software and Services Companies (NASSCOM), 52

National Democratic Alliance (NDA), 131, 169, 170, 171–172
National Development Council, 110
National Family Health Surveys (NFHS), 91
National Health Accounts, 307
National Plan process, 173
National Rural Employment Guarantee Scheme (NREGS). *See* Mahatma Gandhi National Rural Employment Guarantee Act
National Rural Health Mission (NRHM), 301
National Sample Survey (NSS), 69
National Sample Survey Office (NSSO), 239
National Sample Survey Organization (NSSO), 196–197
National Tariff Policy (2006), 49
National Thermal Power Corporation (NTPC), 48
National University of Educational Planning and Administration (NUEPA), 290
National Urban Health Mission (NUHM), 301, 303
Natural disasters (Bihar), 12, 140, 181–184
Negative deficits, 275n2
Nepal, cooperation in flood control, 181
Net State Domestic Product (NSDP), 7, 139, 140
New Andhra Pradesh state (Seemandhra), 4n2, 16, 110, 337
New Comprehensive Scheme of State Incentives (NCSSI, Andhra Pradesh), 44
Nongovernment organizations (NGOs), 79, 86
Nonlinearity of dynamic processes, 152
Non-structural flood management, 182, 184
Non-tax revenue (Gujarat), 281–282
No-Objection Certificate (NOC, Gujarat), 252
Normative statutory transfers, 162n10
North, Douglass C., 199n1
NTR (Rama Rao, N. T.), 25

Oates, Wallace, 1
Octroi (local taxes), 271–272, 274
Oil production (Gujarat), 232
Olson, Mancur, 11n6, 199, 209
"108" emergency services, 305, 310, 313
Organized sector manufacturing (registered manufacturing), 46, 47–48, 50–51, 71–72, 251
Orissa state
  Bengal Presidency, separation from, 153n2
  economic success of, 3
  government per capita expenditures in, 156–158
Other Backward Castes (OBCs), 83, 167
Outsourcing, 51, 53
Own revenues
  in Bihar, 162–163
  in Gujarat, 271, 281–282

Pakistan, flood control in, 184
Panagariya, Arvind, 1, 3, 7, 160n9, 333
Pandey, S., 227n1
Parthasarathy, R., 323
Paswan, Ram Vilas, 171n8, 172
Pataliputra (Patna), origins of, 126
Patel, Anandiben, 16, 319, 339
Patel, Chimanbhai, 317
Patel, Keshubhai, 317
Patna district, use of land revenue, 155
Pearl River Delta (China), urbanization of, 31–32
Per capita GSDP
  in Andhra Pradesh, 30–31
  in Gujarat, 13
Per capita income
  in Bihar, 125f, 131–133, 145, 147t
  in Gujarat, 229
Per capita NDP, for Bihar vs. India, 140–141
Per capita NSDP, for Bihar vs. India, 140–141
Permanent settlement, 153–156, 166, 214
Persson, T., 201
Peugeot, 253
Pipavav, Gujarat, port of, 256
Pitt, M., 81
Planning Commission of India, 132, 159, 213, 329

Polgreen, Lydia, 124, 129
Policy experimentation and reforms, importance of, 103–107. *See also* Reforms
Policy impacts. *See* Bihar, policy impacts
"Policy on Private Participation in Power" (central government), 48
Polio, 196
Politics and politicians. *See also* Governance; Kumar, Nitish; Naidu, Chandrababu; Rao, Narasimha; Reddy, Y. S. Rajshekhar (YSR); Vajpayee, Atal Bihar; Yadav, Lalu Prasad; *names of individual political parties*
  political influence, 159–160, 162t
  political leaders, 102, 167–172, 317–318
  political parties, 208–209
Pollution, 303
Pollution Control Board (Gujarat), 252
Population growth rates, in Bihar vs. in India, 138
Ports (Gujarat), 255–256
Poverty. *See also* Andhra Pradesh, poverty and employment in; Microfinance; Rural poverty; Urban poverty
  in Andhra Pradesh, 8, 9, 24–25, 27, 114–115
  in Bihar, 12, 134–135, 142–143, 213
  data on, 7
  declines in, 60f, 334
  in Gujarat, 13, 238–239, 305
  regional poverty trends (Andhra Pradesh), 114–115
Power sector. *See* Energy
PPPs. *See* Public-private partnerships
Pradhan Mantri Gram Sadak Yojana (PMGSY, Prime Minister's Rural Roads Program), 188
Pratham (NGO), 288, 293
Presidential assent, 2
Primary deficits, 275n2, 276, 277t, 279
Primary Health Centers (PHC), 301, 302t
Primary sector (of GSDP, Gujarat), 230–231, 232. *See also* Agriculture sector

Private schools and universities
　in Andhra Pradesh, 97–98, 99, 100
　in Bihar, 190, 191f
　in Gujarat, 288–289, 291, 293–294
　Right to Education act and, 100
Prosperity (Andhra Pradesh), 8, 25, 26, 56, 104, 106
Protectionism, 337
Public Grievance Redressal System (Bihar), 203
Public-private partnerships (PPPs)
　in Gujarat, 261, 274, 276, 313
　in Gujarat, for healthcare, 303, 304, 305, 310
　in Gujarat Model, 321, 322
　in Kutchh district earthquake reconstruction, 325
Public Sector Undertakings (PSUs), 315–316
Public service delivery, 172–173, 209–210, 215, 267–271
Punjab state
　consumer expenditure inequality in, 240
　per capita income in, 227
　public health spending in, 307
　public investment in, 160, 161t
　total fertility rate in, 149

Quality of life indicators, 241–243. See also Infant mortality rates; Literacy rates

Raiyatwari provinces, 215
Rajasthan state
　labor laws, changes to, 339
　Sardar Sarovar Project and, 323
Rajiv Aarogyasri (health insurance), 91–94, 106
Rajkot, Gujarat
　bus rapid transit system in, 271
　solid waste disposal in, 270
　water supply in, 270t
Rama Rao, N. T. (NTR), 25
Rangarajan Committee on Financial Inclusion, 77n1
Rao, M. G., 157, 159, 160n9, 215n3
Rao, Narasimha, 7, 29
Rao, Parthasarthy, 38, 40, 41
Rashtriya Janata Dal (RJD), 131, 164, 170–172, 215

Ration cards, 92
Rationing rate, for MNREGA, 83, 84f
Ravallion, M., 62, 76
Rayalseema region
　as constituent of new Andhra Pradesh, 16, 337
　growth rate, 111–114
　literacy levels in, 95
　poverty in, 114–115
Real estate sector, 35. See also Land market
Real wages (Andhra Pradesh), 73–74
Reddy, N. Janardhan, 52
Reddy, Y. S. Rajshekhar (YSR)
　election, 9, 56, 104
　growth, recognition of virtues of, 107
　leadership of, 9–10, 26–27, 102, 106, 335–336
　reforms by, 30, 104, 105
Red tape. See Single-window systems
Reforms. See also Bihar, governance and reforms in; Gujarat, economic sectors, policy reform in; Gujarat, fiscal reforms and performance in
　Gujarat judicial reforms, 313–314
　land reforms, 209, 210, 252, 334
　by Naidu, 29–30, 79, 105, 108
　policy experimentation and, importance of, 103, 104, 105, 106, 107
　by YSR, 30, 104, 105
Registered manufacturing (organized sector manufacturing), 46, 47–48, 50–51, 71–72, 251
Regulation of Money Lending (Andhra Pradesh Microfinance Institutions) Ordinance (2010), 80
Regulatory environment, 107. See also Andhra Pradesh Industrial Single Window Clearance Act
Religious groups. See also Buddhism; Hindus; Jainism; Muslims
　poverty in, 67t, 75, 105
Remittances, 196–198, 197n20, 205
Representative democracies, 100, 102, 104, 107
Reserve Bank of India (RBI), 78–79, 80
Revealed comparative advantage, 234, 317, 318
Revenue deficits, 275n2, 276, 277t, 279

Right of Children to Free and
    Compulsory Education Act (Right
    to Education Act, RTE, 2009),
    99–100, 101, 106, 285
Right to Information (RTI), 202
Right to Public Service Act (2011,
    Bihar), 203, 204
River Narmada, Sardar Sarovar
    Project, 247–248, 258, 263, 313,
    323–324
RJD (Rashtriya Janata Dal), 131, 164,
    170–172, 215
Road Construction Department
    (RCD), 188
Roads
  in Bihar, 185, 187, 188–189
  in Gujarat, 257, 270, 273–274
  link roads, 187
Robinson, J. A., 199n2
Roodman, D., 81
Rorabacher, J. A., 181
"Roving bandits," 199
Roy, A., 206
Roy, S., 233n6
Rural areas
  consumer expenditure
    inequality in, 240
  employment guarantees in
    (Andhra Pradesh), 81–87
  in Gujarat, 260, 266, 301–303
  inequality in (Bihar districts),
    143, 144t
  tele-density (Gujarat), 260
  workforce, 69, 70t, 73, 75t
Rural poverty
  in Andhra Pradesh, 60, 75, 104–105,
    106, 114–115
  in Bihar districts, 143, 144t
  in large states, declines in, 60f
  by social groups, 63, 64t
Rural Works Department (RWD), 188
Ryotwari land tenure system, 156, 334
Rythu Bazars (farmer markets),
    40–41, 103
Rythu Chaitanya Yatra (Farmer
    Empowerment Program), 43

Sakala (Karnataka government
    information phone access
    center), 202n4
Salmon, Pierre, 1
Salmon mechanism, 1
Samata Party, 169, 170, 171
Sample Registration
    Survey (SRS), 194
Sardar Sarovar Project (SSP), 247–248,
    258, 263, 313, 323–324
Sarva Shiksha Abhiyan (SSA,
    universalization of elementary
    education program), 190, 285
Saurashtra district (Gujarat), ports
    in, 255
Scheduled Castes (SC)
  in Andhra Pradesh, 27, 44, 45,
    54, 105
  employment, shift from self- to
    casual employment, 66
  in Gujarat, 13, 243, 244t, 245, 283
  job card holders in, 74
  in large states, 65
  MGNREGA participation rates, 83
  poverty ratios, 63, 64t
Scheduled Tribes (ST)
  in Andhra Pradesh, 27, 44, 45,
    54, 105
  employment, shift from self- to
    casual employment, 66
  in Gujarat, 13, 243, 244t, 245, 283
  job card holders in, 74
  MGNREGA participation rates, 83
  poverty ratios, 63, 64t
  rural poverty declines, 64f
Schools and schooling. *See* Andhra
    Pradesh, education in; Education;
    Gujarat, education in; Private
    schools and universities
Secondary sector
    (of GSDP), 230–233.
    See also Industry sector and
    industrialization
Second Backward Classes Commission
    (Mandal Commission), 167, 168
Sectors. *See* Agriculture sector;
    Industry sector; Manufacturing
    sector; Services sector
Seemandhra (new Andhra Pradesh
    state), 4n2, 16, 110, 337
Self-Employed Women's Association
    (SEWA), 78
Self-Help Groups (SHGs), 78–79
Service delivery, 172–173, 209–210,
    215, 267–271

Services sector
  in Andhra Pradesh, 32–33, 35, 36t, 57–58, 70, 71t
  in Bihar, 133–134, 139, 141–142, 146, 148t, 150f, 210, 213–214
  in Coastal Andhra Pradesh, 112–114
  growth rates, 33t
  in Gujarat, 230–233
  in India, vs. other Asian countries, 234
  output shares, 34t, 36t
  in Rayalseema, 112–114
  in Telangana, 112–114
Sewa Yatras (service travels), 208
SEZs (Special Economic Zones), 54, 254–255, 263, 316
Shah, N., 252
Sharma, K. L., 131n3, 134, 135
Sharma, Vijay Paul, 250
SHGs (Self-Help Groups), 78–79
Ship-making industry, 254
Shleifer, A., 164
Shukla, P. R., 50
Sikaria district, public works in, 180
Singh, Manmohan, 110, 172
Singh, N., 157, 159
Singh, N. K., 160n8
Singh, Prabal, 305
Singh, V. P., 168
Single-window systems
  in Andhra Pradesh, 45, 46, 55, 57, 103–104
  in Gujarat Model, 321, 335
Sinha, A., 168n1, 169, 188
Sinha, C. P., 182
Sinhya, Arun, 180
SKS (microfinance company), 79, 80
Slums (Gujarat), 267–269, 273
Small states, problems with study of, 4
Smart cards, 85
Smith, Adam, 201
Social audits, 86
Social sectors
  as Bihar growth determinant, 190–196
  expenditures on, 282f, 283, 284, 306
  poverty reduction among, 63–69, 75
Social unity, 215
Society for Social Audit, Accountability and Transparency (SSAAT), 86

Socioeconomic indicators. *See also* Education; Literacy rates; Poverty
  for Bihar, 135–138
  for Gujarat, 243, 244t, 245
Software technological park (STP), 52
Soil testing, 43, 248
Solar Parks, 259
Solid waste disposal, 270, 273
Somanathan, E., 184
Special category status
  for Bihar, 153
  for new Andhra Pradesh, 110, 337–338
Special Economic Zones (SEZs), 54, 254–255, 263, 316
ST. *See* Scheduled Tribes
State Agricultural Produce and Marketing (Development and Regulation) Act 2003 (Andhra Pradesh), 41, 103
State Auxiliary Police (SAP) force, 179
State Domestic Product (SDP, Bihar), 133–134
State governments. *See* Governance; *specific states*
State List (Indian Constitution), 336
State Planning Boards, 173
State Public Finance Reform Committee (SPFRC, Gujarat), 271, 276, 278
States. *See also* Andhra Pradesh state; Bihar state; Gujarat state; Large states; Uttar Pradesh state; *names of other individual states*
  features of, 6–7
  impact of history on, 6–7, 11
  MGNREGA participation rates, 82
  own revenue, 281–282
  power of, effects of poor utilization of, 209
  role in federal structure, 2
State Wide Attention on Grievance with Application of Technology (SWAGAT, Gujarat), 313
"Stationary bandits," 199, 209
Storage facilities, 259–260
Structural flood management, 182, 184
Sub-Centers (SC, for health care), 301, 302t
Sundararaman, V., 98

Surat, Gujarat
  bus rapid transit system in, 271
  slum population of, 268
  solid waste disposal in, 270
  water supply in, 270t
Sustainability, 28, 283
Systematic neglect (Bihar), 166

Tamil Nadu state
  consumer expenditure inequality in, 240
  exports, 228n2
  infant mortality rate in, 88–89
  life expectancy rates in, 89, 90f
  malnourishment of children in, 298n2
  public health spending in, 307
  total fertility rate in, 149
  urban and slum population of, 267
Target 2000 (Andhra Pradesh industrial policy), 44–45
Targeting differential (TD), for MNREGA, 83
Tata, Ratan, 15
Tata Consultancy Service (TCS), 85n2
Tata motors, 253
Taxes
  computer software sales tax, 54
  Goods and Services Tax, 175, 281
  in Gujarat, 272, 274, 278, 279, 281t, 315
  Minimum Alternate Tax, 316
  minor tax revenue, 281
  in municipal corporations, 271
  profession tax, 315
  property taxes, 272, 274
  revenue collection systems (colonial Bihar), 11
  value added tax, 76, 281, 283–284
Teachers. *See* Education
Technology. *See also* Information technology
  for improving governance (Gujarat), 312–313, 318
  Internet, Gujarat policies supporting, 260–261
  mobile phones, 260–261
  optical fiber infrastructure, 53
Telangana
  creation of, 4n2, 16, 22, 109, 336–337

  economic growth, 27, 111–114
  internal hostilities, 110–111
  literacy levels in, 95
  political opportunities in, 109–110
  poverty in, 114–115
  protectionism in, 337
Telecommunications, 53, 260–261. *See also* Technology
Telugu Desam Party (TDP), 25, 26, 79, 336
Tendulkar methodology (for poverty determination), 8, 59, 60f, 61f, 62f, 114f, 213. *See also* Poverty
Tertiary sector (of GSDP), 230–233. *See also* Services sector
Texas Instruments (TI), 51
Thaker, Hrima, 250
Thakur, Karpoori, 168
Thapar, Romila, 123–124, 125n2, 126, 127
Thirteenth Finance Commission, 159, 279
Tocqueville, Alexis de, 1
Total fertility rate, 148–149, 150
Towns, size-classes of, 238
Trade (Gujarat), 228
Transmission Corporation of Andhra Pradesh Limited (APTransco), 49
Transport and transit systems, 255–257, 270–271. *See also* Roads
  airports, 256–257
  bridges, 187–188
  bus rapid transit system (BRTS), 270–271, 274
  ports, 255–256
Tribal populations, 283. *See also* Scheduled Tribes
Tripathy, R., 152n1
Twelfth Finance Commission, 159, 173, 279

United Progressive Alliance, 171–172
United Provinces, per capita government health expenditures in, 158
Unproductive expenditures (Gujarat), 276, 322
Unregistered manufacturing, 251–252
Upper castes
  (Bihar), 167–168

Urban areas. *See also* Urbanization (urban development); Urban poverty
   in Gujarat, 266, 269, 271, 274, 303
   inequality in, 143, 144t, 240
   urban sprawl, 266
   urban tele-density, 260–261
Urban Development Ministry (MUD), 269
Urbanization (urban development). *See also* Gujarat, urban development; Worker migration
   in Andhra Pradesh, 57
   in Bihar, 215
   growth in, 37
   in Gujarat, 13, 237–238, 245, 273
   Kumar government's goals for, 206
   Naidu on, 26
   urban development projects, 268
   workforce, 69, 70–71, 73, 76
Urban Land Ceiling and Regulation Act (ULCRA, 1976), 269, 273
Urban poverty
   in Andhra Pradesh, 60–61, 74, 104–105, 106, 114–115
   in Bihar districts, 143, 144t
   by social groups, 64t
Uttarakhand state, growth of, 109
Uttar Pradesh state
   agricultural output share, 34
   agricultural workforce share, 36
   Andhra Pradesh, comparison with, 8, 22–24, 102, 106
   infant mortality rates in, 194
   IT sector in, 52
   migration from, 196
   poverty in, 60–61, 62f
   remittances from out-migrants, 197n20
   size of, 340
   urbanization in, 37

Vadodara city (Gujarat)
   slum population of, 268
   solid waste disposal in, 270
   water supply in, 270t
Vadodara district (Gujarat), special economic zones in, 255
Vajpayee, Atal Bihari, 7, 29, 31, 169, 170

Value added tax (VAT), 76, 281, 283–284
Velugu (financial support program for self-help groups), 79
Veterinary services (Andhra Pradesh), 41
Vibrant Gujarat Summit (VGS), 15, 262–263, 264
Violence, 175–176, 177t, 243. *See also* Crime
Virjis republic, as Magadha rival, 126
Vision 2020 (Andhra Pradesh document), 21–22, 52

Waldaeur, C., 127
Warangal district (Andhra Pradesh), health care claims per poor person, 92
Waste disposal, 270, 273
Water. *See also* Irrigation
   city water supplies, 269–270
   conservation and management of, 42–43, 247–248, 257–258, 273, 313
   drinking water, 258
Welfare programs (Andhra Pradesh), 8, 25, 26, 56, 87
West Bengal state
   total fertility rate in, 149
   urban and slum population of, 267
"What Constrains Indian Manufacturing?" (Gupta, Hasan, and Kumar), 46–47
Women. *See* Females and girls
Women and Child Welfare Ministry, 298n2
Worker migration, 27, 31–32, 37, 57, 142. *See also* Urbanization (urban development)
Working of the Reforms in Bihar and Orissa (Indian Statutory Commission), 157
World Bank, 172, 201, 257, 312

Yadav, Lalu Prasad, 16, 131n3, 164, 168–171, 338
YSR. *See* Reddy, Y. S. Rajshekhar

Zamindari system, 154–156, 334